Do You Really Want to T

The 4th Edition

Buckled Up, the Best Viewer's Guide to Area 51 & Beyond and Other Top Secret Adventures

37°14'36.52"N, 115°48'41.16"W

RON P MILIONE
W2TAP // AAR2JD

U.S. ARMY MARS

Do You Really Want to Take A Ride?

4th Edition

Buckle Up, the Best Viewer's Guide to Area 51 & Beyond and Other Top Secret Adventures

37°14'36.52"N, 115°48'41.16"W

WINTER 2019 - FOURTH EDITION PRINTING

Fourth Edition Publication: Winter, 2019

ISBN: 9781706945949

Written, Explored, Researched & Compiled By Ron P. Milione

U.S. Army MARS //AAR2JD

Formerly of the Show, UFO Hunters from the History Channel.

Do You Want to Take a Ride?

4th Edition, Winter 2019

Copyright © 2019 by Ron P. Milione
All rights reserved. This book or any portion thereof may not be reproduced or used in any manner whatsoever without the express written permission of the publisher except for the use of brief quotations in a book review.

Although every precaution has been taken to verify the accuracy of the information contained herein, the author and publisher assume no responsibility for any errors or omissions. No liability is assumed for damages that may result from the use of information contained within.

Printed in the United States of America

Fourth Edition, WINTER 2019

ISBN: 9781706945949

WORLDWIDE DISTRIBUTION

AMAZON / AMAZON PRIME

Books may be purchased by contacting the publisher and author at:

w2tap@arrl.net

4th Edition Printing, Winter 2019

WELCOME ALL TO MY 4th EDITION OF BUCKLE UP BOOK!

HELLO ALL AND WELCOME TO YOUR OWN SELF-GUIDED/VIEWER'S GUIDE AND ADVENTURE TO AREA 51 AND BEYOND!

Introduction

This fourth edition book that I have put together as a self-guided, informative book with actual real locations for legal viewing of the most secret military base in the world, known as Area 51 aka ICAO:KXTA. We will cover Area 51 Historic Chronology in later parts of this book. There will be key locations to getting around the base **(legally)** *for close-ups of the boarder, back gate entrance, camp site viewing, camping out locations and other secret locations in the great state of Nevada. Also there will be additional military complexes to explore including some real old "Ghost Towns" of Nevada and mining areas, so get into your vehicle, Buckle-Up and let's get going on your own adventure with this guide as a backpack reference. Most of all, be extremely safe and take tons of pictures, video's and of course, BYOD (Bring Your Own Drone)!*

RECOMMENDATION NOTE:

Before we dive into this adventure I want to introduce you to SPOT! [THIS IS NOT AN ENDORSEMENT BUT HIGHLY RECOMMENDED TO ANYONE WHO WILL VENTURE OUT IN MOUNTAINS, DESERT, LONG MILE HIKING and especially being SOLO!].

SPOT offers peace of mind by allowing you to track your assets, notify friends and family of your GPS position and status, mark waypoints, track your progress on Google Maps™ or notify rescue officials in an emergency.

Who Needs SPOT?

Anyone who travels by land, sea and air! Since its launch, SPOT's satellite technology has provided peace of mind by helping initiate more than 5,000 rescues and counting and providing GPS tracking services. Over the years, recreational outdoor enthusiasts, athletes, government agency employees, National Geographic explorers and photographers, and researchers are just some of the people that have benefited from using SPOT.

WHEN THE ROOF IS THE SKY
Sleeping bag: check. Food: check. Small tent: check. SPOT Satellite Messenger: check. Leaving everything behind and getting away is one of the greatest forms of adventure. Rays of sunshine among the sweet air, unforgettable sights and a connection with the land draw

you to get out there. You never know what your next backpacking trip might bring. The same goes for worldly epic backpacking trips where you find yourself in corners of countries you could only dream about. That's why having a SPOT is a essential item!

How SPOT Works

SPOT sends your GPS location and data to orbiting commercial satellites.

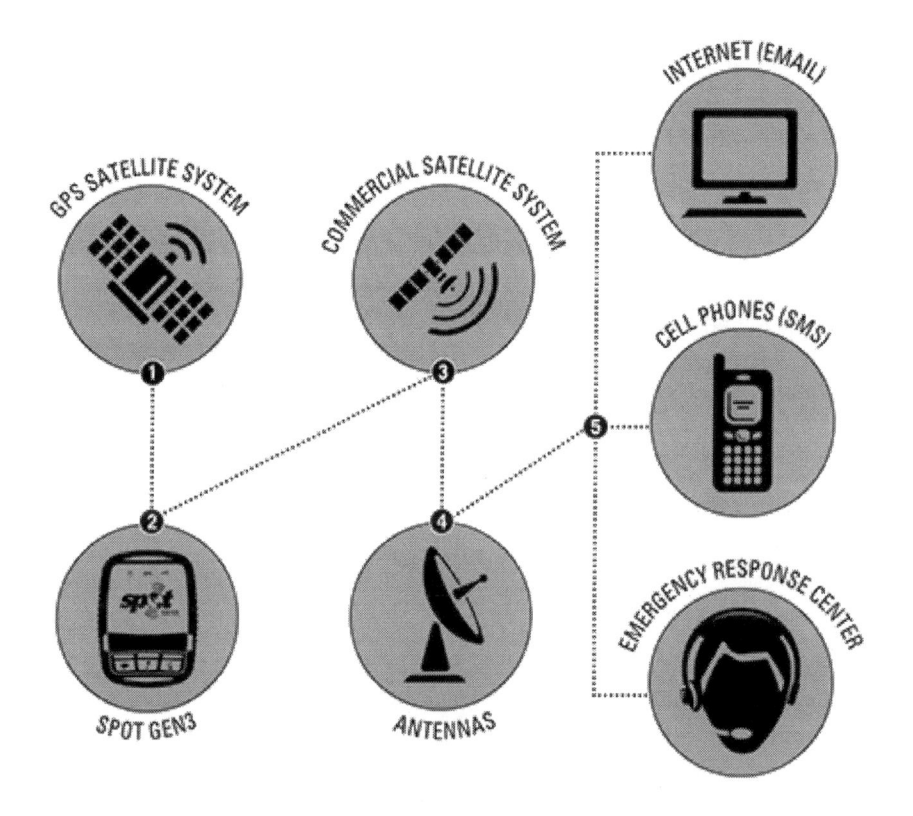

- GPS satellites provide signals
- SPOT messenger's onboard GPS chip determines your GPS location and sends your location and preselected message to communication satellites
- Communication satellites relay your message to specific satellite antennas around the world
- Satellite antennas and a global network route your location and message to the appropriate network
- Your location and messages are delivered according to your instructions via email, text message, or emergency notification to the GEOS Rescue Coordination Center

SPOT Gen3 gives you a critical, life-saving line of communication when you travel beyond the boundaries of cell service. The latest generation of award-winning SPOT devices, SPOT Gen3 lets family and friends know you're okay, or if the worst should happen, sends emergency responders your GPS location - all with the push of a button. Add this rugged, pocket-sized device to your essential gear and stay connected wherever you roam. *Long Live Adventure!*

SPECIFICATIONS

HEIGHT	3.43" (8.72 cm)
WIDTH	2.56" (6.5 cm)
THICKNESS	1" (2.54 cm)
WEIGHT	4.0 oz (114g) with Lithium batteries
OPERATING TEMP	-22F to 140F (-30C to 60C)
OPERATING ALTITUDE	-328ft to +21,320ft (-100m to +6,500m)
HUMIDITY RATED	MIL-STD-810F, Method 507.3, 95% to 100% cond.
VIBRATION RATED	Per SAE J1455
WATERPROOF RATED	IP67 (1 m for up to 30 Minutes and dust proof)

BATTERY TYPE

- 4 AAA Energizer Ultimate Lithium 8x batteries (L92)
- 4 AAA Energizer® NiMH rechargeable batteries (NH12)
- Line Power with a 5v USB connection

SPOT HOME WEB SITE

InReach Product – Recommended Product

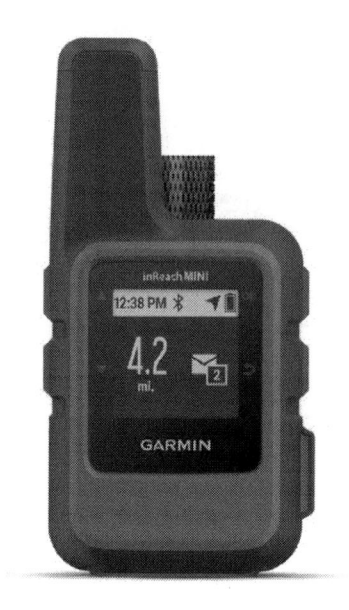

Fit Global Connectivity Into Your Palm

- Small, rugged, lightweight satellite communicator enables two-way text messaging via 100% global Iridium® satellite network (satellite subscription required)
- Trigger an interactive SOS to the 24/7 search and rescue monitoring center (satellite subscription required)
- Access downloadable maps, U.S. NOAA charts, color aerial imagery and more by using the free Garmin Earthmate® app and compatible devices
- Optional inReach weather forecast service provides detailed updates directly to your inReach Mini or paired device; basic and premium weather packages available
- Send and receive inReach messages through compatible Garmin devices, including connected wearables and handhelds
- Internal, rechargeable lithium battery provides up to 90 hours of battery life in 10-minute tracking mode

inReach HOME WEB SIT

InReach Product – Recommended Product

You may venture off the grid, but you can still stay in touch — as long as you're carrying an inReach SE+ or inReach Explorer+. These handheld satellite communicators are designed for the outdoor enthusiast who wants to roam farther and experience more — without compromising their loved ones' peace of mind. From backcountry experiences to international adventures, inReach provides communication, location sharing, navigation and critical SOS functions for anyone who loves getting away from it all, on land, water or in the skies.

Explore Anywhere. Communicate Globally.

Using the worldwide coverage of the Iridium satellite network, these go-anywhere portable devices let you exchange text messages with any cell phone number or email address — while using GPS to track and share your journey's progress. You can also post to social media or even communicate inReach-to-inReach in the field. In case of an at-risk situation, you can also use inReach to trigger an SOS to the 24/7 monitoring center, text back and forth about the nature of your emergency, and receive confirmation when help is on the way.

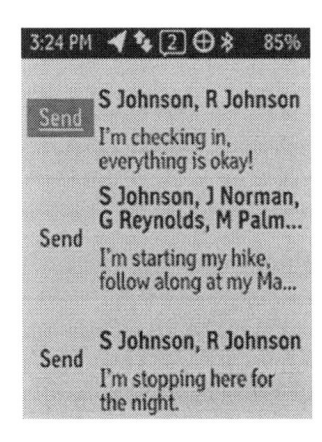

No Cell Tower? No Phone Service? No Problem.

inReach SE+ and Explorer+ give you all the tools to stay totally connected. You don't have to worry about being within range of a cell tower — or encountering spotty coverage in fringe zones or blackout areas. Your inReach communicator offers two-way messaging via the global Iridium satellite network.

Track and Share Your Whereabouts

Turn on the tracking function of your inReach SE+ or Explorer+ communicator, and let family and friends follow your progress on their computers or mobile devices, using the web-based MapShare™ portal. The inReach device will send waypoints at preselected time intervals, so followers can track your whereabouts online. You can also invite your crew back home to use MapShare to ping your inReach unit and see your GPS location, track your movements and exchange messages during your trip. You can even embed your MapShare page on a blog, website or social media.

InReach Product – Recommended Product

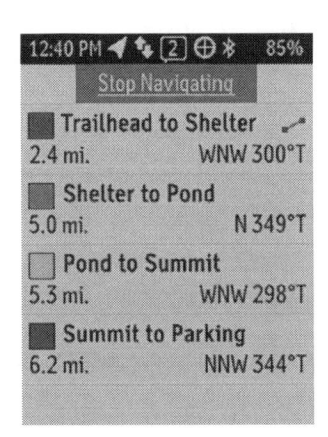

Pair with Your Mobile Device

For even more capability and convenience, the free Earthmate® app syncs your inReach handheld via Bluetooth® with your compatible Apple® or Android™ device[1] so you can access unlimited maps, aerial imagery and U.S. NOAA charts. Plus, Earthmate allows you to conveniently use all of the inReach features on your paired mobile device.For easier messaging, you can also access your phone's contact list from the Earthmate app to connect with fewer keystrokes.
Get Weather Wherever

The optional inReach weather forecast service provides detailed updates directly to your inReach device, compatible smartphone or tablet paired with the Earthmate app, so you'll know what conditions to expect en route. Basic and premium weather packages are offered. And you can request weather forecasts for your current location or any other waypoint or destination on your itinerary.

InReach Product – Recommended Product

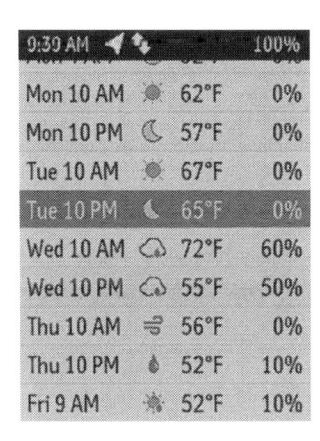

Who Will Answer Your SOS? GEOS Will.

GEOS is the world leader in emergency response solutions and monitoring. They've supported rescues in more than 140 countries, saving many lives in the process. And they're standing by 24/7/365 to respond to your SOS, track your device and notify the proper contacts and emergency responders in your area. Then, while help is on the way, GEOS will continue to text back and forth with you, providing updates and critical information until your situation is resolved.

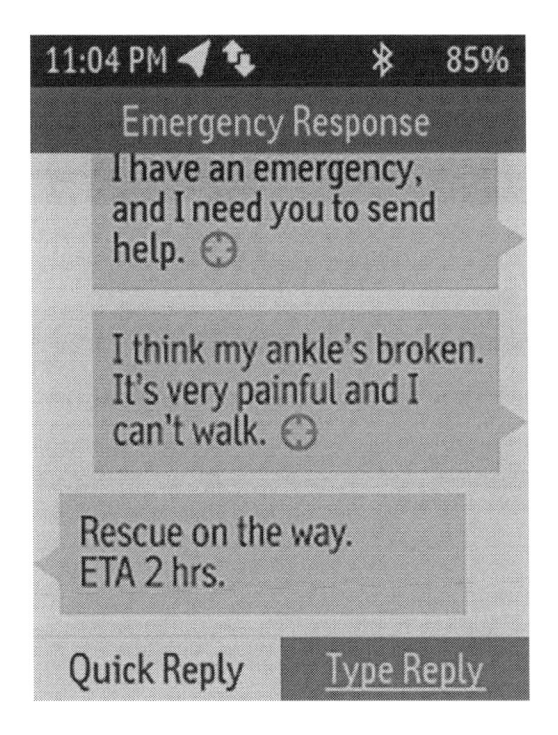

InReach Product – Recommended Product

Which inReach Is Right for You?

As satellite communicators, both the inReach SE+ and Explorer+ offer identical messaging capabilities. However, it's on the GPS navigation side that their differences become apparent. While inReach SE+ uses GPS to provide basic grid navigation and allow you to drop waypoints, mark key locations, track your progress, and follow a breadcrumb trail back to base — the inReach Explorer+ goes a step beyond, providing full-fledged GPS on-map guidance with preloaded TOPO mapping and waypoint routings viewable directly on the unit. Plus, a built-in digital compass, barometric altimeter and accelerometer are included with Explorer+ to help you get and maintain accurate bearings on or off the beaten path.

In the Beginning………

The Angel from Paradise Ranch

In 1954, the Lockheed "Skunk Works" began work on a top secret reconnaissance aircraft, under the codename Project AQUATONE, for the Central Intelligence Agency (CIA). Clarence "Kelly" Johnson designed the single-engine jet to carry its pilot over "denied territory," such as Russia and Cuba, while cruising at altitudes above 70,000 feet and carrying a variety of cameras and sensors. Powered by a Pratt & Whitney J75 engine, the airplane featured long, slender wings and bicycle landing gear. It was officially called the U-2. The "U" for "utility" was meant to obscure the airplane's true mission. The U-2 prototype never carried a serial number, and was referred to simply as Article 341. Johnson called it the "Angel."

Due to the secrecy of the program, a secure test location was required. After a lengthy search, the CIA and Lockheed selected Groom Lake, Nevada because the dry lakebed made a perfect natural landing field. A small airbase with a 5,000-foot paved runway was constructed just off the southwest corner of the playa. It was a primitive facility in a very remote location.

In the Beginning.........

Over-all Shot Of Watertown Area From Hills Shooting Northeast.

With wry humor, Kelly Johnson initially dubbed it "Paradise Ranch," but it was officially named Watertown. In later years it was called Area 51, a name that has come to symbolize government secrecy and exotic aircraft.

Lockheed technicians completed construction of the U-2 prototype on 15 July 1955. On 25 July, Article 341 was shipped to the test site inside a C-124. Static engine runs were completed two days later. Preliminary taxi tests were conducted on 1 August. During the second taxi run (at 70 knots), Lockheed test pilot Tony LeVier noticed that the U-2 had become airborne and was about 35 feet above the lakebed. He brought it down with some difficulty, blowing the tires on the main landing gear, and setting the brakes on fire.

Following additional taxi tests, LeVier made a second flight on 4 August to get a better feel for the airplane's handling qualities. "It flies like a baby buggy," he told chase pilot Bob Matye. The 20-minute flight ended with more landing difficulties.

In the Beginning………

LeVier flew again on 6 August to practice his landing technique. By now, he had determined that the best approach involved landing the airplane like a tail-dragger, tail wheel first.

The official first flight took place on 8 August 1955, with LeVier using the call sign ANGEL 1. Bob Matye and "Kelly" Johnson flew chase in a T-33. The flight lasted nearly an hour and reached an altitude of 32,000 feet. It ended with a low pass over the spectators, including Richard Bissell of the CIA and Col. Osmond J. Ritland.

Tony LeVier went on to make 18 more flights in Article 341, completing Phase I testing. His accomplishments included taking the aircraft to 52,000 feet and a speed of Mach 0.85. After LeVier left the program, Lockheed test pilots Bob Matye and Ray Goudey took over. Robert Sieker joined the program in September 1955. Bob Schumacher followed in November. Through an intense series of flight tests, they expanded the airplanes operating envelope to its design altitude.

On August 1, 1955, during a high-speed-taxi test in the first U-2, Lockheed's chief test pilot, Tony LeVier, inadvertently became airborne at a remote test site in the desert of western Nevada called the Nevada Test and Training Range at Groom Lake. You may know it as Area 51.

LeVier who had conducted the first taxi-test a few days prior, accelerated the U-2 to 70 knots when he suddenly realized he was airborne, leaving him in "utter amazement."

"I had no intentions whatsoever of flying," recalled LeVier in transcripts quoted in "The CIA and Overhead Reconnaissance – the U-2 and OXCART Program, 1954-1974 written by CIA Historians. "I immediately started back toward the ground, but had difficulty determining my height because the lakebed had no markings to judge distance or height. I made contact with the ground in a left bank of approximately 10 degrees."

He was unable to land the U-2 on his first attempt, and it bounced back into the air, but he managed to successfully bring it down on a second try. Damage to the prototype U-2 was very minor. This test would later be considered the first *unofficial* flight of the U-2.

LeVier piloted the U-2's first official test flight a few days later on August 4th, and the first official flight with visiting dignitaries present was on August 8th.

U2 After Flight Lands On Dry Lake.

On August 1, 1955, during a high-speed-taxi test in the first U-2, Lockheed's chief test pilot, Tony LeVier, inadvertently became airborne at a remote test site in the desert of western Nevada called the Nevada Test and Training Range at Groom Lake. You may know it as Area 51.

Why Area 51?

Much of the testing took place at the facility at Groom Lake, a dry lakebed near Las Vegas, Nevada, in an isolated area that came to be known as Area 51 and Watertown. The area was chosen by top officials of the U-2's Development Projects Staff who flew to Nevada in search of a site where the U-2 could be tested safely and secretly.

They spotted what appeared to be an airstrip by a salt flat – Groom Lake – near the northeast corner of the Atomic Energy Commission's (AEC) Nevada Proving Ground, which had been used during World War II as an aerial gunnery range for Army pilots. The site was perfect for testing the U-2 and training its pilots; however, upon further discovery, the U-2 Project Staff learned Groom Lake was not actually part of the AEC proving ground.

They asked the AEC to add the Groom Lake strip to its real estate holdings in Nevada, to which the AEC readily agreed, and the deal was approved by President Eisenhower.

How Area 51 got its various names:

The strip of wasteland was known at the time by its map designation: Area 51. To make the new facility sound more attractive to the pilots and workers who would reside there, Lockheed's famous aeronautical engineer, **Clarence "Kelly" Johnson**, called it "Paradise Ranch," which was soon shortened to just "the Ranch." Many of the workers even referred to themselves as "ranch hands."

Area 51 is also known by the nickname "Watertown," which was rumored to have been inspired by the name of CIA Director Allen Dulles's birthplace of Watertown, New York. Records show that the name was a reference to when rainwater would runoff the nearby mountains and flood the dry lakebed of Groom Lake. Whenever the lakebed flooded, project managers would refer to the facility as "Watertown Strip."

The name "Dreamland" was also commonly associated with the Groom Lake facility. According to Thornton D. (TD) Barnes, president of Roadrunners Internationale, an association of former Air Force, CIA, and contract personnel serving at Area 51 during the Cold War, Dreamland was a radio call sign for the base, introduced in the late 1960s. It replaced the previous name, Yuletide, and referred specifically to the large block of airspace (called a Special Operations Area) surrounding Area 51 and parts of the Nevada Test Site and Nellis Air Force Range (now known as the Nevada Test and Training Range).

Although the commonly preferred official name for the facility today is the Nevada Test and Training Range at Groom Lake, both the names Watertown and Area 51 were used as official names for the facility. According to Barnes, Area 51 may be found on official Nevada Test Site (NTS) maps and other documentation, while some Department of Energy documents indicate that Watertown is legally listed as a member of Alamo Township in Lincoln County, Nevada.

How do you get a super-secret aircraft to a super-secret facility?

For security reasons, primary access to Area 51 was by aircraft. A C-124 would transport the components of a U-2, which were constructed in Burbank, California, then disassembled and transported to Watertown for reassembly and testing. A daily air shuttle also transported personnel and other cargo between Watertown and the "Skunk Works," the Lockheed production facility in Burbank.

The U-2, however, wasn't the only Agency aircraft transported, tested, and flown out of Area 51. The first flight test of the CIA's A-12 **OXCART** took place at the Groom Lake facility on April 25, 1962; the remaining operational aircraft arrived for flight tests through mid-1964. By the fall of 1965, the eleven pilots selected to fly A-12 missions and their aircraft were ready for deployment.

The legacy and sacrifice of those who worked at Area 51:

CIA, Air Force, and private industry personnel from many specialties helped make the U-2 a reality and several lost their lives in the process. Four of those were **pilots** who had known the risks of handling an aircraft that was difficult to fly, even in the best of circumstances. Fourteen members involved in the U-2 project also lost their lives when their transport plane en route from Burbank to Watertown crashed during bad weather into Mount Charleston, a few miles outside of Las Vegas.

The sacrifice these pilots and U-2 project personnel made for their country helped the US win the Cold War. Along with thousands of Americans who worked at Area 51, their patriotism, ingenuity, and willingness to take on a project critics believed was impossible at the time – the creation of the U-2—allowed the US to penetrate the Iron Curtain and gain an unparalleled advantage over the Soviets in intelligence gathering.

Table of Contents

WINTER 2019 - FOURTH EDITION PRINTING 2

Fourth Edition Publication: Winter, 2019 3

ISBN: 9781706945949 3

Written, Explored, Researched & Compiled By Ron P. Milione 3

U.S. Army MARS //AAR2JD 3

Formerly of the Show, UFO Hunters from the History Channel. 3

Do You Want to Take a Ride? 3

4th Edition, Winter 2019 3

4th Edition Printing, Winter 2019 5

WELCOME ALL TO MY 4th EDITION OF BUCKLE UP BOOK! 5

HELLO ALL AND WELCOME TO YOUR OWN SELF-GUIDED/VIEWER'S GUIDE AND ADVENTURE TO AREA 51 AND BEYOND! 5

Introduction 5

This fourth edition book that I have put together as a self-guided, informative book with actual real locations for legal viewing of the most secret military base in the world, known as Area 51 aka ICAO:KXTA. We will cover Area 51 Historic Chronology in later parts of this book. There will be key locations to getting around the base (legally) for close-ups of the boarder, back gate entrance, camp site viewing, camping out locations and other secret locations in the great state of Nevada. Also there will be additional military complexes to explore including some real old "Ghost Towns" of Nevada and mining areas, so get into your vehicle, Buckle-Up and let's get going on your own adventure with this guide as a backpack reference. Most of all, be extremely safe and take tons of pictures, video's and of course, BYOD (Bring Your Own Drone)! 5

RECOMMENDATION NOTE: 5

Before we dive into this adventure I want to introduce you to SPOT! [THIS IS NOT AN ENDORSEMENT BUT HIGHLY RECOMMENDED TO ANYONE WHO WILL VENTURE OUT IN MOUNTAINS, DESERT, LONG MILE HIKING and especially being SOLO!]. 5

SPOT offers peace of mind by allowing you to track your assets, notify friends and family of your GPS position and status, mark waypoints, track your progress on Google Maps™ or notify rescue officials in an emergency. 5

Who Needs SPOT? 5

How SPOT Works 6

SPOT Gen3 gives you a critical, life-saving line of communication when you travel beyond the boundaries of cell service. The latest generation of award-winning SPOT devices, SPOT Gen3 lets family and friends know you're okay, or if the worst should happen, sends emergency responders your GPS location - all with the push of a button. Add this rugged, pocket-sized device to your essential gear and stay connected wherever you roam. **Long Live Adventure!** 7

SPOT HOME WEB SITE 7

InReach Product – Recommended Product 8

Fit Global Connectivity Into Your Palm 8

inReach HOME WEB SIT 8

InReach Product – Recommended Product 9

Explore Anywhere. Communicate Globally. 9

No Cell Tower? No Phone Service? No Problem. 9

Track and Share Your Whereabouts 9

InReach Product – Recommended Product *10*

Pair with Your Mobile Device *10*

Get Weather Wherever *10*

InReach Product – Recommended Product *11*

Who Will Answer Your SOS? GEOS Will. *11*

InReach Product – Recommended Product *12*

Which inReach Is Right for You? *12*

INTRODUCTION *31*

WHAT THE HECK IS AREA 51? THE REAL NAME IS HOMEY AIRPORT (ICAO:KXTA) *31*

WHY IS IT CALLED AREA 51? WHY NOT MILTARY AREA 123, OR BASE GROOM ? ..*31*

Welcome to the Los Alamos Study Group's web site for the Technical Areas (TAs) at Los Alamos National Laboratory (LANL). From here you can either choose a TA from the map from the QR CODE below: *36*

If you can visit only one site of the Top Secret Government, Area 51 in Rachel, Nevada is the one and the most SECRET of any of our military installations. Most of what you have heard about this place is false, most of what you haven't heard is true, and no one wants to talk about the things that aren't entirely true but aren't entirely false either......but the adventure to come close to our most advanced Research & Development Base will get your curiosity flowing and hopefully you will adventure out to Area 51! *37*

Area 51 has been the focus of enormous interest among a significant segment of the public for decades — an interest that inevitably spawned books, articles, and a variety of documentaries.[1] For some enthusiasts Area 51 was a clandestine site for UFOs and extraterrestrials, but it is better understood as a U.S. government facility for the testing of a number of U.S. secret aircraft projects — including the U-2, OXCART, and the F-117. Declassified documents help demonstrate the central role that Area 51 played in the development of programs such as the F-117, and the operational employment of the aircraft. Other declassified documents reveal Area 51's role in testing foreign radar systems and, during the Cold War, secretly obtained Soviet MiG fighters. *37*

VIEWING FROM TIKABOO PEAK AT SUNSET IN THE DESERT *37*

The Great Basin Desert in Nevada using some excellent filtering desert photography and to adventure Area 51 and the surrounding area. *37*

This is a view was taken from the top of Tikaboo Peak with a clear (but far) view of the base...37

Driving directions FROM Las Vegas to Rachel, NV 89001 .... *45*

DESCRIPTION	47
OPERATION	47
HISTORY	51
TECHNICAL ATTRIBUTES	52
EMPLACEMENT CONSIDERATIONS:	56
DANGER WILL ROBINSON: A NEW AREA 51 BAN	77
THE REAL REASON FOR THE BAN	80
THEY CAN'T BAN ON PUBLIC LAND, RIGHT?	83
SEE THE M9 IN ACTION ON YOUTUBE BY CLICKING ON THE QR CODE:	86
WHAT IS TIKABOO PEAK?	94
LET'S START HERE - THE APPROACH	98
ROUTE DESCRIPTION	98
ESSENTIAL GEAR	99
CAMPING	99
Tikaboo Peak, Nevada Weather Station – FOR "LIVE WEATHER INFORMATION: https://wrcc.dri.edu/weather/ntik.html	103
The Mysterious BACK GATE to "The Ranch" aka Dreamland, Watertown, Paradise Ranch, The Base	112
37°20'45.83"N 115°39'34.07"W	112
Introduction and Background History of Area 51	112
Groom Lake	116
Inside Look at the Topology of Area 51	121
The beautiful Mercury, Nevada	122
Groom Lake Topology	123

123

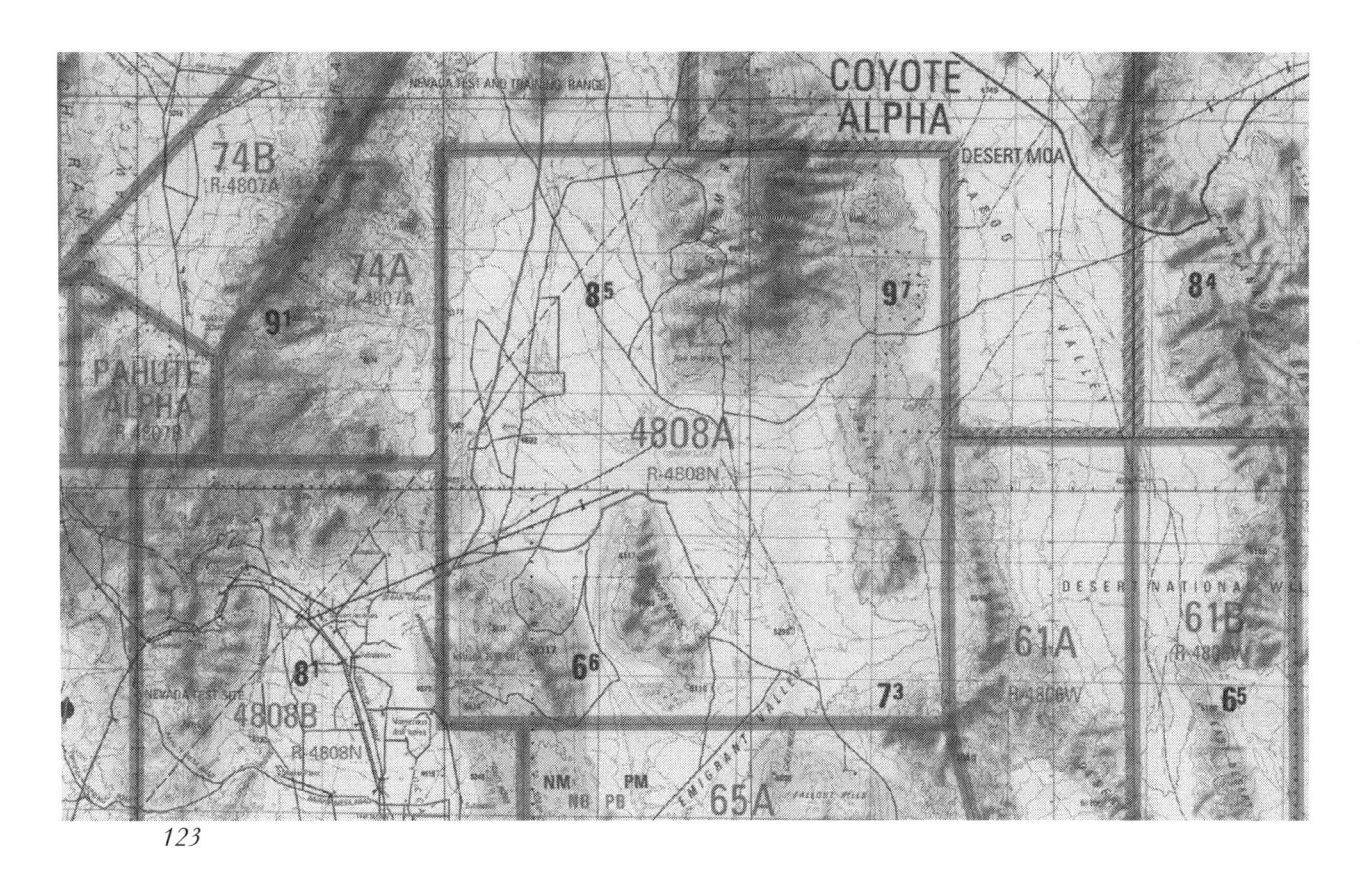

Groom Lake in coordinate section R4808A as shown above. *123*

Restricted Area 51 Airspace (R-4808A) *123*

Groom Lake in coordinate section R4808N as shown above. *124*

The Restricted Area 51 Airspace (R-4808A) *127*

Let Me Tell You all About the "JANET AIRLINES" at McCarran Airport! *127*

FLEET *131*

Not to EXACT SCALE but an estimated distance, street location map… *133*

View of the Janet ramp and terminal from the long-term parking garage of McCarran in the east direction. *133*

The INFAMOUS "JANET AIRLINES"…. *134*

The UNCOVER Jet Airliner from Las Vegas to the Black Projects Playgrounds *134*

Janet Routes to Area 51 .... *134*

Las Vegas - Groom Lake Round Trip Timetables *138*

Driving directions from Las Vegas to Rachel, NV 89001 .... *145*

The Little A'Le'Inn (Previously Rachel Bar and Grill) is a small great bar, restaurant and motel located in Rachel, Nevada on the Extraterrestrial Highway. The business has been running for over 20 years and has been a favorite of mine and to many visitors to the local Area 51 area. The business has a variety of Area 51 and UFO related items for sale such as maps of the area, posters, postcards, toys, etc. and is also famous for its **"Alien Burger"**..........................145

Address: 1 Old Mill St, Rachel, NV 89001..145

Web Address: http://littlealeinn.com/ - WEB 145

Telephone Bus: (775)729-2515 Fax: (775)729-2551 145

GPS Coordinates N37° 38.801' W115° 44.760'..145

Your Adventure begins from the Little A'Le'Inn 146

Don't forget to get your picture or video's on the CAPTURED UFO...147

Only contained at the famous Little A'Le'Inn!..147

Did you bring your drone? 147

Why not FLY IT AROUND HERE AND CAPTURED AWESOME FOOTAGE OF THE FAMOUS "ET HIGHWAY"..147

The "OLD MAILBOX" aka infamous "BLACK MAILBOX" Alien Drop-off 152

There's a new Black Mailbox at Area 51! It was installed on 02/04/2017 per a date found inside the door. The area has been cleaned up and looks a lot better...152

We discovered this on 06/30/2017. 152

"THE NEW BLACK MAILBOX" Alien Drop-off 153

There's a new Black Mailbox at Area 51! It was installed on 02/04/2017 per a date found inside the door. The area has been cleaned up and looks a lot better...153

We discovered this on 06/30/2017. 153

Buckle Up – You're First Road Trip to the mysterious "Black Mailbox" 155

Location of the Black Mailbox - 37°27'25"N   115°28'57"W...155

As you leave the Little A'Le'Inn parking lot you will make a right turn onto Highway 375 also known as the famous "Extraterrestrial Highway." 155

"The Extraterrestrial Highway" to start your first road trip journey. Drive approximately 19.35 miles heading southwest on SR375 from an elevation of approximately 4,846 feet above sea level going past your first landmark called Long Street which is approximately 8.04 miles from your starting point. Keep continuing on SR375 southwest until your second landmark which will be Tempiute Mine Road - Rachel, Nevada which is approximately 2 miles from Long Street that you just past before. Keep continuing on SR375 another 9.5 miles southwest until you see the dirt road off to your

right and the mailbox is right in sight! Soon after mile marker 29 on NV-375, you'll see the Black Mailbox (now white) on the left. 155

Black Mailbox right off CR375 approximately 19.35 miles from your starting point from the 155

Little A'Le'Inn 155

Aerial Satellite View showing the "BLACK MAILBOX" at Mail Box Road & CR375 Intersection 156

The black mailbox is actually inside this white outer box, a mystery wrapped in an enigma, ... 156

BUT NO LONGER EXIST! 156

There is the NEW BLACK MAILBOX as shown above! 156

The NEW "BLACK MAILBOX" at night! 157

Close–up Satellite Aerial of the "BLACK MAILBOX" 157

The box is made of quarter-inch-thick bulletproof metal, and its door is clamped shut with a Master Lock. Its owner, say the black letters printed on its side, is STEVE MEDLIN, HC 61, BOX 80. Over the years, hundreds of people have converged here to photograph this box held up by a chipped metal pole. They camp next to it. They try to break into it. They debate its significance, or simply huddle by it for hours, staring into the night. Some think the mailbox is linked to nearby Area 51, a military installation and purported hotbed of extraterrestrial activity. At the very least, they consider the box a prime magnet for flying saucers. A few visitors have claimed to have seen astonishing celestial oddities, but most seem to enjoy even uneventful nights at the mailbox, about midway between the towns of Alamo and Rachel. 158

TAKE A TRIP TO THE "BACK GATE!" 158

Buckle Up – You're Second Road Trip to The Back Gate Station Area 158

Buckle Up – Your Third Road Trip to the mysterious "Groom Lake Road" aka "Dreamland Lane" to the "FRONT GATE!" 162

Buckle Up – Your Fourth Road Trip to the mysterious "Tikaboo Peak" aka "Peak A Boo" at Dreamland from the summit. 173

Buckle Up – You're Special Road Trip to the mysterious "AREA 6" 184

36.926565, -116.006272 184

3,932' ASL 184

AREA 6 - 36.926565, -116.006272 185

WIDE AREA VIEW OF AREA 6 186

AREA 6 - 36.926565, -116.006272 186

Drone proving ground is what Area 6 is used for. 187

AREA 6 - 36.926565, -116.006272 .... *188*

TOPO MAP 1 .... *188*

Nevada Test Site Area 6 *is in the Locales category for Nye County in the state of Nevada. Nevada Test Site Area 6 is displayed on the Yucca Lake USGS quad topo map. Anyone who is interested in visiting Nevada Test Site Area 6 can print the free topographic map and street map using the link above. The latitude and longitude coordinates of Nevada Test Site Area 6 are 36.924675, -116.076425 and the approximate elevation is 4,537 feet (1,383 meters) above sea level.* 188

For ANY TOPO MAPS, scan the QR CODE ABOVE *188*

AREA 6 - 36.926565, -116.006272 .... *189*

TOPO MAP 2 .... *189*

Nevada Test Site Area 6 Information 189

For ANY NEVADA ONLY TOPO MAPS, scan the QR CODE ABOVE *189*

Buckle Up – Your Fifth Road Trip to the mysterious "Tonopah Test Range" aka "Area 52/Area54." *202*

Russian S-300PS SAM Testing at TTR *203*

That famed MISSILE SIGN! 203

Brainwash Butte 207

FROM LAS VEGAS: *211*

From Las Vegas to TTR (Tonopah Test Range) Directly *211*

S4 - Electronic Combat Ranges around TTR *212*

Tybo Ghost Town and Mine 225

Directions 225

Headworks of one of the more recent mines in Tybo! *226*

The old brick school house, built in 1877 at Tybo! *227*

GPS Coordinates *227*

Update 2017 .... *227*

Buckle Up – Your Sixth Road Trip to the mysterious "Base Camp" aka Area 51 ANNEX *233*

Buckle Up – You're Seventh Road Trip to the mysterious "Nuclear Test Site at Morey Flats." Called "Project Faultless" in NYE County. *239*

26

Introduction... 240

One of the history's largest underground nuclear tests, "Project Faultless," was conducted on Jan 19, 1968, not on the Nevada Test Site but on public land north of Warm Springs. (about 90 miles from Rachel.) You can actually visit **GROUND ZERO** where there is a plaque on a big concrete plug and extensive evidence of ground collapse. (Since the explosion was very deep underground, there is a very little chance of radiation). The site is accessible by roads from US-6. From Warm Springs, go north on US-6 about 25 miles to milepost 76.5, where there is a road on your left and a sign pointing to "Moore's Station." This is a well maintained road suitable for any vehicle. Follow it 12.5 miles until you reach a stop sign. Keep going straight ahead about 1.4 miles until the road ends at perpendicular road. You are very close to the site. Look for a concrete cylinder sticking out of the ground, looking like a water tank! Go right a few hundred yards and then left at the first opportunity to drive right up to the plug. 240

Directions 241

GPS Coordinates 241

Project Faultless with the Concrete Cylinder 242

A Must See! 242

Project Faultless – "The Project Faultless PLAQUE!" 243

Front View at Project Faultless at GROUND ZERO! 243

Google Earth Close Up of Project Faultless at N38° 38.058' W116° 12.920' 244

A Blast from the Past! Ground-Zero 245

Buckle Up – You're Eight Road Trip to the mysterious "Lunar Crater" 246

Lunar Crater National Natural Landmark *is volcanic field landmark located 70 miles (110 km) east-northeast of Tonopah in Nye County, in central Nevada. It was designated a National Natural Landmark in 1973.* .. 246

Aerial View from a rented private plane showing far view of AREA 51 255

History of Groom Lake ..... In the Beginning..... 1950's 256

Watertown Operations 258

Atomic Blasts 260

New Lease on Life 261

OXCART and the Roadrunners 262

Dreamland 263

Red Hats 263

Pioneers of Stealth 264

27

Expansion and Acquisition *266*

Space Invaders *267*

Out of the Black, Into the Blue *267*

Monitoring Military Aircraft **274**

Radio Frequency Reference Information: **275**

RadioReference.com is the world's largest radio communications data provider, featuring a complete frequency database, trunked radio system information, and FCC license data. RadioReference is also the largest broadcaster of public safety live audio communications feeds, hosting thousands of live audio broadcasts of Police, Fire, EMS, Railroad, and aircraft communications. With hundreds of thousands of members, RadioReference is a world leading collaboration platform for public safety communications professionals and hobbyists. 276

FOR COMPLETE UP-TO-DATE DETAIL ON THE LATEST FREQUENCIES PLEASE RESEARCH THE LINK BELOW: 276

Nevada Test and Training Range – GROOM LAKE **286**

TTR SITE DETAILS 286

SITE FREQUENCIES 286

Nevada Test and Training Range – BALD MOUNTAIN **287**

BALD MOUNTAIN SITE DETAILS 287

SITE FREQUENCIES 287

Nevada Test and Training Range – PAPOOSE MOUNTAIN **288**

PAPOOSE MOUNTAIN SITE DETAILS 288

SITE FREQUENCIES 288

Nevada Test and Training Range (Project 25) – PROJECT 25 .... **292**

SYSTEM ID LIST 292

BALD MOUNTAIN SITE DETAILS 294

The *Little A'Le'Inn* 299

How it works – Tracking JANET Airlines 303

ADS-B 304

MLAT 305

North America Radar Data 305

Flarm 306

Estimations 306

Aircraft visible on Flightradar24 (within ADS-B coverage) 306

Aircraft visible on Flightradar24 (within MLAT, radar, or Flarm coverage) 307

Blocking 307

Coverage map example showing all "live" flights at one time. 310

INTRODUCTION TO BASIC TRANSPONDER 101 311

Trailer Parks at Little A'Le'Inn 314

Camping 314

CAMPFIRE HILL 2.26 MILES LINE-OF-SIGHT TO THE GROOM LAKE BORDER! 319

Camp Fire Hill - View from Campfire Hill towards Groom Lake Road 320

THE HIDDEN CAMPSITE 321

THE HIDDEN CAMPSITE 322

THE HIDDEN CAMPSITE 323

COYOTE SUMMIT 325

POWERLINES OVERLOOK	326
CAMPING AROUND RACHEL SUMMARY	329
Trailer Parks	*329*
Camping 329	
MOORES STATION PETROGLYPHS	331
Directions 331	
MOUNT IRISH PETROGLYPH SITE	332
Landforms	*338*
Northern Range	*339*
Eastman Airfield Target	*339*
Southern Range	*339*
Nearby facilities	*339*
Fourth Edition Publication: Winter, 2019	*343*
ISBN: 9781706945949	*343*
Explored, Researched & Compiled By Ron P. Milione	*343*
Formerly of UFO Hunters from the History Channel.	*343*
Do You Wanna Take a Ride?	*343*

INTRODUCTION

WHAT THE HECK IS AREA 51? THE REAL NAME IS HOMEY AIRPORT (ICAO:KXTA)

WHY IS IT CALLED AREA 51? WHY NOT MILTARY AREA 123, OR BASE GROOM ?

Situated in the desert in southern Nevada, within the boundaries of the Nellis Air Force Range (NAFR) and just outside of the northeast corner of the Nevada Test Site (NTS), Area 51 and its neighbors, which also include the Tonopah Test Range (TTR), have hosted some of the most significant weapons testing performed on the planet during the 20th century.

In addition to isolation, the 3.5 million acre region around and including Area 51 boasts other qualities that make it an excellent place to conduct secret tests and training. The dry climate provides superior flying conditions, the variety of terrain helps with gunnery practice, and several dry lake beds are available for emergency landings, including, notably, Groom Lake – situated just north of Area 51.

Therefore, beginning in 1940, public land in the region was set aside and private land was condemned in order to establish the Las Vegas Bombing and Gunnery Range (LVBGR) (today, the NAFR and TTR), which was used throughout World War II "as an aerial gunnery range for Army Air Corps pilots."

As the Cold War began, there was a perceived need for the development and testing of nuclear weapons, and the barren and relatively uninhabited region surrounding Area 51 was identified as an ideal location; as such, a large swath of the southern portion of the LVBGR was set aside as the aforementioned NTS, for testing a variety of nuclear items. Despite the fact that Las Vegas is only 65 miles from its southeast edge, those involved in the site choice minimized any potential danger to the population, with Enrico Fermi opining "that people will receive perhaps a little more [ionizing] radiation than medical authorities say is absolutely safe."

In any event, nuclear testing began at the NTS in its southeastern corner at a place known as Frenchman Flat (FF) on January 27, 1951. After the four remaining devices of the Ranger series were detonated (and studied), also at FF, the locations of nearly all further testing (with a handful of notable exceptions) at NTS were thereafter identified by their "area" numbers, beginning with the Buster-Jangle series in October-November 1951 in Area 7. This was to ensure that it "allowed anyone 'in the know' to know where a test would be conducted . . . [and] the same system is still used today."

Note that not every numeral between 1 and 30 appears on the NTS map. Notably missing are 13, 21, 24 and 28; nonetheless, these numbers were apparently used to designate areas for atomic testing in the region – albeit outside of the set-aside NTS zone. For example, an "Area 13" was designated just northeast of the NTS in the NAFR,[while "Area 24" refers to the North Las Vegas Facility, a satellite site of the NTS managed by the National Nuclear Security Administration's Nevada Site Office (NNSA). "Area 28" was originally designated in the southwestern part of the NTS in the vicinity of areas 25 and 27, into which it was absorbed.

"Area 21" is less easy to identify. Although there is a "Technical Area 21" at Los Alamos National Laboratory (LANL) in north-central New Mexico. However, as that site has its own extensive numbering system, it is doubtful it is the missing NTS area.

Regardless, although the LANL areas may be unrelated, it is clear that NTS-related nuclear testing was done outside of its territorial boundaries, but included within its numbering system. For example, in "Area 13," an experiment called Project 57, was run on April 24, 1957, to explore whether or not the explosive charge of a nuclear warhead could self-destruct the weapon without causing an atomic explosion.

Likewise, four other extra-territorial experiments (Double Tracks and Clean Slate I, II and III) to observe "(nonnuclear) detonation of nuclear weapons" were performed on the TTR, at a site designated as "Area 52," in May and June 1963.[11] Similarly, at "Area 58" on October 26, 1963, near Fallon, Nevada (well outside of the NTS), the Shoal experiment involved the detonation of a 12-kiloton bomb 1,200 feet below the Earth's surface, just to observe earthquake effects.

While not conclusive, the fact that "areas" were designated well-into the 50s supports the inference that "Area 51" was a part of that pattern. Also compelling is the fact that Tonopah's "Area 52" is likely just as close to, yet also just outside of, the NTS.

And while it should come as no surprise that there are no direct records of nuclear testing activities at the secretive Area 51, there is a notable entry on the National Resource Defense Council's (NRDC) comprehensive list of nuclear tests (1945-1992), that may be relevant. Note that this list provides the name of every "event" (e.g., Trinity, Fat Man or Shoal), as well as its date, location (usually detailed, such as "Alamogordo, NM" or "NTS (Area 3)"), the lab that ran the test (e.g., "LA" for Los Alamos), the device type (such as whether it was dropped from a tower or plane, or down a shaft), the height and depth of the burst, and its purpose (e.g., "WR" for "weapons related').

Regarding the NTS-related tests, other than the Frenchman Flat (FF) experiments, only six were not identified on the list by an area number: the four performed at Area 52, which were designated "Bombing Range, NV," the Shoal at Area 58, which was designated "Fallon, NV," and a third, run on May 10, 1962.

This last was a shaft test performed on a weapons related device, attributed to the NTS, but with no "area" or other location designated; in addition, neither the lab that ran the test, nor the height or depth of the burst are recorded, and instead question marks ("?") are inserted under those categories on the list..Obviously this isn't conclusive, and the name of the event is consistent with contemporaneous tests conducted by the Lawrence Livermore National Laboratory (LLNL), but it is curious. And, when combined with Area 51's proximity to the NTS, the site's history of extreme secrecy, its consecutive numbering with neighboring test areas, and the fact that the experiment was conducted in the region one year prior to those performed at Area 52, together these factors present a circumstantial case that Area 51 was designated as part of the NTS numbering system. Map 2 shows different major military areas of boundaries.

See MAP 1 and MAP 3 (Nevada Test Site) for details on the different AREA NUMBERS on the next couple of pages.

MAP 2 shows the basic FEDERAL LANDS sector coverage which includes Nellis Air Force Range; Nevada Test Site and Nellis Air Force Range

The base's current primary purpose is publicly unknown; however, based on historical evidence, it most likely supports the development and testing of experimental aircraft and weapons systems (black projects). The intense secrecy surrounding the base has made it the frequent subject of conspiracy theories and a central component to unidentified flying object (UFO) folklore. Although the base has never been declared a secret base, all research and occurrences in Area 51 are **Top Secret/Sensitive Compartmented Information (TS/SCI)**. On 25 June 2013, following a Freedom of Information Act (FOIA) request filed in 2005, the CIA publicly acknowledged the existence of the base for the first time, declassifying documents detailing the history and purpose of Area 51.

Area 51 is located in the southern portion of Nevada in the western United States, 83 miles (134 km) north-northwest of Las Vegas. Situated at its center, on the southern shore of Groom Lake, is a large military airfield. The site was acquired by the United States Air Force in 1955, primarily for the flight testing of the Lockheed U-2 aircraft. The area around Area 51, including the small town of Rachel on the "Extraterrestrial Highway", is a popular tourist destination.

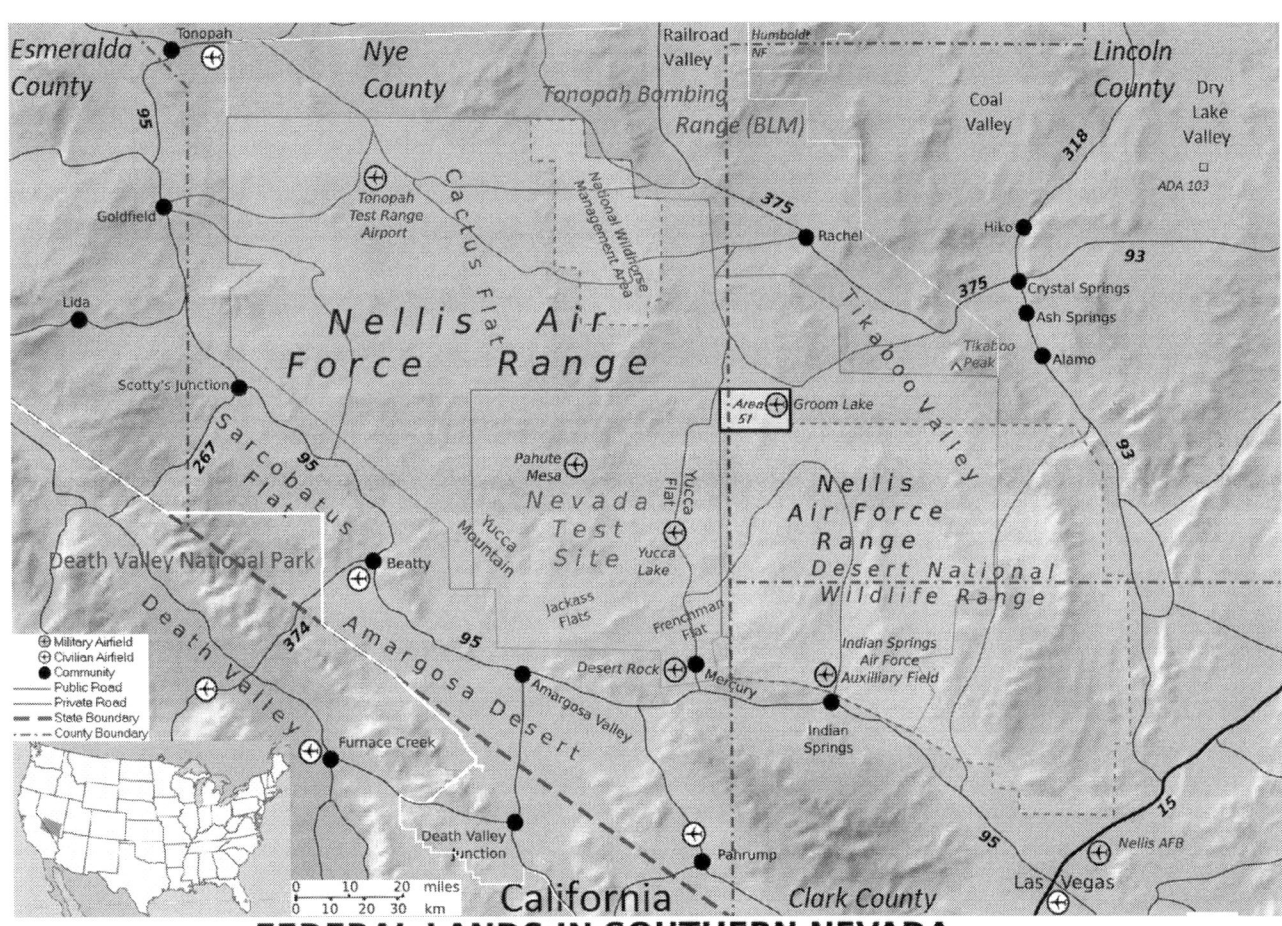

FEDERAL LANDS IN SOUTHERN NEVADA

MAP 2

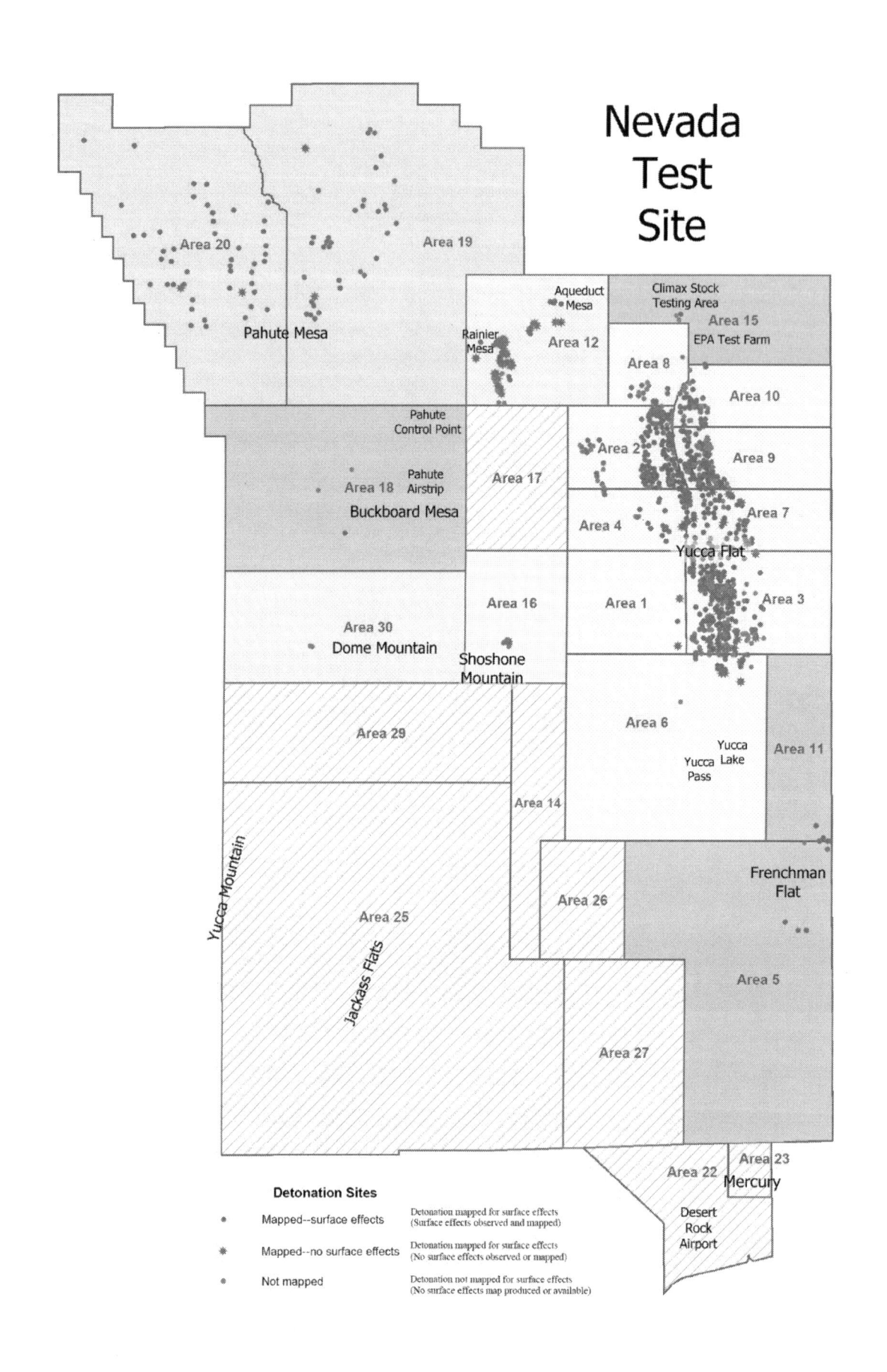

Map 1 – THE NEVADA TEST SITES (AREA NUMBERS BY REGIONS)

Map 3 below showing the "AREA NUMBERS" including the RESTRICTED AREA known as R4808N.

Map 3 – The AREA NUMBERS

Welcome to the Los Alamos Study Group's web site for the Technical Areas (TAs) at Los Alamos National Laboratory (LANL). From here you can either choose a TA from the map from the QR CODE below:

If you can visit only one site of the Top Secret Government, Area 51 in Rachel, Nevada is the one and the most SECRET of any of our military installations. Most of what you have heard about this place is false, most of what you haven't heard is true, and no one wants to talk about the things that aren't entirely true but aren't entirely false either......but the adventure to come close to our most advanced Research & Development Base will get your curiosity flowing and hopefully you will adventure out to Area 51!

Area 51 has been the focus of enormous interest among a significant segment of the public for decades — an interest that inevitably spawned books, articles, and a variety of documentaries.[1] For some enthusiasts Area 51 was a clandestine site for UFOs and extraterrestrials, but it is better understood as a U.S. government facility for the testing of a number of U.S. secret aircraft projects — including the U-2, OXCART, and the F-117. Declassified documents help demonstrate the central role that Area 51 played in the development of programs such as the F-117, and the operational employment of the aircraft. Other declassified documents reveal Area 51's role in testing foreign radar systems and, during the Cold War, secretly obtained Soviet MiG fighters.

VIEWING FROM TIKABOO PEAK AT SUNSET IN THE DESERT

The Great Basin Desert in Nevada using some excellent filtering desert photography and to adventure Area 51 and the surrounding area.

This is a view was taken from the top of Tikaboo Peak with a clear (but far) view of the base.

The white bus shuttles employees of Area 51 to and from the base every day thru the back roads off Highway 375.

NOTE: Look for any U.S. Government Plates on any vehicles in the surrounding area which probably works with secret base!

Notice the BLACKED OUT WINDOWS on the bus to HIDE the base workers, Area 51 DoD Personnel.

If you are camping out by CAMP FIRE HILL, 37°21'6.96"N 115°36'20.76"W. You can see the AREA 51 WHITE BUS passing your viewing area as shown in these pictures.

These will be some of the exciting "UNKNOWNS" you will encounter while driving around the area of Lincoln County, Nevada.

Always Expect the "UNEXPECTED!" – KEEP YOUR EYES FOCUS!

39

INTRODUCTION TO THIS SELF-GUIDED/VIEWER'S GUIDE BOOK

Area 51 is, for obvious reasons, not open to the public but I will still get you to the border! The nearest town is Rachel, Nevada, population 370++. Rachel is home of the Little A'Le'Inn, a great motel with an alien-oriented gift shop that greets visitors of all kinds with an "earthlings welcome" sign out front. *It also houses on-site housing so if you don't have any camping gear you can use the Little A'Le'Inn as a base!*

9631 Old Mill Rd Alamo, NV 89001 - Part of an alien-themed complex, this quirky spot offers trailer-style units with shared bathrooms. Contact (775) 729-2515 - littlealeinn.com

37°38'48.62"N 115°44'45.20"W - Little A'Le'Inn

1.68 MILES West of the infamous "BLACK MAILBOX" Folks!

The Little A'Le'Inn

Earthlings are always WELCOME!

Right off HWY 375 in Rachel, Nevada . You must have that great "Alien Burger"......off the menu.

41

If you need a place to say because you did not bring any CAMPING GEAR, well don't worry, the Little A'Le'Inn has complete housing for all of you explorers and Area 51 personnel!

SOME KEY NOTES TO REMEMBER BEFORE YOU VENTURE OUT:

The gas station in Rachel is closed. The nearest gas stations are 50 miles south in Ash Springs and 110 miles north in Tonopah.

GAS UP IN ALAMO if coming from Vegas!

GAS UP IN TONOPAH if coming from California.

YOU MIGHT WANT TO BRING:

Binoculars, a tripod for your camera, GPS meter, water (or other liquids) and food make these outings a great experience.

Bring proper clothing for warm or hot days and cool or cold nights!!

PLEASE READ THE FOLLOWING WARNINGS FOR YOUR SAFETY!!!

The desert can be dangerous day or night!! Bring liquids and stay hydrated at any rate!!! Even safer is to let someone at the Inn know where you are going when you should be back.

1.) GEOCACHING!!! There are thousands of GeoCache sites along Hwy 375. (Go to www.geocaching.com if you don't know what it is)

2.) ASTRONOMY!! You don't have to walk or drive far to get out of the lights and into the dark to see the stars. The clear night sky makes stargazing easy! The best place is 375 north at the county line, 9 miles away. There is a large pullout well away and safe from the highway traffic. Even on a full moon night the stars are spectacular. Another, closer, spot is go north on 375 only 3.5 miles and on the right hand side is a large, flat spot to set up a telescope

3.) Look out the front door and that mountain slightly to the left is Tempiute. You can drive all the way around it and see a forest on the "back" side. Go south on 375 0.5 miles. Turn left and go through the "S" turns and go another 1.7 miles and bear left at the corral (going right gets you back to 375) at 3.0 miles take the fork that goes to the right. After the fork about another three miles the road is subject to washout, and it can be rough but passable. At the 4 mile mark to the right is the Tempiute Mine. Continue on this road and it becomes paved and gets you back to 375. At 375 turn right and 10.2 miles back to the Little A'Le'Inn. (You lose Verizon coverage soon after passing Tempiute Mine.)

4.) Not too far off of 375 (3.9 miles south of the Inn) is the ghost town of Tempiute which is along the left (north) side of 375 at the 3.9 odometer reading. Turn left on the dirt road and at the 1.3 mile odometer, take the right fork and at the 2.3 mile mark is the town. It is about 1/3 of a mile long but follow the road until you have to stop and walk to the Ghost Town. (Short walk) NOTE: This road was good enough for a 2WD vehicle with decent clearance on 6/30/17 Verizon has good coverage here. NOTE view of Rachel from the ghost town

The Infamous ... Little A'Le'Inn GIFT SHOP & STORE

A must visit and say hello from YOURS TRULY!

WELCOME TO BEAUTIFUL RACHEL, NEVADA

37°38'39.35"N 115°44'20.69"W

DRIVING DIRECTIONS LAS VEGAS, NEVADA!

Driving directions FROM Las Vegas to Rachel, NV 89001
1) Take the ramp onto I-15 N travel about 26 miles
2) Take exit 64 for US-93 N/Great Basin Hwy toward Pioche Ely about 0.2 miles

*******STOP AND FILL YOUR TANK AT ALAMO OR ASH SPRINGS>>>THERE IS NO GAS FOR OVER 150 MILES*****

3) Turn left onto US-93 N/Great Basin Hwy travel about 85 miles

Note: below is a fork in the road watch on-coming traffic before staying left onto NV-375

4) Turn left onto NV-318 N/NV-375 N/State Hwy 375 - Continue to follow NV-375 N/State Hwy 375 about 40 miles
NOTE: AREA 51 BORDER
Take 375 south from The LITTLE A'LE'INN 19.8 miles to Mailbox Road. Turn to your right and go 3.5 miles to the water tank and corral. The road splits 3 ways, take the center road. After another 0.8 miles there is a major dirt road. Turn to the roght and go 8.5 miles to reach the boundary. DO NOT GO PAST THE WARNING SIGNS---- YOU WILL BE ARRESTED!

NOTE: The "ORIGINAL BLACK MAILBOX" no longer exists as of Mid-August 2014! The directions won't change as the road is still there, and it's the only road at that milepost.

There is a back gate nearer to Rachel that you can also go to. Head south on 375 for 1.5 miles to a wide dirt road on the right side and turn on it. You will go behind the town and after a few miles the road will be paved. Follow it to the border gates---you can't miss the border there are red lights and crossing gates there also plenty of room to U-turn.

At mile marker 34.5 on Highway 375, turn onto Groom Lake Road in which we will explore later in detail in this Buckle-Up adventure book. The Area 51 boundary is 13.8 miles down Groom Lake Road.

You will be able to see the warning signs, and most likely the "men in black" security guards.

Do NOT pass the warning signs, or you will be arrested with a $750.00 + fine. We don't want that!

DANGER WILL ROBINSON – "PRIOR ORIGINAL SIGNS"

ROAD SENORS!

AN INTRODUCTION

WARNING: DO NOT CROSS THE BORDER!!!!

BEWARE OF THE FLIR SYSTEM!

PLEASE NOTE:

What is a road sensor?

Description

The MIDS Transmitter (MXMT) as an example unit that is used by Area 51 security which is manufactured by Qual-Tron Inc. located in Tulsa, OK is used to **transmit a digitally encoded ID number, via narrow band VHF (138-174 MHz)** RF frequencies, when activated by various types of attached ground sensors. The transmitter is factory pre-set to a single (customer specified) channel.

ID CODE EXAMPLE BELOW:

Operation

ID Code Set-Up – The ID is the number transmitted when the attached sensor is activated. The ID number transmitted is the sum of the switches, 8A + B. These switches should be set with the screwdriver provided to prevent damage to the plastic slots. Use only even number ID codes between 00-62.

ROAD SENORS!

AN INTRODUCTION

WARNING: DO NOT CROSS THE BORDER!!!!

BEWARE OF THE FLIR SYSTEM!

Operation

ID Code Set-Up – The ID is the number transmitted when the attached sensor is activated. The ID number transmitted is the sum of the switches, 8A + B. These switches should be set with the screwdriver provided to prevent damage to the plastic slots. Use only even number ID codes between 00-62.

Example: ID Code 30
 (A) x8 position = 3; (B) x1 position = 6;
  = (8 x 3) + (1 x 6)
  =   24 + 6 = 30
(ID number **30** will be transmitted)

ID Switch Setting Chart

ID	X8	x1	ID	x8	x1	ID	x8	x1	ID	x8	x1
00	0	0	16	2	0	32	4	0	48	6	0
02	0	2	18	2	2	34	4	2	50	6	2
04	0	4	20	2	4	36	4	4	52	6	4
06	0	6	22	2	6	38	4	6	54	6	6
08	1	0	24	3	0	40	5	0	56	7	0
10	1	2	26	3	2	42	5	2	58	7	2
12	1	4	28	3	4	44	5	4	60	7	4
14	1	6	30	3	6	46	5	6	62	7	6

Note: For all applications use even ID codes only. When a sensor fault occurs (if the connection between the transmitter and sensor is broken for any reason), the transmitter will activate and transmit the next higher odd ID number.
 Example: If the normal ID code is 20, then 21 would be transmitted when a sensor fault occurs. This would advise the user of a special problem, which needs immediate attention.

ROAD SENORS!

AN INTRODUCTION

WARNING: DO NOT CROSS THE BORDER!!!!

BEWARE OF THE FLIR SYSTEM!

As of the Summer 2016 a slightly modified version of these sensors is still in use. There are approximately 30 sensors in Sand Spring Valley and at least 50 sensors in Tikaboo Valley, so beware!

Manufacture: http://www.mcbordersecurityinc.com/

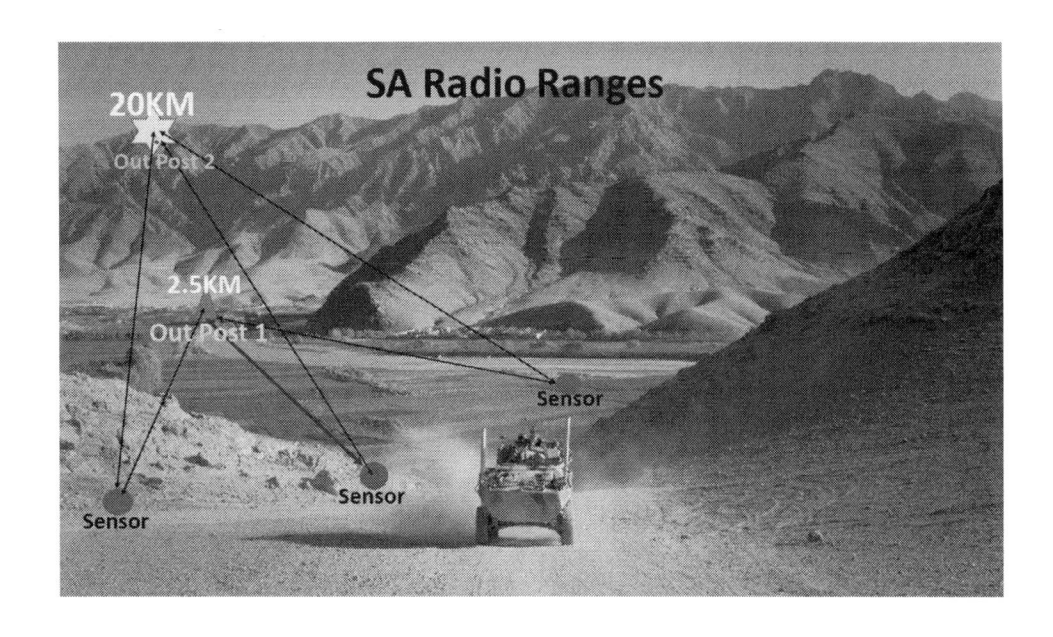

ROAD SENSORS
ROAD SENORS!
AN INTRODUCTION

WARNING: DO NOT CROSS THE BORDER!!!!

BEWARE OF THE FLIR SYSTEM!

QUAL-TRON, INC.

HTTPS://WWW.QUAL-TRON.COM/ABOUT-US

QTI Intrusion Detection Systems are sold exclusively to U.S. and Foreign Military, Government Agencies and Law Enforcement Agencies. They are used for a variety of applications to include perimeter security, conduct surveillance, detect movement, protect resources, and provide site security. Each system includes sensors, transmitters, receivers and relays. They provide instantaneous digitally encoded messages that are displayed on hand held or base station receivers. Data logging systems enhance these systems by providing sensor logs, mapping systems and visual confirmation of sensor activity. See the following pages for more details on this technology.

Qual-Tron, Inc. (QTI) has been providing unattended ground sensors to military and government agency customers since 1986. QTI systems feature an extremely reliable communication link which has been utilized by border professionals around the world. Border security applications include primary detection on avenues of approach, outside the fence, early warning and the cueing of other systems' equipment to augment and enhance effectiveness and save power consumption.

ROAD SENORS!

AN INTRODUCTION

WARNING: DO NOT CROSS THE BORDER!!!!

BEWARE OF THE FLIR SYSTEM!

HTTPS://WWW.QUAL-TRON.COM/ABOUT-US

The robust design of QTI equipment makes it an ideal trigger device to compliment camera systems, ground radar systems, acoustic systems or even systems with higher levels of lethality. QTI produces a range of seismic, magnetic, passive infrared, break beam, break wire, hydrophone, acoustic and other more specialized sensors. QTI sensors and transmitters can boast of three years in the field without a battery change.

QTI sensors possess a very covert profile as these sensors are designed to operate while buried or concealed, making visual detection nearly impossible. The RF profile of much of QTI equipment is designed for maximization of stealth and minimization of power consumption as each transmission sent is a non-repeating short burst message, making it nearly impossible to detect, locate and intercept.

History

Qual-Tron Inc. (QTI) is a major supplier of Unattended Ground Sensors (UGS). QTI has pushed the envelope developing extremely low power sensors. These power needs have made it possible for QTI sensors to remain deployed for as long as two years. QTI has networked its systems with many operations around the globe. QTI sensors are deployed on every Continent and with every major Command. QTI has deployed its sensors in areas of both hot and cold temperatures, while producing outstanding results. QTI sensors have successfully performed, in these areas, for more than 30 years with excellent reliability.

QTI has always been a steady, reliably small business. Striving to provide a technologically advanced product. QTI has proven that the outstanding communications capabilities, of its products, have produced results for the

Warfighter, Special Operations, Border Security, National Parks, The ease of fitting into an existing network or creating a network, has made QTI a go to brand for many organizations worldwide.

ROAD SENORS!

AN INTRODUCTION

WARNING: DO NOT CROSS THE BORDER!!!!

BEWARE OF THE FLIR SYSTEM!

Technical Attributes

- Extremely low power sensors that can provide up to two years of sustainable operations with a small battery package.

- Combine a digital architecture with a broad base of features designed around a modular configuration and you have a Situational Awareness product base that will give you the flexibility to fit most any intrusion need.

- RF communications that allow digital wireless interface from each sensor pushed into a variety of network architectures to transfer critical data to a final destination (C2) for analysis and response evaluation.

- Advanced Artificial Intelligence processing combining features of a learned response format to produce a situational awareness that will produce an extremely accurate picture of the threat. Enabling the operator to make an informed path of interdiction and apprehension.

- Sensor designs that are small, durable and proven in the field of operation. QTI sensors have stood the test of time.

ROAD SENORS!

AN INTRODUCTION

WARNING: DO NOT CROSS THE BORDER!!!!

BEWARE OF THE FLIR SYSTEM!

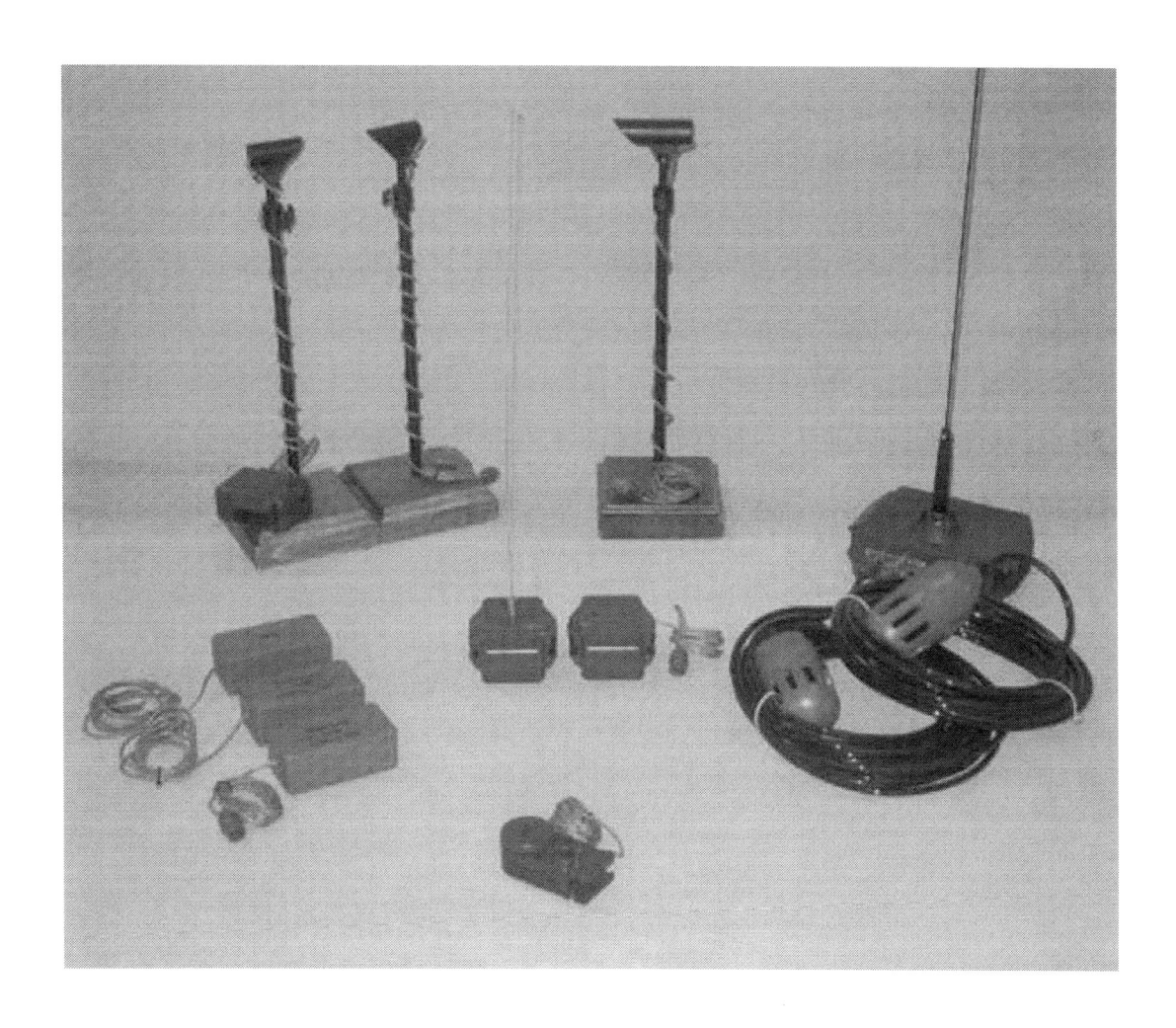

MIDS - Mini Intrusion Detection System is a single channel fixed frequency system capable of monitoring up to 32 sensors. It has a built in sensor fault alarm if the sensor is disconnected from the transmitter. This is the most economical system and consists of the following equipment: MXMT Transmitter, MPDM Hand Held

Receiver, and MRLY Relay. **Note: Frequency is customer specified and factory installed (selected from 138-174 MHz).**

ROAD SENORS!

AN INTRODUCTION

WARNING: DO NOT CROSS THE BORDER!!!!

BEWARE OF THE FLIR SYSTEM!

MIDS-II - Mini Intrusion Detection System (Modified) is a single channel fixed frequency system capable of monitoring up to 999 sensors. It provides additional data messages which include sensor fault alarm, directional information, and transmitter test and low battery message. An "On/Test" switch is included on the transmitter. This system falls in the mid price range. MIDS-II Equipment includes: MXMT-II Transmitter, MPDM-II Hand Held Receiver, and MRLY Relay. **Note: Frequency is customer specified and factory installed (selected from 138-174 MHz).**

ROAD SENORS!

AN INTRODUCTION

WARNING: DO NOT CROSS THE BORDER!!!!

BEWARE OF THE FLIR SYSTEM!

EMIDS - Enhanced Mini Intrusion Detection System is a multi-Channel Synthesized System capable of monitoring up to 999 sensors. It is available in three frequency ranges; low band 138-153 MHz with 600 channels, mid band 154-162 MHz with 1600 channels and high band 162-174 MHz with 1920 channels. This system also provides additional data messages which include sensor fault alarm, sensor directional information, transmitter tamper alarm, and transmitter test and low battery messages. It also provides state of health messages from hourly up to 24 hour intervals. This system includes the following equipment: MMCT Transmitter, MMCR Hand Held Receiver, and MSRY Relay.

ROAD SENORS!
UNDER THE HOOD.

Description

The MIDS Transmitter (MXMT) is used to transmit a digitally encoded ID number, via narrow band VHF (138-174 MHz) RF frequencies, when activated by various types of attached ground sensors. The transmitter is factory pre-set to a single (customer specified) channel. See frequency range below.

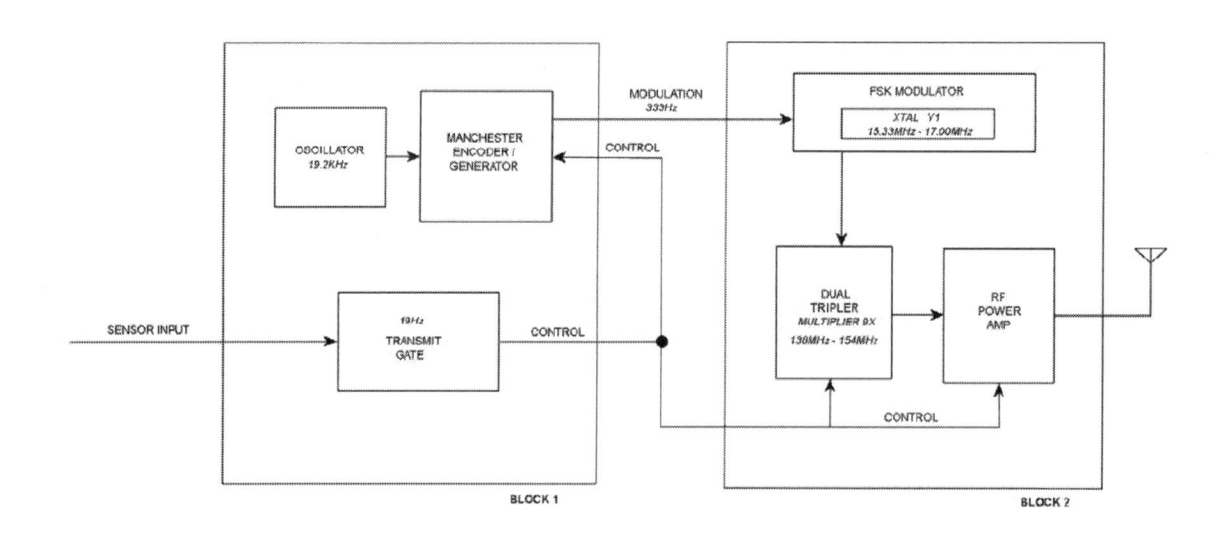

MXMT BLOCK DIAGRAM

Emplacement Considerations:

The MXMT can be buried under one inch of compacted soil. Use caution not to bend the antenna when burying.

MIDS Transmitter (MXMT)

Description
The MIDS Transmitter (MXMT) is used to transmit a digitally encoded ID number, via narrow band VHF (138-174 MHz) RF frequencies, when activated by various types of attached ground sensors. The transmitter is factory pre-set to a single (customer specified) channel. See frequency range below.

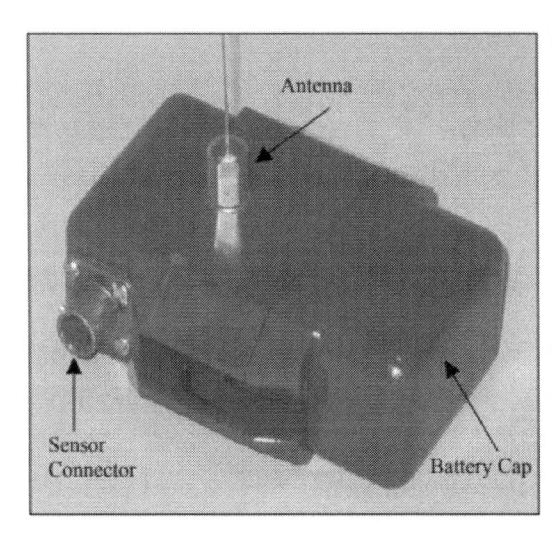

Channel:	Factory Pre-Set Single Channel
ID Codes:	00-63 (Even numbers only for normal use, all numbers for special applications.)
Antenna:	Wire Whip, ¼ Wave
Frequency Range:	138-174 MHz
Power Supply:	1-2 each 9 V DC Batteries (MN1604)
Battery Life:	4-6 months in temperate climate
Sensor:	Any Qual-Tron sensor
Pin Connections:	A: Ground B: +9 VDC C: Tx Trigger D: ID Code Control (do not use)

Design Features
- ID code selection (Switches inside battery compartment)
- Internal power ON – Normal operation – Antenna up
- Internal power OFF – Non operating – Battery cap down
- Internal power ON – Sensor alignment – Battery cap up
- Transmit ID code alarms
- Sensor Fault alarms
- Sealed battery compartment
- Four pin Mil-Type (sensor) connector
- Potted and sealed electronic components
- Injection molded lexan plastic housing
- Metal battery cap clamps with heat welded screw inserts
- Frequency matched antenna

RF Link

The operational range of the RF link is dependent upon various conditions. The high frequency of the RF link works best under line of sight conditions. Transmission can range from a few hundred yards to several miles, depending on terrain. Non line-of-sight can play a part in decreasing the transmission range. The transmission range can be extended with the use of relays, or by elevating the antenna at either the transmitter or receiver position.

ROAD SENORS!
DATA RECEIVER
UNDER THE HOOD.

MCDR Multi-Channel Data Receiver

Description

The Multi-Channel Data Receiver (MCDR) is an OEM modular modem for users who need low power and small size with serial communications. The MCDR is a smaller version of the MCDT-R and is fully compatible. The MCDR is equipped with a RS-485 communications port which is a simple, low cost interface, utilizing few components and allows for daisy-chaining multiple receivers. The MCDR is capable of receiving SEIWG-005 data messages, which includes a distinct ID and a status code, over a selectable frequency range. This frequency is selectable via the synthesizer control circuit, providing a selection of up to 1920 RF channels, depending on the model's frequency range. The MCDR comes in Low-Band, Mid-Band, and High-Band models, having the following frequency ranges:

Low Band Medium Band High Band
Channel 001 = 138.025 MHz
Channel 001 = 154.005 MHz
Channel 001 = 162.00625 MHz
Channel 640 = 154.000 MHz
Channel 1600 = 162.000 MHz
Channel 1920 = 174.000 MHz

Channel Spacing: 25 kHz Channel Spacing: 5 kHz Channel Spacing: 6.25 kHz

ROAD SENORS!
HOW TO FIND THEM WITH RDF

Radio Direction Finder Introduction

A **radio direction finder** (**RDF**) is a device for finding the direction, or *bearing*, to a radio source. The act of measuring the direction is known as **radio direction finding** or sometimes simply **direction finding** (**DF**). Using two or more measurements from different locations, the location of an unknown transmitter can be determined; alternately, using two or more measurements of known transmitters, the location of a vehicle can be determined. RDF is widely used as a radio navigation system, especially with boats and aircraft.

RDF systems can be used with any radio source, although the size of the receiver antennas are a function of the wavelength of the signal; very long wavelengths (low frequencies) require very large antennas, and are generally used only on ground-based systems. These wavelengths are nevertheless very useful for marine navigation as they can travel very long distances and "over the horizon", which is valuable for ships when the line-of-sight may be only a few tens of kilometres. For aerial use, where the horizon may extend to hundreds of kilometres, higher frequencies can be used, allowing the use of much smaller antennas. An automatic direction finder, often capable of being tuned to commercial AM radio transmitters, is a feature of almost all modern aircraft.

The **KN2C DF2020T** is an economical but very sophisticated Doppler DF "kit" with a GPS input, and RS232 output to provide the ability to indicate its location and draw bearing automatically or manually on Google Earth map to find the RF transmitter more conveniently.

KN2C-2020T kit Includes eight assembled / tested PC boards: MAIN board and 2 Sub boards in the main unit, and five antenna boards in the antenna modules (one for each of four antennas and one for auxiliary antenna). Completion work is required by the user to finish the DF main unit. Guidelines for the completion work are provided.

The user must provide a NB FM receiver, antennas and a PC for DF bearing (Windows OS). DF2020 display program further requires a GPS receiver with NMEA 4800 baud output.

ROAD SENORS!

HOW TO FIND THEM WITH RDF

- VHF Doppler DF – 4 Antennas primarily for mobile DF, 100~1000 MHz
- Economy, high performance DSP / micro processor design, software intensive
- Sold as a kit – Main unit, antenna unit and associated cables
- Accepts **NMEA RS232** GPS input data (4800 baud, $GPRMC, $GPGGA and / or $GPVTG sentences) for "Plotting map on Windows PC display"
- RS232 output for Windows PCs (Agrello format)
- Uses modified **Joe Moell Wideband Antenna** design
- 9 ~ 28 VDC operation
- Optional **GPS Receiver** available

DF2020T (Kit)

DF2020T Radio Direction Finder kit requires minimum assembly for 10~15 Minutes

The Stealth DDF2020T/GPS is an economical but very sophisticated Doppler Direction Finder with GPS and can connect a PC or Laptop, to position and draw plots on GoogleEarth™ display window accompanied with "Navi 2020" plotting program.

** Required only minimum assembling for 10 ~ 15 minutes with the tested components in the case

http://www.kn2c.us/ - WHERE TO PURCHASE THE RDF!

ROAD SENORS!
HOW TO FIND THEM WITH RDF

The receiver and antennas are not included
FUNCTIONS

- Multi Display – Numeric & 36 LED pelorus display
- Compatible with APRS software

- Can use with **"Navi2020"** map plotting display program (with the optional GPS Receiver)
- Uses GoogleEarth™ viewer for displaying map of ploiting.
- Automatic or manual operation
- Accepts standard $GPRMC NMEA GPS message
- Archive Navi files are auto-saved

ROAD SENORS!

HOW TO FIND THEM WITH RDF

SPECIFICATIONS

- Microcomputer / DSP Doppler DF
- DF Antenna Module with built-in magnetics on the bottoms for easy install
- GPS input for "moving map" Windows display
- RS232 output for PCs (can use with Serial to USB conveter)
- Uses **Any Type of FM Receiver and Scanner, Wideband Antenna** design
- 12 - 28 VDC operation
- Pre-assembled External Antenna Unit for Plug and Play
- 4 antenna elements and new circuit design for improving the sensitivity and accuracy
- Suitable from 100 to 1000 Mhz and beyond
- Useful from 88 to 100 MHz with reduced sensitivity

MAJOR FEATURES

- VHF/UHF Doppler type DF, (4 antennas) primarily for mobile DF operation, 100 to 1000 MHz
- The user must provide additional equipment (PC or laptop) to use the DDF2020T DF System:
- A VHF/UHF FM receiver is required. (For receiving a signal for DF)
- Pre-assembled antena unit for Plug and Play

1. Comes With DDF2020T, Antenna Unit, GPS Receiver, Navi2020 Program, 3.5mm Audio Cable Set, Antenna Control Cable(4.5 m), RG174 Cable(4.5 m), Bracket, Cigar Cord. - **Not Include Receiver and antennas**
2. The appearance of product may be different from the picture

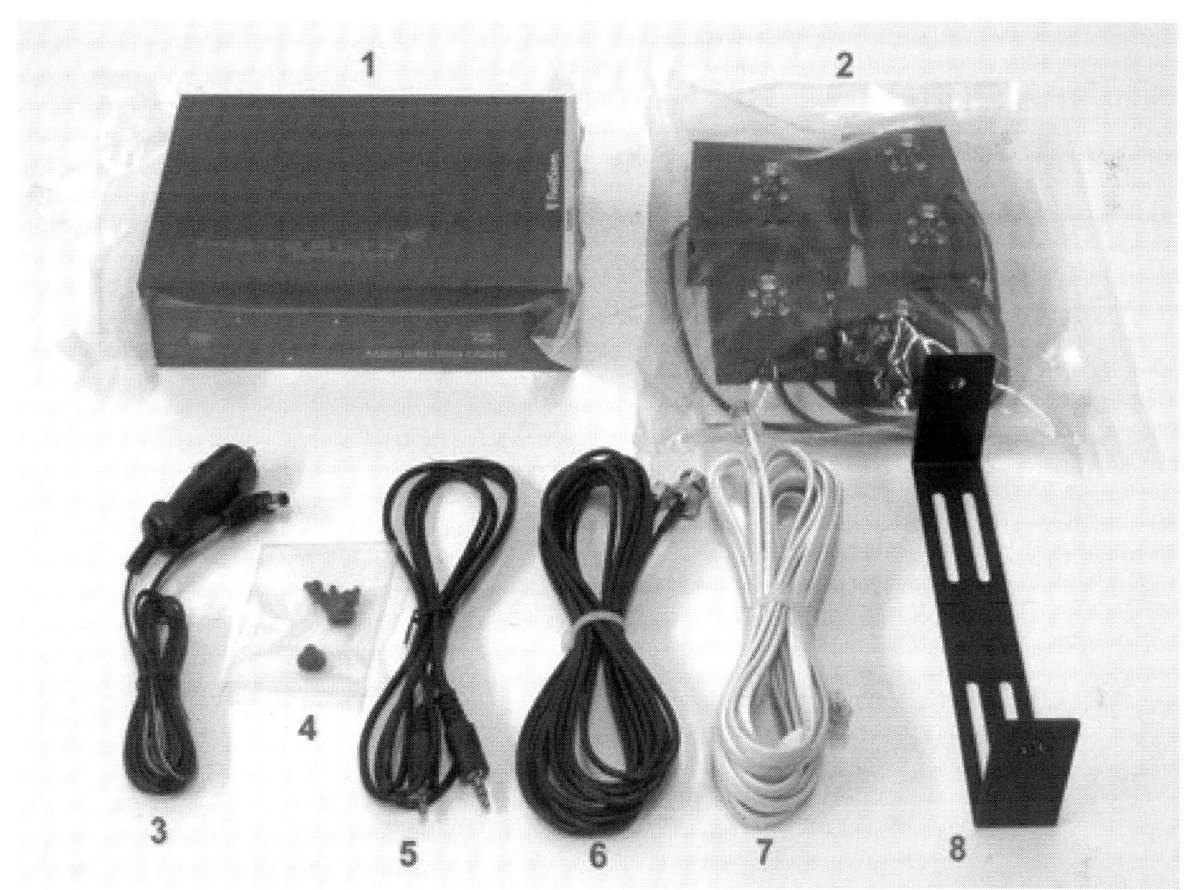

ROAD SENORS!
HOW TO FIND THEM WITH RDF

Cotents in the Package

1. Case with assembled parts - requires a minimum assembly

63

2. The Antenna Module with magnetics on the bottoms
3. Cigar Jack Power Cord
4. Screw pack
5. 3.5 mm Audio Cable Set
6. RG-174 cable
7. Antenna Control Cable
8. Bracket

ROAD SENORS!

HOW TO FIND THEM WITH RDF

Receiver Frequency: Determined by user-provided FM

- receiver, range 100 to 1000 MHz
  - Antenna : Four elements, wave vertical with ground plane (recommended)
  - Ant Scan : Scan rate 430 Hz, rotation clockwise (viewed from above antenna)
  - Ant Switch : Modified Joe Moell Wideband Doppler DF antenna design
  - Employs Agilent HSMP3893 SMT PIN diodes
  - SMT / stripline circuit design, BNC output connector
  - Audio Input : FM receiver speaker audio, 1.0 K ohm
- load. 25 db dynamic range.

  - GPS Input : 4800 baud RS232 input, NMEA $GPRMC,
- $GPGGA and / or $GPVTG messages.
  - Output : RS232 Agrello DF message, 4800 baud, 8N2.
- (15 messages / second)
  - Ant Outputs : Four discrete active HIGH outputs for

DDF2020T Antenna (one per antenna) and 1 auxiliary antenna for improving it sesitivity and accuracy.

- Voice Filter: Switched-capacitor filter, (SCF) 4

sections. Bandwidth 0.2 Hz

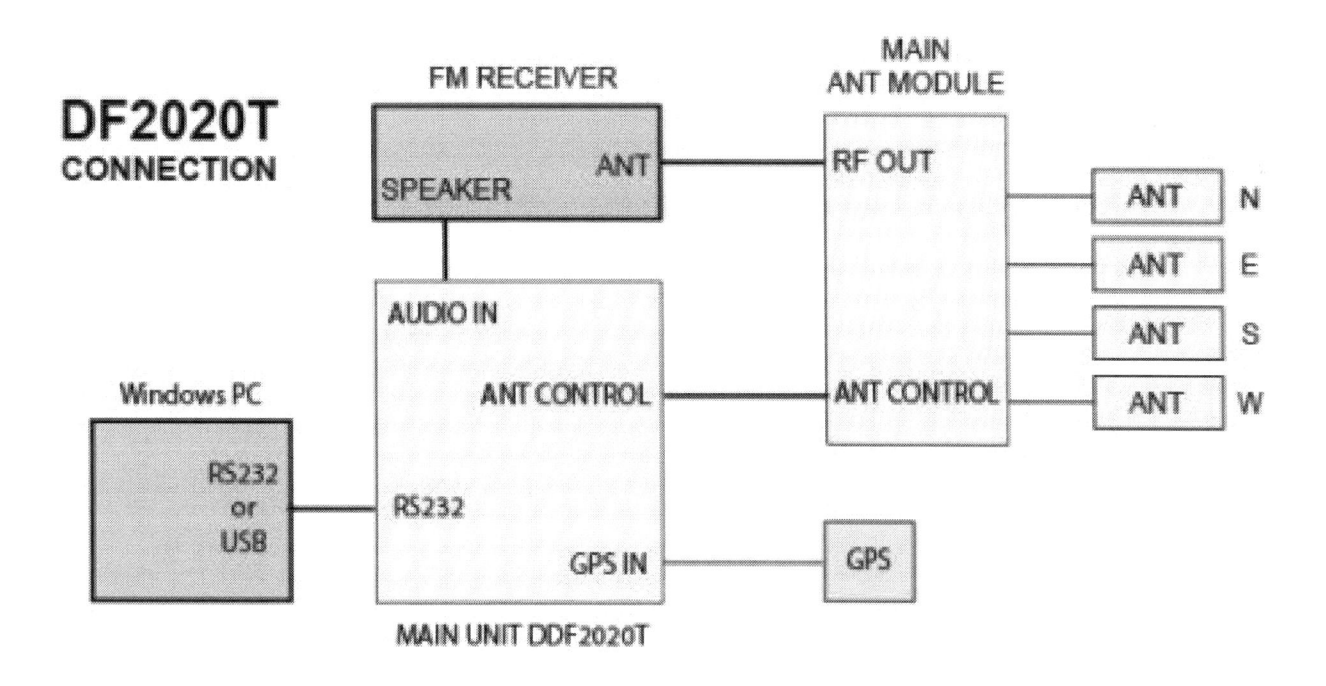

ROAD SENORS!
HOW TO FIND THEM WITH RDF

ROAD SENORS!
HOW TO FIND THEM WITH RDF
PICTURES OF THE RDF UNIT
WITH THE ANTENNA ARRAY

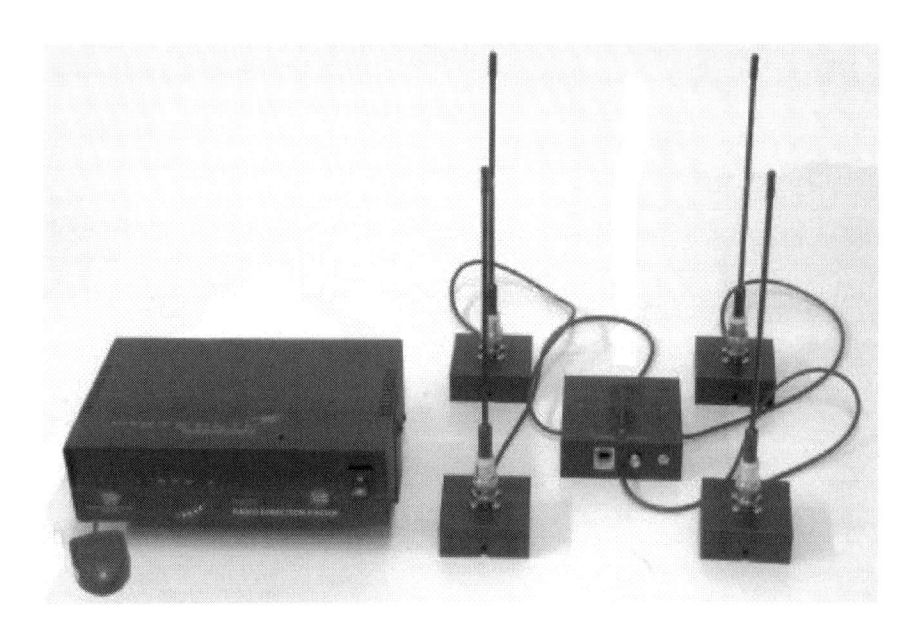

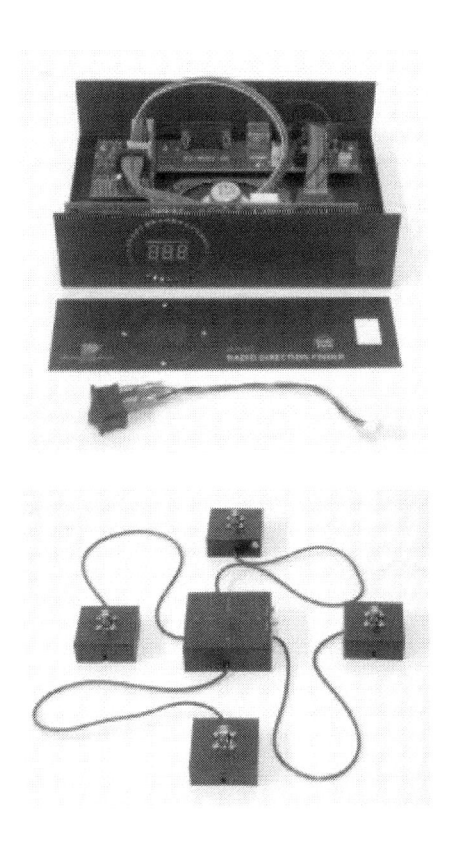

ROAD SENORS!
HOW TO FIND THEM WITH RDF
PICTURES OF THE RDF UNIT

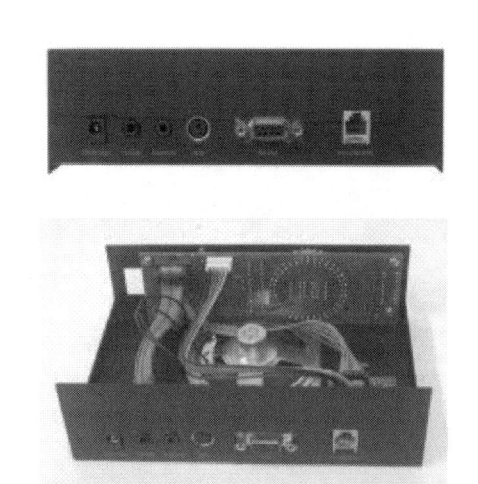

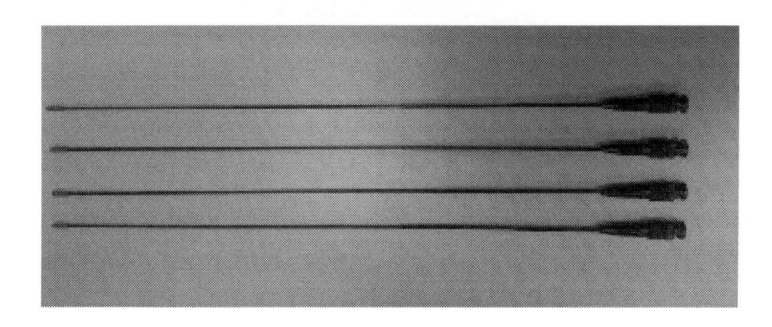

ROAD SENORS!

HOW TO FIND THEM WITH RDF

GOOGLE EARTH INFO BELOW:

ROAD SENSOR COORDINATES:

37°22'41.67"N 115°31'3.90"W

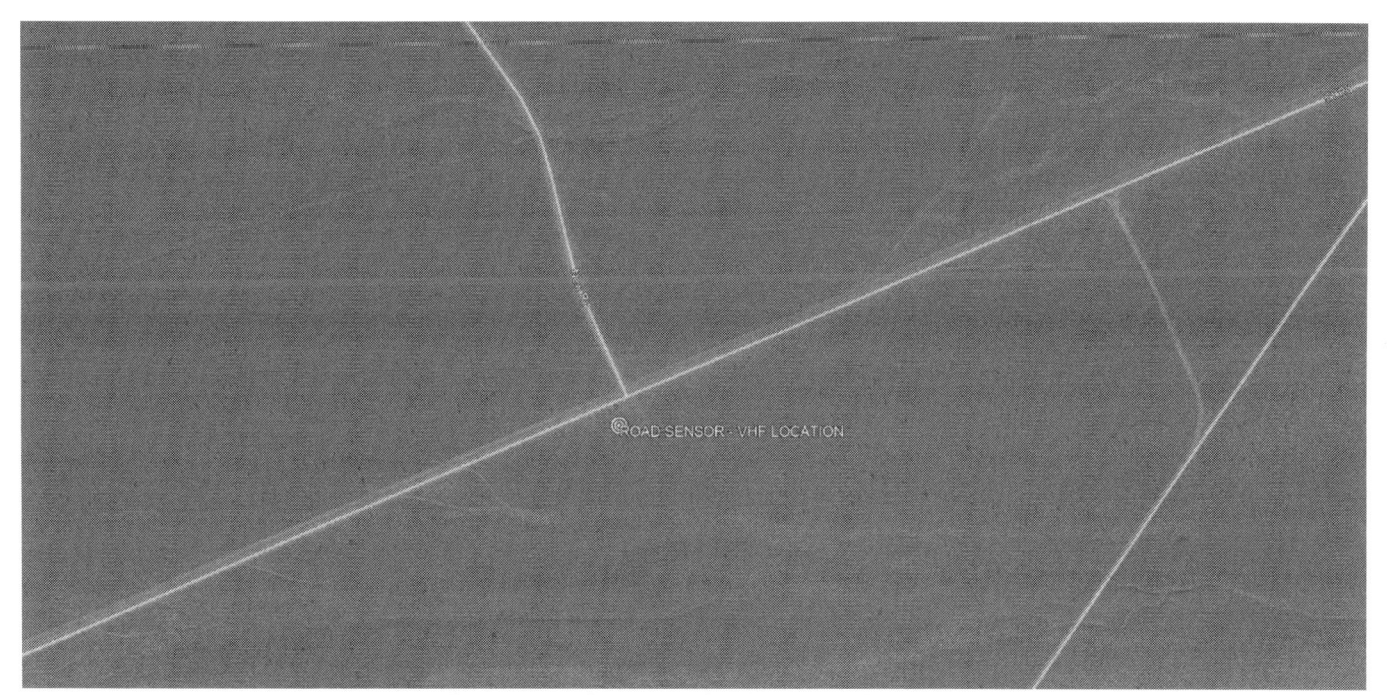

THE ROAD SENSOR IS AT THE INTERSECTION OF NEW RD AND GL ROAD. IT IS JUST BY THE TREE ON THE SOUTH SIDE OF GL ROAD.

ROAD SENORS!

HOW TO FIND THEM WITH RDF

GOOGLE EARTH INFO BELOW:

MERLIN RANCH COORDINATES:

37°24'6.17"N 115°32'9.21"W

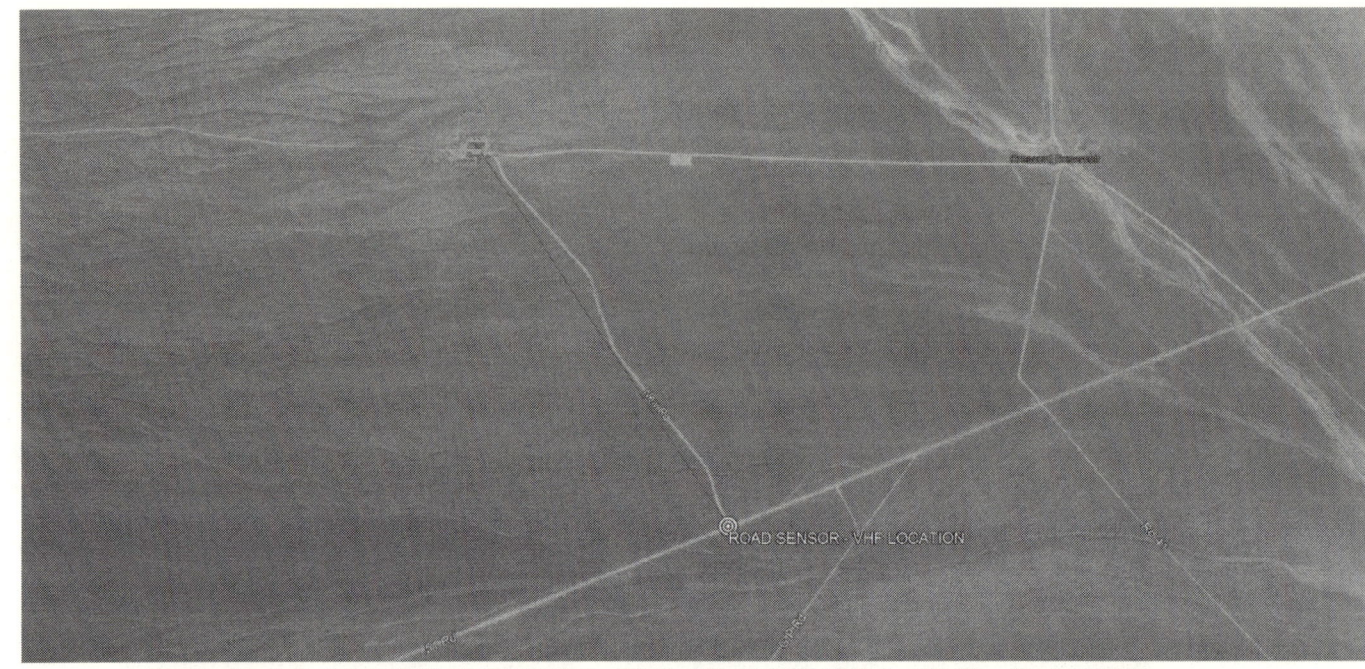

FROM THE MERLIN RANCH TO 51 GL ROAD VIA NEW ROAD IS APPROXIMATELY 1.88 MILES.

37.378421°, -115.517825°

ROAD SENORS!

HOW TO FIND THEM WITH RDF

GOOGLE EARTH INFO BELOW:

375 & GL ROAD COORDINATES:

37°24'53.49"N 115°24'35.27"W

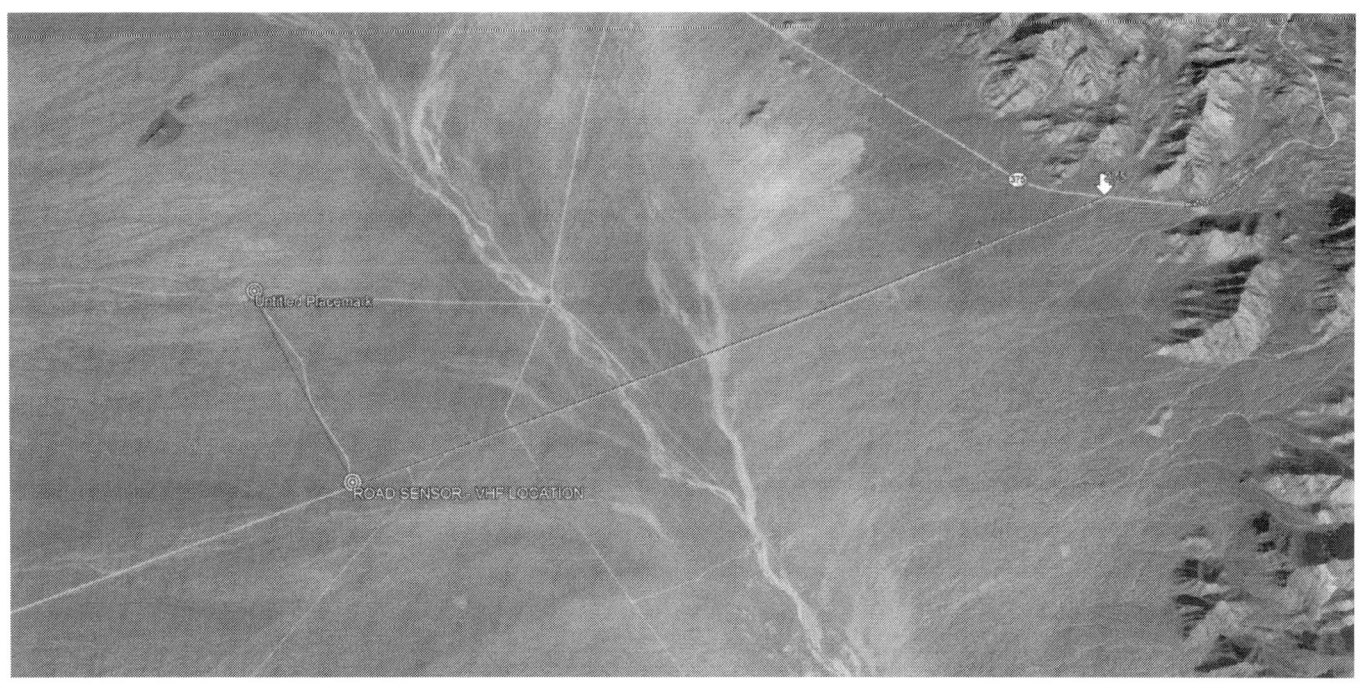

FROM ROAD SENSOR / NEW ROAD TO HWY 375 IS APPROXIMATELY 6.44 MILES

Radiolocation Methods – ROAD SENSORS or SIMILAR

There are two broad methods for locating the source of a radio transmission. The first, Trilateration, uses multiple geographically-separated omnidirectional receiving stations while the second, Triangulation, uses one or more directional receiving stations.

Trilateration

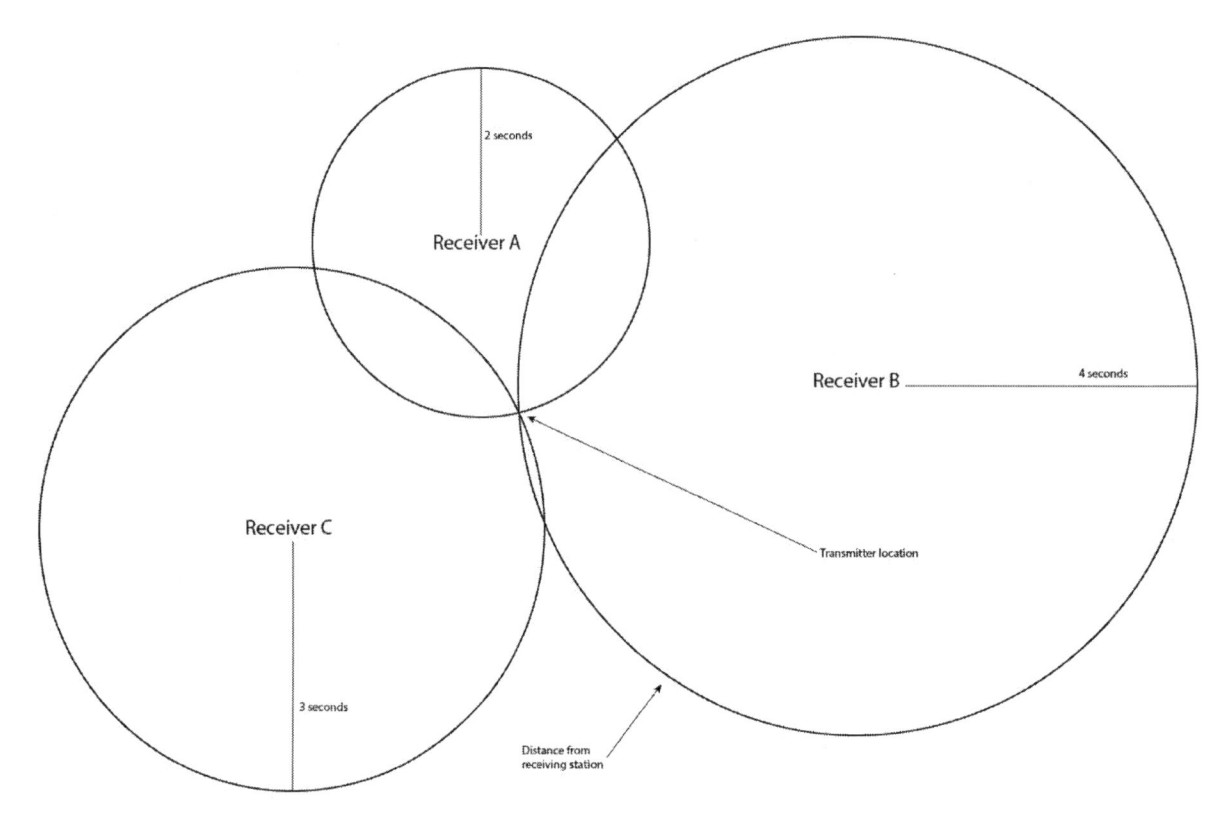

[Diagram: Three overlapping circles showing Receiver A (2 seconds), Receiver B (4 seconds), and Receiver C (3 seconds), intersecting at the Transmitter location. An arrow labelled "Distance from receiving station" points to the radius of Receiver B's circle.]

The first method uses a technique called trilateration. Each receiving station measures the length of time taken for the radio signal to reach their position, and when the times from three or more receiving stations are known, a position for the receiver can be calculated. The advantage of this method is that each receiving station is equipped with a simple, omnidirectional antenna (the received signal strength is the same from all directions), however you need multiple fixed receiving stations, and each station must be equipped with a very precise clock in order to have any accuracy (since we're timing things travelling at the speed of light here).
Triangulation

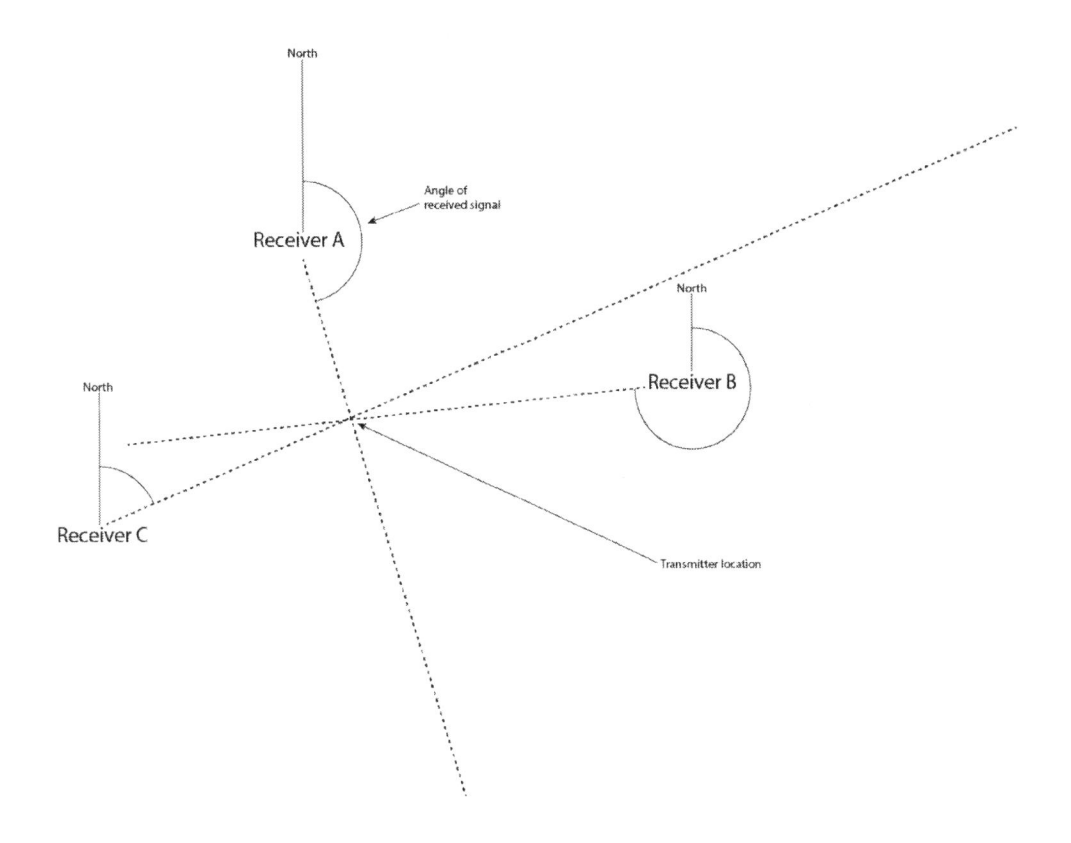

The second method uses the slightly more familiar-sounding triangulation. It can be used with multiple fixed-position receiving stations, as with trilateration, or it can be used with a single mobile receiving station. The station is equipped with a directional antenna (the received signal strength is much higher when the antenna is pointed toward the transmitter), and determines the angle which the signal is received from. When this angle is taken from three or more different locations, the location of the transmitter can be calculated.

The advantage of this method is that a single receiving station can be placed at each location in turn, and take a bearing to the signal. No clocks are involved; you just need to measure your position and the angle to the signal from a reference point (i.e. magnetic north) with reasonable accuracy.

When using triangulation manually in real life, the operator would typically select 3+ good sites on a map (ideally at on top of some nearby hills), go to each location, take a bearing, and plot the lines on a map. As shown in the diagram above, the transmitter should be where the lines meet.

This is the process I plan to implement with the drone, with the added advantage that we can select arbitrary points in space (as long as they're above ground) to take the bearings from!

Radio Direction Finding (RDF)

To get a bearing on a signal, you need a way to find the direction the signal was transmitted from - this is the field of Radio Direction Finding, which has had lots of development thanks to its use in aircraft navigation for most of the 20th century. Rather than looking at professional aerial navigation systems however, at this point we'll be going off into the world of amateur radio and the sport of "Foxhunting". Not surprisingly, radio nerds have made a sport out of searching for hidden radio transmitters and dedicate quite a bit of effort to the equipment they use to help them.

Again, there are two main methods of RDF used in the foxhunting world - using a directional antenna (a "directive gain antenna" to be more precise), or using a direction-finding (DF) system.

Directive Gain Antennas - In electromagnetic, **directivity** is a parameter of an antenna or optical system which measures the degree to which the radiation emitted is concentrated in a single direction. It measures the power density the antenna radiates in the direction of its strongest emission, versus the power density radiated by an ideal isotropic radiator (which emits uniformly in all directions) radiating the same total power.

An antenna's directivity is a component of its gain; the other component is its (electrical) efficiency. Directivity is an important measure because many antennas and optical systems are designed to radiate electromagnetic waves in a single direction or over a narrow angle. Directivity is also defined for an antenna receiving electromagnetic waves, and its directivity when receiving is equal to its directivity when transmitting.

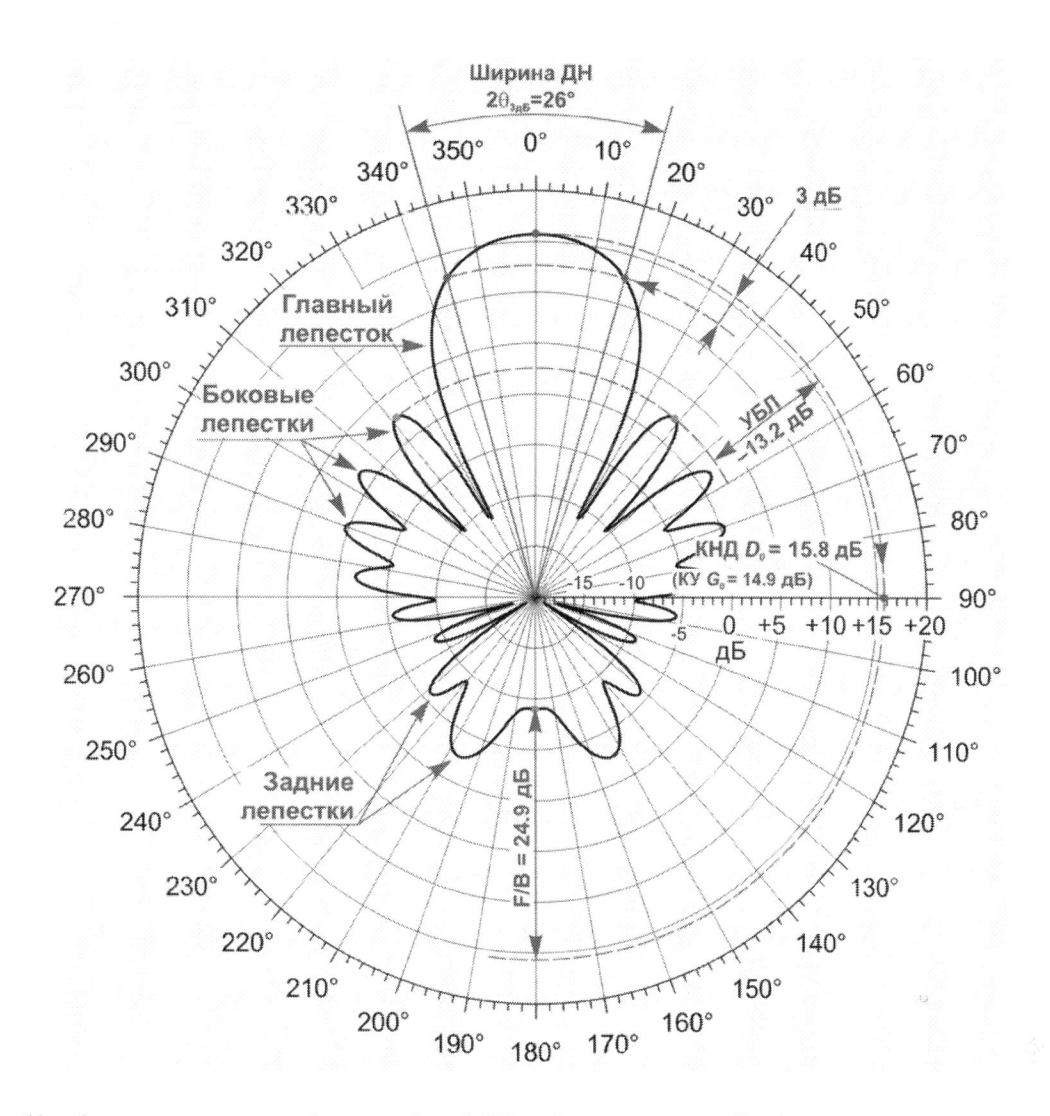

Radiation pattern of a typical Yagi antenna (ignore the Russian!)

As the name suggests, directive gain antennas achieve their directionality by applying gain (increasing the received signal strength) in the direction the antenna is pointing. Think of this in the same way you can focus the light from a light bulb by using a reflector - it's the same amount of light, but concentrated in a direction rather than going out in all directions.

The most common example of this sort of antenna is a Yagi antenna, which looks like your standard long-and-pointy TV antenna. These are simple, really easy to make, and can have reasonable directionality (10-20 degrees beamwidth). Unfortunately they're quite large and ungainly, which could present problems mounting it to the drone, although that can probably be worked around.

The fact that these antennas have a high gain is both good and bad - if the signal is weak, or far away, having a high gain directional antenna is a real advantage. However, as you get closer to the signal and it gets stronger, having a high gain antenna can be a pain if it is your only method of determining direction - it can become less sensitive to direction. Using a stepped attenuator (see later) can help overcome this somewhat.

A directional Yagi antenna seems like a good plan B for the drone. It has quite a few downsides for typical expected use cases - it's bulky, has quite a wide beamwidth, and taking a bearing requires the drone to hover and rotate a full 360 degrees. The high gain makes it harder to use when close to the transmitter, however it could also be really useful in situations involving a transmitter which is weak or far away. So for now I'll focus elsewhere, but eventually it might be useful to integrate a yagi as a third antenna.

Direction Finding (DF) Systems

DF systems use multiple antennas to determine the direction of the signal. These come in two types, "homing" DF units which tell you which way (left or right) you need to rotate the antenna to be pointing directly at the transmitter, and doppler DF units which constantly tell you which direction the signal is in, regardless of which direction the receiver is pointing.

Doppler DF units work using the Doppler Effect - the same effect which causes a car horn to change pitch as it approaches you. A "true" Doppler DF antenna consists of a single antenna, rotating around a point in space at a high rate. As the antenna moves towards the transmitter, the frequency of the radio signal increases, as the antenna moves away from the transmitter the frequency decreases, and as the antenna moves perpendicular to the transmitter the frequency is the actual frequency of the transmission. So by observing the frequency changes of the received signal as the antenna rotates, you can determine the direction of the transmitter.

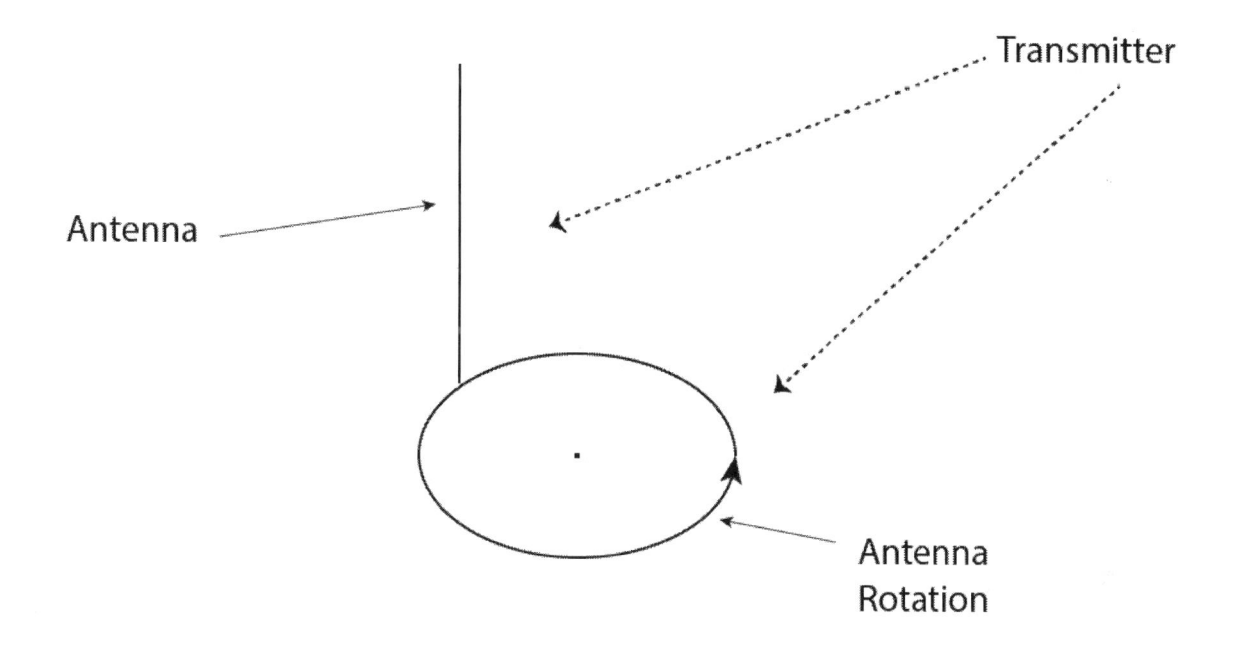

Making a rotating antenna like that is pretty hard, but luckily you can approximate the effect by making a circle of 4 or more static antennas and electronically switching between them at a high rate. This signal is then fed into a special receiver which analyses the frequency shifts and, traditionally, outputs to a ring of LEDs to show the direction the signal was received from.

Of the various homing DF designs, one stands out as being highly directional, lightweight and, crucially, easy to implement in an SDR - the "TDOA" DF antenna. This DF system consists of three dipole antennas, mounted a quarter-wavelength apart. A circuit switches between the two antennas at a high rate, and is fed into an FM radio receiver. If the switching frequency is in the audible range, the radio receiver outputs a tone at that frequency. When the two antennas are in-line with the transmitter, the tone is at its loudest, and when the two antennas are perpendicular to the transmitter the tone is a it's quietest, or is not there at all.

DO NOT CROSS THE BORDER!!!!

37°21'4.06"N 115°38'48.29"W

DANGER WILL ROBINSON: A NEW AREA 51 BAN

CAUTION: THERE IS NEW "BARB WIRE" AROUND BOTH SIDES OF THE GROOM ROAD BORDER WHERE THE BLACKTOP TAKES OVER.

***********NO DRONE AREA**********

Below are United States FEDERAL Code of Regulations

RESTRICTED FLIGHT AREA. NO PERSON MAY OPERATE AN AIRCRAFT WITHIN THIS RESTRICTED FLIGHT AREA WITHOUT PERMISSION OF THE CONTROLLING AGENCY. 14CFR73.13

PROHIBITED MAN UNMANNED VEHICLE OPERATION. NO PERSON MAY OPERATE AN UNMANNED VEHICLEWITHIN THIS AIRSPACE. LINCOLN COUNTY ORDINANCE 2015-02.

PHOTOGRAPHING DEFENSE INSTALLATIONS. NO PERSON MAY PHOTOGRAPH WITH THIS AIRSPACE RESERVATION OR DEFENSE INSTALLTION WITHOUT THE WRITTEN PERMISSION OF THE INSTALLTION COMMANDER. 18 U.S. CODE 795.

37°21'3.70"N 115°38'47.77"W

WATCH THE NEW BORDER MARKERS, SEE ABOVE!

NO DRONE ZONE

Restricted Flight Area. No person may operate an aircraft within this restricted flight area without the permission of the controlling agency. 14 CFR 73.13.

Prohibited unmanned vehicle operation. No person may operate an unmanned vehicle within this airspace. Lincoln County Ordinance 2015-02

Photographing Defense Installations. No person may photograph within this airspace reservation or defense installation without the written permission of the Installation

Drones? Now they're banned too AT THE BORDER!

We don't just mean the remote-piloted planes the US uses in the Middle East to take out terrorists and wedding parties. We're talking about the drone you got for your birthday, the one that can go a thousand feet up, the one with the GoPro attachment, the one that (if you're in the US) you had to register with the FAA like myself.

Now that consumer drones are widely available, you knew *someone* was going to try and fly one over Area 51. We don't have reports of anyone's drone being shot down over the base as of 2017, but that may just mean that the drone flight was successful. Or, maybe the base management realized what could happen and is merely being proactive.

Subpart B—Restricted Areas § 73.11 Applicability. This subpart designates restricted areas and prescribes limitations on the operation of aircraft within them. § 73.13 Restrictions. No person may operate an aircraft within a restricted area between the designated altitudes and during the time of designation, unless he has the advance permission of (a) The using agency described in §73.15; or (b) The controlling agency described in §73.17.

THE REAL REASON FOR THE BAN

Some have suggested this new drone bad is strictly for safety: they *do* test aircraft (and probably other kinds of, ahem, craft) at Area 51, and the borders are patrolled by helicopter.

A consumer drone flying out of control nearby could cause a catastrophe for sure. We don't believe that's the real reason for ban, though. The real reason: these drones have cameras mounted in them. Video cameras especially equipped with 4K resolution. 4K resolutions are technically, "Ultra High Definition" is actually a derivation of the **4K** digital cinema standard. However while your local multiplex shows images in native 4096 x 2160**4K resolution**; the new Ultra HD consumer format has a slightly lower **resolution** of 3840 X 2160.

Most consumer-grade drones can't go 20-odd miles away from their remote controls, so one would need to be modified in order to reach the base. Most DRONES have a 25-30 minute battery flying time life and if the battery is less than 40% of full charge, your DRONE will make a grave en route back to "HOME RETURN" and will never make it back, it will crash! But it is within the realm of possibility if modifications are made to your DRONE. And if someone got a drone into base territory, some 500 feet up, the drone could take some nice pictures of things that are not supposed to exist. That is what Area 51 officials are afraid of. That is what prompted this ban.

Drones? Now they're banned away from the BORDER!

At these coordinates **37°21'24.34"N 115°35'0.11"W** exists a new warning sign, informing you of entering "Restricted Airspace," and not to operate any sort of UAV//Aircraft!!

I find it particularly "cool," as it isn't typical to find any sort of signs informing you of such information!!

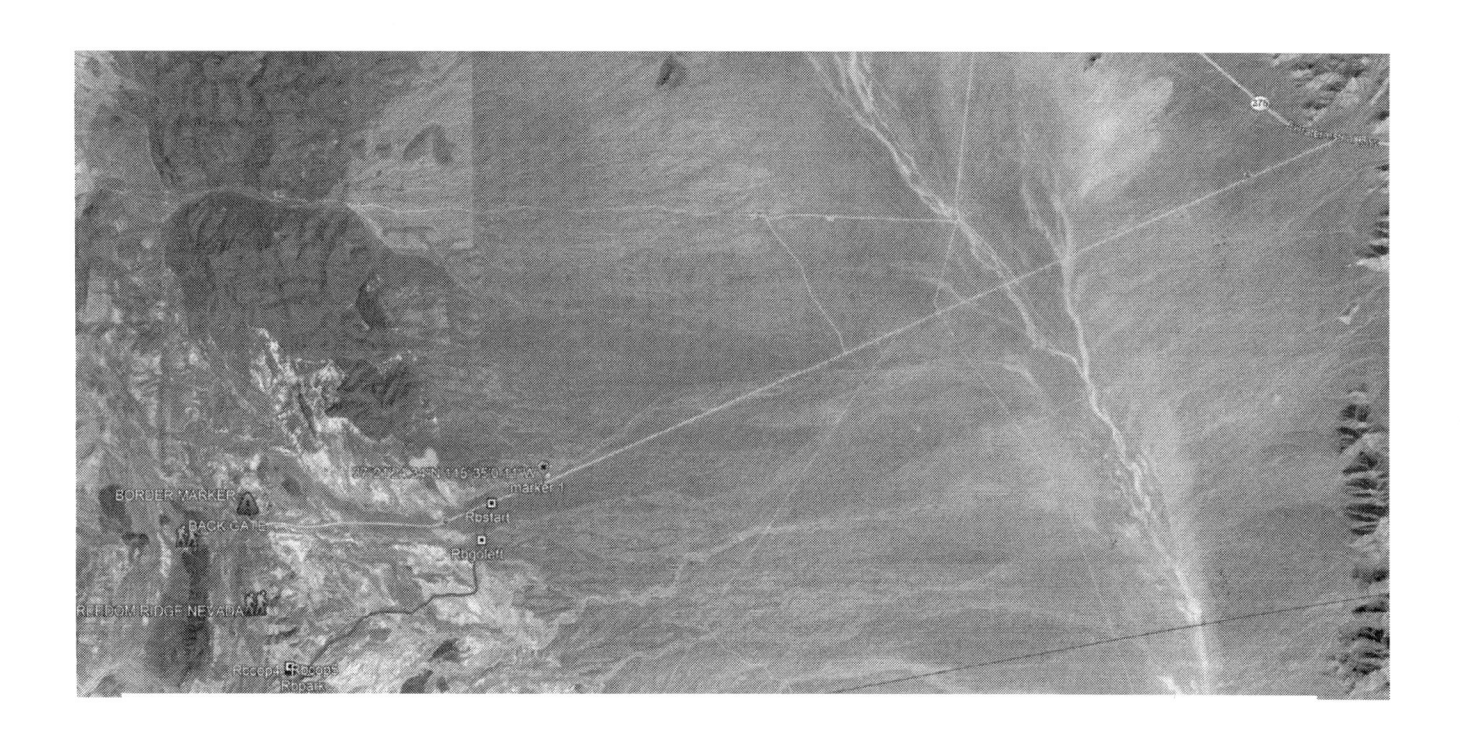

37°21'24.34"N 115°35'0.11"W – Sign on Page 81

Approximately 3.58 miles to the MAIN BORDER MARKER.

Approximately 10.36 miles to Highway 375 from the Drone Sign.

WARNING

MILITARY INSTALLATION

OFF LIMITS TO UNAUTHORIZED PERSONNEL

AUTHORITY: Internal Security Act, 50 U.S.C. 797
PUNISHMENT: Up to one year imprisonment and $5,000. fine.

THEY CAN'T BAN ON PUBLIC LAND, RIGHT?

The nearest legal observation point to the base is Tikaboo Peak, and, being public land, there is still no drone ban there as well, but who is going to know!

Tikaboo Peak is the closest publicly accessible mountain peak that allows hikers to see the buildings comprising the Area 51 military installation. The trail to the top is not always well-defined, so please use extra caution.

DO NOT CROSS THE BORDER!!!!
BEWARE OF THE FLIR!

37°21'4.06"N 115°38'48.29"W

Do you think at anytime you can sneak into Area 51 at the darkest of the night skies? Well, think again! A network of remote controlled security cameras was installed along the Area 51 perimeter between 2012 and 2015. By the end of 2015 the system was operational. It is made up of about a dozen so-called FLIR cameras mounted on mobile camera towers. FLIR stands for *Forward Looking InfraRed*. These cameras are designed to see intruders even at night.

There is one camera each at the Groom Lake Road Gate and at the Back Gate locations. A network of at least 9 more cameras on concrete pads was installed in a valley east of the Groom Mountain Range and Bald Mountain. This part of the Area 51 boundary faces Hwy 375 and is most likely to be visited by curious tourists like yourself. Trenching for the camera cables all the way from the GL Rd Guard Shack to the "Bald Mountain Gates" can be seen in a recent satellite image. A January 2013 satellite image shows the pads complete and camera towers on at least some of the pads.

There is two more camera pads further north, at what is known as the "Bald Mountain Gates." They were installed around late 2012 or 2013. However, there is no trenching for wires leading to these pads, and as of June 2018 there are no cameras on the pads, just an electrical panel.

What is a FLIR System?

Forward-looking infrared (**FLIR**) cameras, typically used on military and civilian aircraft, use a thermographic camera that senses infrared radiation.

The sensors installed in forward-looking infrared cameras, as well as those of other thermal imaging cameras, use detection of infrared radiation, typically emitted from a heat source (thermal radiation), to create an image assembled for video output.

They can be used to help pilots and drivers steer their vehicles at night and in fog, or to detect warm objects against a cooler background. The wavelength of infrared that thermal imaging cameras detect is 3 to 12 μm and differs significantly from that of night vision, which operates in the visible light and near-infrared ranges (0.4 to 1.0 μm).

FLIR Design

Infrared light falls into two basic ranges: *long-wave* and *medium-wave*. Long-wave infrared (LWIR) cameras, sometimes called "far-infrared", operate at 8 to 12 μm and can see heat sources, such as hot engine parts or human body heat, several kilometers away. Longer-distance viewing is made more difficult with LWIR because the infrared light is absorbed, scattered, and refracted by air and by water vapor.

Some long-wave cameras require their detector to be cryogenically cooled, typically for several minutes before use, although some moderately sensitive infrared cameras do not require this. Many thermal imagers, including some forward-looking infrared cameras (such as some LWIR Enhanced Vision Systems (EVS)) are also uncooled.

Medium-wave (MWIR) cameras operate in the 3–5 μm range. These can see almost as well, since those frequencies are less affected by water-vapor absorption, but generally require a more expensive sensor array, along with cryogenic cooling.

Many camera systems use digital image processing to improve the image quality. Infrared imaging sensor arrays often have wildly inconsistent sensitivities from pixel to pixel, due to limitations in the manufacturing process. To remedy this, the response of each pixel is measured at the factory, and a transform, most often linear, maps the measured input signal to an output level.

Some companies offer advanced "fusion" technologies that blend a visible-spectrum image with an infrared-spectrum image to produce better results than a single-spectrum image alone

Original Design

The term "forward-looking" is used to distinguish fixed forward-looking thermal imaging systems from sideways-tracking infrared systems, also known as "push broom" imagers, and other thermal imaging systems such as gimbal-mounted imaging systems, handheld imaging systems and the like. Pushbroom systems typically have been used on aircraft and satellites.

Sideways-tracking imagers normally involve a one-dimensional (1D) array of pixels, which uses the motion of the aircraft or satellite to move the view of the 1D array across the ground to build up a 2D image over time. Such systems cannot be used for real-time imaging and must look perpendicular to the direction of travel.

AREA 51 FLIR PROTECTION UNIT SUMMARIES

The M9 Is the Pinnacle of Super Ultra Heavy Duty, Image Stabilized Extreme long range cooled MWIR Thermal Imaging FLIR EOIR camera system. The system has incredible detection ranges up to **_60 Kilometers_**. THE SYSTEM IS THE WORLDS MOST RUGGED, HAS THE BEST GYRO STABILIZATION + OFFERS THE HIGHEST PERFORMANCE, BEST SENSITIVITY & LONGEST DETECTION RANGES. This Long Range Thermal Imaging PTZ FLIR Thermal Camera system plays a vital role in todays security, law enforcement, military and industrial arenas. The need to see at long distances in day and night is crucial for a wide variety of applications. PTZ FLIR Thermal Imaging Pan and Tilt thermal camera systems consist of rugged all weather housing and positioners that pan and tilt the camera housings. A plethora of sensor options are available with SPI M series camera that fills a void in wide (WSTI) Short (SRTI) Medium (MRTI) Long (LRTI) and Ultra Long (ULRTI) Detection, identification and detection Ranges. The Optional remote operated thermal flir PTZ camera also has long range slew to cue radar capabilities.

See the M9 IN ACTION on YouTube by clicking on the QR Code:

The "M9" from SPi Infrared Systems

The "M9" "Follow-Me" option with PTZ at the main gate on Groom Lake Road.

The "M9" with "Follow-Me" option with PTZ at the main gate on Groom Lake Road close-up view.

BACK GATE "M9" FLIR SYSTEM

The "M9" with "Follow-Me" option with PTZ at the back gate on Groom Lake Road close-up view.

"M9 FLIR CAMERA SYSTEM"
AT THE BACK GATE, AREA 51 ENTRANCE

The "M9" with "Follow-Me" option with PTZ at the back gate on Groom Lake Road close-up view.

MORE ON THE BACK GATE:

About 1.5 miles southeast of Rachel a dirt road intersects with the Highway, leading roughly west. If you follow that road for a good 10 miles, you get to the North Gate of Area 51, also known as the Rachel Back Gate. Unlike the Groom Lake Road border, here you get to see a real guard shack, a gate and a fence marking the perimeter. There is actually an old fence a few hundred yards before the boundary, but it is ok to pass it and drive right up to the black and white gate.

WARNING: A similar setup can be found at <u>Cedar Gate</u>, a little further north. There, however, it is NOT OK to drive past the first fence.

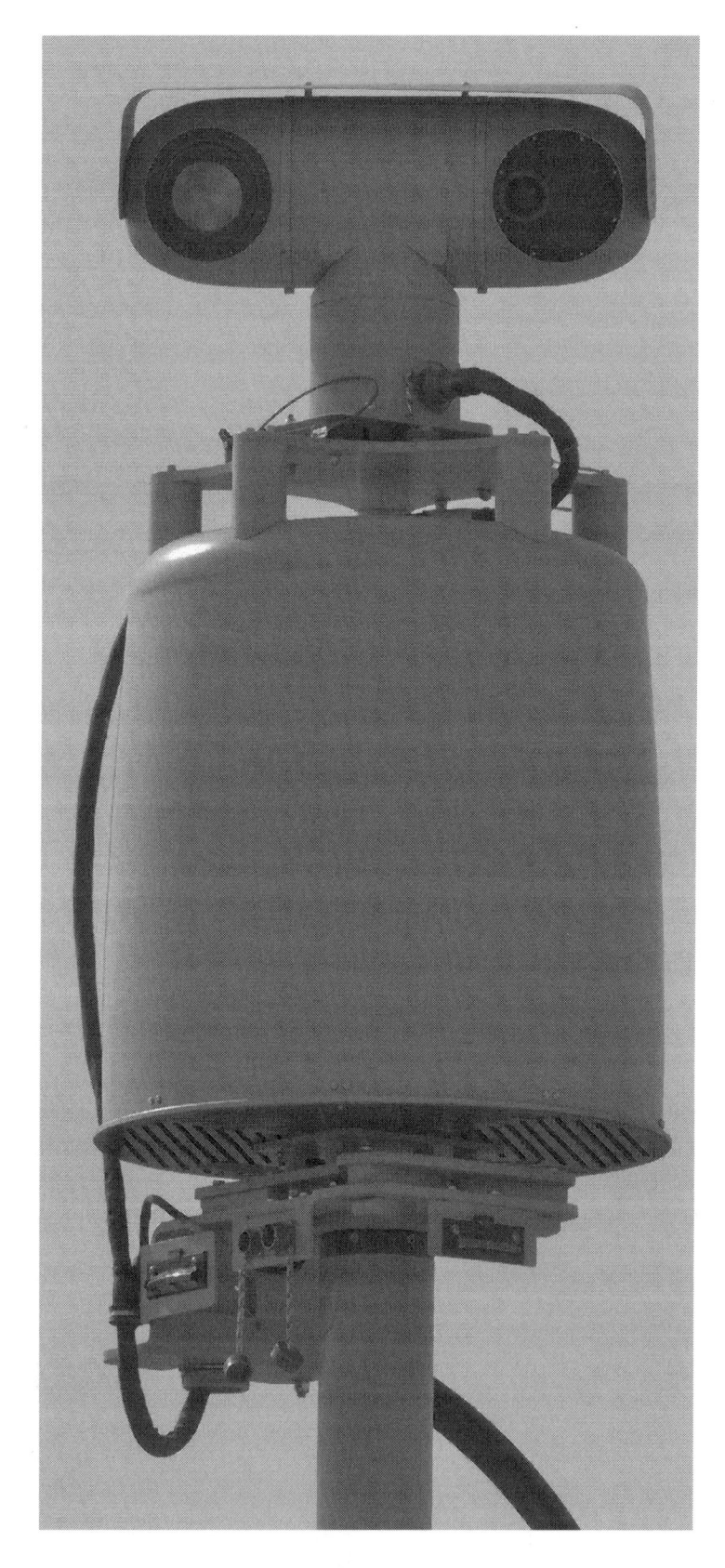

"M9 FLIR SYSTEM," ASSEMBLY CLOSE-UP

MORE ON THE BACK GATE:

There are several small buildings, warning signs similar to the ones on Groom Lake Road, and a double gate with a chain link fence marking the border. Usually at least one guard is inside the guard shack, and a security vehicle is parked behind the building. The ground is level here for several miles, so there is no need for patrol cars sitting on a lookout hill like by Groom Lake Road. However, there are several tall poles with with floodlights and various cameras around the guard shack. The cameras can be monitored from inside the guard shack, as well as from a central security station in a different location.

Life as a cammo at the Back Gate is good. There is a barbecue behind the building, and a large satellite dish next to it. On several occasions we caught the guard watching TV (they seem to like old Western movies). The only downside has to use a port-a-potty when nature calls. There is no septic system or running water, and power is provided by a generator inside one of the buildings.

In October 2000 the Gate was upgraded to new security standards. A new Guard Shack, about 30 yards behind the old white Guard Shack, was added. A new fence was set up and the old barrier was replaced by a black-and-white double gate with red lights, similar to the one at the hidden guard shack on Groom Lake Road. The area between the gates is enclosed by a chain-link fence. Apparently the idea is to have a lock gate for increased security. When a vehicle checks in, they are boxed in between the gates while the guard checks their paperwork. This way they are no longer directly exposed to public view during check-in, and also a potential intruder would be "trapped" between the gates.

The three main buildings have black building numbers: 997, 998 and 999. The old white Guard Shack is still there, but it looks completely abandoned and does not have a number. There are several Russian radar sites and various support buildings northwest of the guardhouse, about 1-2 miles inside the perimeter. See the link below for more information. One of the buildings near the radar sites has the building number 980, and likely the other buildings in that vicinity also have numbers in the high 900's that are not visible from outside the perimeter.

It is interesting to note that the road leading to the gate from Highway 375 is a dirt road. However, from the Gurad Shack on into Area 51 it is paved.

MORE ON THE BACK GATE:

Update April 2006: A new remote-controlled camera was added in late 2005 or early 2006. (see some photos below)

Update 8/21/2010: The Area 51 Back Gate Road has been partially paved. The pavement extends for 2.2 miles from the Guard Shack to the intersection with a road leading north and eventually back to Hwy 375. The pavement continues up that road for another 0.8 miles and then ends. There is no indication for plans to extend the pavement past that point.

Update 1/07/2011: A large new Guard Shack has been built at the Rachel Back Gate to Area 51. The building is about five times the size of the current guard shack, which was built in October 2000. It is located between the current guard shack and the original pre-2000 guard shack. After the paving of part of the Back Gate road last August (see below), this is the second major upgrade to the Back Gate in six months.

WHAT IS TIKABOO PEAK?

TIKABOO PEAK

LOCATION COORDINATES: 37°20'39.39"N 115°21'31.98"W (SUMMIT)

Tikaboo Peak is essentially a side peak of Badger Mountain, which is part of the Pahranagat Range, one of the seemingly endless series of north-south ranges in the Great Basin desert. The surrounding terrain is barren scrub, but the approach to the summit passes through a thin evergreen forest that can be cool and pleasant in the summer in which is the one of the best time of the year to camp out!
The most popular hike takes less than an hour each way, trailhead-to-summit, but the full expedition from Las Vegas usually ends up taking all day and of course my advice is suggest to make your exploration overnight.

On a recent return visit, nothing much has changed in the past 20 years this trail has been in use - with one exception. There is now a "weather station" at the summit. It is producing real weather data but the real reason is has been placed there is to allow the Air Force to install a surveillance camera at the peak, take some pictures please! If your intention is the viewing of our famous secret activity at Area 51, you may want to take this into account first and scout the area. There is also another "weather station" in the Badger Spring Valley, less than 5 miles away, within view of the road approach to the trailhead. (My, there sure is a lot of "weather" around here!)

The dirt road from US-93 to the trailhead has deteriorated considerably in recent years. The first 18 miles are very sandy and deeply rutted. You need an SUV, 4x4 or other high-clearance vehicle. Do not stop your car in the sand or you might never move again.

TIKABOO PEAK

LOCATION COORDINATES: 37°20'39.39"N 115°21'31.98"W

A BRIEF LOOK INSIDE THE HISTORY OF TIKABOO PEAK

There is a USGS survey marker at the summit, so humans have visited here for years, but the peak was first "discovered" as an Area 51 viewpoint in the early 1990s. At the time, the Groom Lake airbase could be seen from two much closer hills -- Freedom Ridge and White Sides (**now both closed to the public**). When the Air Force threatened to withdraw this land, base watchers felt challenged to find another viewpoint to replace it.

The first to visit the peak as a potential viewpoint into Area 51 was probably my good friend Peter Merlin, who says he visited the summit around 1993. However, at the time the closer viewpoints were still public, so Tikaboo was unnecessary. There was interest in Tikaboo only when the Air Force announced plans to withdraw the closer viewpoints in 1994.

The Interceptors Trail was first blazed by Mr. Tom Mahood in the Spring of 1994. Since then, there have been hundreds expeditions to the summit, especially after the closer viewpoints were finally closed in April 1995. Visitors have included several large public outings and dozens of TV crews. Lately, interest has waned, and the peak is probably visited only a couple of times per month in the summer.

Other potential viewpoints, including Badger Mountain and Mt. Irish, have been surveyed, and none seem to offer a satisfying view of the base. Short of chartering a plane and flying along the edge of the restricted airspace either by DRONE or other means, Tikaboo offers the best legal view of the base.

TIKABOO PEAK – THE INTERCEPTORS TRAIL – BUCKLE-UP!

THERE ARE ADDITIONAL SELF-GUIDED TOURS IN THIS BOOK BUT IF YOU GOT THIS FAR EARLY IN THE BOOK WHY NOT GIVE THIS A WHIRL! GOOD LUCK!

Trail: Trails are paths laid out, developed, and maintained to greater or lesser degrees by land management agencies such as the U.S. Forest Service, the BLM, and the National Park Service. Trails usually have signs, a wide tread, switchbacks on steep hillsides, and water bars to direct water off the tread. When necessary, trails might have safety features such as railings or chains.

This is the quickest route to the summit.

From the great city of Las Vegas, the trailhead is reached by about 90 miles of paved road, followed by 23 miles of minimally maintained dirt road. Any sturdy car can handle the dirt road, except perhaps in bad weather. **A four-wheel-drive vehicle with an experienced driver might get about 1/2 mile closer to the peak.** Keep in mind, however, that this is area is very remote and the dirt road is lightly traveled.

NOTE: If you break down, you'll probably be hiking 23 miles back to the paved highway.

The hike itself is about a mile, climbing no more than 1000 feet of elevation, and taking about 1 to 2 hours up and 45 minutes down. (The exact distant depends on how far you can drive on the 4WD road.)

The dirt road from US-93 to the trailhead has deteriorated considerably in recent years. The first 18 miles are very sandy and deeply rutted. You need an SUV or other high-clearance vehicle. Do not stop your car in the sand or you might never move again. At 6 miles from US-93, you may encounter a wire gate. **You can legally pass it, but you must leave it in the same position you found it, which can be a challenge.**

REPEAT: YOU MUST HAVE AN SUV OR OTHER HIGH-CLEARANCE VEHICLE.

A sturdy car might be able to make it, but there is a high risk you'll scrape the underbody of your car or get stuck in the sand. Don't risk it! 4WD is desirable but not necessary, as long as you keep moving on sandy stretches and don't stop.

BE PREPARED TO HIKE 23 MILES TO SAFETY IF YOUR CAR BREAKS DOWN OR GETS STUCK.

GPS INFO: - A GPX file is a GPS data saved in the GPS Exchange format, an open standard that can be freely used by GPS programs. It contains longitude and latitude location data, which includes waypoints, routes, and tracks. GPX files are saved in XML format that allows GPS data to be more easily imported and read by multiple vendors GPS models.

IMPORT TO GOOGLE EARTH: *Import GPS data from a* **file**. *If you have GPS data stored in a* **GPX** *or other type of* **file**, *you* **can open** *it in* **Google Earth**. *Also, if you have a GPS device for which* **Google Earth** *does not support direct connections, but which* **can** *export data to a* **file**, *you* **can** *still view your GPS data in* **Google Earth**.

WHAT ARE THE BENEFITS OF GPX?

Here are some of the benefits that GPX provides:

GPX allows you to exchange data with a growing list of programs for Windows, MacOS, Linux, Palm, and PocketPC.

GPX can be transformed into other file formats using a simple webpage or converter program.

GPX is based on the XML standard, so many of the new programs you use (Microsoft Excel, for example) can read GPX files.

GPX makes it easy for anyone on the web to develop new features which will instantly work with your favorite programs.

Reference: http://www.topografix.com/gpx_resources.asp

GPS Visualizer: Do-It-Yourself Mapping

This is an excellent resource (free to use) to provide many different map conversions.

GPS Visualizer is an online utility that creates maps and profiles from geographic data. It is **free** and easy to use, yet powerful and extremely customizable. Input can be in the form of GPS data (tracks and waypoints), driving routes, street addresses, or simple coordinates. Use it to see where you've been, plan where you're going, or quickly visualize geographic data (scientific observations, events, business locations, customers, real estate, geotagged photos, etc.).

Reference: http://www.gpsvisualizer.com/

Let's Start Here - The Approach

The following directions were valid in 2018...

From Las Vegas, take I-15 north (in the Salt Lake City direction). Go about 15 miles and take the US-93 exit. Head north on US-93 for about 75 miles until you pass a shallow lake on the left (Lower Pahranagat Lake). Watch the milepost markers along the side of the road. Look for Milepost LN-32, which is near the Wildlife Refuge headquarters. About 2/10 mile after Milepost 32.2, there is a gated dirt road on the left. The gate may be open or closed, but it should not be locked, you may enter and open the gate if it is closed.

(If you find a locked gate, it is probably not the right one -- There are several other gated roads in this area.) Turn here, and reset your odometer.

Immediately after entering the dirt road, you may see a symbolic "No Vehicles" sign. This sign refers to a side road to the right, and not the main road you are on. Continue on the main road across a narrow strip of the wildlife refuge into the desert hills. This is now public (BLM) land. At about 5.5 miles from the paved highway, slow down! There may be a primitive barbed-wire cattle gate across the road at about 5.9 miles. You have the right to pass this gate, but you need to leave it in the same position you found it. Disengaging and reengaging the gate could be the most difficult technical challenge of your trip. Study the gate carefully before you try to open it, and try to put it back the same way.

Proceed on the main road for 18.7 miles from the paved highway. Along the way, be on alert for stray cattle and the cattle gate. The road heads southwest at first, then at 8.5 miles, the main road takes a sharp and unexpected turn to the right (northwest). (Do not keep going straight, or you might get stuck in sand.) Along the next 10 miles, you will pass several side roads (mostly leading to water troughs). If you come to any ambiguous fork, keep left.

At 18.7 miles, the main road turns hard right, with a smaller road going straight. Keep going straight ahead on the smaller road. This road is no longer graded and could be damaged. It is likely to be covered with snow or mud in winter and may be impassible at mile 22.2; you will come to Badger Spring, where there is a cattle trough and the remains of a developed spring. Shortly after Badger Spring, the road degenerates and becomes impassible for most vehicles about 1/2 mile beyond the spring. Parking anywhere that doesn't block the road. The "official" trailhead is no longer accessible by car unless you are an extreme 4WD-er, but there is a new unofficial trailhead just below it where most cars park. There are comfortable parking spots here for about 4 cars.

Route Description

This short, but fairly tough 1.1-mile hike leads to one of the quintessential Las Vegas hiking experiences: a view into Groom Lake and the secret military base at Area 51.

The official trailhead is a clear in a saddle where there is a wooden monument. It is about 100 yards up a washed-out road from the place you park. The trail begins at the saddle, heading up a ridge to the south on a primitive dirt road. The trail is evident from use and from intermittent trail markings. Many people have attempted to mark the trail over the years, but no one marking system is complete. A good rule of thumb is to never proceed from your current position until you see the next trail marker.

From the saddle, a newly blazed 4WD road goes left up a ridge. Extreme drivers who have somehow managed to make it to the official trailhead can keep going to cut a further 1/4 mile off the hike; others can hike. Eventually, the drivable road ends, and you must proceed on foot. Look for various trail markers and evidence of previous foot traffic.

From this point the trail gets steeper and steeper and eventually turns to scree. This stretch of the hike can be very strenuous and painful for anyone who is out of shape or dwells at sea level. (You are starting from 7000 feet.).

As you climb the steepest part of the scree slope, watch for a point where the trail bears to the right for an easier route. You are only going about 2/3rd up the first slope, then the trail cuts right and the worst of the hike is over. You will stay at a fairly steady elevation to the right to a lower saddle, then continue up the next ridge. If you lose the trail (which is likely after the second saddle) your goal is to reach the highest point in the area. If you follow your nose and just try going up, you shouldn't go wrong, but be careful to note the route by which you came so you can retrace your steps going back.

When you can't get any higher, you have reached the summit. There will be plenty of evidence of previous visitations, and you will have a full view in all directions. (Also a new "weather station" installed in 2011.)

Your greatest risk of getting lost is on the return leg, so pay careful attention to the topography and follow the trail markers.

Essential Gear

Bring binoculars or a telescope to view the base. If you expect to take photos of it, you will need a high-power telephoto lens to capture any detail.

4WD drivers intending to push beyond Badger Spring should bring one or more full-size shovels for possible road repair. A camp saw might also be helpful for clearing brush.

There is Verizon cellphone service on the peak and on portions of the first 18 miles of the approach road. Cellphone service is unlikely at the trailhead. **BUT if you have a Satellite Phone you will have no coverage problems at all!**

Camping

The weather is ideal for camping in the summer, with pleasant days and cool nights. Desert conditions are mitigated by the 7000-foot altitude. At other times of year, temperatures can get very cold at night and possible very windy.

This is public land and you can legally camp virtually anywhere along the route (as long as you are away from any cattle water trough). The official and unofficial trailheads are the preferred camping spots because there is plenty of flat space. Camping here lets you arrive on the summit very early in the morning, which is the best time to view the base.

You can also camp at the summit, if you insist on hauling your camping gear up there, but beware of lightning and possible high winds. If the exposure makes you uncomfortable, there are more protected camping spots just before the peak -- but unfortunately out of view of the base. People without experience in backpack camping shouldn't try it here. It is much more comfortable to camp at the trailheads near your car.

There should be adequate firewood in the area. Be sure to bring a saw to cut it.

INTERCEPTORS TRAIL – SATELLITE VIEW FROM GOOGLE EARTH

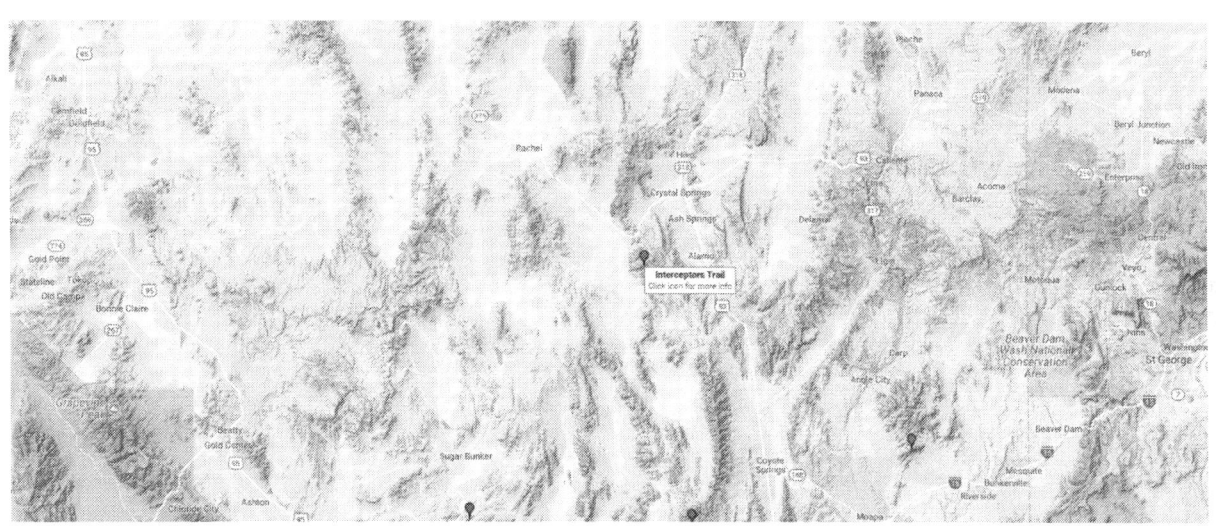

INTERCEPTORS TRAIL – MAP VIEW

TRAIL MAP

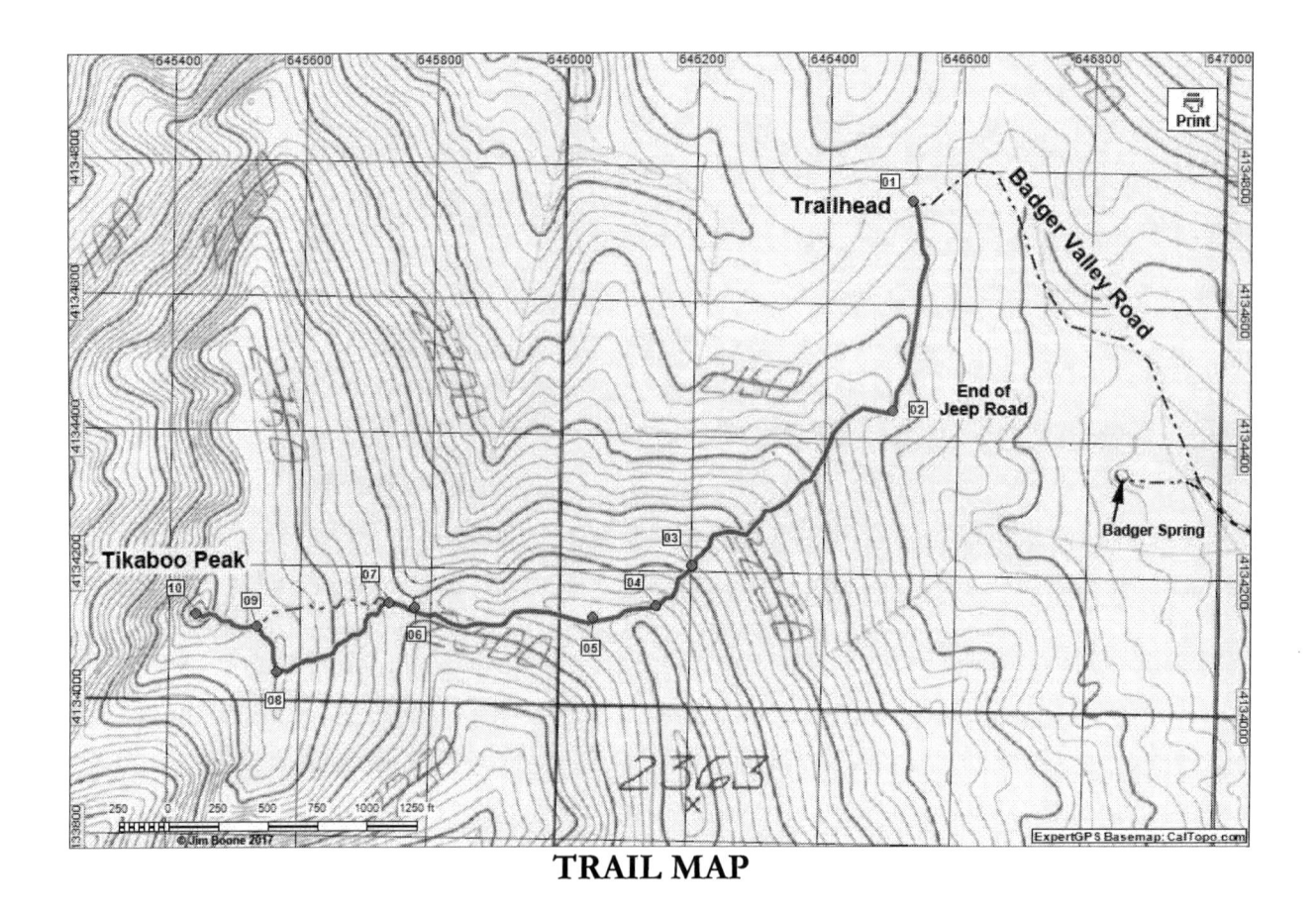

Note: Map based on USGS 7.5 minute topo map, which may have red grid lines and various numbers. North is at the top. Grid is UTM NAD27 CONUS. Roads are black (solid = paved; dashed = unpaved; width implies quality). Trails and routes are red (solid = main; dashed = adjacent or alternate). BLM areas (no color overlay) based on BLM data

ELEVATION PROFILE of TIKABOO PEAK

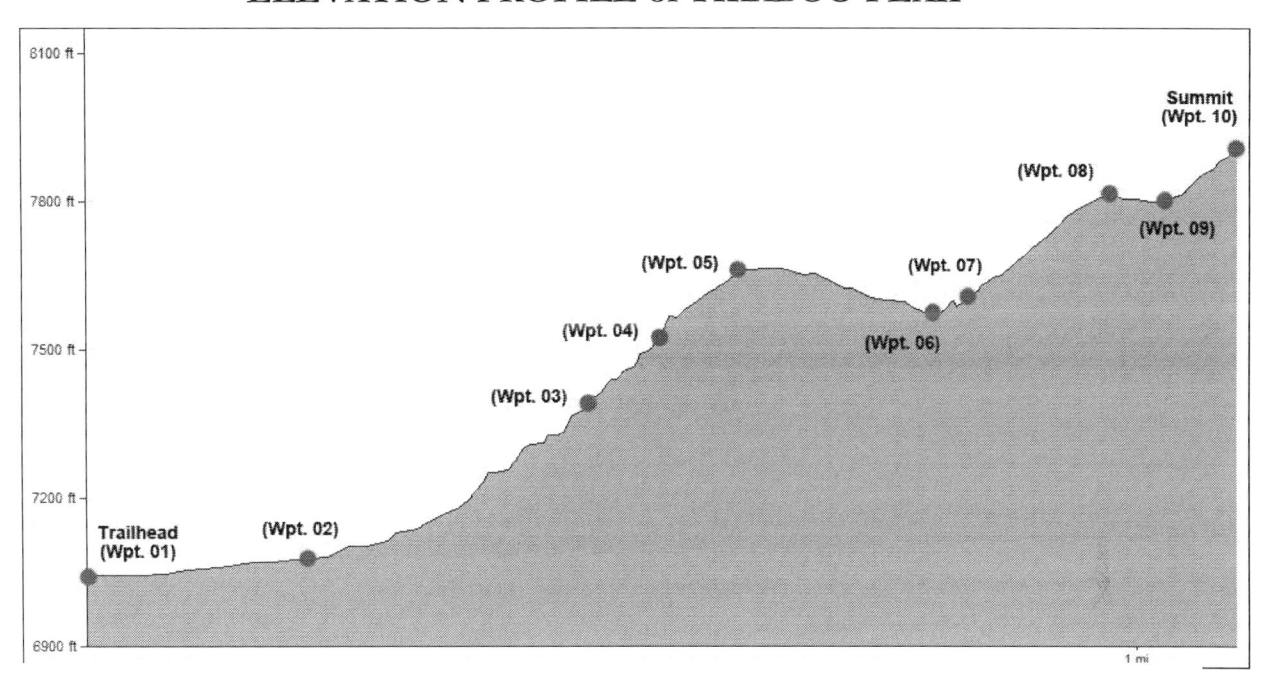

Note: Elevation profile based on raw GPS data.

Please note the ELEVATION HEIGHTS BELOW:

SUMMIT: 7,927' AMSL

AVERAGE: 7,563' AMSL

GATE: 4,395' AMSL

INTERSTATE 93: 4,148' AMSL

Tikaboo Peak, Nevada Weather Station – FOR "LIVE WEATHER INFORMATION: https://wrcc.dri.edu/weather/ntik.html

Tikaboo Peak, Nevada Weather Station

INTERCEPTORS TRAIL – GOOGLE EARTH VIEW

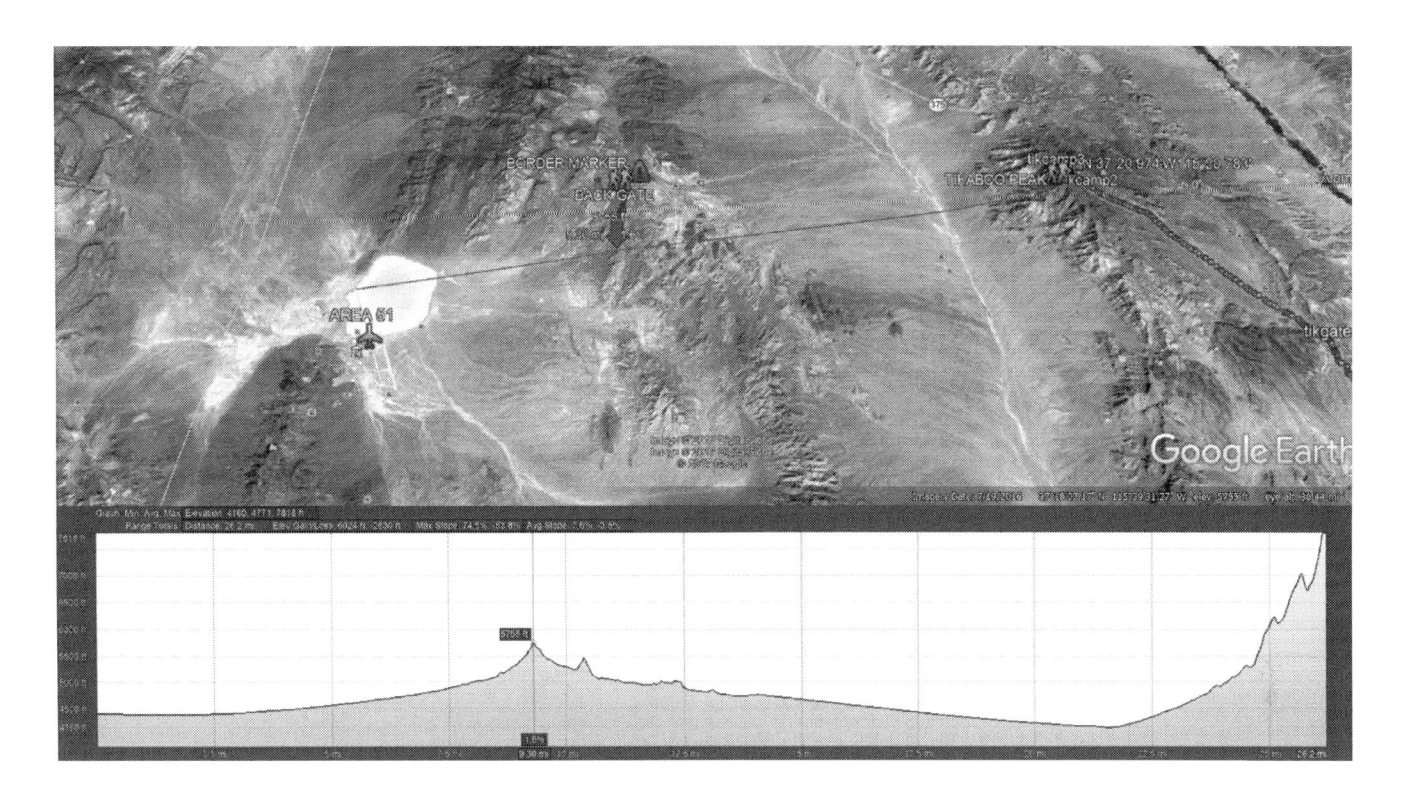

This distance from the SUMMIT of Tikaboo Peak [37°20'39.36"N 115°21'31.86"W] to AREA 51 [RUNWAY 32L OVERUN] by exact Line-of-Sight is 26.0 miles.

The highest EVEVATION OBSTRUCTION is 5,755', 9.30 miles from the base.

Runway 32L OVERRUN sits 4,409' ASL

BACK IN THE GOOD OLD DAYS WHEN FREEDOM RIDGE & WHITE SIDES WAS AVAILABLE TO THE PUBLIC FOR CAMPING & VIEWING THE RANGE AT ~ 12 MILES AWAY!

The PUBLIC AERIAL viewpoints at White Sides and Freedom Ridge Mountain ranges were seized by the government in 1995, and are *no longer open to the public at all*.

These are NOW ALL USAF DoD properties!

The closest publicly-accessible viewing spot is now at Tikaboo Peak in which we will have you take a road trip there, it is about 26 miles east. It takes a four-wheel-drive vehicle and some rock climbing just to get there, and you'll need a good powerful binoculars or a spotting scope to see anything at all, but pictures is worth a thousand words!

TIKABOO PEAK AT THE SUMMIT

LOCATION COORDINATES: 37°20'39.39"N 115°21'31.98"W

FREEDOM RIDGE – THIS IS OFF LIMITS – U.S. GOVERNMENT PROPERTY!

LOCATION COORDINATES: *37°20'4.62"N 115°38'40.74"W*

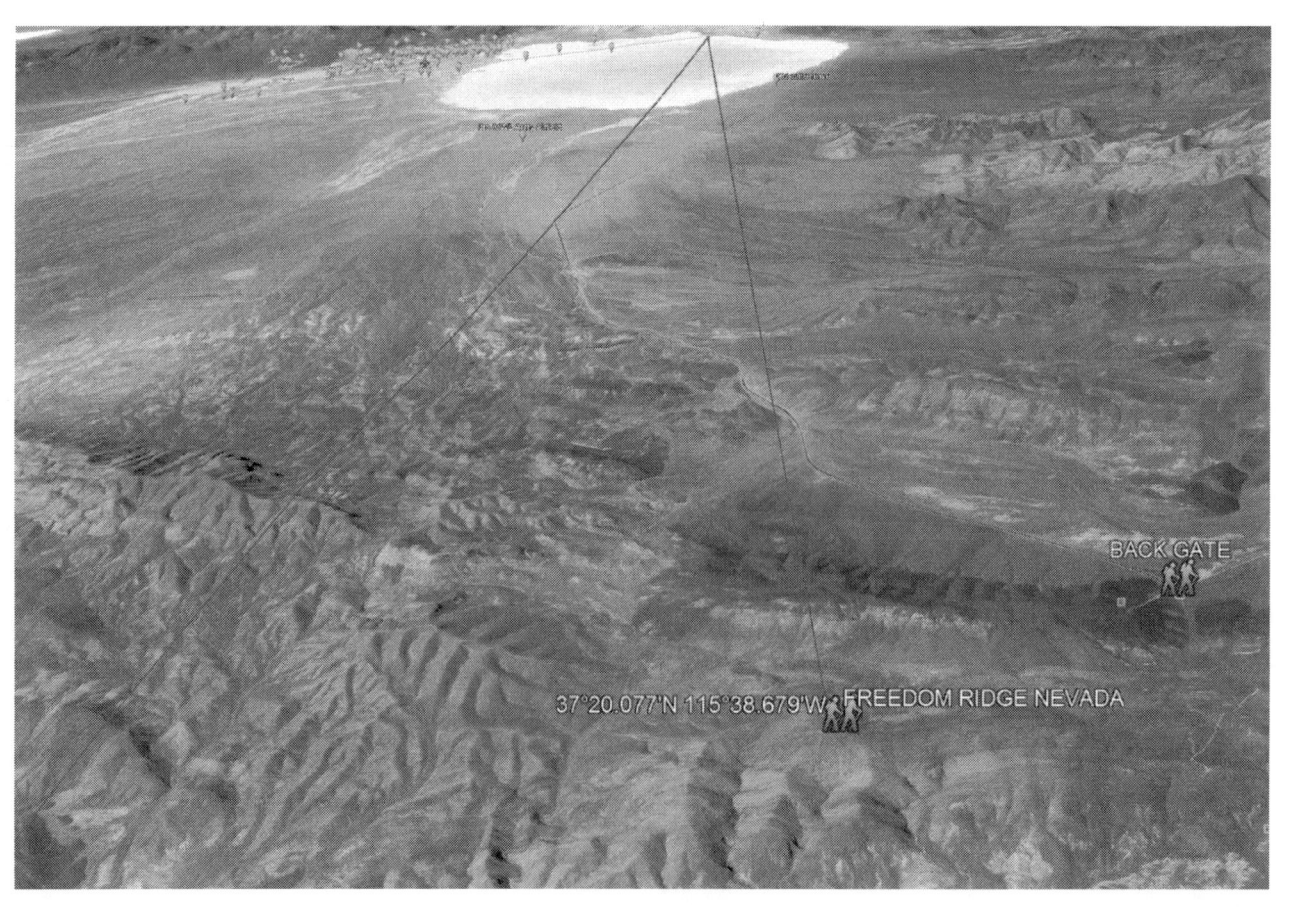

***WHITE SIDES MOUNTAIN RANGE* – THIS IS OFF LIMITS – U.S. GOVERNMENT PROPERTY!**

LOCATION COORDINATES: *37°22'6.84"N 115°37'40.86"W*

AN EXCELLENT VIEWING SPOT to VIEW ON THE BASE!

FOR THAT AREA 51 EXPLORER

This is an excellent high elevation, 5874 feet ASL view point in the mountains behind the infamous Black Mailbox right off Highway 375. I highly recommend a 4WD vehicle for this adventure!

"THE POWER LINES OVERLOOK MOUNTAIN RANGE" AN APPROVED VIEWING AREA

LOCATION COORDINATES: *37°27'32.46"N 115°25'26.22"W*

CAMPING AT POWER LINES OVERLOOK: 37°27'32.15"N 115°25'25.57"W

"THE POWER LINES OVERLOOK MOUNTAIN RANGE" AN APPROVED VIEWING AREA

LOCATION COORDINATES: *37°27'32.46"N 115°25'26.22"W*

CAMPING AT POWER LINES OVERLOOK: 37°27'32.15"N 115°25'25.57"W

"THE POWER LINES OVERLOOK MOUNTAIN RANGE" AN APPROVED VIEWING AREA

LOCATION COORDINATES: *37°27'32.46"N 115°25'26.22"W*

CAMPING AT POWER LINES OVERLOOK: 37°27'32.15"N 115°25'25.57"W

The Mysterious BACK GATE to "The Ranch" aka Dreamland, Watertown, Paradise Ranch, The Base

37°20'45.83"N 115°39'34.07"W

Introduction and Background History of Area 51

Area 51, also officially known as **Groom Lake** or **Homey Airport** (ICAO - International Civil Aviation Organization) **KXTA**) is a remote detachment of Edwards Air Force Base. According to the Central Intelligence Agency (CIA), the correct names for the Area 51 facility are the Nevada Test and Training Range and Groom Lake, though the name Area 51 has been used in official CIA documentation. Other names used for the facility include *Dreamland, Paradise Ranch, "The Ranch" Home Base, Watertown Strip, The Square* and most recently *Homey Airport*. The area around the field is referred to as (R-4808N). The Federal lands in Southern Nevada "OFFICIALLY" states "AREA 51 on Nellis Air Force Range shown on the map below.

On April 12, 1955 Richard Bissell and Col. Osmund Ritland flew over Nevada with Kelly Johnson in a small Beechcraft plane. Johnson was the director of the Lockheed Corporation's Skunk Works, which, as part of a secret CIA-Air Force project, codenamed AQUATONE by the CIA and OILSTONE by the Air Force, was building a revolutionary spy plane, designated the U-2. Bissell, CIA head of the project, Ritland his Air Force deputy, Johnson, and Lockheed's chief test pilot, were looking for a site where the plane could be tested safely and secretly.

During the trip they discovered, near the northeast corner of the Atomic Energy Commission's (AEC) Nevada Proving Ground, what appeared to be an airstrip near a salt flat known as Groom Lake. After examining the location from the ground, the four agreed that it "would make an ideal site for testing the U-2 and training its pilots." Upon returning to Washington, Bissell discovered that the land was not part of the AEC's proving ground — leading him to ask the commission's chairman to make the Groom Lake area an AEC possession, a request which was readily granted. President Eisenhower approved the plan, and the territory, known by its map designation — Area 51 — was added to the Nevada Test Site.

The site acquired several other designations. Kelly Johnson, in order to make the remote location seem more palatable his workers began referring to it as Paradise Ranch, which was then shortened to the Ranch. An additional unofficial name would be Watertown Strip — a consequence of the need to build a paved runway so that testing could continue when rainwater runoff from nearby mountains made it impossible to land on Groom Lake. By July 1955, the base was ready and personnel from the CIA, Air Force, and Lockheed began to arrive.

Within a year the U-2 program would transition to an operational program, with flights initially over Eastern Europe and then the Soviet Union. Bissell and other senior officials anticipated that the U-2 would have a limited life before becoming vulnerable to Soviet air defense systems. Before the end of 1958 they had launched Project GUSTO to find a successor to the U-2, which resulted in the selection of another Lockheed-designed plane, the A-12 or OXCART— which was to fly higher than the U-2, far faster (over Mach 3), and be harder for air defense radars to detect.

In November 1959, a little over two years before the first A-12 arrived at Area 51 in late December 1961, a radar test facility was established there — the result of contractor Edgerton, Germeshausen & Greer (EG&G) agreeing to move its Indian Springs, Nevada test facility to Area 51. Its purpose was to determine the vulnerability of an OXCART mockup to detection. Area 51 would also become the home to testing programs for two OXCART derivatives — the YF-12A KEDLOCK fighter plane and the Air Force's Project EARNING, which ultimately produced the SR-71 (also designated SENIOR CROWN) reconnaissance aircraft — as well as the D-21 TAGBOARD drone that was expected to be launched from A-12 aircraft.

In September 1961, a few months before the first OXCART arrived, the site was visited by CIA Inspector General Lyman Kirkpatrick, who conveyed his findings (Document 1) to Richard Bissell — who had become the CIA's Deputy Director of Plans in the summer of 1958, with continued responsibility for the CIA's secret aircraft projects through his directorate's Development Projects Division (DPD). Kirkpatrick wrote that his "visit left reservations in my mind." One was that the "'Area' appears to be extremely vulnerable in its present security provisions against unauthorized observation" — including air observation.

In addition, Kirkpatrick suggested that the project had reached a stage "where top management at the 'Area 51' needs consolidation with clear and precisely defined authority." Finally, he questioned "the survivability of the program's hardware when and if employed in actual operations."

Bissell's off-the-cuff reactions were reported in an October 17 memo (Document 2) from Bissell's assistant to the acting chief of the DPD. The author reported Bissell's belief that Kirkpatrick's points about area security were "well taken," his lack of strong reaction to the comment about site management, and his questioning whether the inspector general's comment about OXCART vulnerability was "appropriate" for Kirkpatrick "to get himself involved in." With regard to the issue of security Bissell "was particularly interested in why we have not yet been able to eject the various holding property around the Area."

Concern about maintaining secrecy for activities at the site persisted as illustrated by an April 6, 1962 memo (Document 3) from DPD executive officer John McMahon to the division's acting chief. He reported that he and another DPD official (John Parangosky) had earlier discussed the idea of employing a U-2 to produce images of the area and asking photographic interpreters to determine what was happening at the site. But given, the upcoming scheduled launches of CORONA reconnaissance satellites, McMahon noted that "it might be advisable" to include a pass crossing the Nevada Test Site, "to see what we ourselves could learn from satellite reconnaissance of the Area." That and later missions could be used to assess what deductions the Soviets could make "should Sputnik 13 have a reconnaissance capability."

A dozen years later, it was not Soviet reconnaissance that resulted in interagency discussions and memos concerning exposure of Area 51 activities via overhead imagery. Rather it was the inadvertent imaging of the area by American SKYLAB astronauts. Among the memos was one (Document 4) from Robert Singel, the National Reconnaissance Office's deputy director, concerning the on-going internal government controversy. Another memo (Document 5) provided Director of Central Intelligence William Colby with the latest information on the internal debate and identified key questions that needed to be answered before a final decision was made.

During the mid-1970s another issue was whether the CIA should continue Area 51; its major aerial reconnaissance programs, such as the U-2 and OXCART, no longer needed the site, but the Air Force still needed the site for radar testing, development of stealth aircraft, and exploitation of Soviet MiG aircraft that the U.S. had acquired. The National Security Council decided that the Air Force should take over the site. According to a memo (Document 6) from deputy director of central intelligence, E.H. Knoche to the Air Force's chief of staff, David C. Jones. Knoche, the National Security Council's Committee on Foreign Intelligence had approved the recommendation "that management of Area 51 be transferred from CIA to Air Force by FY-78."

Eventually, the transfer would take place, and the Groom Lake facility became Detachment 3 of the Air Force Flight Test Center, whose headquarters were at Edwards Air Force Base, California.

By the mid-1990s, the existence of Area 51 had become widely known — and the subject of threatened legal action because of environmental concerns. Seeking to prevent that from resulting in revelations about activities conducted at the site President Bill Clinton signed a presidential determination exempting the "Air Force's operating location near Groom Lake, Nevada from any Federal, State, interstate, or local hazardous or solid waste laws that might require disclosure of classified information concerning that location to unauthorized persons" a determination he reported to congressional leaders (Document 8) on January 30, 1996. In September 2003 President George W. Bush made a similar determination, in the form of a memorandum (Document 9) to the administrator of the Environmental Protection Agency.

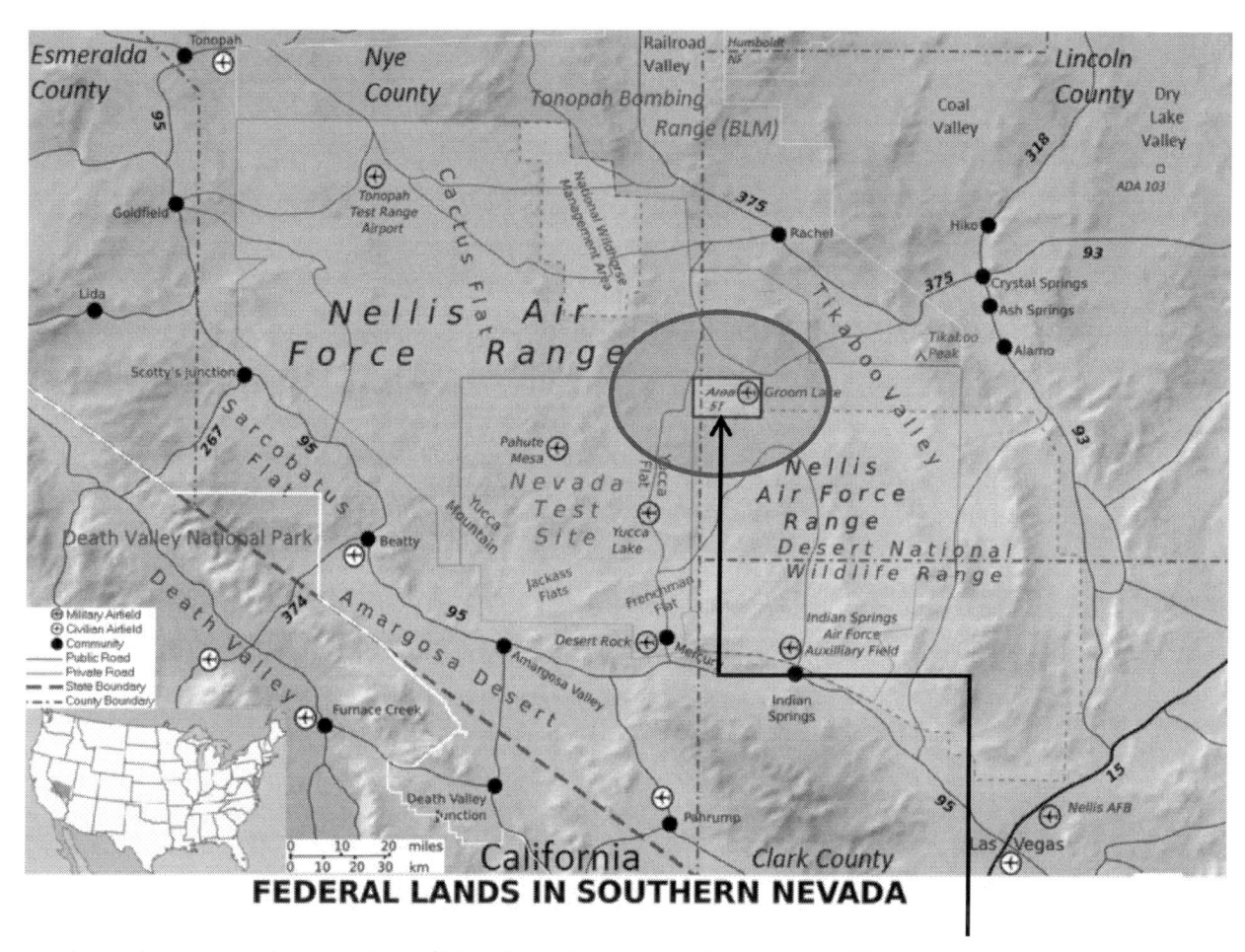

FEDERAL LANDS IN SOUTHERN NEVADA

It is located in the southern portion of Nevada in the western United States, 83 miles (133 km) north-northwest of Las Vegas.

Its exact GPS Coordinates are 37°14'36.52"N, 115°48'41.16"W which will put you smack right on in the middle of the adjacent taxi runway off from 32L runway.

Your Destination: Dreamland, the Ranch, Watertown

Area 51 (**also known as** *Dreamland,* **or** *Groom Lake*) is a military base that operates as Detachment 3 of the Air Force Flight Test Center, which is headquartered at Edwards Air Force Base. It is located in the southern portion of Nevada in the western United States, 83 miles (133 km) north-northwest of Las Vegas. Situated at its center, on the southern shore of Groom Lake is a large military installation. The primary purpose of the base is undetermined; however, based on historical evidence, it appears to support development and testing of experimental aircraft and weapons systems.

The Area 51 base lies within the United States Air Force's vast Nevada Test and Training Range (NTTR), formerly called the Nellis Air Force Range (NAFR). Though the name Area 51 is used in official Central Intelligence Agency (CIA) documentation, other names used for the facility include *Dreamland, Paradise Ranch, Home Base, Watertown Strip, Groom Lake,* and most recently *Homey Airport.* **The area is part of the Nellis Military Operations Area, and the restricted airspace around the field is referred to as (R-4808N), known by military pilots in the area as "The Box" or "The Container".**

The facility is not a conventional airbase, as frontline operational units are not normally deployed there. It instead appears to be used for highly classified military/defense Special Access Programs (SAP), which are unacknowledged publicly by the government, military personnel, and defense contractors.

Its mission may be to support the development, testing, and training phases for new aircraft weapons systems or research projects. Once these projects have been approved by the United States Air Force or other agencies such as the CIA, and are ready to be announced to the public, operations of the aircraft are then moved to a normal air force base. Everything that happens at Area 51 is classified Top Secret/Sensitive Compartmented Information (TS/SCI), or higher.

Groom Lake

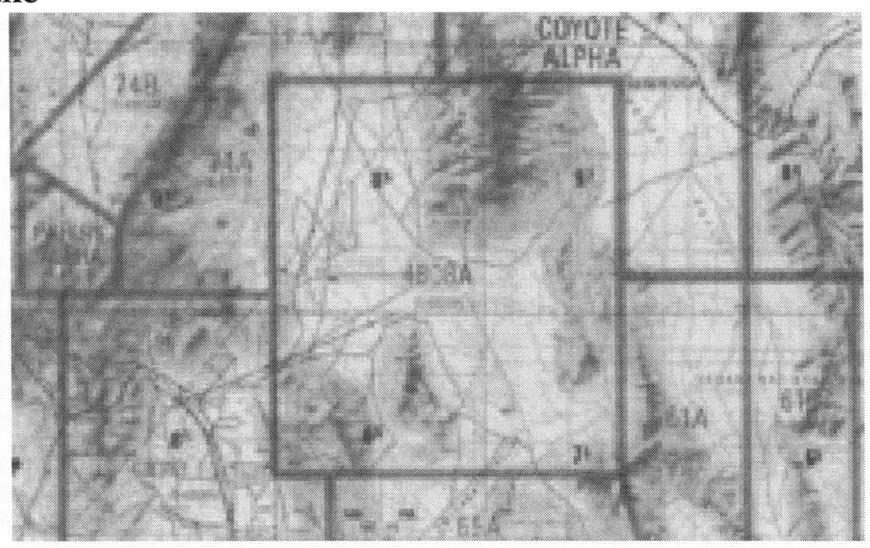

Nevada Test Range topographic chart centered on Groom Lake

Groom Lake is a salt flat in Nevada used for runways of the Nellis Bombing Range Test Site airport (KXTA) on the north of the Area 51 USAF military installation. The lake at 4,409 ft (1,344 m) elevation is approximately 3.7 miles (6.0 km) from north to south and 3 miles (4.8 km) from east to west at its widest point. Located within the namesake Groom Lake Valley portion of the Tonopah Basin, the lake is 25 mi (40 km) south of Rachel, Nevada.

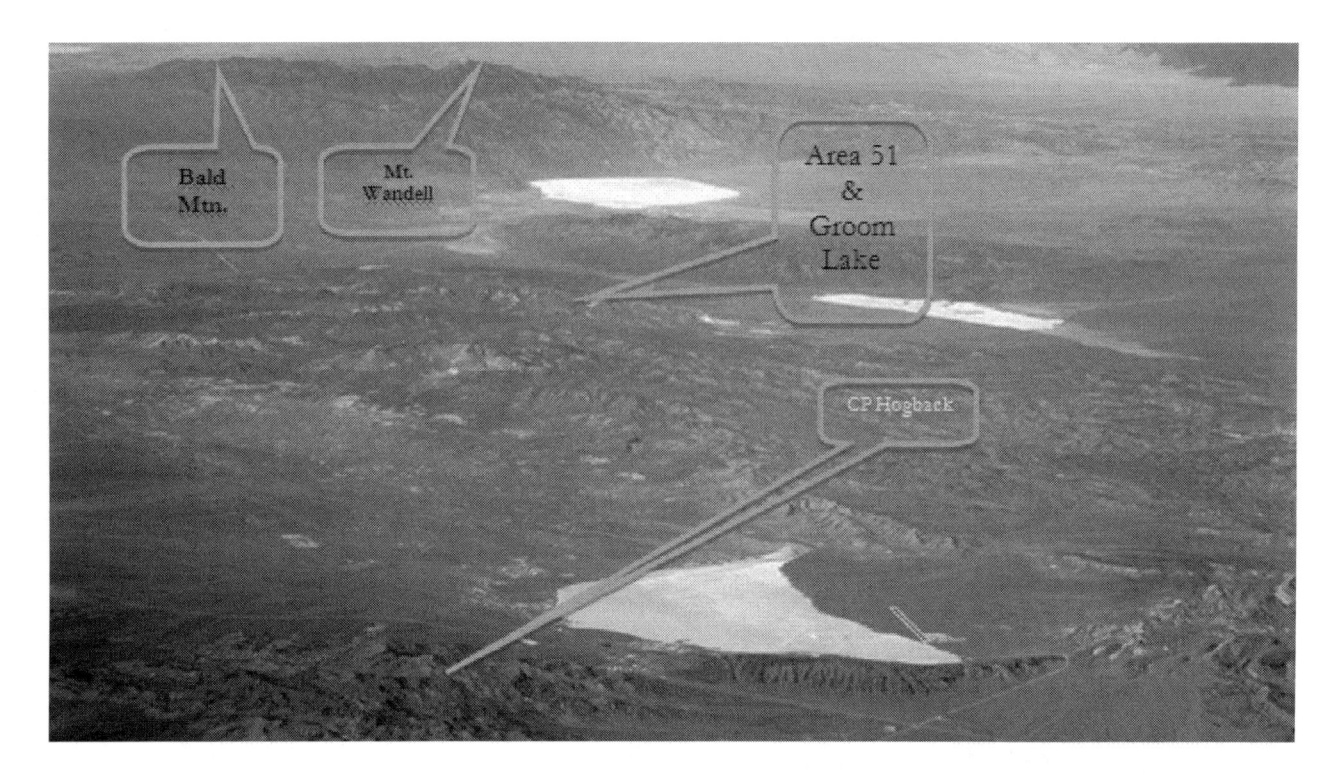

Aerial View of the Nevada Test Site above, where many dozens of atomic bomb tests were conducted in the 1950s and '60s. Yucca Flat is in the foreground and Area 51, part of the Nevada Test and Training Range, is at the round Groom Lake, above. In the middle is Papoose Lake.

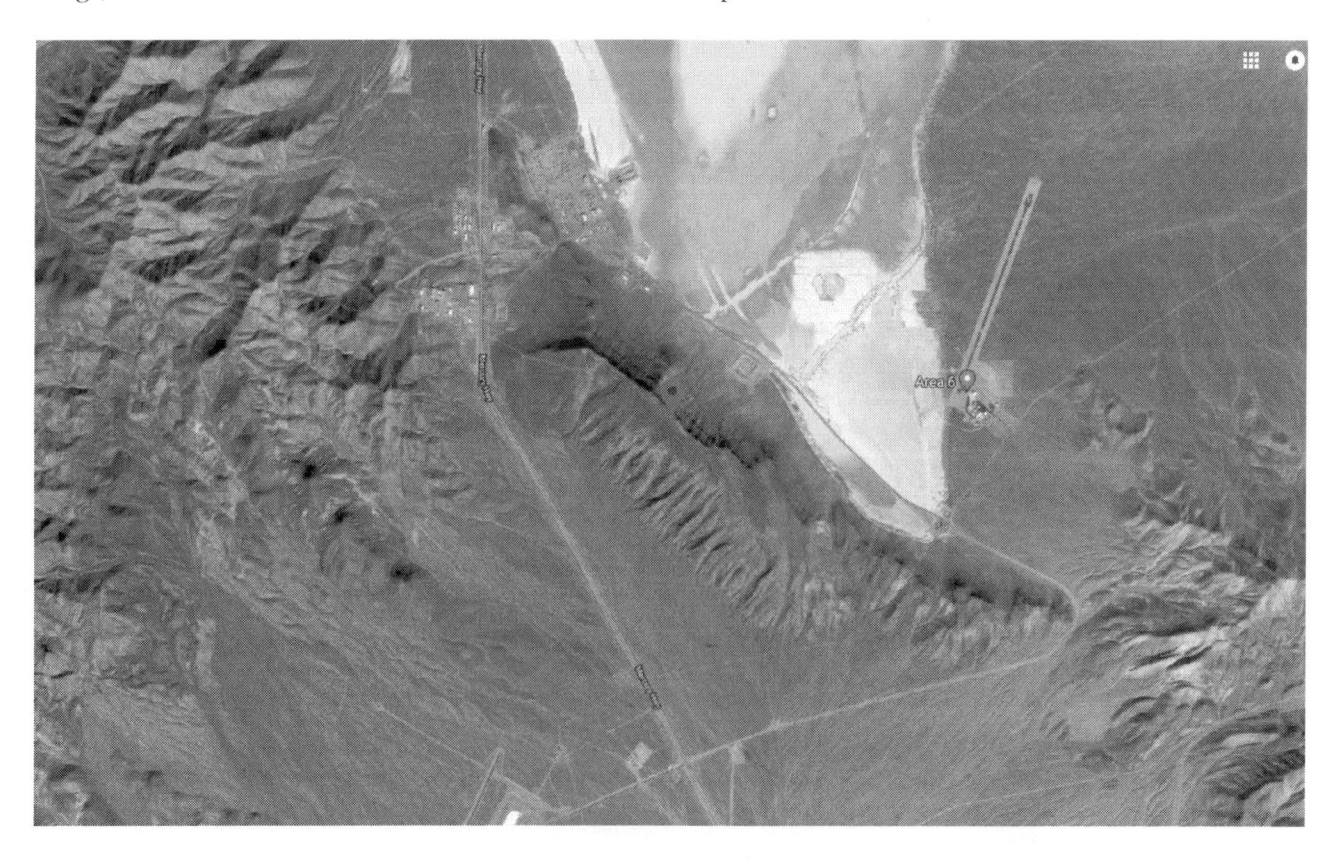

Aerial view of CP HOGBACK

C P Hogback is a mountain within Nevada and is southeast of News Nob and C P Canyon and east of C P Hills. C P Hogback has an elevation of 4,482 feet.

- Type: Mountain
- Location: Nevada
- Latitude: 36° 55' 32.8" (36.9258°) north
- Longitude: 116° 2' 4.1" (116.0345°) west
- Elevation: 4,482 feet (1,366 meters)

AREAS OF INTEREST BELOW FROM CP HOGBACK.......

Yucca Airstrip
1.4 miles or 2.3 km -> North
Type: Airport

Yucca Airstrip is a private-use airport located 17 miles north of the central business district of Mercury, in Nye County, Nevada, United States. The airport is located on the Nevada Test Site and is owned by the United States Department of Energy. On the sectional chart it is depicted as an unverified airstrip.

Bren Tower
15.3 miles or 24.7 km -> SouthWest
Type: Unclassified

BREN Tower was a guyed steel framework mast, 1527 ft high, on the Nevada Test Site in Nevada, USA. "BREN" stands for "Bare Reactor Experiment, Nevada." The structure was owned by the Department of Energy and maintained by National Security Technologies. Access to the tower area had been closed since July 2006. No reason for the closure has been given. As part of the Nevada Test Site, it was also located in restricted airspace.

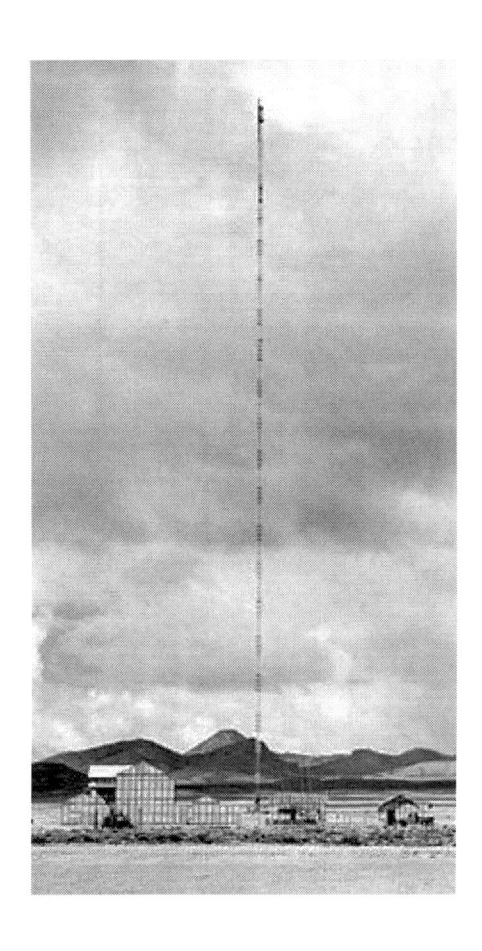

AREA 25
17.1 miles or 27.5 km -> SouthWest
Type: City

Area 25 is the largest named area in the Nevada National Security Site at 254 sqmi,; and has its own direct access from Route 95. Area 25 is commonly called "Jackass Flats" because it is composed primarily of a shallow alluvial basin by that name.

JACKASS FLATS
23.2 miles or 37.3 km -> SouthWest
Type: Landmark

Jackass Flats is a shallow alluvial basin located in the southwest portion of the Nevada National Security Site in Nye County, Nevada. The area lies east of Yucca Mountain, south of the Calico Hills and Shoshone Mountain and northwest of Skull Mountain. The valley drains to the southwest via the Tonopah and Fortymile washes into the Amargosa Valley across US Route 95 at Amargosa Valley. The "flat" covers an area of approximately 120 square miles and ranges in elevation from about 2800 ft just north of US 95 to 4000 ft at the mountain bases to the north and east.

Yucca Mountain
24.9 miles or 40.1 km -> West
Type: Mountain

Yucca Mountain is a mountain in Nevada, near its border with California, approximately 100 mi northwest of Las Vegas. Located in the Great Basin, Yucca Mountain is east of the Amargosa Desert, south of the Nevada Test and Training Range and in the Nevada National Security Site. It is the site of the Yucca Mountain nuclear waste repository, which is currently identified by Congressional law as the nations spent nuclear waste storage facility. However, while licensure of the site through the Nuclear Regulatory Commission is ongoing, political maneuvering led to the site being de-funded in 2010.

Gold Center, Nevada
40.7 miles or 65.5 km -> West
Type: City

Gold Center was a mining town in Nye County, Nevada. Located in the Bullfrog Mining District south of Tonapah, Gold Center was established in December 1904 with a United States Post Office being authorized on January 21, 1905. The town began publishing its own newspaper in 1907. The location of the town was ideal as it was on the stagecoach route to Rhyolite and Beatty. It was also near the Amargosa River, allowing sufficient water for drinking and for two mills and an ice house. Gold Center also sold water to Rhyolite and Carrara. The Tonopah and Tidewater Railroad, the Las Vegas & Tonopah Railroad and the Bullfrog Goldfield Railroad all ran through Gold Center. Gold Center also had the first brewery in the area which was built underground to maintain a cool temperature.

Papoose Lake (below) is a dry lake bed located in Lincoln County, Nevada, USA. The lake lies within the plot of land referred to as the Groom Lake facility (aka Area 51) and is a restricted area. The lake is located a few miles southwest of the Groom lake facility nestled adjacent the Papoose Range.

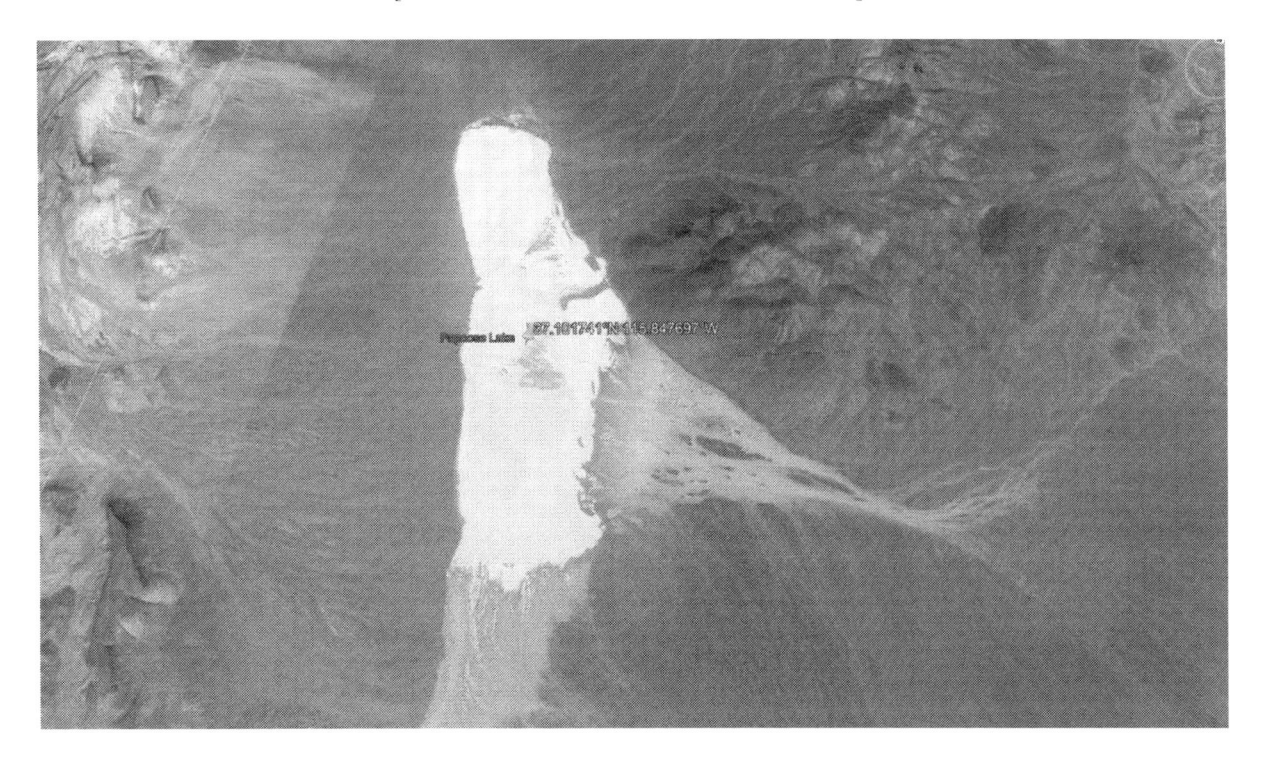

[Coordinates: **37.101741°N 115.847697°W**]

37°14'36.52"N, 115°48'41.16"W

Central Location of Downtown Area 51

Want to take a visit here?

Situated at its center, on the southern shore of Groom Lake is a large military airfield. The base's current primary purpose is officially undetermined; however, based on historical evidence, it most likely supports development and testing RCS (Radar Cross Sectional Testing); Stealth Skin Technologies; Kill Radar Systems; High Target Reconnaissance UAV Systems; Mobile Radar Systems; Foreign Technologies research from Jamming, Electronic Warfare and weapon systems including advanced X-series experimental aircraft. The intense secrecy surrounding the base has made it the frequent subject of conspiracy theories and a central component to unidentified flying object (UFO) folklore.

Although the base has never been declared a secret base, all research and occurring's in Area 51 are Top Secret/Sensitive Compartmented Information (TS/SCI) levels from Department of Defense. In July 2013, following a FOIA request filed in 2005, the Central Intelligence Agency publicly acknowledged the existence of the base for the first time by declassifying documents detailing the history and purpose of Area 51.

Inside Look at the Topology of Area 51

The original rectangular base of 6 by 10 miles (9.7 by 16 km) is now part of the so-called "Groom box", a rectangular area measuring 23 by 25 miles (37 by 40 km), of restricted airspace. The area is connected to the internal Nevada Test Site (NTS) road network, with paved roads leading south to Mercury, Nevada and west to Yucca Flat. Leading northeast from the lake, the wide and well-maintained Groom Lake Road runs through a pass in the Jumbled Hills.

The road formerly led to mines in the Groom basin, but has been improved since their closure. Its winding course runs past a security checkpoint, but the restricted area around the base extends further east.

After leaving the restricted area, Groom Lake Road descends eastward to the floor of the Tikaboo Valley, passing the dirt-road entrances to several small ranches, before converging with State Route 375, the "Extraterrestrial Highway", south of Rachel, Nevada.

Area 51 shares a border with the Yucca Flat region of the Nevada Test Site, the location of 739 of the 928 nuclear tests conducted by the United States Department of Energy at NTS. The Yucca Mountain nuclear waste repository is 44 miles (71 km) southwest of Groom Lake.

About Mercury, Nevada

Mercury, Nevada is a closed city in Nye County, Nevada, United States, 5 miles north of U.S. Route 95 at a point 65 miles further northwest of Las Vegas. It is situated within the Nevada Test Site and was constructed by the Atomic Energy Commission to house and service the staff of the test site. The specific site was known as Jackass Flats, NV and near-by Nevada Test Site 400. Today, the site is governed by the United States Department of Energy. As part of the test site, the town is not accessible to the general public. It was named after the mercury mines which flourished in its general vicinity a century before the town itself was established. The current population is very small.

The beautiful Mercury, Nevada

Groom Lake Topology

Nevada Test Range topographic chart centered on Groom Lake

Groom Lake is a salt flat in Nevada used for runways of the Nellis Bombing Range Test Site airport (KXTA) on the north of the Area 51 USAF military installation. The lake at 4,409 ft (1,344 m) elevation is approximately 3.7 miles (6.0 km) from north to south and 3 miles (4.8 km) from east to west at its widest point. Located within the namesake Groom Lake Valley portion of the Tonopah Basin, the lake is 25 mi (40 km) south of Rachel, Nevada.

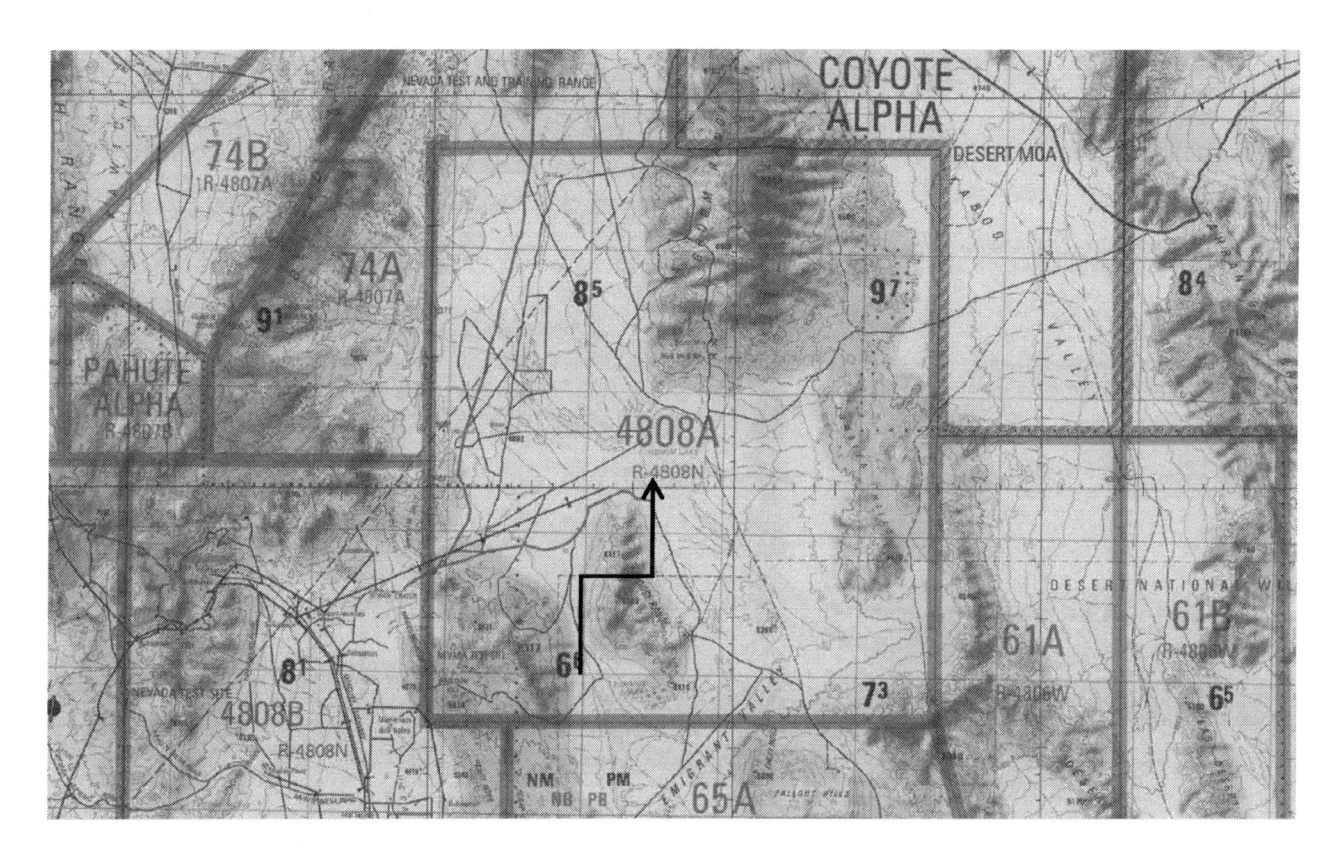

Groom Lake in coordinate section R4808A as shown above.

Restricted Area 51 Airspace (R-4808A)

The coordinates of the no-fly zone (even for military aircraft) around Area 51, also known as "the Box" or "the Container" is as follows:

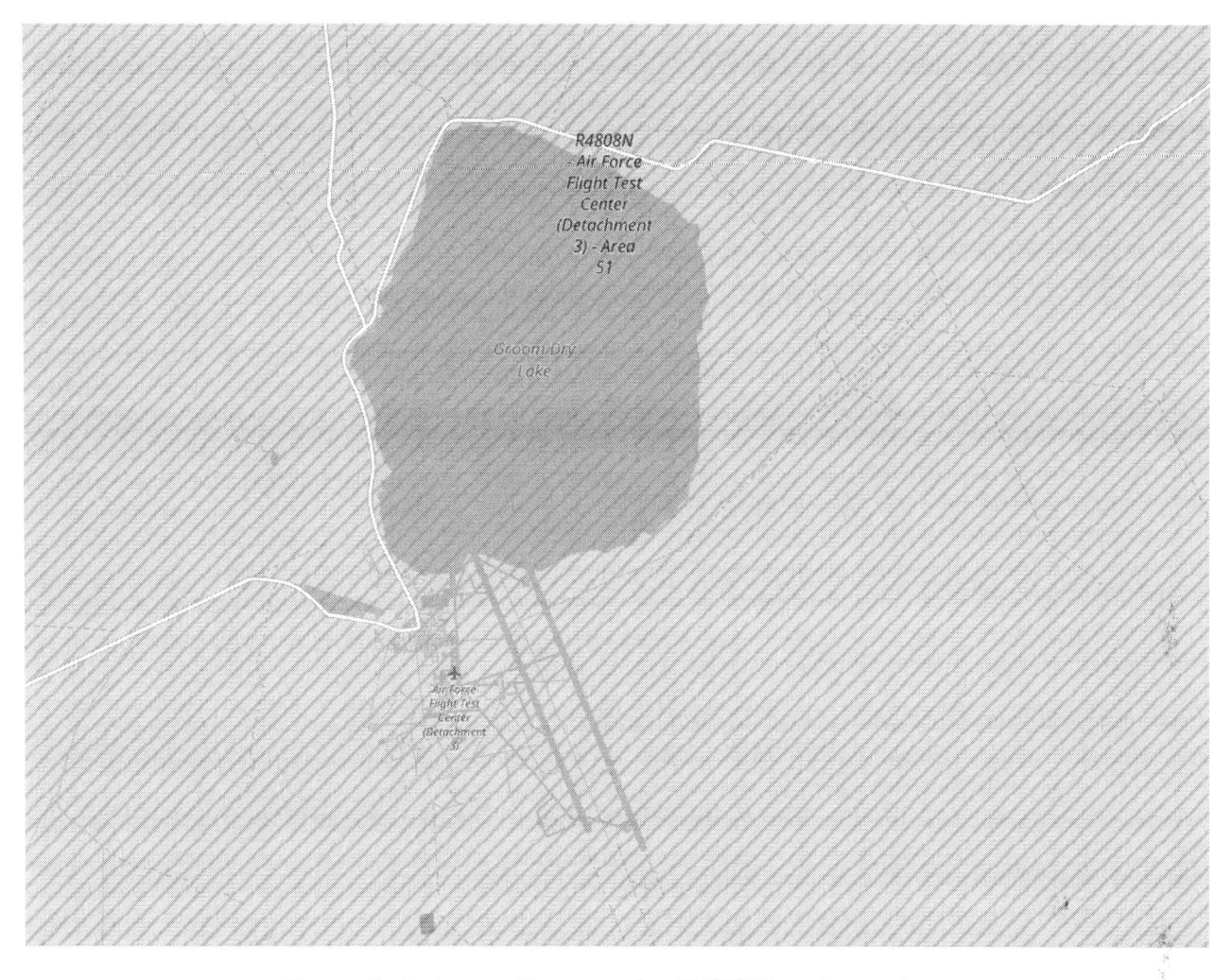

Groom Lake in coordinate section **R4808N** as shown above.

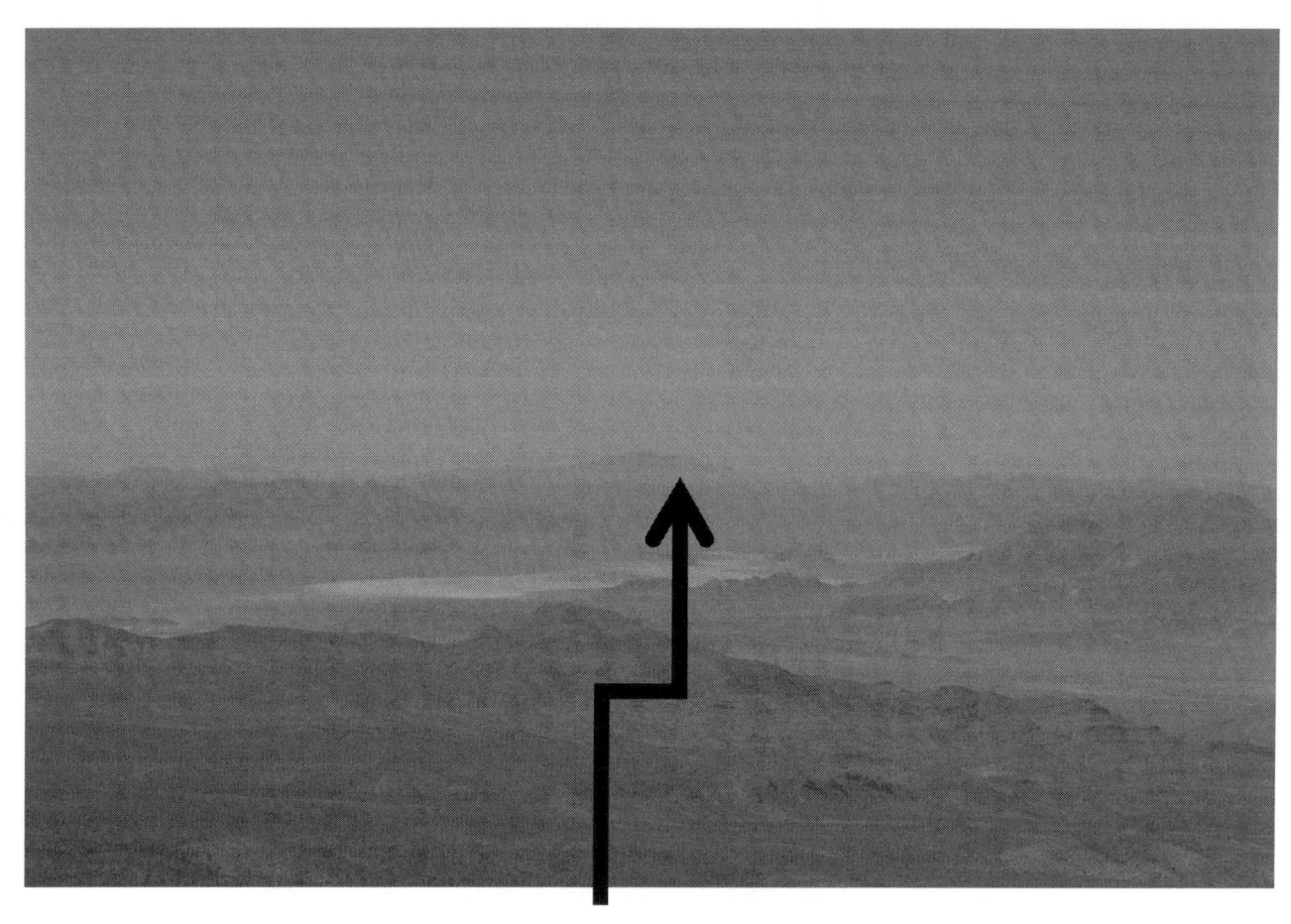

This is Angel Peak Looking at R-4808N

The view of Bald Mountain from Angel Peak.

This is R-4808N, the Restricted Airspace over Area 51!

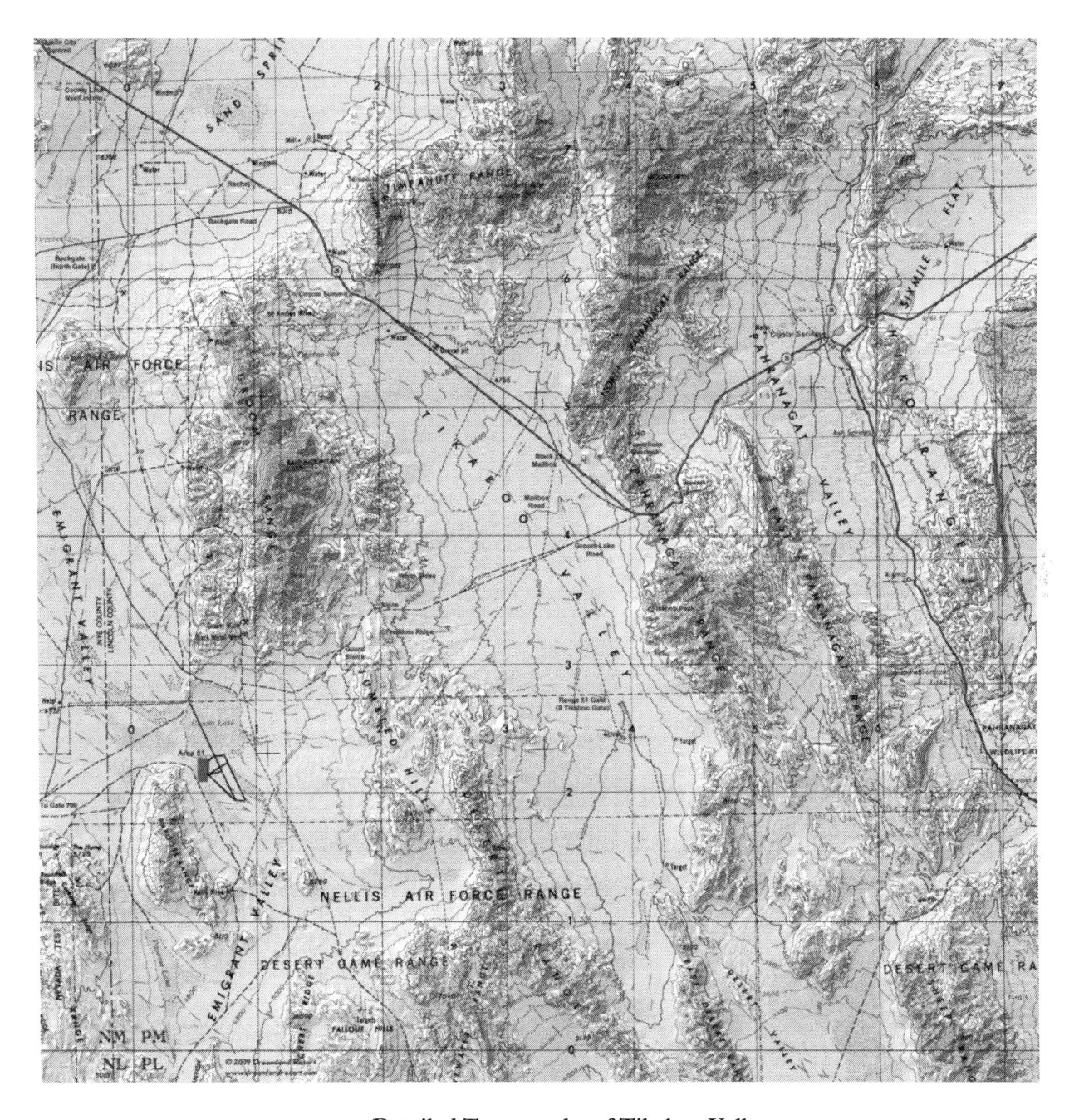

Detailed Topography of Tikaboo Valley

The Restricted Area 51 Airspace (R-4808A)

The coordinates of the no-fly zone (even for military aircraft) around Area 51, also known as "the Box" or "the Container" is as follows:

NW Corner   37-28-00N / 116-00-03W
NE Corner   37-28-00N / 115-35-03W
SE Corner   37-06-00N / 115-35-03W
SW Corner   37-06-00N / 116-00-03W

Let Me Tell You all About the "JANET AIRLINES" at McCarran Airport!

The Janet terminal is located in a fenced-off area in the northwest corner of Las Vegas McCarran Airport. It is surrounded by a large parking lot, with approximately 1740 marked parking spaces for cars and 72 spaces for motorcycles. Lately the parking lot has been about 85% full on any given workday. With an estimated 10% car-pooling and 60% of flights going to Groom, we can assume over 1000 workers commuting to Area 51 and almost 700 to TTR.

The Terminal is located in the 400 block of S.Haven St., only a couple of blocks east of the Las Vegas Strip. Access is possible from the north via E.Hacienda Ave. (marked "Mandalay Blvd." at the Strip) and from the south via E.Diablo Dr. (marked "Four Seasons Dr." at the Strip). It is safe to drive by, although along the entire block there are "No Parking" signs on both sides of the road. There is some open space off the road, though. Despite obvious efforts to block the view, you can still get a decent view of the terminal, and the parked Janets on the other side. If you do go there, please be careful not to violate the law and ***try to play it low-key***. I would hate to see more fences coming up.

About 10 minutes after a Janet plane lands you can see a convoy of workers leaving the large parking lot (about 2000 spaces) through the two guarded access roads, and proceeding to the Strip via E.Hacienda Ave. and E.Diablo Dr. Please don't bother them as they come out, on their daily commute home from work.

There used to be a good view spot at E.Diablo Dr. and S.Haven St., marked by a blue dot. However, recently, after publishing that location on this web site, I found the view blocked by mothballed planes, that are now parked just inside the fence. Coincidence??? Hmmmm!
Another good view spot is near the gate at the end of E.Hacienda Ave. You get very close to the parked Janets there, but it is not immediately clear whether this dead-end road is still a public road, and on one occasion we were told in rather clear words to leave there by a security guard, dressed as a construction worker, but wearing a security badge. We have been told that on weekends there is no security, and it is possible to get close to the parked Janets for some good closeup shots. Make sure that you are not trespassing, though.

The terminal can be seen from the higher floors of the hotels around the LV Blvd & Tropicana Ave. intersection, especially from rooms on the east side of the Luxor and in the south tower of the Tropicana.

RANGE 61

WHAT IS RANGE 61?

37° 9'31.64"N 115°25'47.05"W

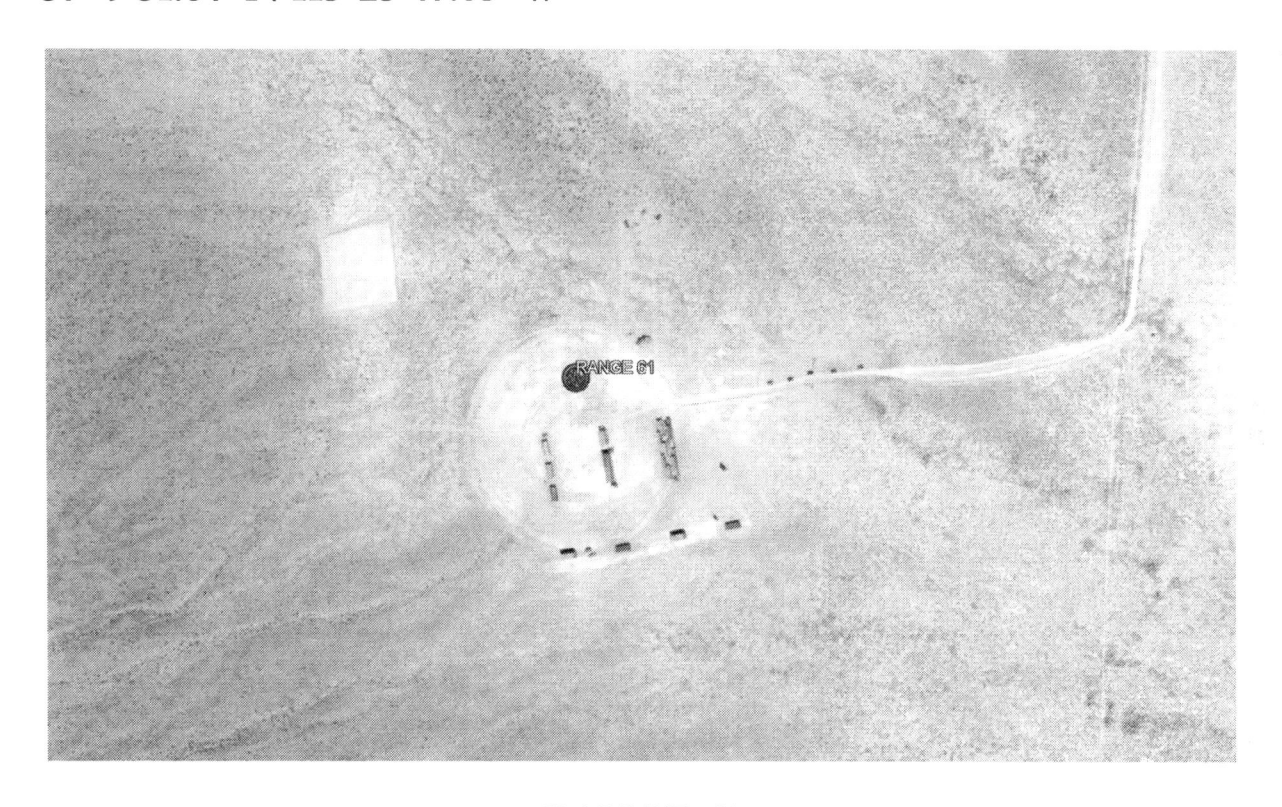

RANGE 61

Range 61: Range 61 is located North of a small Dry lake bed inside the border. There are targets located at 213° of your position which are located only 8 miles from Tikaboo Peak. The boundary of Range 61 is only 6 miles away. A perfect place to watch Range 61 traffic during day and night. More targets are located at 195° which works out to be 13 miles away from Tikaboo Peak and these are located actually south of the nearer targets. Further south but probably out of sight is Dogbone Lake Gunnery and Bombing Range. This is Range 62 centered over the dry lake. There are also targets here but you will not see them without extremely powerful optics.

RANGE 61

37° 9'31.64"N 115°25'47.05"W

Range 61. Located in the northwest corner of R-4806. The single target is a simulated ICBM site located on the eastern side of the range.

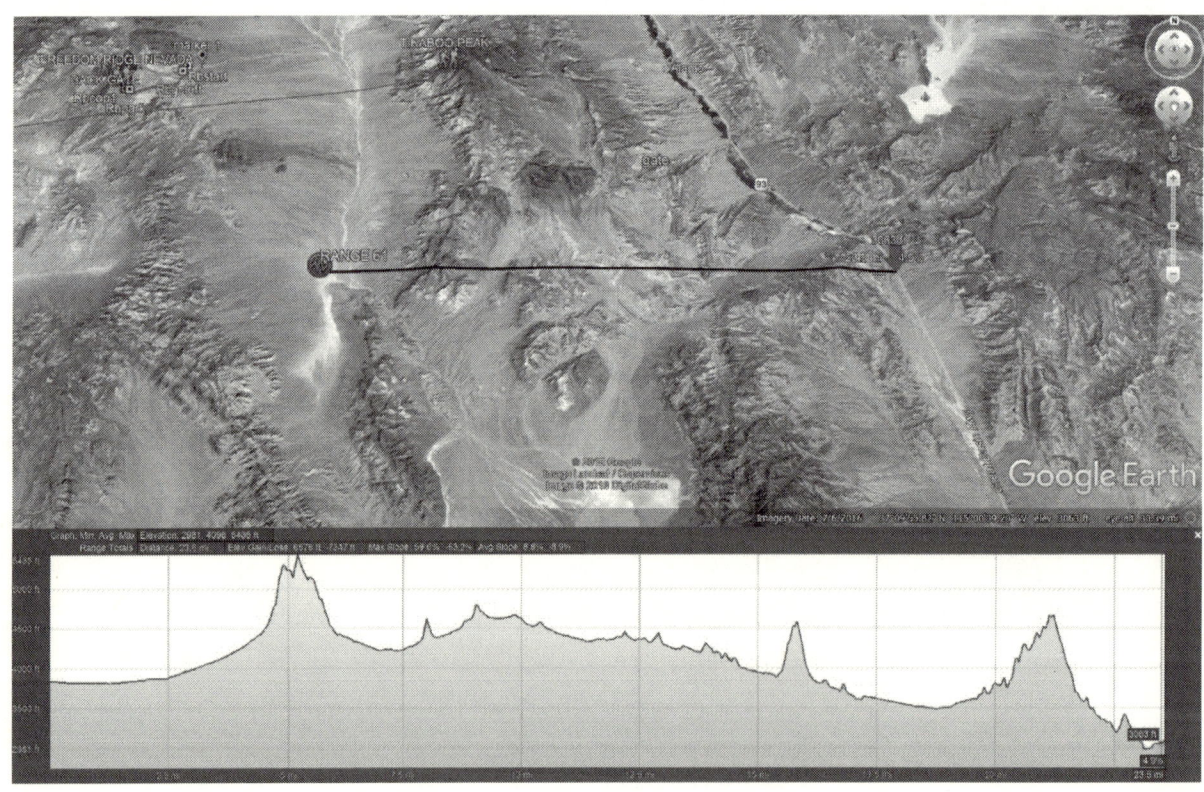

Range 61 to Highway 93 by Line-of-Sight is 22.23 miles

The elevation at Highway 93 is 3,078 feet ASL.

RANGE 61

37° 9'31.64"N 115°25'47.05"W

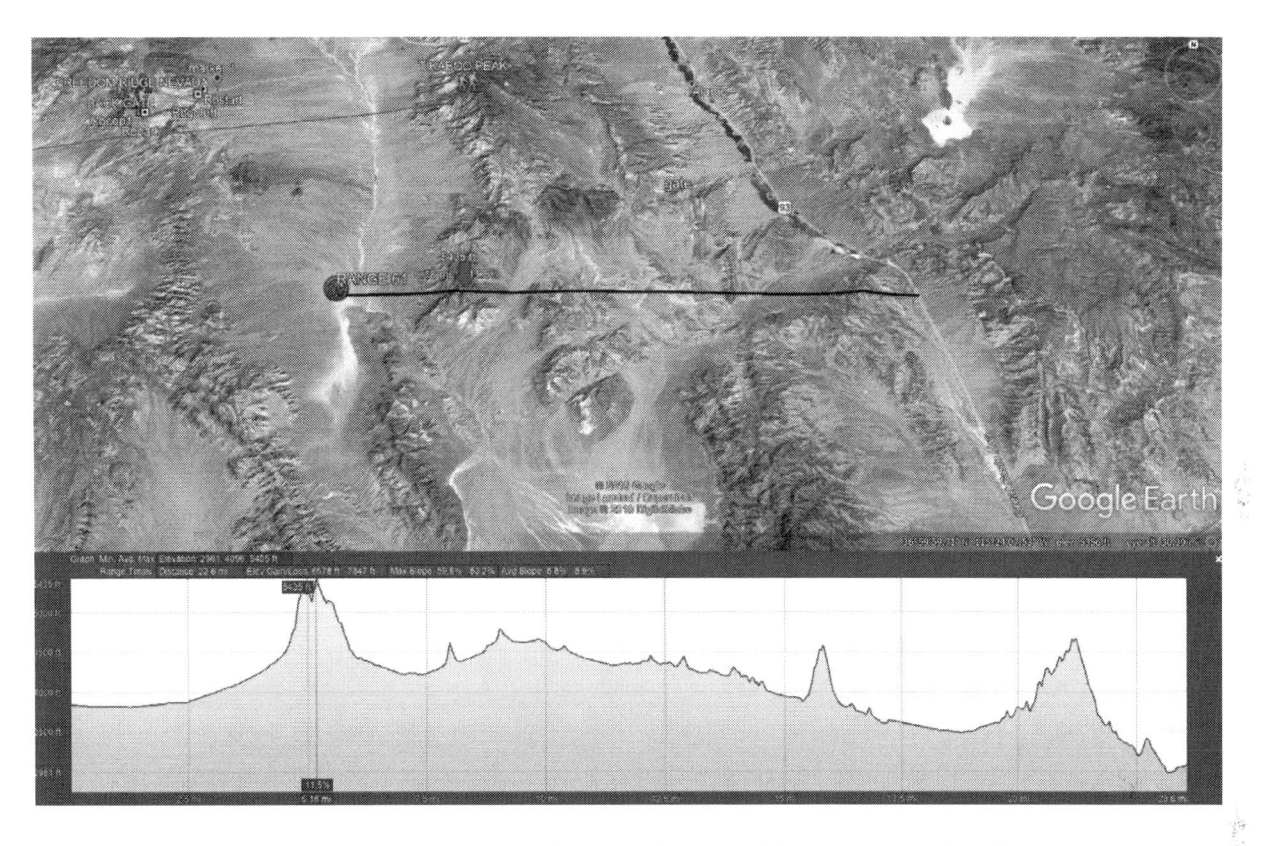

Range 61 to Highway 93 by Line-of-Sight is 22.23 miles

The highest elevation along that path from Range 61 to Highway 93 is 5,435 feet ASL.

Welcome to the World of JANET!

Due to the airline's secretive nature, little is known about its organization. It is operated for the USAF by infrastructure and defense contractor AECOM through AECOM's acquisition in 2014 of URS Corporation, which acquired EG&G Technical Services in 2002, as derived from URS's history of providing this service to the Air Force and job openings published by URS. For example, in 2010, URS announced it would be hiring Boeing 737 flight attendants to be based in Las Vegas, requiring applicants to undergo a Single Scope Background Investigation in order to be able to obtain a Top Secret security clearance. More recently, AECOM has posted similar openings.

Janet flights operate with a three-digit flight number and a *WWW*-prefix. In the official publication of ICAO airline codes, this specific three-letter designator is listed as being blocked.[9]

Common Janet destinations, mostly military, include:

Fleet

The first flights from Las Vegas to Area 51 were performed in 1972 by a Douglas DC-6 operated by EG&G. A second Douglas DC-6 was added in 1976 and this type remained in use until 1981.[5]

As of mid-2015, the Janet fleet consists of six Boeing 737-600s painted white with a prominent red cheatline. There are also five smaller executive turboprops (two Beechcraft 1900s and three Beechcraft 200Cs) painted white with less prominent blue trim stripes. The fleet is registered to the Department of the Air Force, while some earlier aircraft were registered to several civil aircraft leasing corporations. Before the arrival of the 737-600s, Janet operated Boeing 737-200s, some of which were modified from military T-43A aircraft. One of the 737-200s with registration N5177C in the 1980s was briefly based in Germany at Frankfurt International Airport (which was at the time also home to a USAF base, Rhein-Main Air Base), and operated by Keyway Air Transport, apparently a front company for a US government operation. It was retired on 6 March 2009. Together with the other 737-200s, it was sent to AMARG at Davis–Monthan Air Force Base in Arizona for storage.

All the 737-600 aircraft are ex-Air China and with the exception of N273RH and N365SR were previously operated by the now defunct China Southwest Airlines before being acquired for US Air Force operations starting in 2008. The aircraft were initially taken to Wright-Patterson Air Force Base before being transferred to Las Vegas. Most of the Beechcraft airplanes were sold directly to the Air Force, except for two, which had civilian owners first.

The aircraft livery is similar to that of the defunct Western Airlines.

JANET Fleet Information

Fleet information

Model	Registration	MSN	C/N
Boeing 737-66N	N319BD	28649	887
Boeing 737-66N	N869HH	28650	932
Boeing 737-66N	N859WP	28652	938
Boeing 737-66N	N273RH	29890	1276
Boeing 737-66N	N365SR	29891	1294
Boeing 737-66N	N288DP	29892	1305
Beech 1900C	N20RA	UB-42	–
Beech 1900C	N623RA	UC-163	–
Beech King Air B200C	N654BA	BL-54	–
Beech King Air B200C	N661BA	BL-61	–
Beech King Air B200C	N662BA	BL-62	–

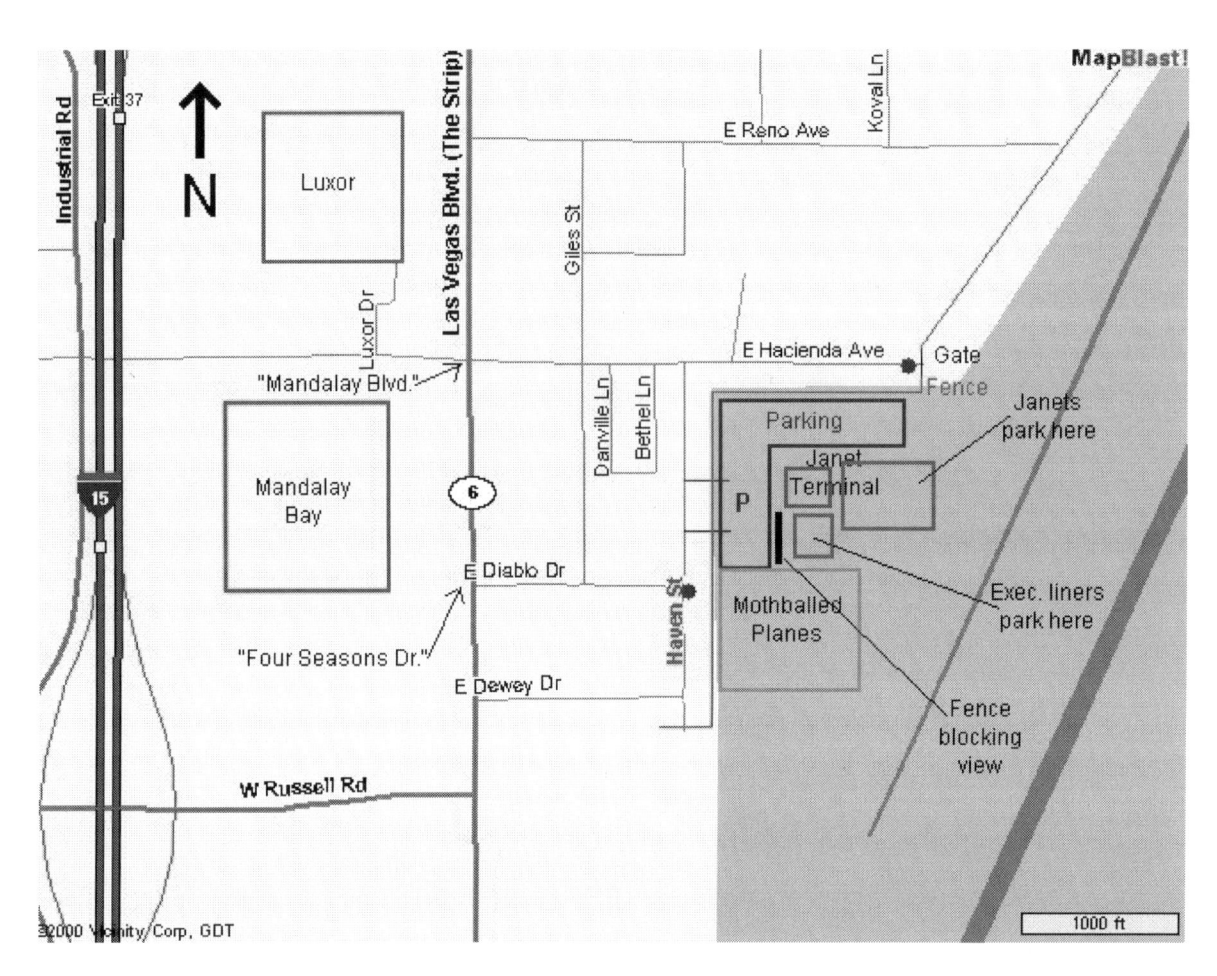

Not to **EXACT SCALE** but an estimated distance, street location map…

View of the Janet ramp and terminal from the long-term parking garage of McCarran in the east direction.

The INFAMOUS "JANET AIRLINES".....

The UNCOVER Jet Airliner from Las Vegas to the Black Projects Playgrounds

Janet Routes to Area 51

Janet Airline Terminal shown below from Google Earth

LOCATION: 36° 5'30.06"N 115° 9'53.35"W

LOCATION: 36° 5'30.06"N 115° 9'53.35"W – LV AIRPORT

Route: LAS -> Groom

Filed Flight Plan	FIDOE SHOWW BTY060030
Normal Route	LAS - FIDOE - MCY - Pyramid - Visual Approach Groom Rwy.32
Keyhole (Direct)	LAS - FIDOE - MCY (Planet) - TEDDY - Visual Approach Groom Rwy.32
Red Flag	LAS - FIDOE - MCY (Planet) - ABBIE - Visual Approach Groom Rwy.32
ILS Yankee Appr.	LAS - FIDOE - MCY (Planet) - SMOKY - ILS Rwy.32

Route: Groom -> LAS

Filed Flight Plan	BTY060030 SHOWW FIDOE BLD260033 BLD
Normal Route	Groom Departure Rwy.14 - Pyramid - MCY (Planet) - FIDOE - LAS
Keyhole (Direct)	Groom Departure Rwy.14 - TEDDY - MCY (Planet) - FIDOE - LAS
Red Flag	Groom Departure Rwy.14 - ABBIE - MCY (Planet) - FIDOE - LAS

Groom typically uses Rwy 32 for arriving Janet 737's, and Rwy 14 for departures. The smaller Beechliners often use the shorter Rwy 30 for arrival and Rwy 12 for departure. The old Rwy 14R/32L is no longer used. Rwy 32 is equipped with an ILS.

Flights to and from Groom do not follow the filed flight plan. They enter the restricted area over Mercury as filed, apparently in an effort to conceal the fact that they are going to Groom instead of TTR, as filed.

But from Mercury, where they are handled by Groom Control on an unpublished frequency and under a different call sign, they take different routes, depending on activity within the Ranges:

The normal route goes north from Mercury to a fix referred to as "Pyramid", and from there north-east, across the NW corner of the 60's Ranges, to the Groom Approach to Rwy 32.

During Red Flag, when the 60's Ranges are used for live bombing and air-air combat, Janets circumnavigate the bombing ranges via the ABBIE fix in the northern part of the NTS, near the SW corner of the Groom airspace. The route goes north from Mercury, then east at ABBIE for the approach to Groom.

During public events at the NTS (NTS tour, media day etc., referred to as "Keyhole" condition) the TEDDY fix in the southern part of Range 64A is used. This way the Janets do not fly over the NTS, where they could easily be identified by visitors as being in approach to an air field that officially does not exist. This more direct route is also often used as a shortcut, when the Ranges are cold, especially in the early mornings and evenings.

For an ILS approach to Rwy 32, also referred to as "ILS Yankee Approach", a routing via the SMOKY fix is used. This fix is believed to be in line with the Groom runway 32, approximately 16 miles out. Janets intercept the 3 degree glide slope here from 11,000ft AMSL to the Groom runway at 4,500 AMSL.

In the early mornings and late evenings, sometimes a more direct route is used. It leads from the FIDOE fix via Indian Springs and the SMOKY fix into Groom. This route leads right across the bombing ranges 64 and 65. It is only available if the ranges are "cold" (no exercise activity scheduled in the ranges).

Inbound Janets are typically handed off to Groom Control before they reach MCY, while they are still in open airspace.

At that time they change their callsign from Janet to the Groom "callsign of the day".

The handoff to Groom tower is usually near the fix used for the routing between MCY and Groom. Outbound flights are handled similar, in reverse order.

The schedule below shows the matching LAS outbound and return flights, or the round trips a given Boeing 737 Janet makes from LAS. The schedule is different on Mondays and Fridays because of the extra flights to Palmdale. For the Groom callsigns see the Janet Flight Schedule below.

Boeing 737-600, registration N319BD

"UNMARKED COMMERICAL AIRLINER"

Las Vegas -> Area 51 (14,000 ft.)			
Callsign	Time	Groom Callsign	Notes
Janet 211	3:40am - 4:05am	... 26	
Janet 772	4:10am - 4:35am	... 87	
Janet 456	5:10am - 5:35am	... 71	
Janet 738	6:10am - 6:35am	... 53	
Janet 621	7:10am - 7:35am	... 36	
Janet 866	7:55am - 8:20am	... 81	Mondays only, other days occasionally at different times
Janet 652	8:10am - 8:35am	... 67	
Janet 451	9:10am - 9:35am	... 66	
Janet 876	11:10am - 11:35am	... 91	
Janet 675	2:00pm - 2:25pm	... 90	
Janet 331	3:00pm - 3:25pm	... 46	
Janet 812	4:00pm - 4:25pm	... 27	

Janet 555	5:00pm - 5:25pm	... 70	
Janet 362	6:35pm - 7:00pm	... 77	
Janet 482	(varies)	... 97	Only occasionally no set schedule
Janet 634	(varies)	... 49	Only occasionally no set schedule

Las Vegas - Groom Lake Round Trip Timetables

History of Area 51

In 1942 an auxiliary airfield was established at Groom Lake in Nevada, 83 miles north-northwest of Las Vegas.

A Time Line of Events at Area 51

"The Ranch"

The following is a time line beginning soon after Area 51's construction in 1957 up to present day:

- **1957** – The AEC distributes "Background Information on Nevada Nuclear Tests" to the press. The booklet describes a small base at Groom Lake called the Watertown Project. The booklet claimed the facility was part of a project to study weather.

- **1961** – The restricted airspace expands upwards, but not outwards — it measures five by nine nautical miles in size, but extends up to space and is designated R-4808. A year later, the Department of the Air Force expands the space again, but this time the perimeter grows to 22 by 20 nautical miles. This forms the "Groom Box," or just "the Box," as it is known today. No flights, whether commercial or military, are allowed in the restricted space (except the test flights from the base itself).
- **1962** – The first A-12 arrives at Groom Lake. The first test flight takes place two months after the aircraft's arrival to the base. CIA pilots arrive at the base nearly a year later to begin flight training.
- **1967** – The first Mig 21, a Soviet aircraft, arrives at Groom Lake. Officials name the testing program of Mig aircraft "Have Donut." Some pilots begin to call the restricted air space above Groom Lake "Red Square."

A Time Line of Events at Area 51

"The Ranch" "Watertown" "Dreamland"

The F117-A Nighthawk Stealth Fighter

1977 – Years before the public became aware of the Stealth Fighter, the first F117 prototype arrives at Area 51. It's called the "Have Blue." That same year, the United States Geological Survey takes an aerial photo of the base. The photo appears in numerous publications and is available until 1994, when the government withdraws it from release.

1982 – The first flight of the vehicle known as "Tacit Blue" takes place at Groom Lake. Like the F-117A, Tacit Blue is a stealth vehicle.

A Time Line of Events at Area 51

"The Ranch" ....

1984 – The base petitions for an additional 89,000 acres of land to increase the size of restricted space around the facility. Guards had previously discouraged the public from entering this area before it was officially withdrawn, raising concern and criticism from locals and tourists. The request is ratified by Congress three years later.

1988 – A Soviet satellite photographs Area 51. "Popular Science" runs the photograph, giving most U.S. citizens their first chance to glimpse the secret base. That same year, Robert Frost, a civilian employee at Area 51, dies. An autopsy shows that his body contained high levels of dangerous chemicals like dioxin, trichloroethylene and dibenzofuran. His widow, Helen, files a lawsuit against several government officials, claiming her husband died as a result of exposure to dangerous chemicals.

1989 – Robert Lazar appears on television and claims to have worked on reverse engineering alien technology at a site not far from Groom Lake.

1995 – Area 51 acquires two locations popular with tourists and curious locals. Freedom Ridge and White Sides Peak. President Clinton signs an executive order exempting Area 51 from legislation and investigation in order to preserve national security.

1996 – Nevada names Route 375, formerly known as the "loneliest highway in America," the "Extraterrestrial Highway." Skeptics around the world groan in unison.

1997 – Area 51 is declassified, though all operations at the facility are still kept secret.

2007 – It appears that crews are building a new hangar, much larger than the existing hangar. The hangar's size is approximately 200 by 500 feet and 100 feet tall

2009 - A newer satellite image, taken on June 29, 2009, for the first time shows the completed new hangar. Other significant changes include the newly paved north ramp, a new running track, several smaller new buildings and the two new radio sites that we discovered in June of 2008.

2009: Between 12/15/09 and 12/30/09 the remaining 9-mile dirt section of Groom Lake Road inside the restricted area between the warning signs and the old cattle fence near the north end of the dry lake bed was paved. Groom Lake Road is now a paved road from Area 51 all the way to the warning signs. The 13.8-mile section outside the restricted area, between the warning signs and Hwy 375, remains still a dirt road.

A Time Line of Events at Area 51

"The Ranch"..............

2010: Another large new hangar was added at the South Ramp of Area 51 between 11/05/09 and 05/24/10. Ground preparation for the foundation can be seen in a June, 2009 Satellite Image at www.dreamlandresort.com . The hangar is located just west of the old Hangar 20-23 storage building. It is most likely connected to the ramp on the south side, opposite another hangar that was added in early 2005. Photo by Jeff Gregos, with friendly permission.

2010: The Area 51 Back Gate Road has just been partially paved. The oil pavement is covered with a thin layer of very fine gravel or sand. The pavement goes for 2.2 miles from the Guard Shack to the intersection with a road leading north and eventually back to Hwy 375. The pavement continues up that road for another 0.8 miles and then ends. There is no indication for plans to extend the pavement past that point.

2011: A large new Guard Shack is currently being built at the Rachel Back Gate to Area 51. The outside of the sheet metal building is complete, and contractors are busy finishing the inside. The building is about five times the size of the current guard shack, which was built in October 2000. It is located between the current guard shack and the original pre-2000 guard shack. After the paving of part of the Back Gate road last August, this is the second major upgrade to the Back Gate in six months. Clearly this gate is going to see more traffic.

A Time Line of Events at Area 51

"The Ranch"..............

2011: There were road improvements at the Groom Lake Road gate and the and Back Gate back in 2010. A newer satellite photo shows that some of the roads inside the restricted area have also been improved during the same time period, including Groom Lake Road, the Backgate Road, the road to the engine test cells on the far south end of the base and the access road to a fairly new radio site on a hill on the northwest side of Groom Lake.

2011: A satellite image shows a new very large building near the new Base Headquarters and the Janet Ramp in the final stages of construction. It measures approximately 255x184', and appears to be fairly tall. The building, located just south-east of the new Base Headquarters could be a new dining hall or administrative offices. Google Earth imagery dated 6/28/2010 shows the previously vacant area being graded in preparation for the construction. Built between August of 2010 and August of 2011.

2012: One of the latest new satellite photo shows beginning construction of a new hangar east of the existing North Ramp. We believe this hangar will be used for the base security helicopters, based on the proximity to the helicopter ramp and two security helicopter hangars at Nellis AFB with a very similar footprint.

About State Route 375 (SR 375)…ET Highway…Extraterrestrial Highway

State Route 375 (**SR 375**) is a state highway in south-central Nevada in the United States. The highway stretches 98 miles (158 km) from State Route 318 at Crystal Springs northwest to U.S. Route 6 (US 6) at Warm Springs. The route travels through mostly unoccupied desert terrain, with much of its alignment paralleling the northern edges of the Nellis Air Force Range. The road originally traversed through what is now the northern reaches of the air force range in the 1930s, when it was previously designated **State Route 25A** and later part of State Route 25.

The top-secret Area 51 government base is near SR 375 and many travelers have reported UFO observations and other strange alien activity along this road. Such stories prompted the state to officially designate the route as the **Extraterrestrial Highway** in 1996. The small town of Rachel, located near the center of the highway, caters to tourists and UFO seekers with alien-themed businesses. Although the area receives some tourism due to alleged extraterrestrial activity, SR 375 remains a lightly traveled route.

SR 375 with the infamous

"EXTRATERRESTRIAL HIGHWAY SIGN" looking northwest.

Major Intersections of SR375 aka "The Extraterrestrial Highway"

County	Location	Mile	km	Destinations	Notes
Lincoln	Crystal Springs	**98.41**	158.38	SR 318 to US 93	Southern terminus
Nye	Warm Springs	**0.00**	0.00	US 6 – Tonopah, Ely	Northern terminus

1.000 mi = 1.609; 1.000 km = 0.621 mi

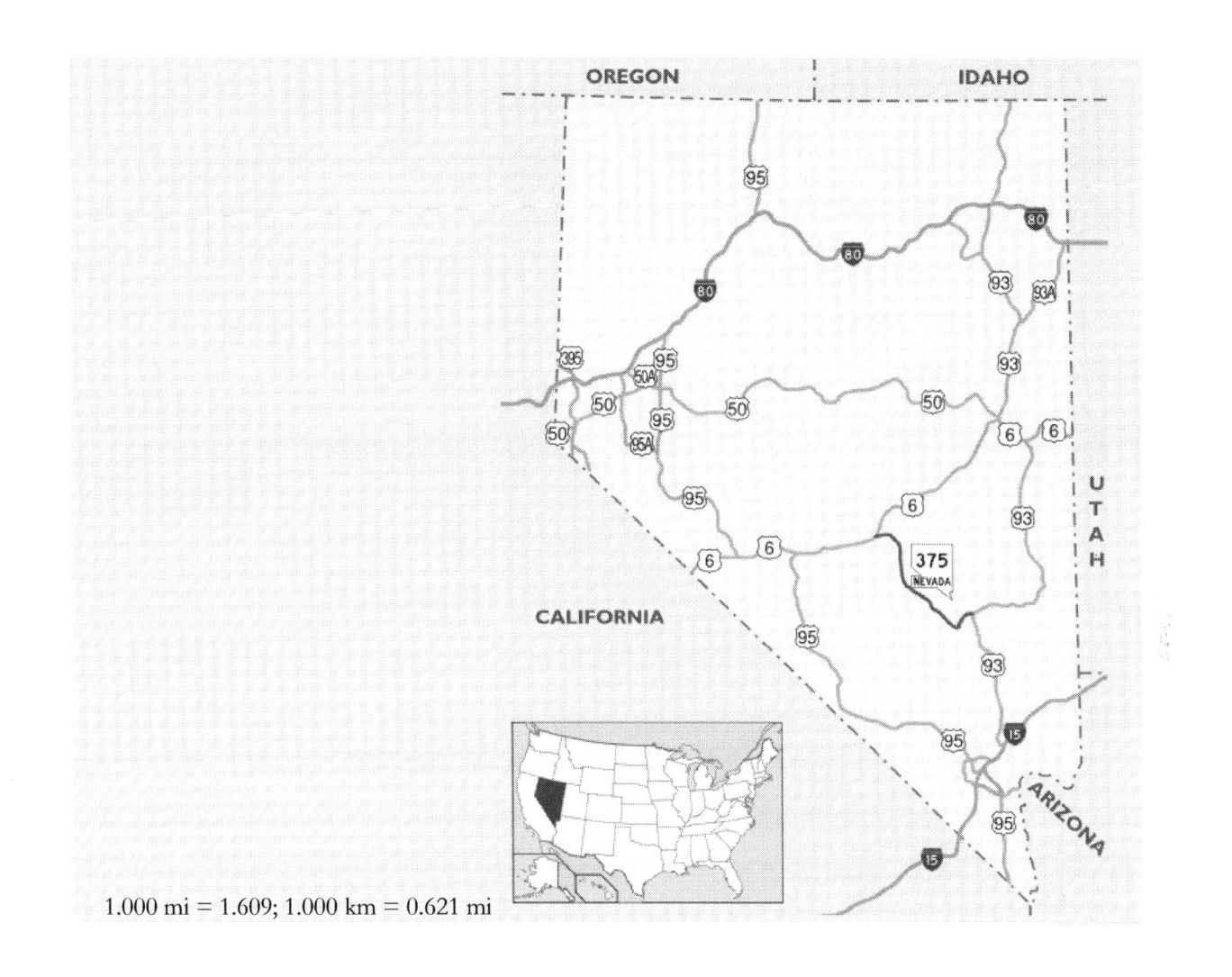

STARTING Your Road Trip from Little A'Le'Inn

145

Rachel, Nevada.

FOR SMARTPHONES/MOBILE BAR CODE SCANNERS

Driving directions from Las Vegas to Rachel, NV 89001

1) Take the ramp onto I-15 N travel about 26 miles
2) Take exit 64 for US-93 N/Great Basin Hwy toward Pioche Ely about 0.2 miles
3) Turn left onto US-93 N/Great Basin Hwy travel about 85 miles
Note: below is a fork in the road watch on-coming traffic before staying left onto NV-375
4) Turn left onto NV-318 N/NV-375 N/State Hwy 375 - Continue to follow NV-375 N/State Hwy 375 about 40 miles

The Little A'Le'Inn (Previously Rachel Bar and Grill) is a small great bar, restaurant and motel located in Rachel, Nevada on the Extraterrestrial Highway. The business has been running for over 20 years and has been a favorite of mine and to many visitors to the local Area 51 area. The business has a variety of Area 51 and UFO related items for sale such as maps of the area, posters, postcards, toys, etc. and is also famous for its *"Alien Burger"*.

Address: 1 Old Mill St, Rachel, NV 89001

Web Address: http://littlealeinn.com/ - WEB

Telephone
Bus: (775)729-2515
Fax: (775)729-2551

GPS Coordinates
N37° 38.801'
W115° 44.760'

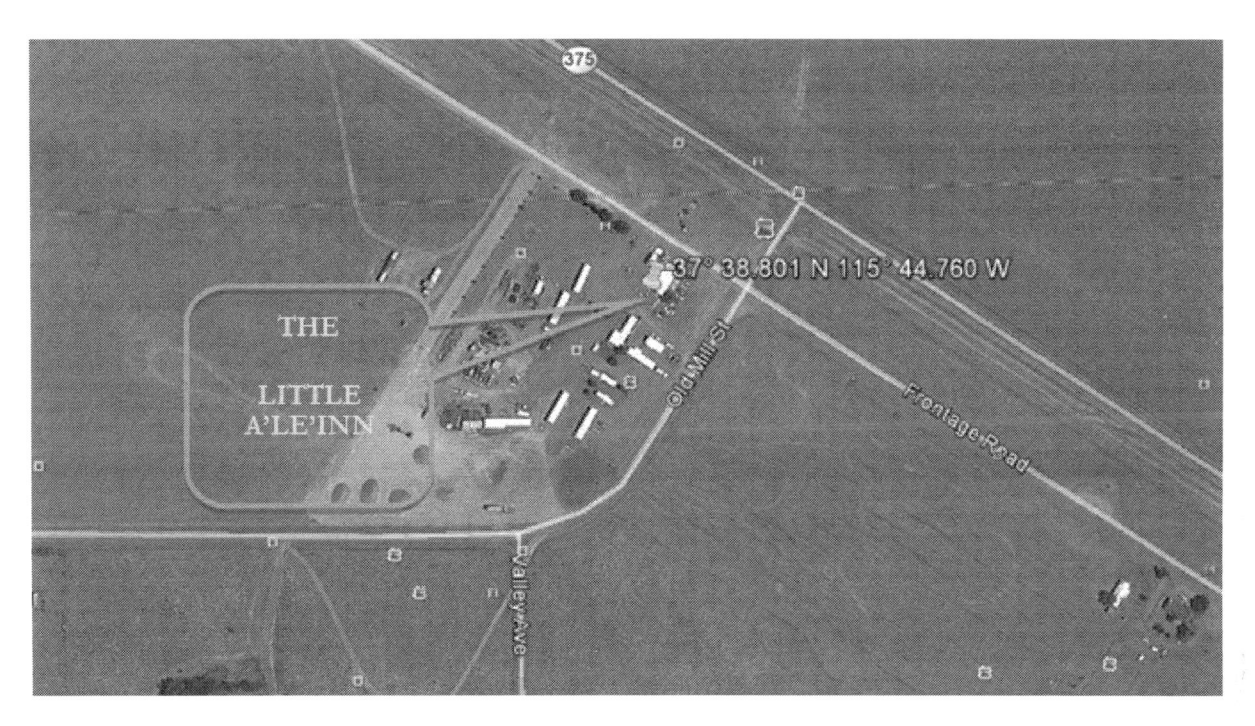

Your Adventure begins from the *Little A'Le'Inn*

Don't forget to get your picture or video's on the CAPTURED UFO

Only contained at the famous *Little A'Le'Inn!*

Did you bring your drone?

Why not FLY IT AROUND HERE AND CAPTURED AWESOME FOOTAGE OF THE FAMOUS "ET HIGHWAY"

Say Hello to Connie & Pat

and

The Great Staff of the Famous Alien Burger Team!

From Pat (Owner of Little A'Le'Inn) said .... Back in 1990 we decided to aspire to the surrounding area and embrace what this town of Rachel was really all about during this period in history. Thus the name of the Little A'Le'Inn was born. Some believe the name to sound like an inn that serves ale (ale inn), while others believe it to mean alien. We leave this up to you to decide. We like the sounds of both.

There are so many memories, so many wonderful people, and so many good times that have been had here in our little establishment. Thank you all for what you have allowed us to do here. This has been my life's dream. Some of those who have shared this dream have passed on and will be remembered forever each and every day as we pass through the Little A'Le'Inn's front doorway on our way ...... to serve you.

Look up as the truth lies there. Always keep your eyes to the skies whenever you can. You just never know when that special event will happen. At those times there may be no answers, leaving you only to wonder what just happened or what you saw, and having to ask more questions... getting no answers. Life is a mystery, enjoy the ride.

The events and unidentified flying objects we see and only hear at times in this area often leave us shaking our heads. The unknown is what we live for. The times when logic escapes us and the knowledge of things to come are before us. We welcome it all.

Shown below for your reference is a area view map of Sand Spring Valley, Rachel, NV and Tikaboo Valley. It shows the location of Area 51, the Main Gate and the Back Gate, the Black Mailbox, and several other locations that may be of interest you to visit to these areas. In the table below NY... and LN... refers to the Nye and Lincoln County mile markers along Hwy. 375.

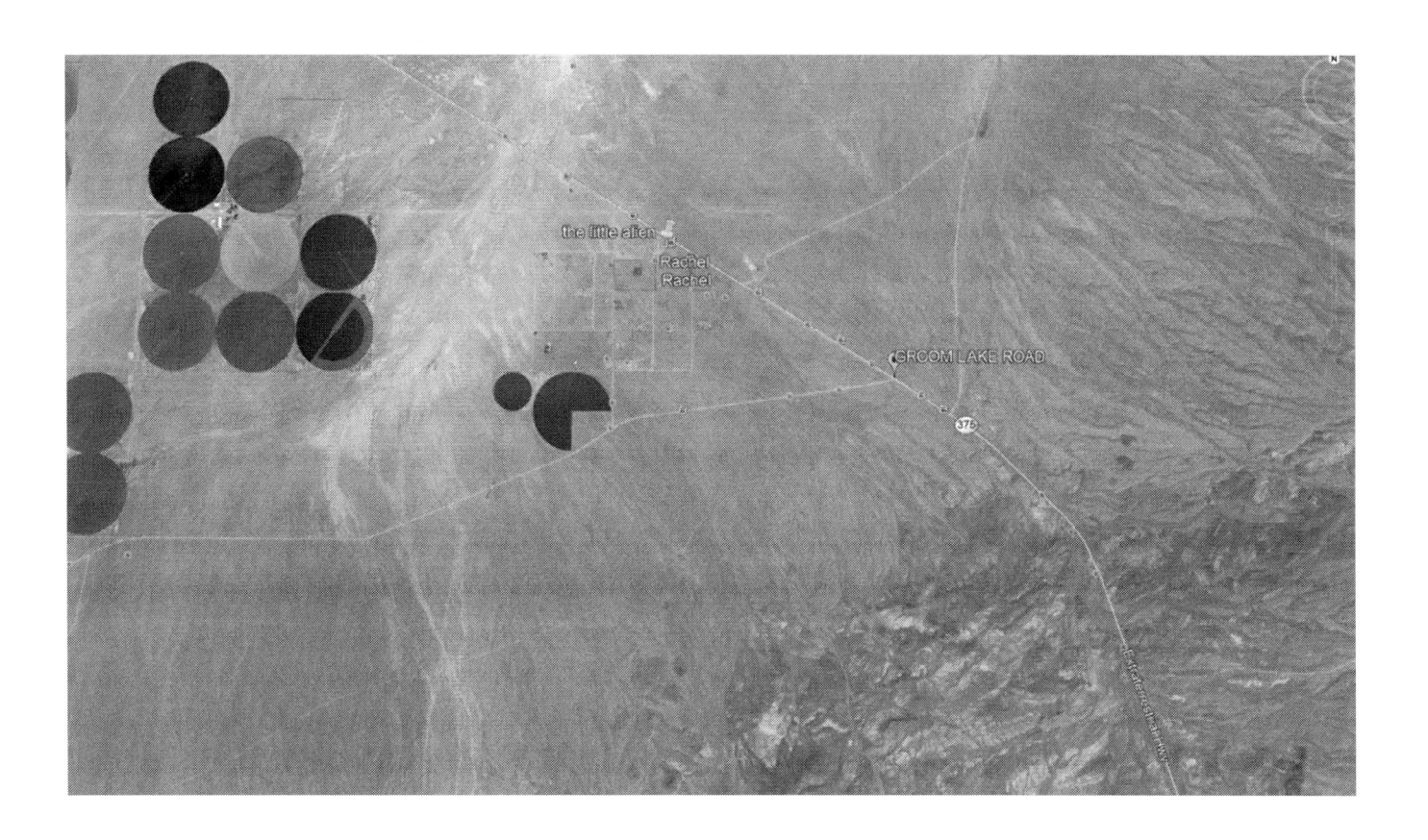

Latitude and Longitude are the GPS coordinates of the location.

#	Description Details	Location	Latitude North (N)	Longitude West (W)
0	Area 51 (Tower)		37°14.428'	115°48.528'
1	Queen City Summit (5960 ft.)	NY 45.85	37°45.129'	115°56.733'
2	Nye / Lincoln County Line	LN 0 / NY 49.36	37°43.329'	115°53.671'
3	Town of Rachel	LN 10.0	37°38.801'	115°44.760'
4	Intersection of Hwy. 375 and Back Gate Road	LN 11.4	37°38.063'	115°43.181'
5	Area 51 Back Gate (Rachel Back Gate) - Here you get to see the guard shack. It is legal to drive right up to the barrier	10.2 mi from 4	37°35.641'	115°53.924'
6	Coyote Summit (5591 ft.)	LN 16.6	37°34.331'	115°40.123'
7	Black Mailbox (now white), intersection of Hwy. 375 and Mailbox Road - Good viewing location. However, the base is right behind White Sides (the mountain with 'shoulders' on both sides) from here	LN 29.6	37°27.432'	115°28.962'
8	Crescent Reservoir - 5-way intersection. Make sure you get the right turn here. The main road leads around the reservoir and to the ranch; to get to Groom Lake Road take the second road from the right.	3.9 mi from 7	37°24.063'	115°29.573'
9	Gravel Parking Area south of Hwy. 375 - Excellent viewing location, slightly higher than the Mailbox, and better angle	LN 32.3	37°25.931'	115°26.689'
10	Intersection of Hwy. 375 and Groom Lake Road	LN 34.6	37°24.892'	115°24.586'
11	Intersection of Groom Lake Road and Ranch Road	4.2 mi from 10 / 1.0 mi from 8	37°23.456'	115°28.823'
12	Intersection of Groom Lake Road and Mailbox Road - Coming from the Mailbox, turn right onto Groom Lake Road here	5.2 mi from 10 / 1.1 mi from 8	37°23.137'	115°29.826'
13	Area 51 Main Gate - Do not continue past the warning signs. Look for the cammo boys on nearby hills. Security cameras on the hill to your left	13.8 mi from 10	37°21.068'	115°38.813'
14	Hancock Summit (5592 ft.)	LN 37.5	37°25.832'	115°22.432'
15	Horneys Rest Stop - Roadside rest near Hancock summit, some shade, picnic tables	LN 38.1	37°26.372'	115°22.614'
16	Powerlines Overlook - Excellent high elevation view point in the mountains behind the Black Mailbox. Requires 4WD	4.3 mi from 15	37°27.541'	115°25.437'
17	Tikaboo Peak - The closest view spot for Area 51. Requires 4WD and a somewhat strenuous hike	25.6mi from .Area 51	37°20.654'	115°21.543'

18 Groom Lake Road Guard Shack - Hidden behind a curve well inside the restricted area, do not attempt to go there.	0.85 mi from 13	37°20.750'	115°39.610'
19 Bald Mountain Radio and Surveillance Facility	15.0 mi f.rom Area 51	37°26.967'	115°44.023'
20 White Sides *(Former Area 51 View Spot)*	13.3 mi from .Area 51	37°22.114'	115°37.681'
21 Freedom Ridge *(Former Area 51 View Spot)*	11.1 mi from .Area 51	37°20.077'	115°38.679'

The "OLD MAILBOX" aka infamous "BLACK MAILBOX" Alien Drop-off

There's a new Black Mailbox at Area 51! It was installed on 02/04/2017 per a date found inside the door. The area has been cleaned up and looks a lot better.

We discovered this on 06/30/2017.

THE NEW BLACK MAILBOX
37°27'25.77"N 115°28'57.38"W

"THE NEW BLACK MAILBOX" Alien Drop-off

There's a new Black Mailbox at Area 51! It was installed on 02/04/2017 per a date found inside the door. The area has been cleaned up and looks a lot better.

We discovered this on 06/30/2017.

THE NEW "BLACK MAILBOX"
37°27'25.77"N 115°28'57.38"W

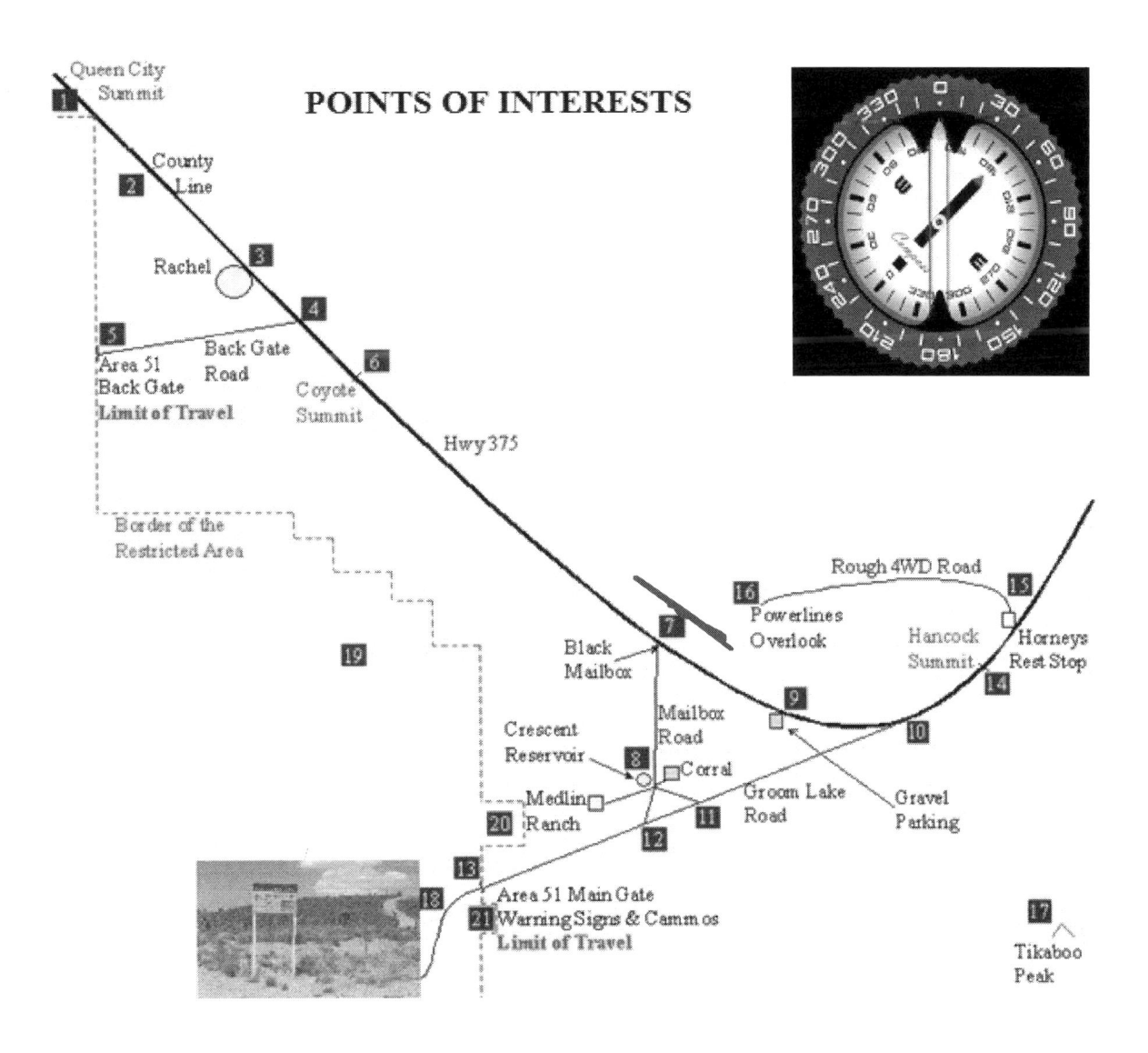

Map Schematic of Major Main Points of Interest from the **Latitude and Longitude** in ref with **GPS** coordinates of the locations.

Buckle Up – You're First Road Trip to the mysterious "Black Mailbox"

Location of the Black Mailbox - 37°27'25"N   115°28'57"W

As you leave the Little A'Le'Inn parking lot you will make a right turn onto Highway 375 also known as the famous *"Extraterrestrial Highway."*

"The Extraterrestrial Highway" to start your first road trip journey. Drive approximately 19.35 miles heading southwest on SR375 from an elevation of approximately 4,846 feet above sea level going past your first landmark called Long Street which is approximately 8.04 miles from your starting point. Keep continuing on SR375 southwest until your second landmark which will be Tempiute Mine Road - Rachel, Nevada which is approximately 2 miles from Long Street that you just past before. Keep continuing on SR375 another 9.5 miles southwest until you see the dirt road off to your right and the mailbox is right in sight! Soon after mile marker 29 on NV-375, you'll see the Black Mailbox (now white) on the left.

Black Mailbox right off CR375 approximately 19.35 miles from your starting point from the

Little A'Le'Inn

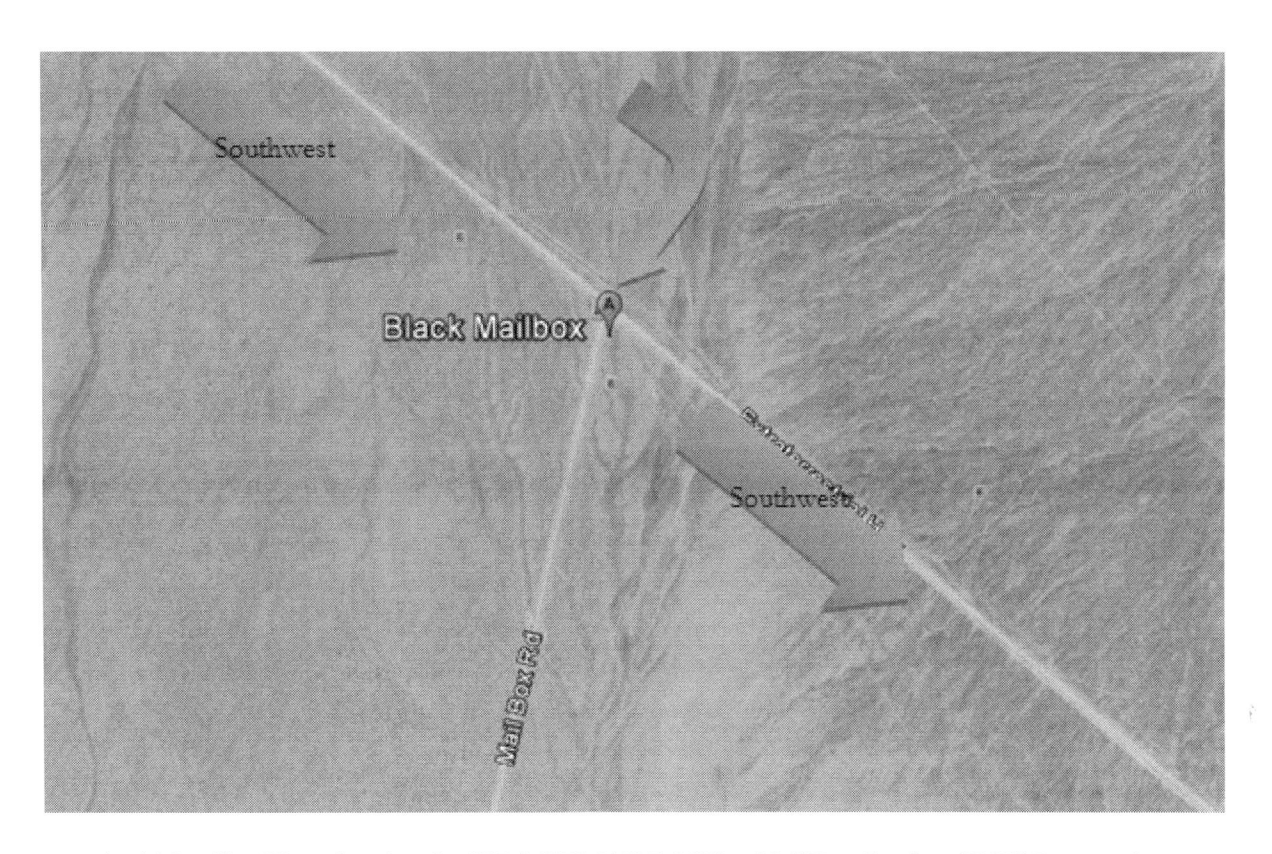

Aerial Satellite View showing the "BLACK MAILBOX" at Mail Box Road & CR375 Intersection

THE NEW "BLACK MAILBOX"
37°27'25.77"N 115°28'57.38"W

The black mailbox is actually inside this white outer box, a mystery wrapped in an enigma,

BUT NO LONGER EXIST!

There is the NEW BLACK MAILBOX as shown above!

The NEW **"BLACK MAILBOX"** at night!

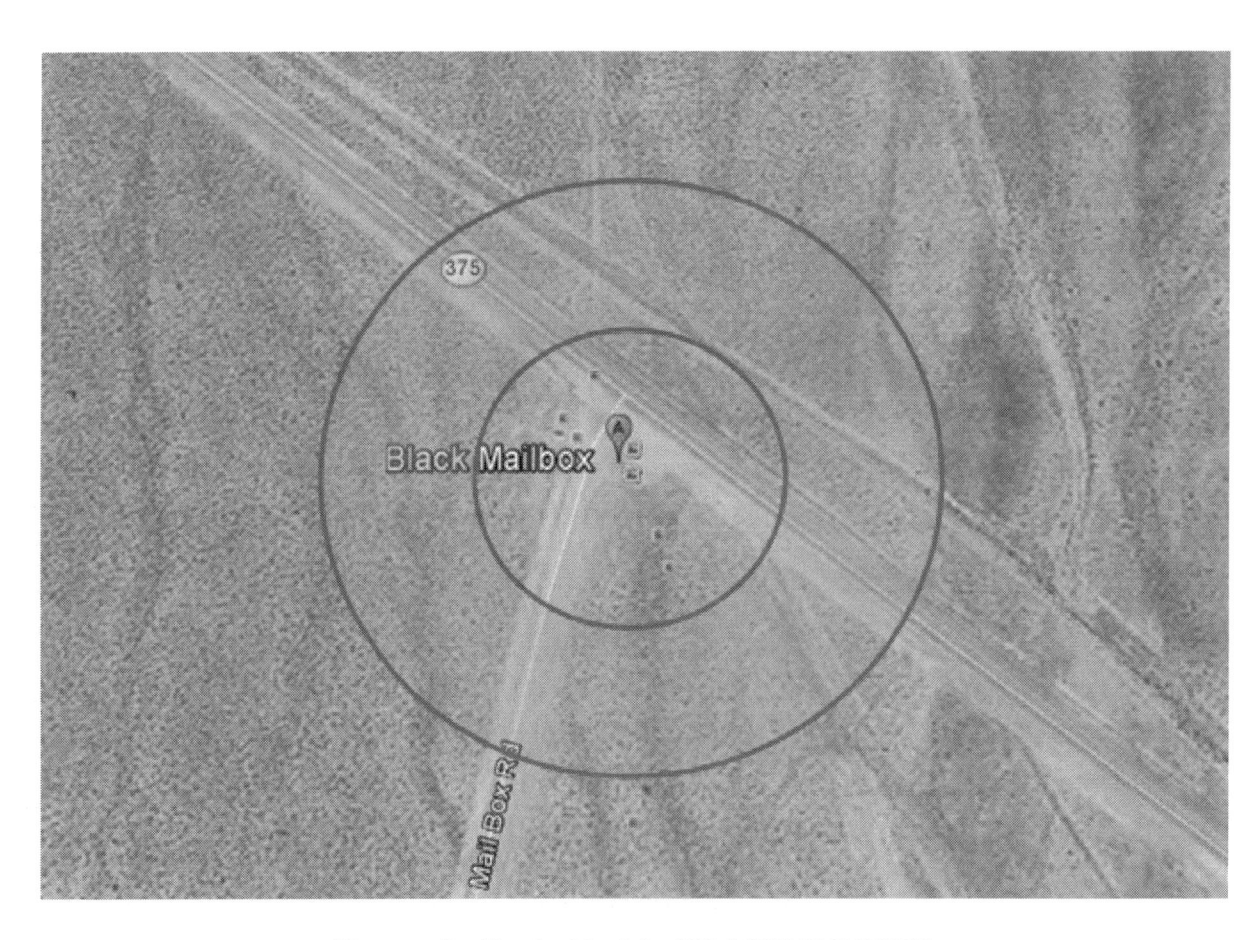

Close–up Satellite Aerial of the "BLACK MAILBOX"

The box is made of quarter-inch-thick bulletproof metal, and its door is clamped shut with a Master Lock. Its owner, say the black letters printed on its side, is STEVE MEDLIN, HC 61, BOX 80. Over the years, hundreds of people have converged here to photograph this box held up by a chipped metal pole. They camp next to it. They try to break into it. They debate its significance, or simply huddle by it for hours, staring into the night. Some think the mailbox is linked to nearby Area 51, a military installation and purported hotbed of extraterrestrial activity. At the very least, they consider the box a prime magnet for flying saucers. A few visitors have claimed to have seen astonishing celestial oddities, but most seem to enjoy even uneventful nights at the mailbox, about midway between the towns of Alamo and Rachel.

TAKE A TRIP TO THE "BACK GATE!"

Buckle Up – You're Second Road Trip to The Back Gate Station Area

As you leave the Little A'Le'Inn parking lot you will make a right turn onto Highway 375 also known as the famous *"Extraterrestrial Highway"* to start your second road trip journey. Drive approximately 1.68 miles southwest until you see the Back gate Road which intersects with CR375.

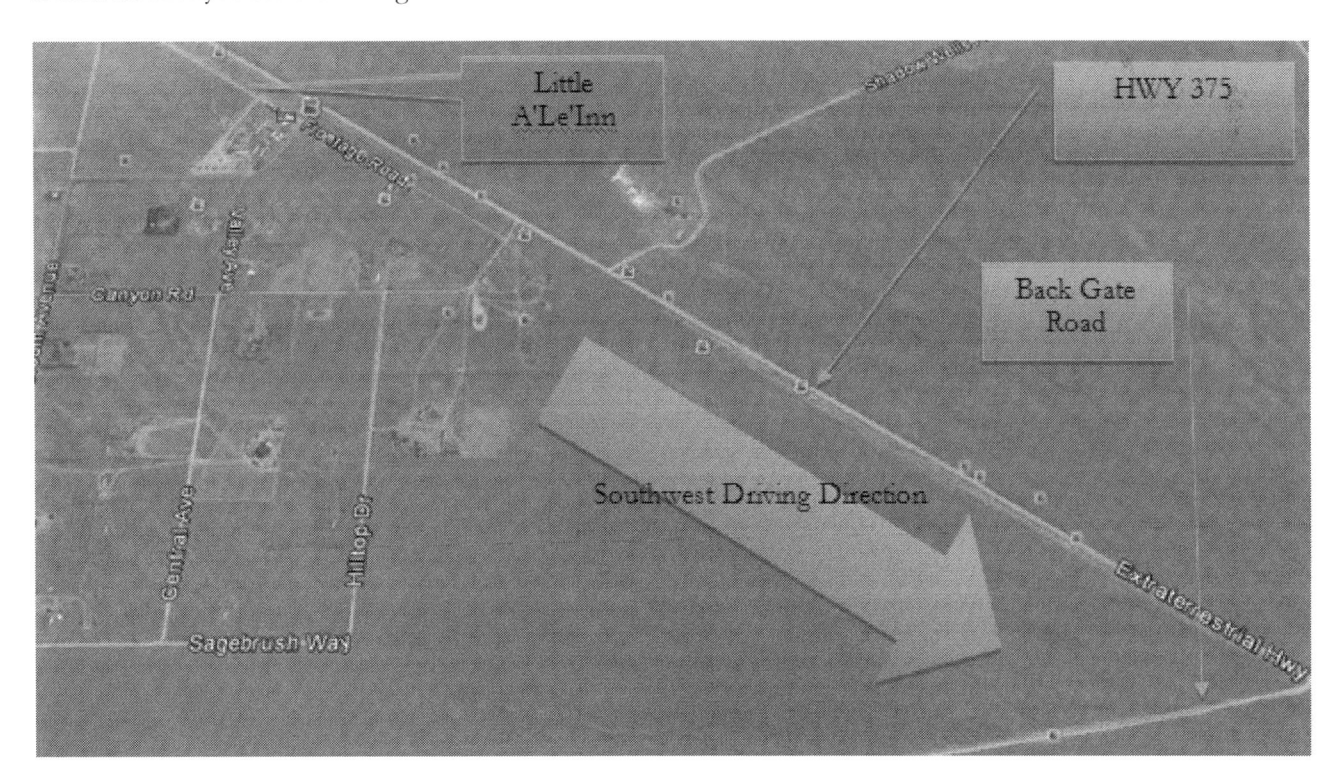

Road access to the facility is with Nevada State Route 375 at ***37°38'4.04"N 115°43'10.35"W*** where an access road called Back Gate Road connects to the public highway system which is CR375. The security gate and a parking facility is at ***37°35'38.67"N 115°53'56.02"W*** (figure 3) about 10.25 miles west-southwest of the road turnoff which was Back Gate Road. *DO NOT PASS THE BACK*

GATE! You can take a car or of course a jeep depending on your ride. The gate is approximately 25 miles from the main support base (Area 51) along a winding road. It shows that once road traffic reaches the base, vehicles are routed to a large facility *37°14'28"N 115°49'26"W* where imagery shows below a large number of tractor-trailers and other vehicles that are parked. This facility processes incoming shipments and presumably issues security credentials for personnel for their movement on the base. Several storage areas are around the facility, in which are used for outside storage of large items. The road then continues to the west, eventually going into the Nevada Test Site, and southward to Mercury, Nevada, an restricted access community some 40 miles to the south-southeast where the road connects to the public highway system at U.S. Route 95.

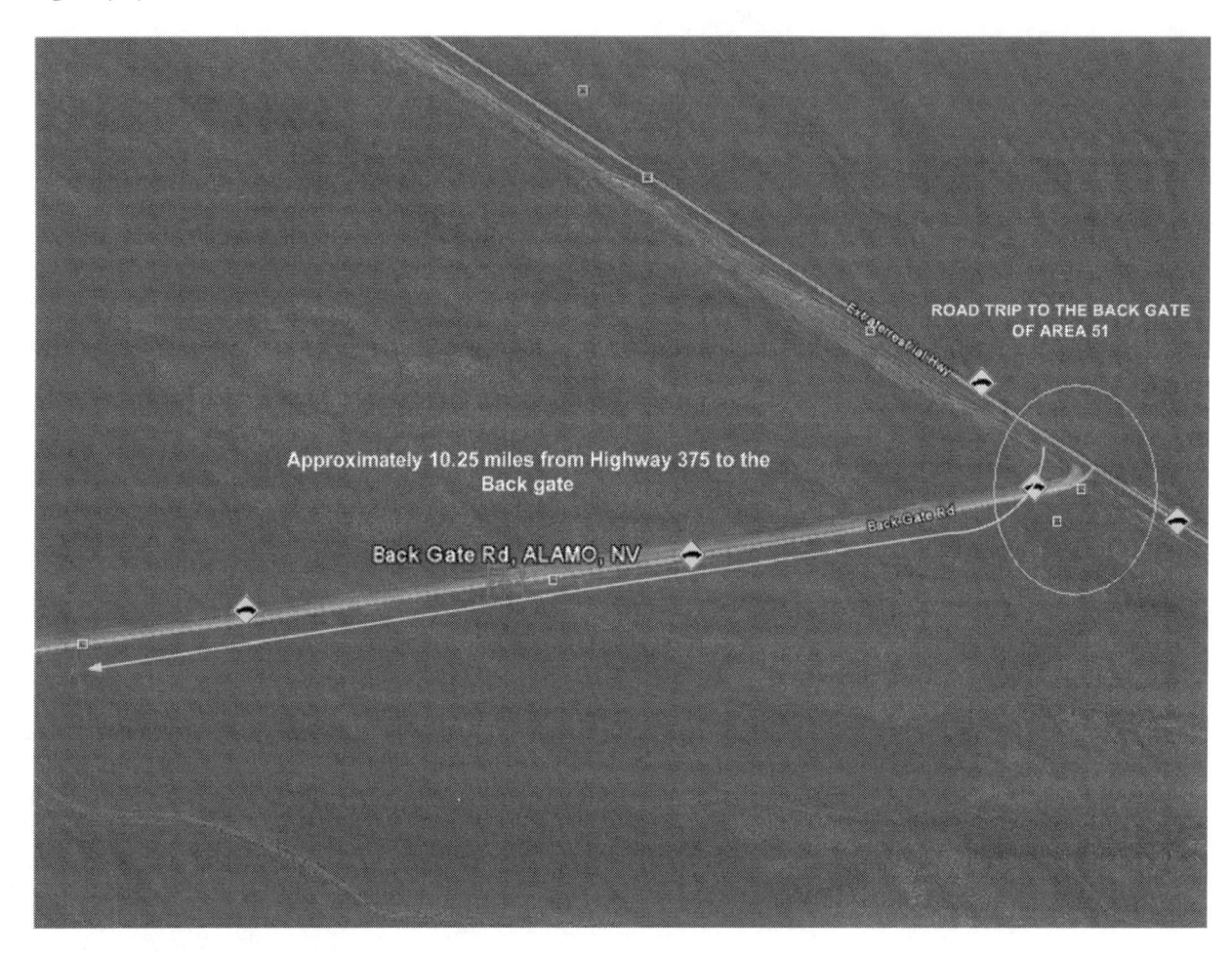

HWY 375 and Back Gate Road Intersection. This is the road access to the back gate facility.

This is reference at *37°38'4.04"N 115°43'10.35"W*

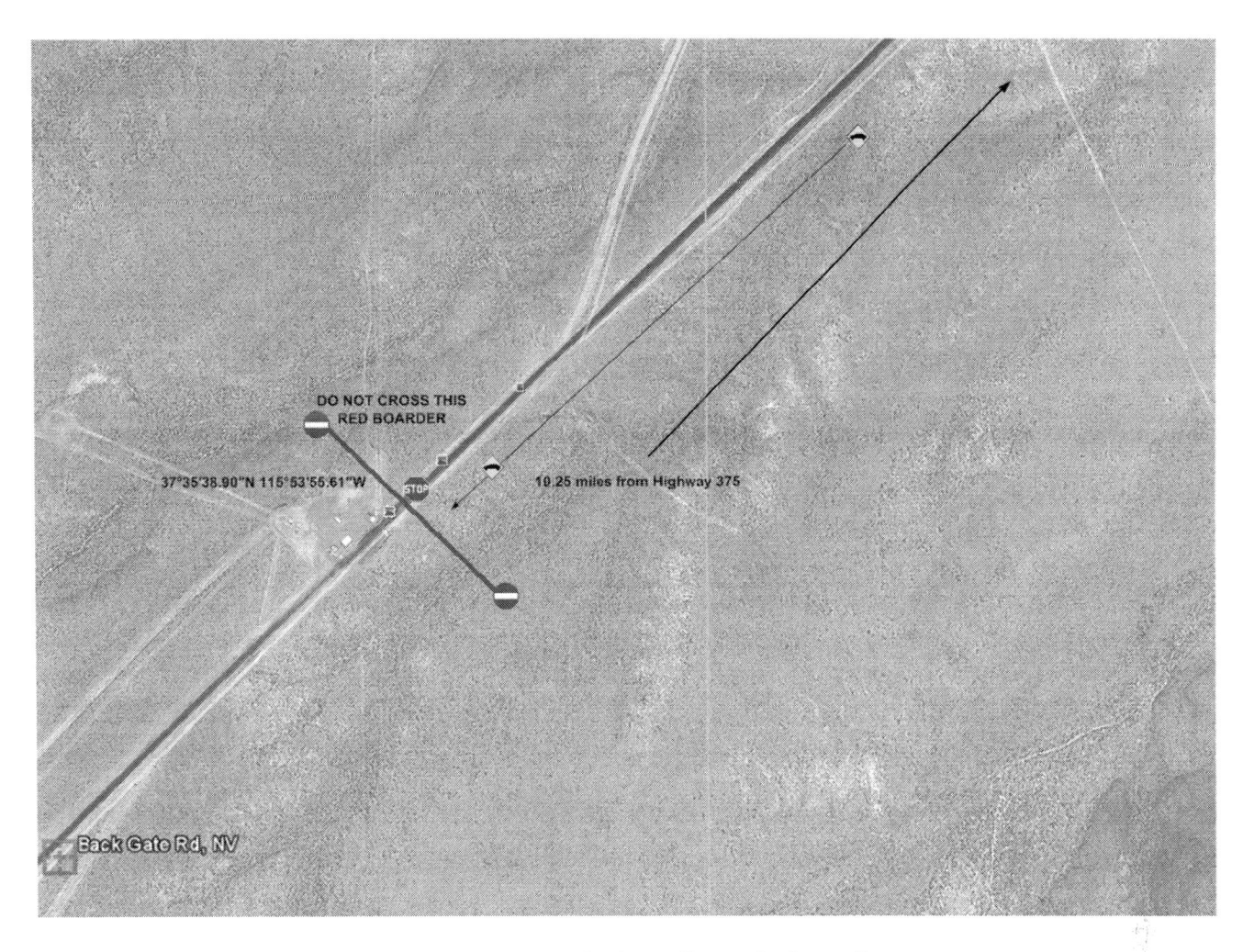

The Back Gate at 37°35'38.67"N 115°53'56.02"W

You can approach the Back Gate but

DO NOT PASS!

The Back Gate entire trip starts from Highway 375 and the Back Gate Road showing the entire route which runs approximately 10.25 miles. There are no speed limits but I recommend to cruise no more than *40MPH to not cause a giant sand/dust storm*. Keep your eyes and wits about you as you are getting to the *9 mile marker*. Again take lots of pictures of the country side and anything else that you may come across.

The Back Gate is located at 37°35'38.67"N 115°53'56.02"W.

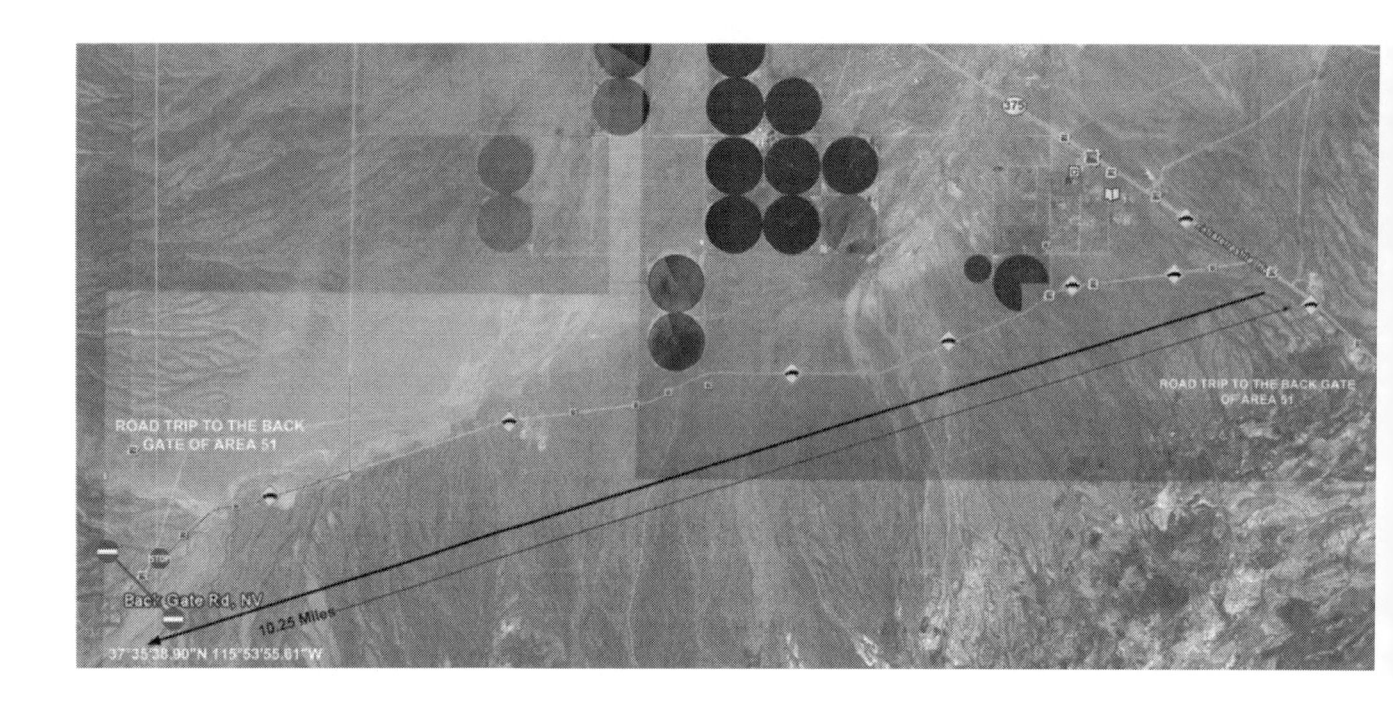

The Back Gate entire trip starting from Highway 375 and the Back Gate Road to the Back Gate at

37°35'38.67"N 115°53'56.02"W.

DO NOT PASS!

The Main Security Building at Area 51 is located approximately 25 miles beyond the Back Gate check point. This Main Security Building is inside Area 51. This building is for all check-ins before proceeding to any facility on the base. All levels of security clearances are checked and verified so the vehicle is only directed to their authorized location only. The location of this Security Building A51 is located at 37°14'28"N 115°49'26"W

(ONLY CAN BE VIEW FROM GOOGLE EARTH).

Buckle Up – Your Third Road Trip to the mysterious "Groom Lake Road" aka "Dreamland Lane" to the "FRONT GATE!"

As you leave the Little A'Le'Inn parking lot you will make a right turn onto Highway 375 also known as the famous *"Extraterrestrial Highway"* to start your third road trip journey. Drive approximately 24.45 miles southwest until you see the Groom Lake Road also which is called 51 RD which is located at 37°24'53.22"N 115°24'35.18"W which intersects with CR375. Make a RIGHT TURN onto Groom Lake Road.

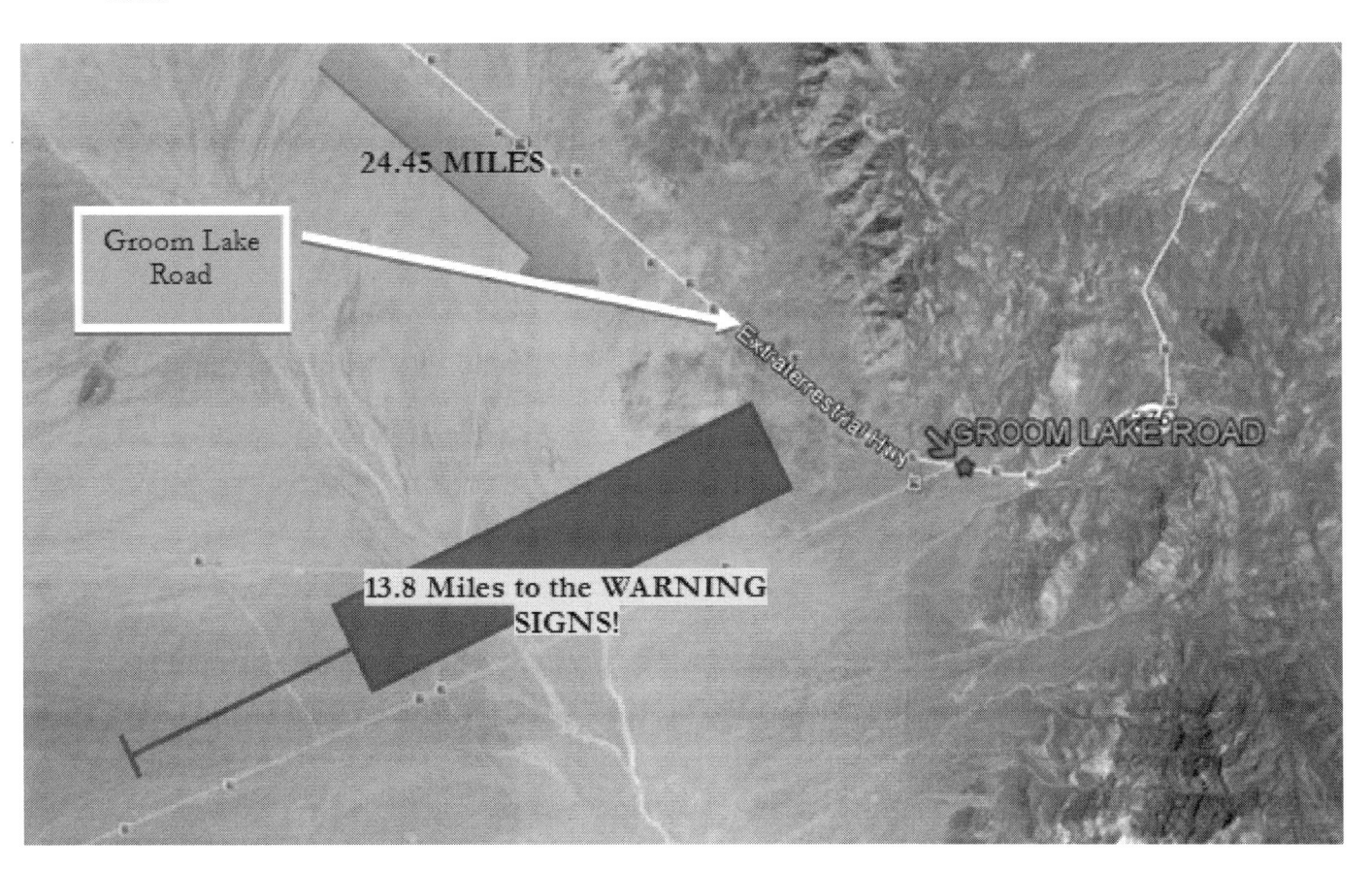

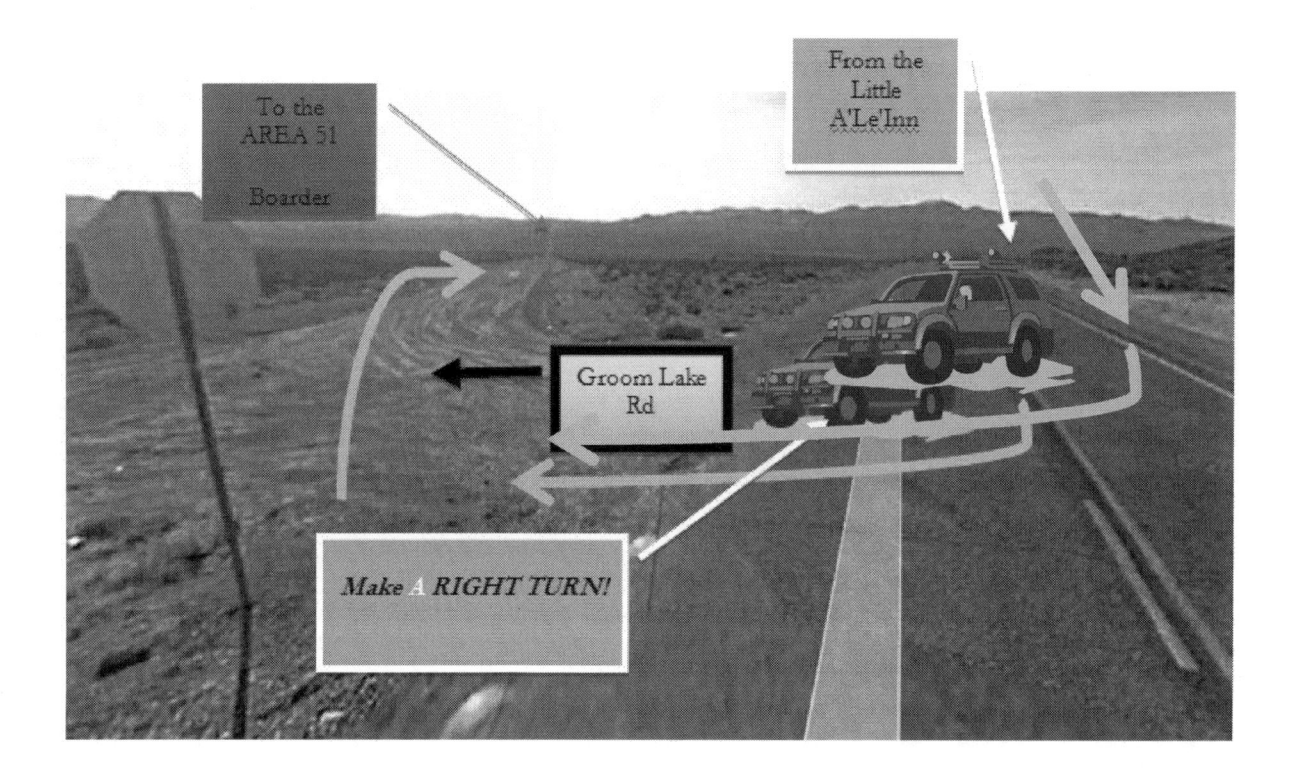

You will be making a RIGHT TURN onto GROOM LAKE ROAD as shown above.

Groom Lake Road leads from Hwy. 375 (between mile marker 34 and 35) west for about 13.8 miles through the desert towards Area 51 sign markers.

Make sure that you set your ODOMETER first to ZERO before heading down Groom Lake Road.

DO NOT MAKE ANY DETOURS ALONG THE WAY.

REMEMBER 13.8 MILES TO THE WARNING SIGNS!!!!!!

It is a well-maintained dirt road, suitable for all cars in decent shape. There are hidden road sensors buried in the ground along the road, to give Area 51 security team an very early warning of approaching vehicles. And of course you are watched from the surveillance installation on Bald Mountain nearby, and by the special perimeter security guards that we all call them "The Cammo Dudes" at the end of Groom Lake Road public road. The road to the front gate is long and dusty, but good enough to travel at the rated speed (40 MPH +/-) most of its length. When you hit the 12 mile marker (ODOMETER TRACKING) begin to cruise back to only 20MPH.

This view below is from route 375 looking down Groom Road. The puffs of smoke are the dust trails from vehicles going down the road. You can park near the entrance of the road for about an hour just to see if anyone official looking used the road. After collecting a quarter inch of dust on your rear bumper, you will eventually arrive at the front gate of Area 51.

The warning signs will be the first thing you see!

Traveling Down on Groom Lake Road

****BE ALERT –**

THERE IS NO FENCE AT THE BORDER**

There are ROAD SENSORS located down Groom Lake Road!

37°21'3.38"N 115°38'47.47"W – Public Side of the Boarder

Looking down Groom Lake Road from the junction at Nevada Route 375. The Area 51 perimeter is 13 miles down Groom Lake Road, about where the road ends in this photo. The dust cloud is from an unmarked white pickup truck, which blasted by us about a minute after I took this photo and through the stop sign just behind the camera. We reasoned that the driver must have been a "Cammo Dude" who didn't want to be photographed. Indeed, we heard a local tell a story about having his camera confiscated when he did manage to take a photograph of a "Cammo Dude".

Mountain side view of Groom Lake Road – Notice the traveling dust storm along Road 51!

The CAMMO DUDES on the move!

NEW BOARDER SIGNS – PLEASE DO NOT CROSS OVER THESE SIGNS!

These signs mark the beginning of the restricted government land and THE USE DEADLY FORCE IS AUTHORIZED if you cross on to military property. There have been no cases reported of anyone being shot for crossing the border but they would be well within their rights to open fire should you decide to do so. Crossing the border will most definably result in a trip to the Lincoln County Jail usually accompanied by a $750+ fine.

THE OLD SIGNS AT THE BORDER, SEE BELOW:

BOARD SIGNS – PLEASE DO NOT CROSS OVER THESE SIGNS!

These signs have been updated to NO DRONE FLYING

NEW SECURITY CAMERA AT THE GROOM LAKE BORDER!

THIS FLIR CAMERA WILL FOLLOW YOU!

BOARD SIGNS – PLEASE DO NOT CROSS OVER THESE SIGNS!

They drive FORD RAPTORS!

As you can see once you are within a good mile of the boarder the security perimeter boys already have you tracked and recorded! As you get RIGHT NEAR the BOARDER SIGNS they are ENGAGED to see what your next move is! DO NOT even put your foot over the border because at that point you have crossed over the border and have violated SECTION 21, INTERNAL SECURITY ACT of 1950, 50 U.S.C. 797!

PLEASE READ ON THE NEXT PAGE THE EXACT PENALTY FOR VIOLATING SECTION 21, INTERNAL SECURITY ACT OF 1950, 50 U.S.C. 797.

VIOLATION OF SECTION 21, INTERNAL SECURITY ACT of 1950, 50 U.S.C. 797!

<u>Security regulations and orders; penalty for violation</u>

(a) Whoever willfully shall violate any such regulation or order as, pursuant to lawful authority, shall be or has been promulgated or approved by the Secretary of Defense, or by any military commander designated by the Secretary of Defense, or by the Director of the National Advisory Committee for Aeronautics, for the protection or security of military or naval aircraft, airports, airport facilities, vessels, harbors, ports, piers, waterfront facilities, bases, forts, posts, laboratories, stations, vehicles, equipment, explosives, or other property or places subject to the jurisdiction, administration, or in the custody of the Department of Defense, any Department or Agency of which said Department consists, or any officer or employee of said Department or Agency, or of the National Advisory Committee for Aeronautics or any officer or employee thereof, relating to fire hazards, fire protection, lighting, machinery, guard service, disrepair, disuse or other unsatisfactory conditions thereon, or the ingress thereto or egress or removal of persons therefrom or otherwise providing for safeguarding the same against destruction, loss, or injury by accident or by enemy action, sabotage, or other subversive actions, shall be guilty of a misdemeanor and upon conviction thereof shall be liable to a fine of not to exceed $5,000 or to imprisonment for not more than one year, or both.

A Suggestion:

I suggest having a telephoto lens on your camera or if you are using your smart phone if you want to take any photographs and videos. Since photographs of these signs are all over the internet, you can suspect the prohibition of photography rule is not strictly enforced.

CAUTION:

There is a small turnout spot by the signs, on the right side of the road. Please be sure to park off the Groom Lake road. When you take a look around you will see two **UHF** (Ultra High Frequency) surveillance cameras watching you from a hill to the left. PLEASE …. Do not hike up to the cameras at all! They are inside the restricted area and could result in very serious consequences including **A POTENTIAL DHS** Terrorist Arrest.

This view above is from route 375 looking down Groom Road

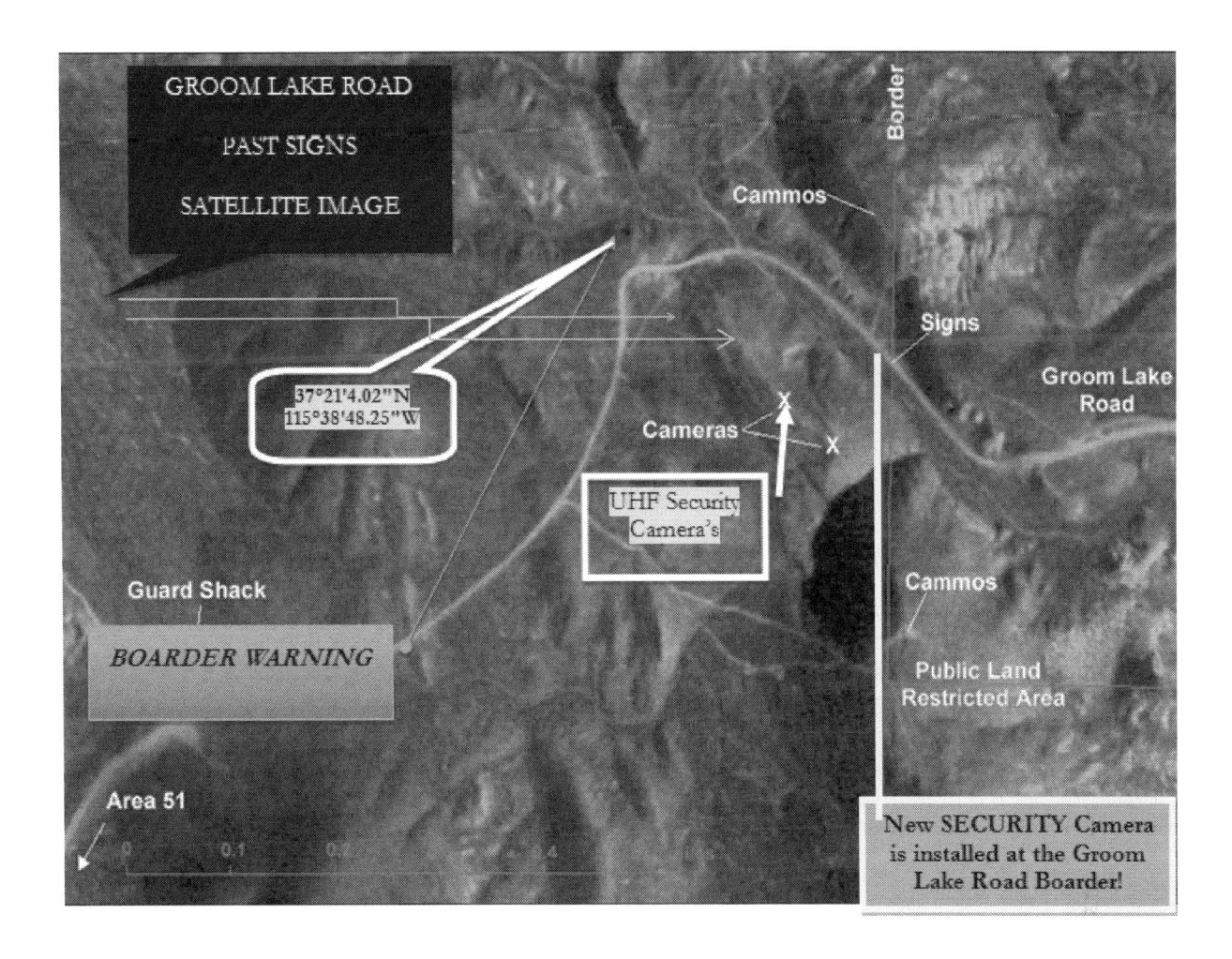

A topology aerial view of Groom Lake Road to the border warning line! There are UHF (Ultra High Frequency) -**Ultra-high frequency** (**UHF**) designates the ITU radio frequency range of electromagnetic waves between 300 MHz and 3 GHz (3,000 MHz), also known as the **decimetre band** or **decimetre wave** as the wavelengths range from one to ten decimeters; that is 1 decimetre to 1 metre. They are designed for Line-Of-Sight communications and send the video signals back to the Guard Shack for any in coming notifications of near approaches on Groom Lake Road near the border.

THE BORDER - 37°21'4.02"N 115°38'48.25"W

Buckle Up – Your Fourth Road Trip to the mysterious "Tikaboo Peak" aka "Peak A Boo" at Dreamland from the summit.

Story:

Tikaboo Peak is an 8,000 ft mountain approximately 26 miles from the infamous Air Force Flight Test Center at Groom Lake, NV -aka Area 51. Tikaboo Peak is one of the last places where you can actually see the base legally. The summit is exactly located at 37.3442° N, 115.3588° W. The exact height above sea level is 7,915 feet.

The turn off for Tikaboo Peak is between the Upper and Lower Lakes in the Pahraganat Valley near Alamo, NV. From there you travel down a well maintained dirt road until a few hundred yards from the trailhead. Depending on what type of vehicle you have you may want to hike in. If you have a high clearance 4WD vehicle you can drive right to the "Lower Staging Area" where you can camp for the night before the hike.

If you got a pair, you can drive up to the "Upper Staging Area" and save yourself about 500 feet of the climb. From there it is a somewhat strenuous 1.2 mile hike up 1,000 feet in elevation.

The first 2,500 feet is the worse climbing up a the steepest part of the hill covered in loose shale. From there it actually becomes fun as you past the "False Summit" and "Rocky Outcrop" to the "Saddle." From there you start back up the hill until you reach the first view of the base and another good spot to camp. The last 600 feet is my favorite part as you climb up the hill covered with boulders and not that dangerous loose shale! At the end you are rewarded with a magnificent view of the Tikaboo Valley and of course Area 51!

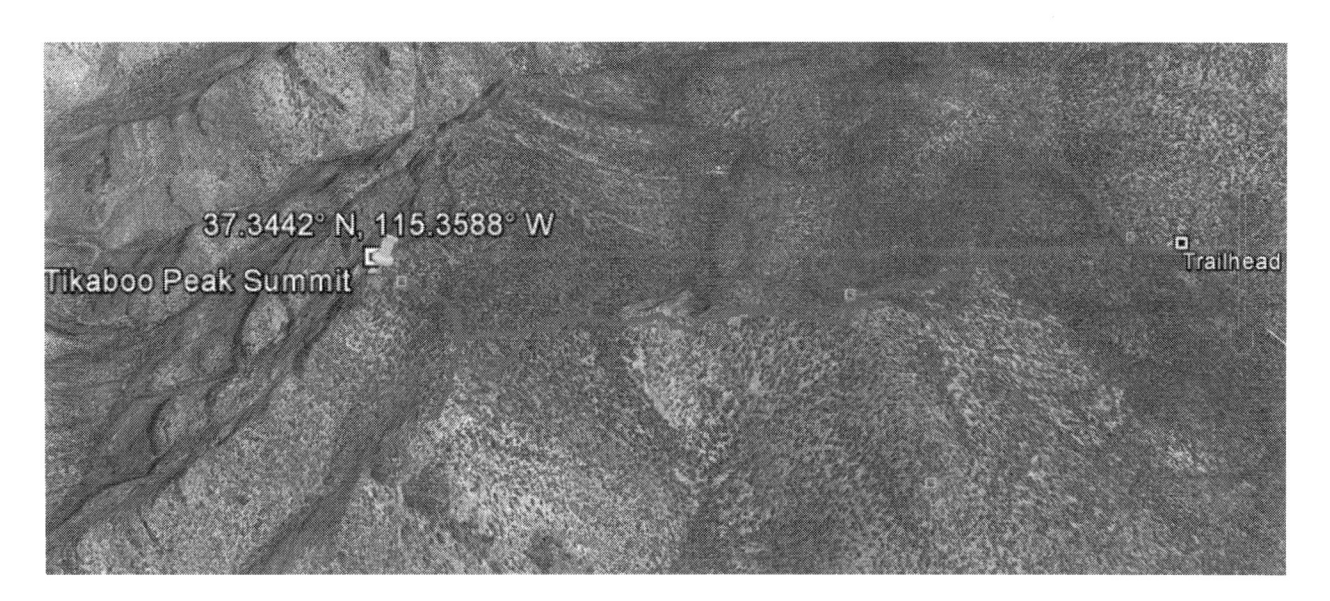

How DO we get to get there?

A Little Background for your ride to Tikaboo Peak - After the 1995 land grab, in which the closer Area 51 view spots "White Sides" and "Freedom Ridge" were seized by the FEDS, Tikaboo Peak, 26 miles from the Groom Lake Base, is now the closest view point. However, to get a glimpse of Area 51 you have to do some four-wheeling and serious hiking. And it takes a clear day to make out details with your binoculars or spotting scope. The best time is early in the morning, when you have the sun in the back, and there is not too much atmospheric heat distortion so check the weather before you head out. – www.wunderground.com

Tikaboo - http://wrcc.dri.edu/weather/ntik.html

Latest Updated Tikaboo Photo's Updated every 10 minutes - http://wrcc.dri.edu/weather/ntik/

Tikaboo Historical data - http://wrcc.dri.edu/cgi-bin/rawMAIN.pl?nvntik

Before you start, please consider that it takes you into a **very remote area**, with virtually no traffic (and except for the top of Tikaboo no cell phone service, unless you have a Satellite Phone). If your vehicle breaks down you are looking at a very long 22-mile hike back to US-93. Bring plenty of drinking water and food, as well as tools for minor repairs and at least one good spare tire especially if you are renting a vehicle from Las Vegas. Also, you will be in almost 8000 ft. elevation, which means that even in summer the nights are cool. In spring and fall the nights can be very cold, even if it is hot in the valley. In winter, usually between November and March or early April, snow prevents any access to Tikaboo Peak.

It is not possible to drive all the way up to Tikaboo Peak. Even as a daring four-wheel driver you are looking at a one to three hour hike each way, depending on what shape you are in and how much gear you are carrying with you. That includes steep climbs, partially on loose shale, in 8000 ft. elevation, where the air is much thinner than at sea level. If you are in less than average shape you should seriously reconsider your plans and tour it from Google Earth.

There is no water on Tikaboo or anywhere on the way, and you need to take **at least** one gallon of drinking water per person and day.

Try not to make the hike alone which is always the recommended buddy system when hiking, and make sure to let someone know where you are going, and when you expect to be back.

Easiest access to Tikaboo Peak is from mile marker LN 32.2 on US-93. This unmarked turnoff to the west is easy to miss. Look for a stop sign about 0.4 miles north of the marked entrance to the Pahranagat Wildlife Refuge. There is another, shorter, access road further north, but it has some steep climbs and requires 4WD. After you turn off at LN 32.2 you get on a maintained dirt road, which is passable for most sturdy cars. However, after rains the road may be washed out and require 4WD. In the above map all mile markers along the dirt road are driving distance to the intersection with US-93 by the stop sign. Always follow the main road to get to Badger Spring.

0.0 mi.	N 37°16.823' W115°07.159'	Unmarked gate to the Pahranagat Wildlife Area at the intersection with US-93, approx. 0.35 miles north of the marked road to the ranger station. If you find the gate closed it is ok to open it to drive through, as long as you close it after you. If it is open leave it open.
5.7 mi.	N 37°14.542' W115°11.950'	Fence and gate. Again, if the gate is closed it is ok to open it, drive through and close it. When closed, the gate looks like a solid fence, but it can be opened. If you can't figure out how to open it, you probably should not be out there in the first place. Be careful not to damage the gate, and be sure to close it properly behind you.
8.2 mi.	N 37°12.425' W115°11.709'	Fork. Follow the main road, which makes a sharp right turn here.
18.2 mi.	N 37°18.907' W115°17.823'	Road intersects from the right. That is the rugged shortcut mentioned earlier. Continue straight on the main road. From here on the road may require 4WD at certain times, or be completely impassable.
21.6 mi.	N 37°20.760' W115°20.495'	Badger Spring. Keep right here. From here on the road becomes more difficult, and is only passable for 4WD vehicles. You can camp here and hike the rest of the way. Only about 0.5 miles from here the road ends anyway.
21.85 mi.	N 37°20.888' W115°20.625'	A road intersects from the left. Keep right and stay on the main road.
22.0 mi.	N 37°21.000' W115°20.687'	The road forks here, keep left. The road continues steep uphill, and only experienced 4WD drivers with a high clearance vehicle should continue.
22.1 mi.	N 37°20.974' W115°20.783'	End of the passable road. There is a clearing with enough room to camp and park your vehicle, if you made it up here. From here on a very rugged dirt road and then a hiking trail, marked by rock cairns, leads up to Tikaboo Peak. Depending on your shape, and the amount of gear you are carrying, the hike will take between one and three hours.

The first part of the hike leads up to a "false summit", first moderately steep and near the summit quite steep, on loose shale. This is the hardest part of the hike, especially if you are carrying a heavy pack. About 50 yards below the summit the trail turns right, towards a rock outcropping. The trail is mostly level here.

Follow it around the left side of the rocks, and then downhill on the other side.
You come to a saddle, that offers plenty of room to camp. The trail continues uphill on the other side, up to the real Tikaboo Peak. This part is moderately steep, and leads through bushes and trees. It is easy to loose

the trail here, but if you keep going uphill you will eventually get to the peak. There is a small rocky platform on top, from where you can see the base, behind the Jumbled Hills and Freedom Ridge. Right below the peak is plenty of camping space in between the trees.

The mile markers in the table below are hiking distance to the parking area.

0.0 mi.	N 37°20.974' W115°20.783'	Parking area. Only accessible for 4WD high-clearance vehicles.
0.2 mi.	N 37°20.827' W115°20.842'	End of the rugged dirt road, and start of the hiking trail. **Do not attempt to drive up to here**, unless you are a very experienced 4WD driver with a familiar high clearence vehicle in excellent shape. There is a good chance that you will cause serious damage to your vehicle (as two of my friends have) and/or get yourself hopelessly stuck.
0.45 mi.	N 37°20.667' W115°21.044'	Just below "false summit". Turn right here.
0.7 mi.	N 37°20.667' W115°21.301'	Saddle. Good camp site.
1.0 mi.	N 37°20.654' W115°21.543'	Tikaboo Peak. >>>>>>>>>>**YOU HAVE DONE IT! CONGRATS!**

You can see most of the base in its entire format from the high peak from beautiful Tikaboo Summit at 7,915 feet.

I recommend climbing this mountain in the late spring to early fall to avoid the excessive heat as I recommended earlier. *I also climb just before sunset to arrive at the campsite just below the summit and spend the night watching the base for activity.* I finish the hike in the early morning to get the best pictures of the base before the heat distorts the atmosphere. There is no water source anywhere along the trip so pack all you can carry!!!!!!!

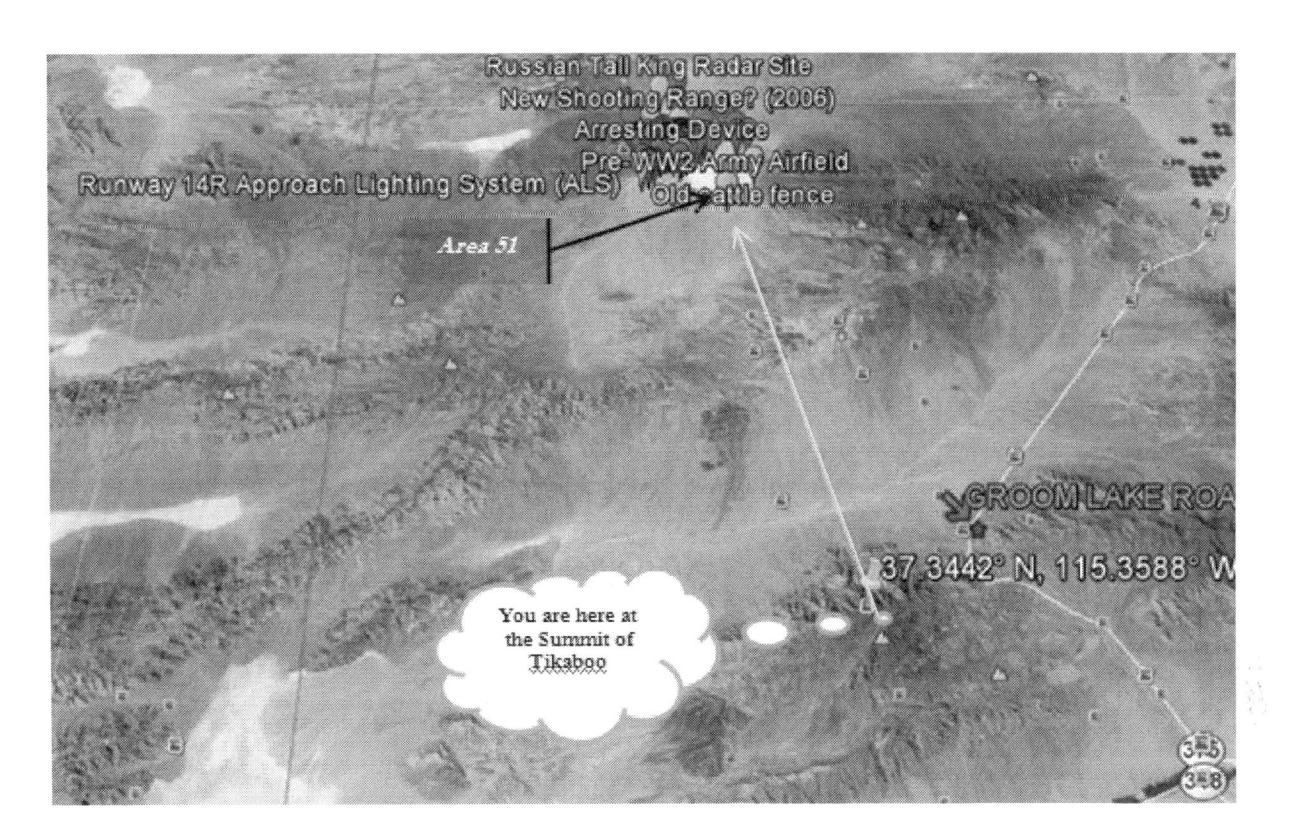

As you can view with a good telephoto system look WEST at a distance of approximately 24.85 miles from Tikaboo Summit at a direction of 257.50° the entire base in smoke in the middle of your view.

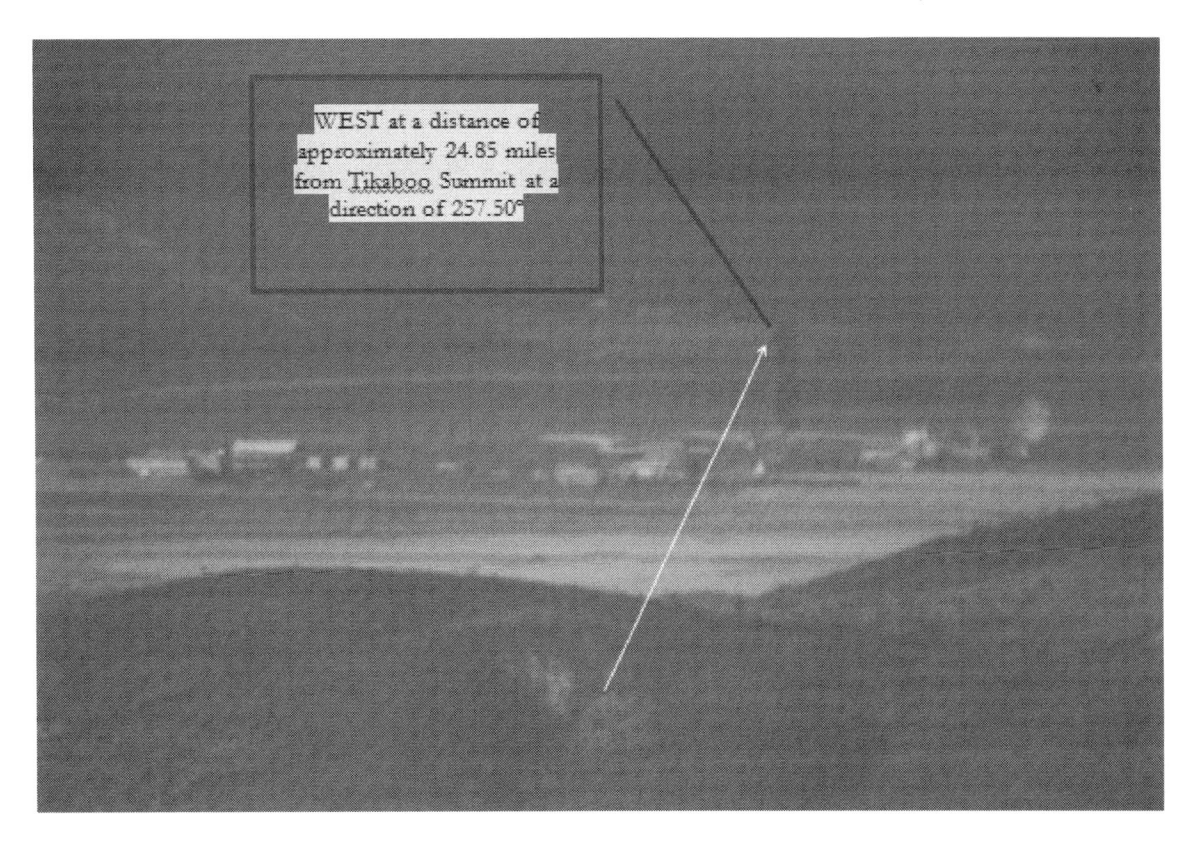

37.2464° N, 115.8234° W

Viewing from Tikaboo Peak

37.2359° N, 115.8139° W

Viewing from Tikaboo Peak looking at Hanger 18 at Area 51

Tips AGAIN:

Carry lots of H2O!

Temperatures can dip down into the 40s in summer months

Carry lots of H2O! RESEARCH this trip.

Did I mention to carry lots of H2O?

South

Desert Lake

Mt. Charleston

This awesome 270° Panorama was taken by Tom Mahood, one of the original Groom Lake Interceptors, in the morning of May 10, 2002 from Tikaboo Peak. It covers an angle from about 160° (true north heading, left) clockwise to 70° (right). The image is quite large. You will need to view up and down on these few pages to see the full panorama.

West

Papoose Range

Groom Base

Guard Shack

181

This awesome 270° Panorama was taken by Tom Mahood, one of the original Groom Lake Interceptors, in the morning of May 10, 2002 from Tikaboo Peak. It covers an angle from about 160° (true north heading, left) clockwise to 70° (right). The image is quite large. You will need to view up and down on these few pages to see the full panorama.

North

Hiko

Badger Mt.

This awesome 270° Panorama was taken by Tom Mahood, one of the original Groom Lake Interceptors, in the morning of May 10, 2002 from Tikaboo Peak. It covers an angle from about 160° (true north heading, left) clockwise to 70° (right).

Hiko - Hiko Range is a mountain range in Lincoln County in the state of Nevada (NV). Hiko Range climbs to 4,495 feet (1,370.08 meters) above sea level. Hiko Range is located at latitude - longitude coordinates (also called lat - long coordinates or GPS coordinates) of N 37.485239 and W -115.157796.

Anyone attempting to climb Hiko Range and reach the summit should look for detailed information on the Hiko Range area in the topographic map (topo map) and the Ash Springs USGS quad. To hike and explore the Nevada outdoors near Hiko Range, check the list of nearby trails.

- **Peak Type:** Range

- **Latitude:** 37.485239

- **Longitue:** -115.157796

- **Peak Elevation:** 4,495 feet (1,370.08 m)

- **Nearest City:** Ash Springs (8.2 miles away)

Badger Mountain is a mountain summit in Lincoln County in the state of Nevada (NV). Badger Mountain climbs to 7,966 feet (2,428.04 meters) above sea level. Badger Mountain is located at latitude - longitude coordinates (also called lat - long coordinates or GPS coordinates) of N 37.351627 and W -115.326133.

Anyone attempting to climb Badger Mountain and reach the summit should look for detailed information on the Badger Mountain area in the topographic map (topo map) and the Badger Spring USGS quad. To hike and explore the Nevada outdoors near Badger Mountain, check the list of nearby trails.

- **Latitude:** 37.351627
- **Longitue:** -115.326133
- **Peak Elevation:** 7,966 feet (2,428.04 m)
- **Nearest City:** Tempiute (10.1 miles away)

As seen from highway 93 near Alamo Nevada.

Buckle Up – You're Special Road Trip to the mysterious "AREA 6"

36.926565, -116.006272

3,932' ASL

A mysterious, mile-long landing strip in the remote Nevada desert could be the home base for testing sensors on a top-secret fleet of drones, security experts speculate.

It's approximately 51.70 miles south of the Little Alien

As seen in images from Google Earth, the asphalt landing strip is in Area 6 of the Yucca Flat test site, about 12 miles (19 kilometers) northeast of the infamous Area 51 that has long been the subject of conspiracy theories. In Area 6, a handful of hangars with clamshell doors are clustered at one end of the airstrip, the Google Earth images reveal.

The area, which does not have a name, is fenced off and can be seen from the road by those touring the pockmarked Nevada National Security Siteof Yucca Flat, where the military conducted hundreds of nuclear tests over several decades.
While little is known about Area 6, the Yucca Airstrip is used by both the Department of Defense and the Department of Homeland Security, Darwin Morgan, a spokesperson for the National Nuclear Security Administration, told the Las Vegas Review-Journal.

"They come here to test their own sensors," he recently said after evading questions from the newspaper about Area 6 for months.

Drone base?

Though officials with the government have been extremely reticent to reveal any details about the site, a few details have leaked out.

A 7,500-page tome on nuclear safety at the Yucca Mountain nuclear wasteproject includes a brief paragraph describing Area 6 as an "aerial operations facility."

"The purpose of this facility is to construct, operate, and test a variety of unmanned aerial vehicles. Tests include, but are not limited to, airframe modifications, sensor operation, and onboard computer development. A small, manned chase plane is used to track the unmanned aerial vehicles," according to a 2008 report in the Yucca Mountain repository license application filed by government contractor Bechtel

SAIC, which built the airstrip for $9.6 million.

The airspace above the strip is controlled, which reduces the risk of planes or satellites in space getting a detailed look at the surroundings. It also prevents the public from unintentionally stumbling upon the site, Morgan told the Review-Journal.

Based on its size, the hangars could house up to 15 MQ-9 Reaper planes, the type of drones used to perform reconnaissance, Tim Brown, an imagery analyst at the defense information website GlobalSecurity.org, told the Review Journal. The runway is too small for fighter jets or bombers, he added.

One possibility is that the remotely piloted planes do practice runs for reconnaissance work. Yucca Flat's high desert terrain echoes that found in the most remote regions of Libya, where Al Qaeda or ISIS operatives could be hiding out, he said.

If that's the case, the government may be testing out sensor arrays — essentially fields of hundreds of smartphone-type cameras that are mounted on planes such as the MQ-9 Reaper to take time-lapse photography. The idea is that anything out there that's moving could, in fact, be moved by a potential terrorist or bad actor

AREA 6 - 36.926565, -116.006272

WIDE AREA VIEW OF AREA 6

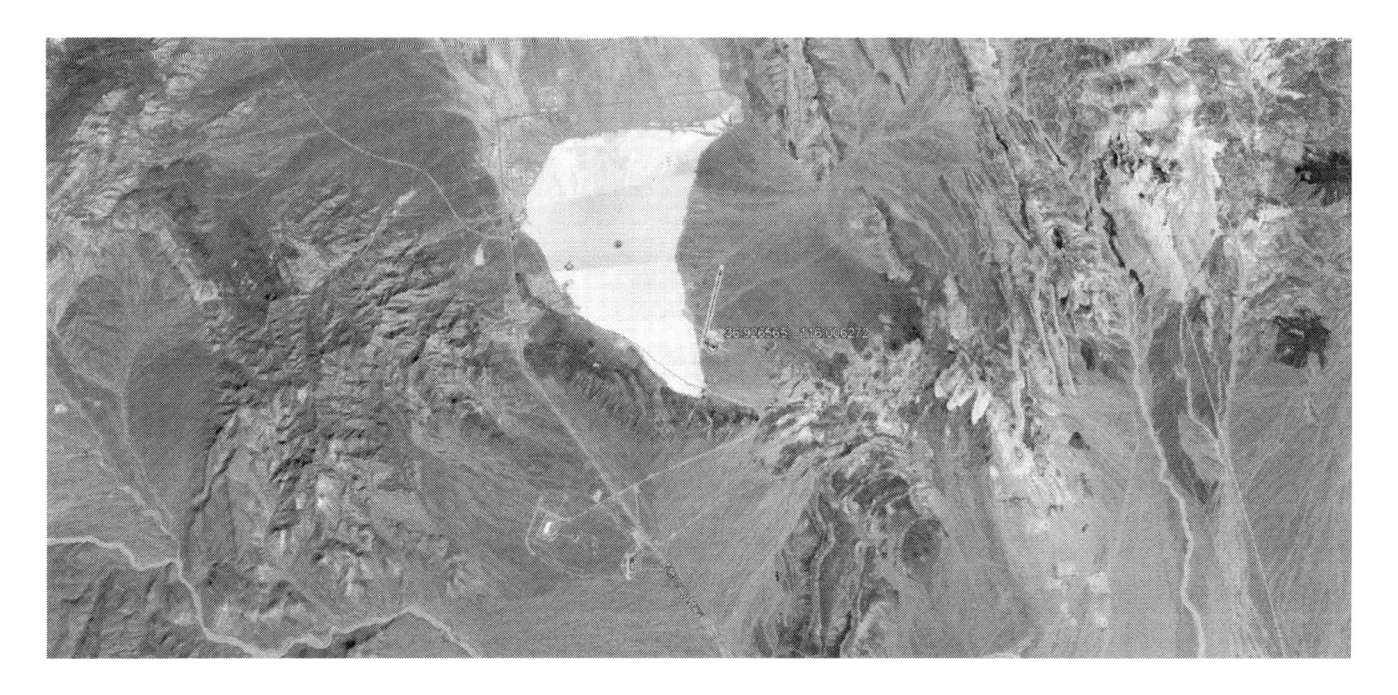

AREA 6 - 36.926565, -116.006272

The asphalt runway stretches for a mile on Yucca Flat, deep in the Nevada National Security Site about 80 miles northwest of Las Vegas.

Built in 2005, the runway covers a dirt landing strip from the 1950s, when the wide, flat valley was used for atomic bomb test shots. A small complex of buildings dominated by a large hangar with unusual clamshell doors dominates the southern end of the asphalt strip.

The complex has no official name. Not many people even know it's there.

As secret airbases go, the single runway in the test site's Area 6 is easily overshadowed by the world's most famous secret military base, Area 51, a dozen miles northeast. Area 51's existence was only recently acknowledged, even after decades of speculation by UFO enthusiasts that the aircraft development and test facility also houses space aliens and extraterrestrial technology.

Unlike Area 51, which is protected by shoot-to-kill security and shielded from outside view by mountain ranges, Area 6 has only fences and visitor checkpoints. It can be seen at a distance from tour buses on the highway to historic bomb craters at the northern end of Yucca Flat.

But exactly what goes on at the much smaller and much newer Area 6 is still top-secret defense research-and-development work. It's so hush-hush that the security site's spokesman can say little about it.

Darwin Morgan, a spokesman for the National Nuclear Security Administration, said the low-key Area 6 facilities have been used by the Defense and Homeland Security departments.

"They come here to test their own sensors," he recently said after spending months fending off questions about the Area 6 runway from the Review-Journal.

Drone proving ground is what Area 6 is used for.

AREA 6 - 36.926565, -116.006272

TOPO MAP 1

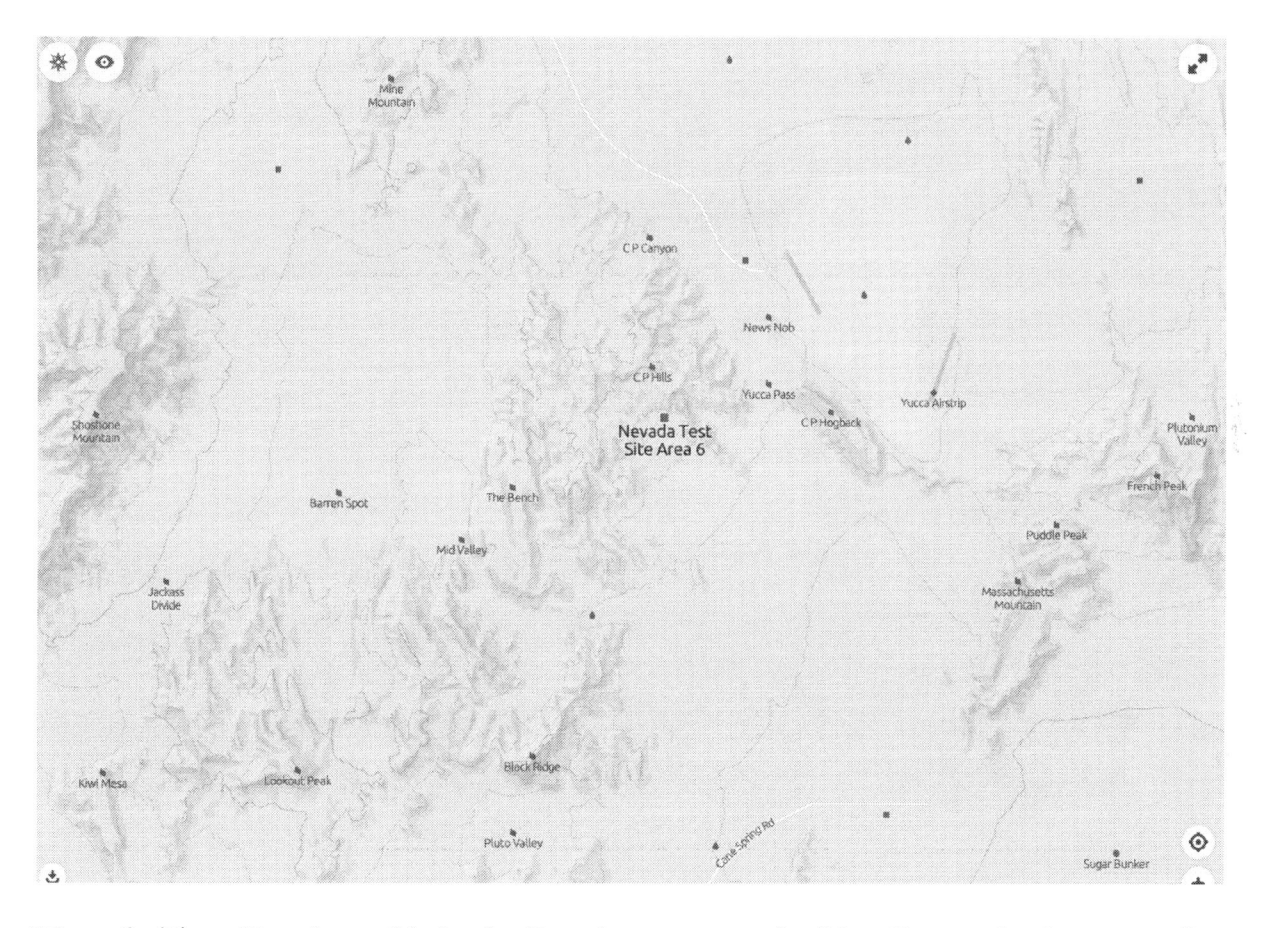

Nevada Test Site Area 6 is in the Locales category for Nye County in the state of Nevada. Nevada Test Site Area 6 is displayed on the Yucca Lake USGS quad topo map. Anyone who is interested in visiting Nevada Test Site Area 6 can print the free topographic map and street map using the link above. The latitude and longitude coordinates of Nevada Test Site Area 6 are 36.924675, -116.076425 and the approximate elevation is 4,537 feet (1,383 meters) above sea level.

For ANY TOPO MAPS, scan the QR CODE ABOVE

AREA 6 - 36.926565, -116.006272

TOPO MAP 2

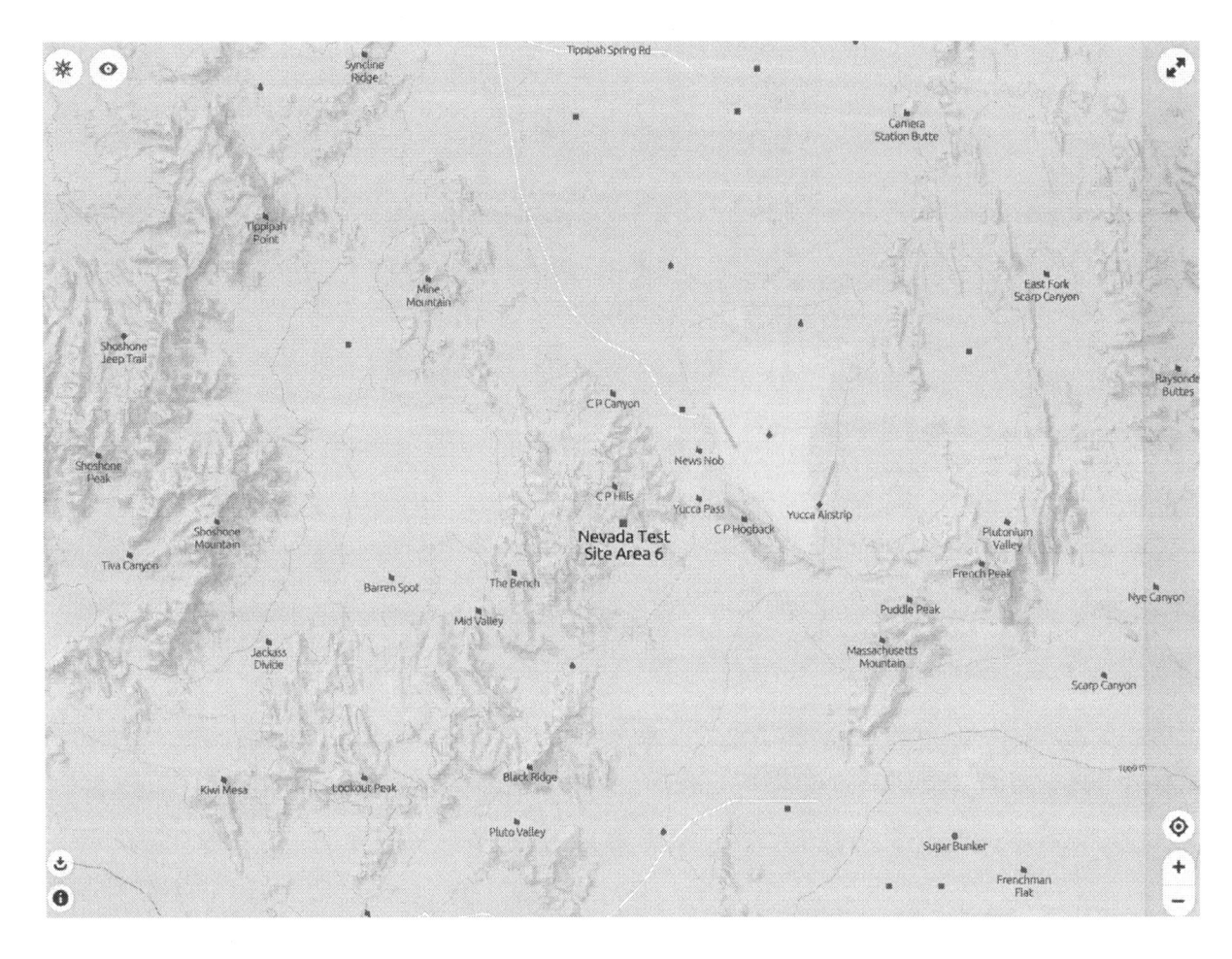

Nevada Test Site Area 6 Information

Coordinates: 36.924675°N, -116.076425°W
Approx. Elevation: 4,537 feet (1,383 meters)
USGS Topo Map Quad: Yucca Lake **Feature Type:** Locale

For ANY NEVADA ONLY TOPO MAPS, scan the QR CODE ABOVE

Areas of Areas of NEVADA TEST SITE

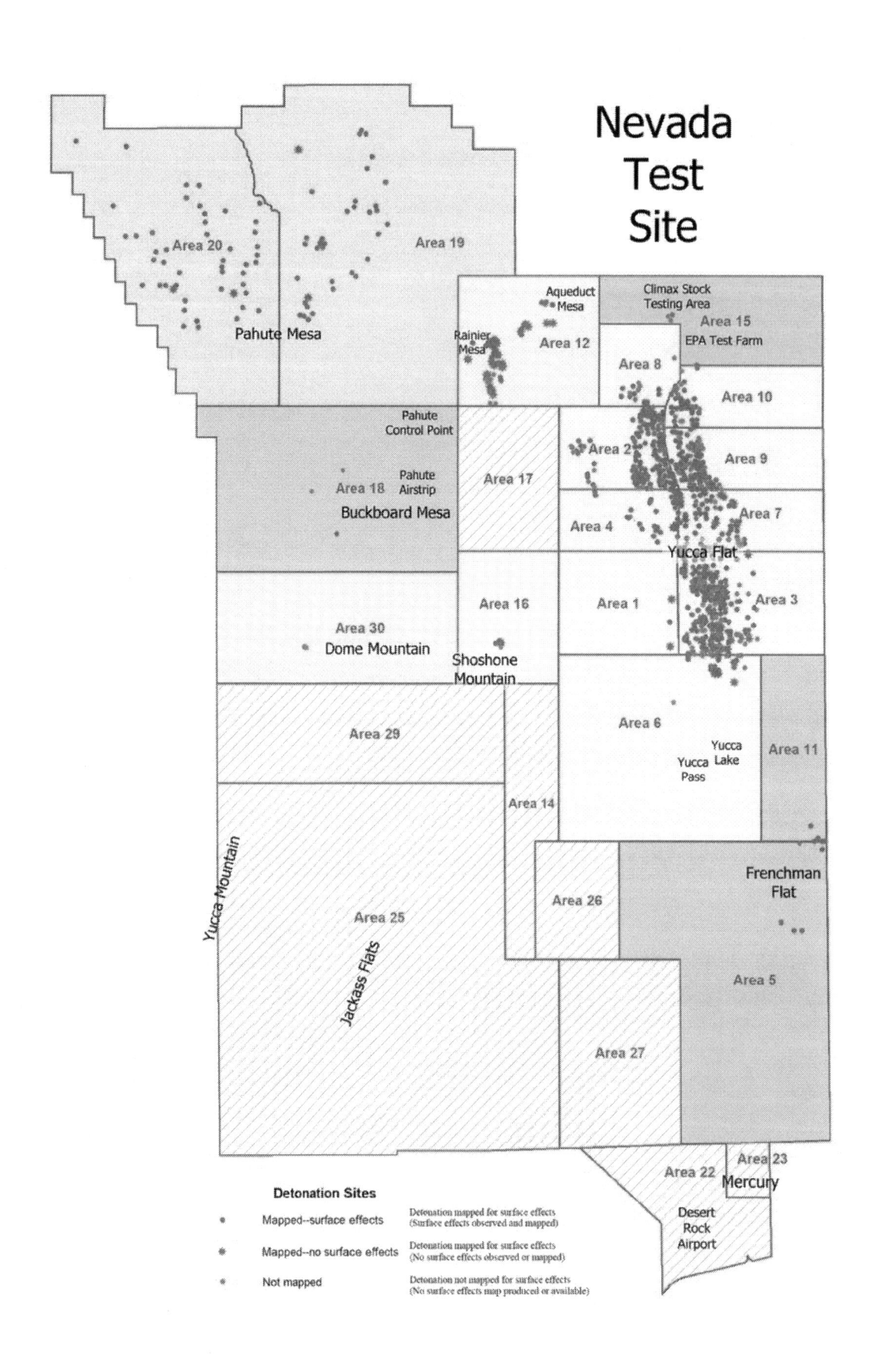

Nuclear explosions in various areas of NTS

The Test Site is broken down into areas. Some of the areas and their uses include the following:

Area 1

Area 1 held eight nuclear tests for a total of nine detonations. Four early atmospheric tests were conducted above Area 1 in the early 1950s, as well as three underground tests in 1971 and 1990. In 1955, a Civil Defense experiment (called Operation Cue in the press) studied nuclear blast effects on various building types; a few structures still stand.

Heavy drilling equipment and concrete construction facilities are sited in Area 1. Non-destructive X-ray, gamma ray, and subcritical detonation tests continue to be conducted in Area 1.

The radioactivity present on the ground in Area 1 provides a radiologically contaminated environment for the training of first responders.

Area 2

Area 2 (Nevada National Security Site)

Area 2 is a division of the Nevada Test Site in the Mojave Desert. The area is located 18 miles south-west of Area 51.

Area 2 was the site of 144 tests comprising 169 detonations. Shot "Gabbs", intended for 1993, was abandoned in place.

Area 3

Area 3 held 266 nuclear tests for a total of 288 detonations, more than in any other area of the NTS.

As part of Operation Tinderbox, on 24 June 1980, a small satellite prototype (DSCS III) was subjected to radioactivity from the "Huron King" shot in a vertical line-of-sight (VLOS) test undertaken in Area 3. This was a program to improve the database on nuclear hardening design techniques for defense satellites.

The final nuclear test detonation at Nevada Test Site was Operation Julin's "Divider" on 23 September 1992, just prior to the moratorium temporarily ending all nuclear testing. Divider was a safety experiment test shot that was detonated at the bottom of a shaft sunk into Area 3.

In 1995 and 1997, plutonium-contaminated soil from "Double Tracks" and "Clean Slate 1" of Operation Roller Coaster (1963) was picked up from the Tonopah Test Range and brought to the Area 3 Radioactive Waste Management Site as a first step in eventually returning Tonopah Test Range to an environmentally neutral state. Corrective action regarding the contaminated material from the "Clean Slate 2" and "Clean Slate 3" tests has yet to be agreed upon.

Area 4

Big Explosives Experimental Facility (BEEF) in Area 4

Area 4 held 40 nuclear tests for a total of 44 detonations.

It is home to the Big Explosives Experimental Facility (BEEF).

Area 5

Main article: Area 5 (Nevada National Security Site)

Area 5 held 19 nuclear tests. Five atmospheric tests were detonated, starting on 27 January 1951 at Area 5 as part of Operation Ranger. These were the first nuclear tests at NTS. Further tower detonations were studied at Area 5, and the Grable shot which was fired from a M65 Atomic Cannon located in Area 11 exploded in Area 5. The Priscilla test was conducted at Area 5 on 24 June 1957.

Five underground tests were set up at Area 5; four of those suffered accidental release of radioactive materials.

On 16 March 1968, physicist Glenn T. Seaborg toured the upcoming Milk Shake shot of Operation Crosstie. Milk Shake's radioactive release was not detected outside of NTS boundaries.

Area 6

Device Assembly Facility in Area 6

Control Point in Area 6

Area 6 held four nuclear tests for a total of six detonations. The only two towns to be established within the boundaries of NTS prior to 1947, BJ Wye and Mule Lick, are located in Yucca Flats, in Area 6. The area features an asphalt runway, that was constructed on top of a dirt landing strip, that existed since the 1950s. Some buildings, including a hangar, are situated near the runway.

The Device Assembly Facility (DAF)[31] was originally built to consolidate nuclear explosives assembly operations. It now serves as the Criticality Experiments Facility (CEF).

The Control Point[31] is the communication hub of the NTS. It was used by controllers to trigger and monitor nuclear test explosions.

In 1982, while a live nuclear bomb was being lowered underground, the base came under attack by armed combatants. The combatants turned out to be a security team conducting an improperly scheduled drill.

Area 7

Area 7 held 92 nuclear tests.

During Operation Buster, four successful tests were conducted via airdrop, with bomber aircraft releasing nuclear weapons over Area 7.

It is also the site of Matthew Reilly's book called Area 7.

Shot "Icecap" planned for 1993 was abandoned in Area 7 following 1992's testing moratorium. The tower, shaft and wiring remain in place, along with a crane intended to lower the nuclear test package into the shaft.

Area 8

Radioactive materials were accidentally released from the 1970 Baneberry shot in Area 8.

Area 8 held 13 nuclear tests for a total of 15 detonations.

Area 8 hosted the "Baneberry" shot of Operation Emery on 18 December 1970.

The Baneberry 10 kt (42 TJ) test detonated 900 feet (270 m) below the surface but its energy cracked the soil in unexpected ways, causing a fissure near ground zero and the failure of the shaft stemming and cap. A plume of fire and dust was released, raining fallout on workers in different locations within NTS. The radioactive plume released 6.7 megacuries (250 PBq) of radioactive material, including 80 kCi (3.0 PBq) of Iodine131.

Area 9

Area 9 held 115 nuclear tests for a total of 133 detonations.

In Area 9, the 74 kt (310 TJ) "Hood" test on 5 July 1957, part of Operation Plumbbob, was the largest atmospheric test ever conducted within the continental United States; nearly five times larger in yield than the bomb dropped on Hiroshima. A balloon carried Hood up to 460 meters above the ground where it was detonated. Over 2,000 troops took part in the test in order to train them in conducting operations on the nuclear battlefield. 11 megacuries (410 PBq) of iodine-131 (131I) were released into the air.

Area 10

North end of Yucca Flat, where most tests have been conducted.

Area 10 held 57 nuclear tests for a total of 71 detonations.

The first underground test at NTS was the "Uncle" shot of Operation Jangle. Uncle detonated on 29 November 1951 within a shaft sunk into Area 10.

The "John" shot of Plumbbob, on 19 July 1957, was the first test firing of the nuclear-tipped AIR-2 Genie air-to-air rocket designed to destroy incoming enemy bombers with a nuclear explosion. The 2 kt (8.4 TJ) warhead exploded approximately three miles above five volunteers and a photographer who stood unprotected at "ground zero" in Area 10 to show the apparent safety of battlefield nuclear weapons to personnel on the ground. The test also demonstrated the ability of a fighter aircraft to deliver a nuclear-tipped rocket and avoid being destroyed in the process. A Northrop F-89J fired the rocket.

The "Sedan" test of Operation Storax on 6 July 1962, a 104 kt (440 TJ) shot for the Operation Plowshare which sought to discover whether nuclear weapons could be used for peaceful means in creating lakes, bays or canals.

The explosion displaced twelve million tons of earth, creating the Sedan crater which is 1,280 feet (390 m) wide and 320 feet (100 m) deep.

Area 11

Main article: Area 11 (Nevada Test Site)

Area 11 held 9 nuclear tests.Four of the tests were weapons safety experiments conducted as Project 56; they spread so much harmful radioactive material around the test sites that Area 11 has been called "Plutonium Valley". As is the case with Area 1, background radiation levels make Area 11 suitable for realistic training in methods of radiation detection.

Area 12

Main article: Area 12 (Nevada National Security Site)

Area 12 held 61 nuclear tests between 1957 and 1992, one of which involved two detonations. All tests were conducted below Rainier and Aqueduct mesas.

Area 12 was the primary location for tunnel tests and used almost exclusively for that purpose. The tunnel complexes mined into Rainier and Aqueduct Mesa include the B-, C-, D-, E-, F-, G-, I-, J-, K-, N-, P-, and T-Tunnel complexes, and the R- and S- shafts.

Area 13

There is no Area 13 within NNSS, though such a name is attached to a section of Nellis Air Force Range which abuts the northeastern corner of Area 15. Project 57's weapons safety test was conducted here on 24 April 1957, spreading particles emitting alpha radiation over a large area.

Area 14

Area 14 occupies approximately 26 square miles (67 km2) in the central portion of the NNSS. Various outdoor experiments are conducted in this area. No atmospheric or underground nuclear tests were conducted in Area 14.

Area 15

EPA Farm in Area 15

Three underground detonations took place in area 15 in the 1960s.

Pile Driver was a notable Department of Defense test. A large underground installation was built to study the survivability of hardened underground bunkers undergoing a nuclear attack. Information from the test was used in designing hardened missile silos and the North American Aerospace Defense Command facility in Colorado Springs.

The abandoned Crystal and Climax mines are found in Area 15. Storage tanks hold contaminated materials.

From 1964 to 1981, the Environmental Protection Agency operated a 36-acre (150,000 m2) experimental farm in Area 15. Extensive plant and soil studies evaluated the uptake of pollutants in farm-grown vegetables and from the forage eaten by a dairy herd of some 30 Holstein cows. Scientists also studied horses, pigs, goats, and chickens.

Area 16

Area 16 held six nuclear tests.

Area 17

No nuclear tests took place in Area 17.

Area 18

Area 18 held five nuclear tests.and includes the Pahute Mesa Airstrip.

Area 19

Pahute Mesa

Pahute Mesa is one of four major nuclear test regions within the Nevada National Security Site (NNSS). It occupies 243 square miles (630 km2) in the northwest corner of the NNSS. The eastern section is known as Area 19 and the western section as Area 20.

A total of 85 nuclear tests were conducted in Pahute Mesa between 1965 and 1992. Three of them — Boxcar, Benham and Handley — had a yield of over one megaton. Three tests were conducted as part of Operation Plowshare and one as part of Vela Uniform.

Area 20

Main article: Pahute Mesa

Area 22

No nuclear tests took place in Area 22. Area 22 once held Camp Desert Rock, a staging base for troops undergoing atmospheric nuclear blast training; as many as 9,000 troops were camped there in 1955. Desert Rock Airport's runway was enlarged to a 7,500 ft (2,300 m) length in 1969 by the Atomic Energy Commission. It is a transport hub for personnel and supplies going to NNSS and also serves as an emergency landing strip.

Area 23

No nuclear tests took place in Area 23. The town of Mercury, Nevada lies within Area 23. The area is the main pathway to and from NNSS test locations by way of U.S. Route 95. An open sanitary landfill is located to the west of Mercury, and a closed hazardous waste site abuts the landfill. Mercury is also the main management area for the site which includes a bar and large cafeteria, printing plant, medical center, warehousing, fleet management, liquidation and recycling center, engineering offices, dormitories, and other administrative areas for both the O&M contractors, LLNL, LANL, and SNL personnel. At its height in the 1950s and '60s it also held several restaurants, a bowling alley, a movie theater, and a motel.

Area 25

Area 25 (Nevada National Security Site)

Area 26

Mostly abandoned buildings and structures at Port Gaston

No nuclear tests took place in Area 26, the most arid section of the NNSS. An old abandoned mine, the Horn Silver Mine, was used for waste disposal between 1959 and the 1970s; some of the waste is radioactive. Water flow past the shaft could pose a human health risk, so corrective action has been planned.

In 1983 the Department of Defense, the Department of Energy, and the Federal Emergency Management Agency performed the NUWAX-83 tests near Port Gaston in Area 26, simulating the explosion of a nuclear-armed helicopter and the resulting spread of nuclear debris over 65 acres. The radioactive material used to simulate the accident became inert in less than six months.

An eight-square-mile complex was constructed in Area 26 in support of Project Pluto. It consisted of six miles of roads, the critical assembly building, the control building, the assembly and shop buildings, and utilities. Those buildings have been used recently as mock reactor facilities in the training of first responders.

Area 27

Main article: Area 27 (Nevada National Security Site)

Area 28

Area 28 no longer exists; it was absorbed into Areas 25 and 27.

Area 29

No nuclear tests took place in Area 29. The rugged terrain of Area 29 serves as a buffer between other areas of NNSS. A helipad is present at Shoshone Peak.

Area 30

The Crosstie Buggy test.

Area 30 occupies approximately 59 square miles (150 km2) at the center of the western edge of the NNSS. Area 30 has rugged terrain and includes the northern reaches of Fortymile Canyon. It is used primarily for military training and exercises.

Area 30 was the site of a single nuclear test, the Crosstie Buggy row charge experiment, part of Operation Plowshare, which involved five simultaneous detonations.

Buckle Up – Your Fifth Road Trip to the mysterious "Tonopah Test Range" aka "Area 52/Area54."

Introduction & History

Site - http://ttr.sandia.gov/

Weather - http://www.wrcc.dri.edu/weather/wnd3.html

Located approximately 35 road miles SW of the town of Tonopah.
Driving along Hwy 6 west you will actually come to a sign showing you the way to this Semi-Secret Airbase. The sign you cannot miss! As it is a Rocket pointing in the direction of TTR down a road for 35 miles!

1. Head **east** on **Old Mill St** toward **Valley Ave**

    0.2 mi

2. Turn left onto **NV-375 N/Extraterrestrial Hwy**

    59.0 mi

3. Turn left onto **US-6 W**

    49.2 mi

4. Turn right onto **Erie St**

    0.5 mi

5. Continue onto **N Main St**

    0.1 mi

6. Turn right onto **Brougher Ave**

    177 ft

7. Turn left onto **Mineral St**

    344 ft

Tonopah, NV

Tonopah Test Range (TTR), is a restricted military installation located about 30 miles (48 km) southeast of Tonopah, Nevada. It is part of the northern fringe of the Nellis Range, measuring 625 sq mi (1,620 km²). Tonopah Test Range is located about 70 miles (110 km) northwest of Groom Dry Lake, home of the Area 51 facility as you are now very acquainted by now. Like the Groom Lake facility, Tonopah is a site of interest to conspiracy theorists, mostly for its use of experimental and classified aircraft. As such, it is not the focus of alien enthusiasts, unlike its neighbor. It is currently used for nuclear weapons stockpile reliability testing, research and development of fusing and firing systems, and testing nuclear weapon delivery systems. The airspace comprises restricted area R-4809 of the Nevada Test and Training Range and is often used for military training. This region of 625 sq miles is broken into Area 52 and Area 54.

The Tonopah Test Range is owned by the United States Department of Energy and is managed by Sandia National Laboratories, a division of Lockheed-Martin, which operates the Tonopah Test Range under an

Air Force permit with the National Nuclear Security Administration. The range is part of the Great Basin Desert and lies mostly within the Cactus Flat valley, consisting of horst and graben geology. It is flanked by the Cactus Range hills to the west and the Kawich Range to the east, which is home of Silverbow, one of the largest mining ghost towns in Nevada. The vegetation consists mostly of black sagebrush and creosote bush. It holds a sizable wild horse and burro population, closely monitored by the Bureau of Land Management. Common denizens of the TTR include the gray fox, pronghorn, coyote, and mule deer, along with the native birds sage thrasher, sage grouse, and sage sparrow. One of the primary facilities on the TTR is a large airfield (Area 10), consisting of a 12,000-foot (3,700 m) runway and numerous hangars. About five minor abandoned airfields exist throughout the TTR which were primarily used during World War II by units based at Tonopah Army Air Field (now serving as Tonopah's municipal airport). Only **Mellan Airstrip**, 11 miles (18 km) southeast of Tonopah Test Range Airport, survived past the 1960s, upgraded to a 5,000-foot (1,500 m) concrete runway. A US Air Force assessment published in 2000 indicated it was a minimally adequate airfield which was used to support tactical C-130 and C-17 training. Below is a very early late 60's early 70's of the entrance to Sandia Laboratories.

Russian S-300PS SAM Testing at TTR

The TTR has also been the site of US testing of foreign-made surface to air missiles systems. Satellite imagery confirms the US secretly acquiring the Russian made S-300PS surface to air missile system from an unknown supplier in order to test UAVs as well as other advanced aircraft based at nearby airbases. According to OSGEOINT, these bases include Creech Air Force Base, the Yucca Lake UAV testing facility, and Nellis Air Force Base, operating the MQ-1-9, MQ-170, and the F-35 Joint Strike Fighter in addition to other aircraft.

The testing of aircraft is executed under the direction of the 53rd Wing Test and Evaluation Group based at Nellis.

PLEASE NOTE: Nuclear explosions in various areas of NTS will be broken down in different AREA's later on in this book. For example AREA 1, AREA 2, AREA 3, AREA 4 and so on............

That famed MISSILE SIGN!

The Tonopah Test Range doesn't get much attention because the government makes no attempt to keep it a secret. As you can see, they even have a sign by the road. Nothing like a missile to get someone's attention! Thanks to the efforts of rec.aviation.military usenet readers, the consensus is this missile is a combination of a Nike Ajax booster (bottom half) and a B57 bomb (top half). It probably never flew as shown, but rather was put together because it looked cool.

[GPS coordinates of the entrance sign are N38 04 46.0 W117 00 38.0]

Anything left long enough in the desert will get a bullet hole or gather graffiti. You can see the sign in the above photo is plastered with stickers. This one is interesting in that the group is part of the Navy and based in Norfolk Virginia, so what are they doing in the desert?

Aerial View of Tonopah Air Strip

Aircraft seen and may be seen at and around the area are:

B-2A Spirit   B-1B Lancer, Various UAV's from Creech Air Force Base
B-52H Stratofortress   A-10 Thunderbolt II
F-15 Eagle   F-16 Falcon
F-117 Nighthawk   Various Black Projects from Groom / Area 51 as well as Tonopah also.

At TTR some of the activities around the test ranch include B2 and much more!

At TTR some of the other cool activities around the test ranch includes Missile testing and much more!

At TTR some of the other cool activities around the test ranch includes Missile testing and recovery that you may see and much more!

Brainwash Butte

The observation point where you can see more of the base is known for some reason as Brainwash Butte. To get to the area shown in this photo BELOW, you will need to drive about 25 miles over pretty good dirt roads. A 4WD isn't needed, but as always, you are on your own if you get in trouble this far from the main road. [Directions to the area is discussed below on this page.] It is a relatively easy walk up the hill, though the camera makes it look a bit easier than reality. The shrub on the left of the trail is known as "GW"; use it appropriately. Follow the trail up to the first plateau, turn right and head up the next hill, then take a left along the top of the hill to see the base.

The GPS coordinates where this trail starts are N37 54 20.1 W116 33 23.2. While driving along the main road, this trail is easy to miss.

You can see that more than a few 4WD vehicles have gone up this hill, but I wouldn't suggest it. The rocks look kind of nasty. Further, security will notice a SUV on top of this hill. If you insist on driving up the hill, stop at the first plateau, so at least your truck won't show up on the radar screen. Note that while you are on top of the hill, the numerous planes flying overhead can certainly fink you out. So if security doesn't want you on this hill, I suppose they could make a trip and ask you to leave. The hill is public land, so I doubt this is likely!

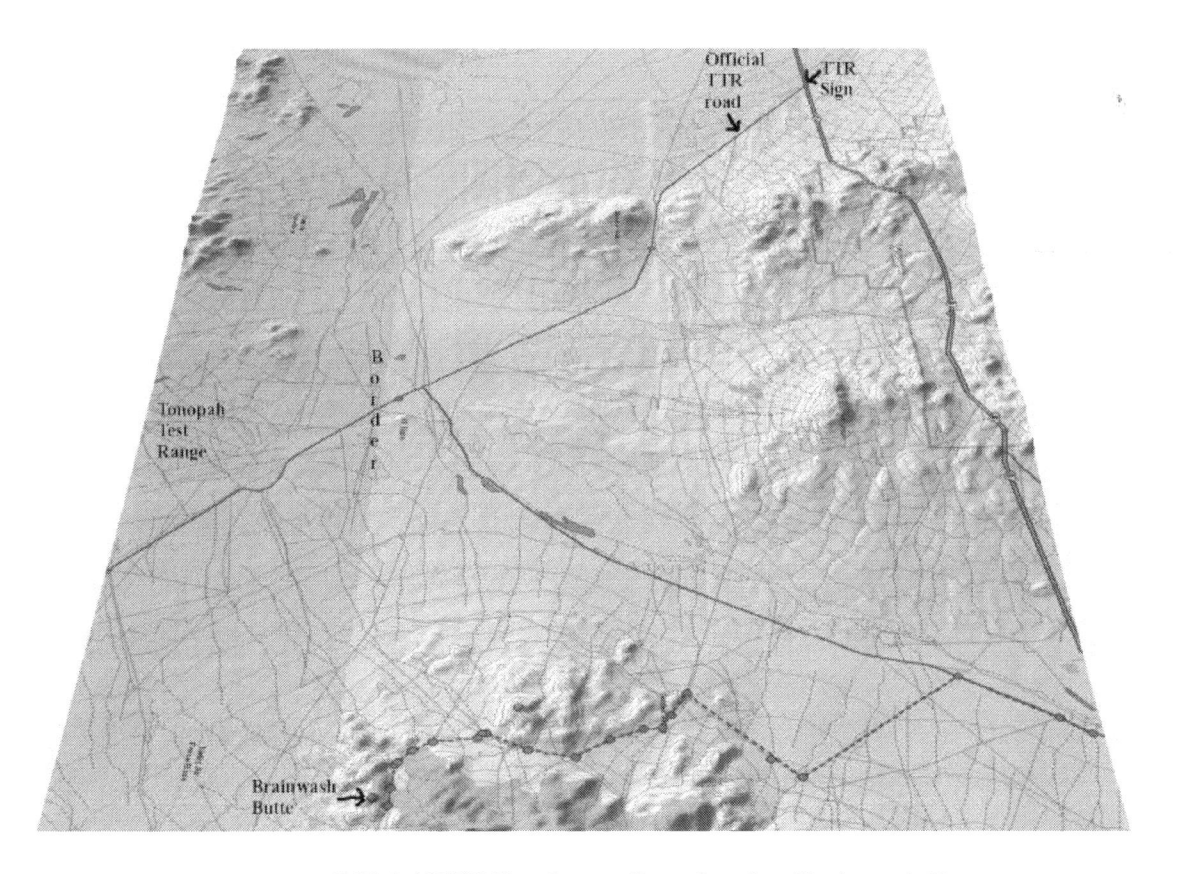

Official TTR Road as well as showing Brainwash Butte

Getting There:

The Road to Brainwash Butte!

The following is one of several possible routes to the top of Brainwash Butte.

The location:

Sits to the north of the Tonopah Test Range, as well as Site 4, and provides an outstanding view of the area. It is approximately 1 mile north of the base boundary and is on BLM land.

This particular route was mapped due to the fact it may be travelled without being seen from the TTR facility. The GPS coordinates listed are for various points and intersections along the route, and are given in decimal degrees in the WGS84 datum. With the exception of the last rocky climb up to the Brainwash Saddle, it should be passable by any vehicle with reasonable clearance. 4WD is only necessary for pressing on to the saddle or summit.

Miles from start	Intervening Distance	GPS coordinates	Comments
0		N38.14946 W116.57967	Silverbow Road junction with Hwy 6 at Milepost NY 38.7, approx 37 miles east of Tonopah. Turn south.
	10.2		
10.2		N38.01607 W116.64914	Four way intersection...turn left (East)
	2.0		
12.2		N38.00692 W116.61616	Four way intersection...go straight thru
	0.5		
12.7		N38.00332 W116.60314	Stay left at fork, then at four way intersection...go straight thru (East)
	0.3		
13.0		N38.00249 W116.60040	Pass 4wd route on left
	0.9		
13.9		N37.99475 W116.58762	Fork...keep right
	1.3		
15.2		N37.97604 W116.58187	Pass poor 4wd route on right
	0.9		
16.1		N37.96560 W116.57428	Pass poor 4wd route on left, route curves south
	0.3		
16.4		N37.96024 W116.57558	Pass old 4WD route on right
	1.0		
17.4		N37.94660 W116.57877	Pass old mining operation on right
	2.0		

19.4		N37.92021 W116.58367	First good view of TTR on right
	0.2		
19.6		N37.91755 W116.58251	Pass road on right
	1.2		
21.0		N37.90606 W116.56380	Nice camping area on right
	0.6		
21.6		N37.90565 W116.55654	**Right turn to Brainwash Butte:** The very poor 4wd route to the right climbs to the top of the hill (6,928') for a fine view. Little cover is available however.

For the next 0.3 miles, the rocky 4WD route climbs directly to Brainwash Saddle (N37.9018, W116.55601), which is the low point visible in the ridge to the south. This route can be traveled by a capable, high-clearance 4wd vehicle with good tires.

At the saddle, the 4wd route turns right (southwest) and climbs to the very summit of Brainwash Butte in 0.25 miles. This route is rocky, so it's advisable to park at the saddle and walk up first to see if the route is passable by the vehicle being used.

Note that any vehicle on top of Brainwash Butte is very exposed and may be seen from within the TTR property. If desired, it is possible to continue on the main road past the Brainwash Butte turnoff another 1.8 miles to reach Stinking Spring (N37.89403,W116.52693), a corral with open water on the right side of the road. This is 23.4 miles from Hwy 6

N38 08 58.8
W116 34 47.3

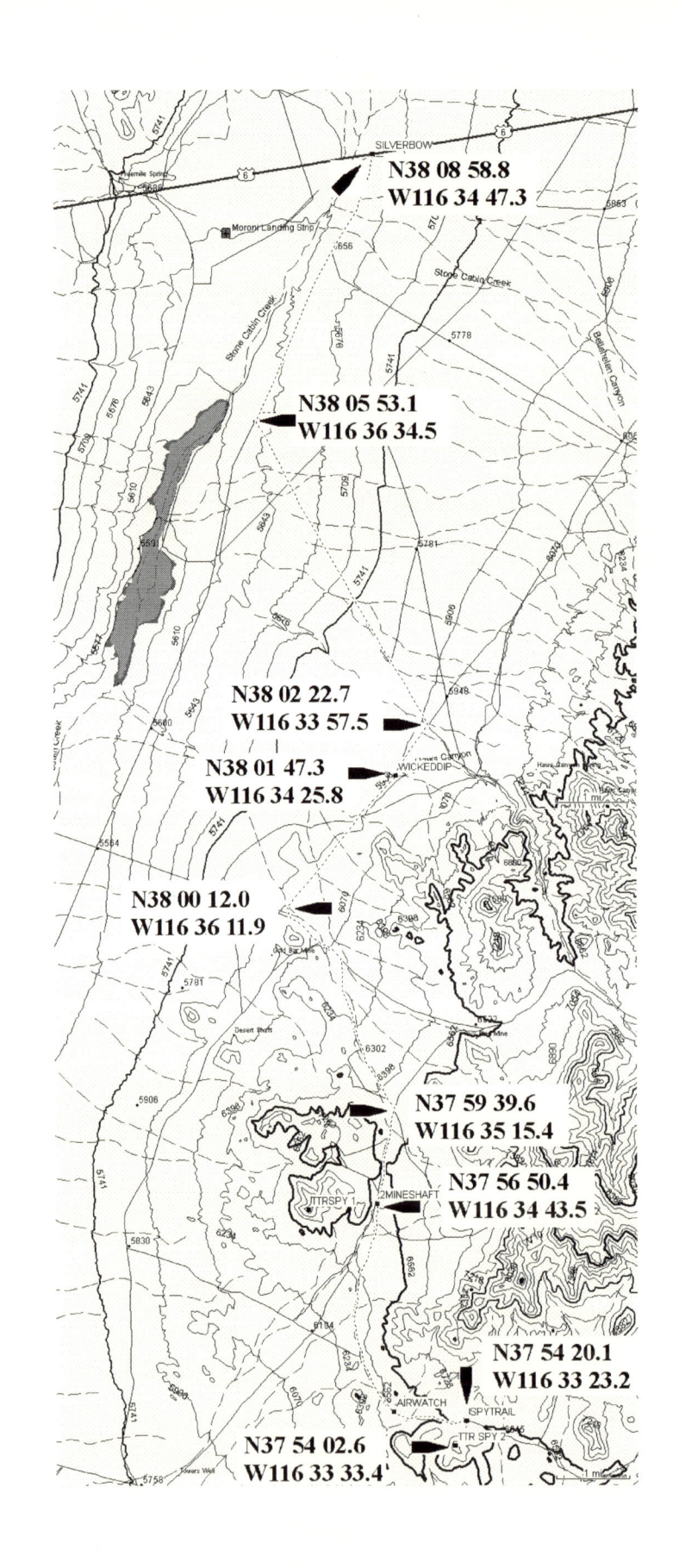

N38 05 53.1
W116 36 34.5

N38 02 22.7
W116 33 57.5

N38 01 47.3
W116 34 25.8

N38 00 12.0
W116 36 11.9

N37 59 39.6
W116 35 15.4

N37 56 50.4
W116 34 43.5

N37 54 20.1
W116 33 23.2

N37 54 02.6
W116 33 33.4

FROM LAS VEGAS:

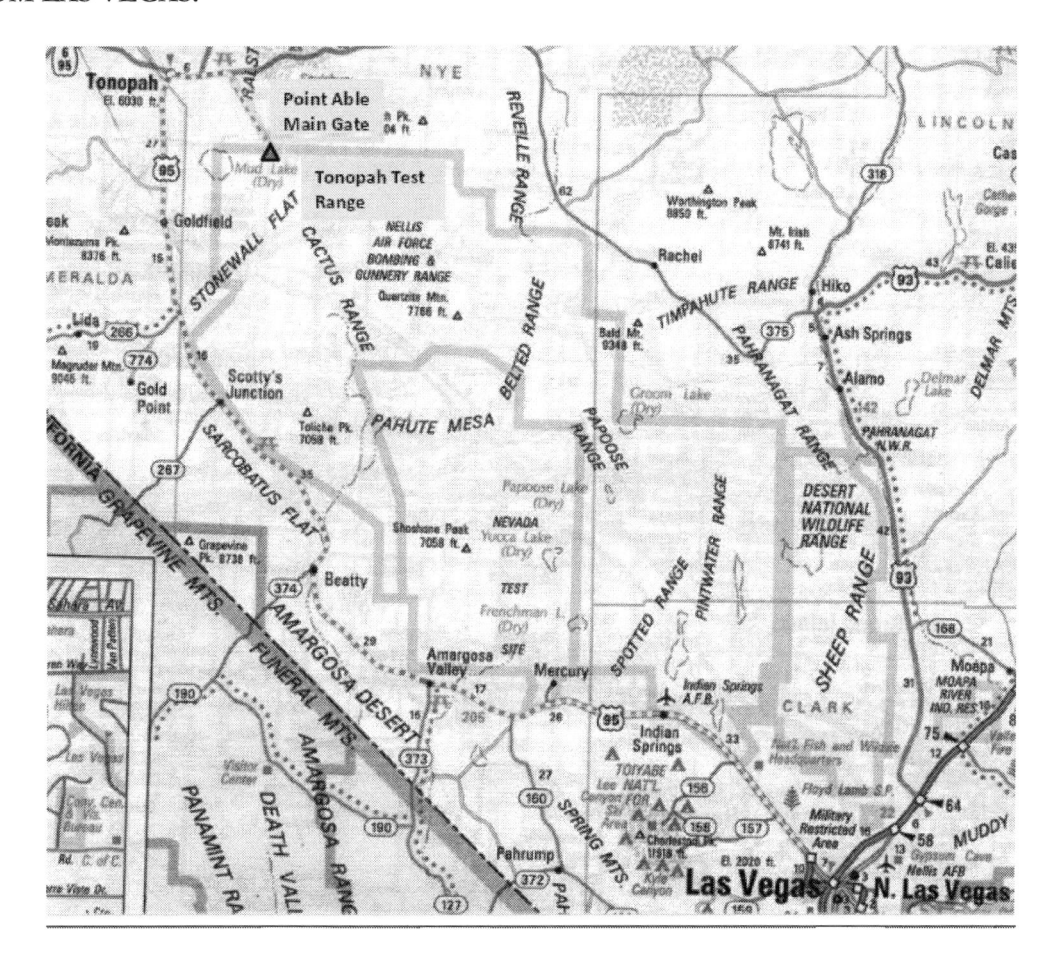

From Las Vegas to TTR (Tonopah Test Range) Directly

Interstate 15 North (towards Downtown LasVegas)

Highway 95 North (Tonopah/Reno)

•Indian Springs: 40 miles

•Beatty: 115 miles-Turn right at the stop sign/light in the middle of the town

•Goldfield: 26 miles from Tonopah

•TONOPAH-Turn right onto Highway 6 (after Cal-Nevada)

-Travel approx. 11 miles to Sandia "rocket"

- Turn right onto AR 504

-Travel approx. 30 miles to the TTR Main Gate

S4 - Electronic Combat Ranges around TTR

Outside of the Base itself, on the vast ranges of the TTR is an area/facility called 'Site-4'. Site-4 is part of the TECR or Tonopah Electronic Combat Range. This Range is used by the USAF for Training pilots against Electronic warfare such as Surface-to-Air Missile (SAM) threats, AAA threats and also Electronic Counter Measure and Electronic Support Measure (ECM and ESM) training. Dotted around the base are real threats, including many actual Russian made systems such as SA-6 SAM's, ZSU-23-4 AAA systems and other Russian, Iraqi and Eastern European systems. Site-4 is owned and operated by the 554th Range Squadron, which has its Headquarters located in the center of the site.

Tonopah ECR operates in conjunction with Tolicha Peak ECR (TPECR) located Southwest of TTR. Tonopah ECR as well as Tolicha Peak ECR are also used by Tonopah Test Range, Area 51 and Edwards AFB for testing stealth aircraft against real-time threats such as the foreign systems mentioned above. The Stealth capabilities of the aircraft are tested by flying the aircraft over the threats to see if the enemy radar can detect it.

The SAM and AAA Radar are not the only radar systems to avoid. Also used at the ECR's are EWRS or Early Warning Radar Systems. These are the 'real' threats that in a conflict need to be disabled first, because many EWRS can actually detect Stealth by changing tracking/scanning frequency and modes. These radars can pass information to the smaller targeting radars, to give away the Stealth location, enabling them to make a "kill".

Another use of the ECR sites is during Red Flag. These aerial war-game exercises are operated out of Nellis AFB with some deployments actually operating from the TTR base itself. During Red Flag, U.S. and allied pilots are trained in extremely realistic aerial combat situations, including the enemy systems of the ECRs.

Welcome to Sandia Landia Laboratories

One of the primary facilities at TTR is a large airfield, consisting of a 12,000-foot (3,700-m) runway and numerous hangars. TTR offers a wide array of signal-tracking equipment, including video, high-speed cameras, and radar-tracking devices. This equipment is used to characterize ballistics, aerodynamics, and parachute performance for artillery shells, bomb drops, missiles, and rockets and lot's more to see!

Day Trip Exclusions leaving from *Little A'Le'Inn*

Following are some suggested day excursions leaving from the Little A'Le'Inn as your starting point. Since most of the excursions involve leaving the paved highway (375), up to date maps are very encourage. For example topographic maps, local area maps or using Google Earth (best method) if you have a data connection. Unless stated, all traveling information mentioned below are listed by direction from the Little A'Le'Inn as your point of starting reference.

North and West of Rachel, Nevada

Driving on the Sand Spring Dry Lake Bed

Location: 37°41'19"N 115°46'25"W

This lake is approximately about 3.6 miles northwest of Rachel, NV. This dry lake bed is equivalent of Bonnievielle Salt Flats in the fall and summer. No matter which type of vehicle you are renting you will have a great time exploring around here. In the background you can see Rachel and the north end of the Groom Mountain Range. You can get to the lakebed on a dirt road past the old dumpsite. Cruising on the smooth surface is a lot of fun, but remember where you came in; the exit is hard to find once you are on the lakebed. The north end of the lakebed is a good place to look for arrowheads as well.

Spring Lake Valley Dry Lake Bed

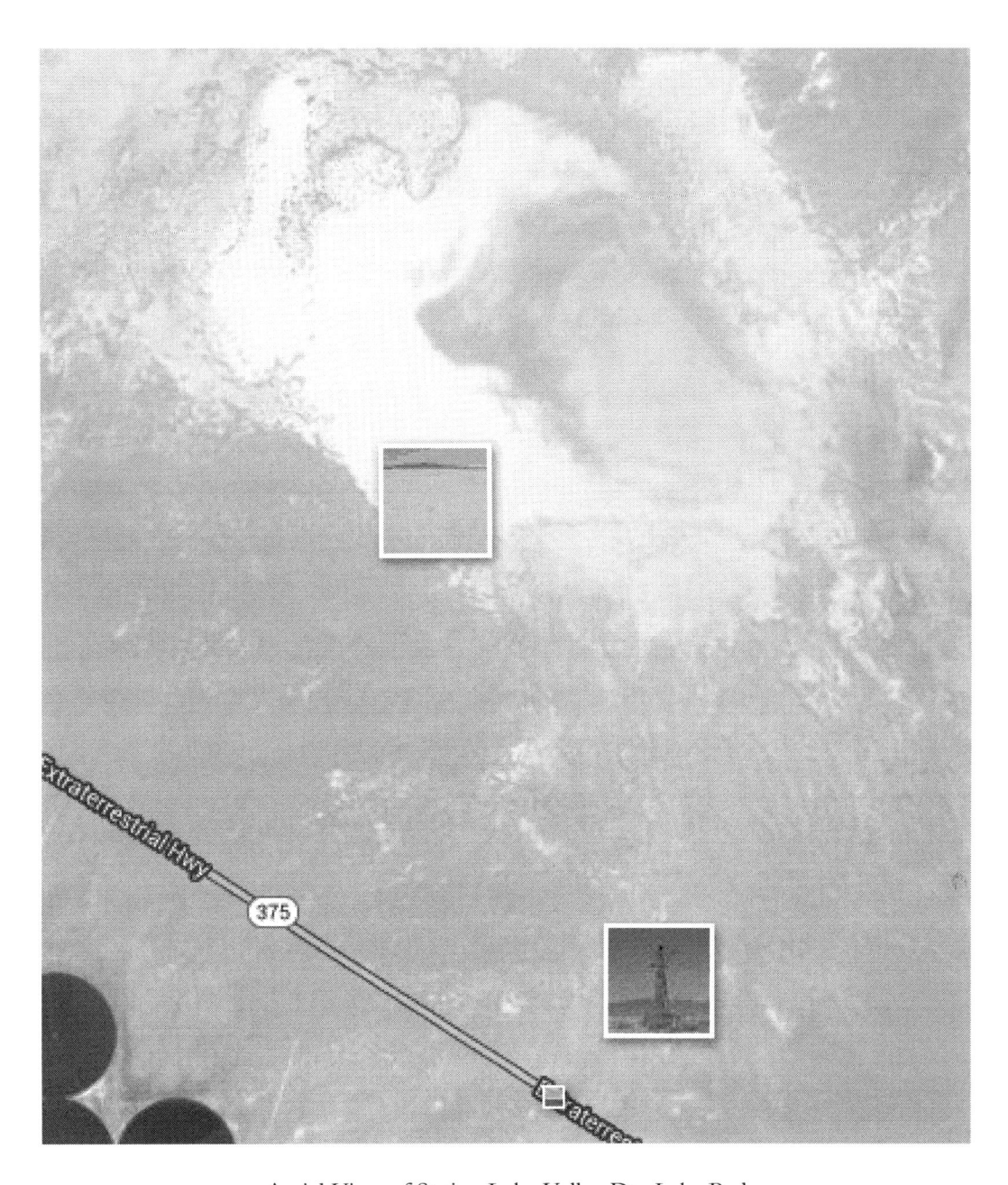

Aerial View of Spring Lake Valley Dry Lake Bed

Leaving the Little A'Le'Inn make a right turn onto Highway 375 of course traveling west. You will be traveling approximately 3.6 miles and look for the intersection Desert Dog Road & Windmill Road which is at coordinates 37°40'30.92"N 115°48'2.97"W. Make a right turn onto Windmill Road and drive 1.40 miles. You will come to an intersection which is a secondary dirt path road. Keep going straight passing the secondary dirt road another .41 tenths of a mile and you will hit the dry lake road.

Once you reach the lake bed, you'll find a wide area of complete flatness the equivalent of Bonnieville Salt Flats. Again be sure to note where you have entered the lake bed, because it is so vast that if may be hard to find your way out! The surface will be okay for sailboarding, quading, drag racing or test your rental car/vehicle to the MAX! You can certainly push the metal to the pedal especially in the middle of the lake! Be careful sometimes of survey markers which sometimes happens may be in the surrounding area's so survey before you race. The best time of the year to take advantage is in the summer and the fall.

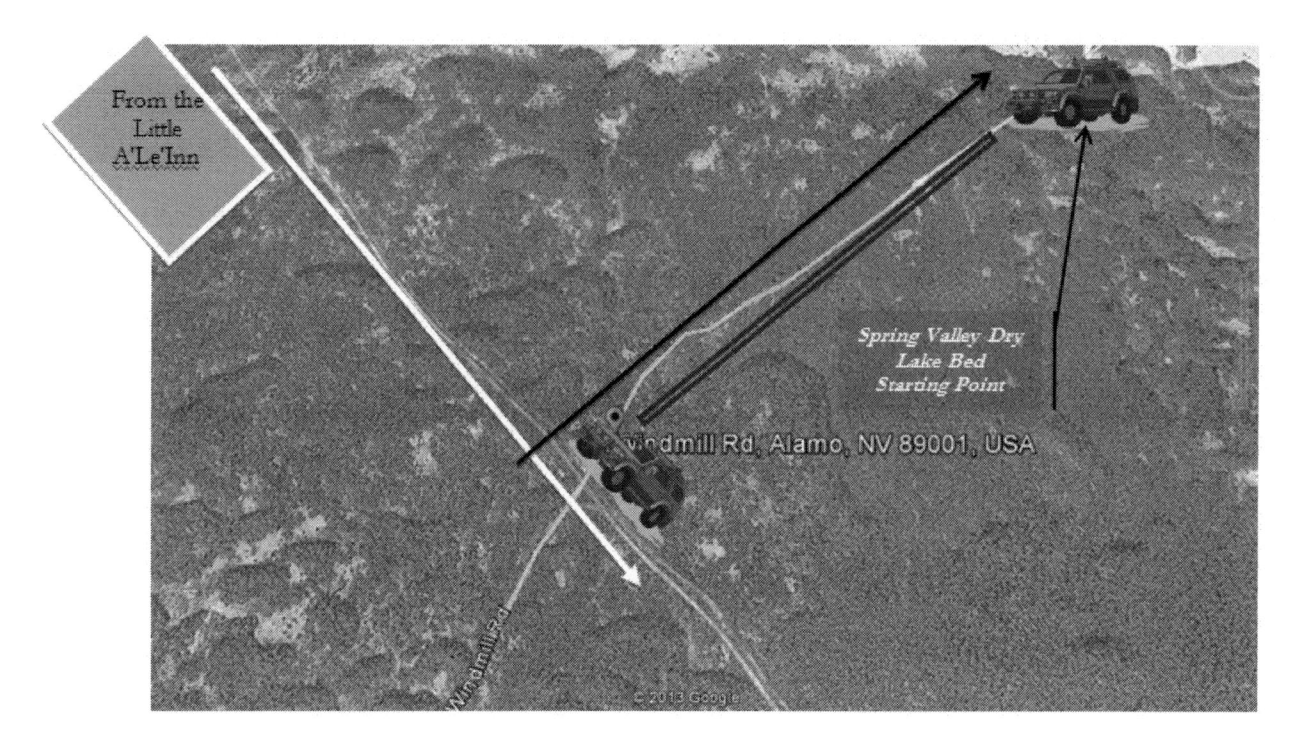

Make at RIGHT TURN and continue approximately 1.81 miles total from 375 until you are on the starting point of the dry lake bed as shown above.

Dry Lake Bed View

Day Trip Exclusions leaving from *Little A'Le'Inn*

Following are some suggested day excursions leaving from the Little A'Le'Inn as your starting point. Since most of the excursions involve leaving the paved highway (375), up to date maps are very encourage. For example topographic maps, local area maps or using Google Earth (best method) if you have a data connection. Unless stated, all traveling information mentioned below are listed by direction from the Little A'Le'Inn as your point of starting reference.

Indian Caves in Rachel

Shallow caves where Indians once camped at the south end of the Worthington Mountains. The **Worthington Mountains** is a mountain range in Lincoln County, Nevada at an elevation of approximately 2,368 m (7,769 ft) at location N 37°53'07 W115°36'23". This area is accessible by dirt roads about a 20 mile drive from the Little A'Le'Inn. The Worthington Mountains Wilderness is located in a remote part of the Ely District within Lincoln County in east-central Nevada. The nearest paved highway is about 15 miles to the south, and the nearest town is Alamo, 38 miles southeast. To access this wilderness area from Hiko, Nevada head northwest on State Highway 375 toward Rachel. Approximately 1.5 miles before Rachel take a right (north) on Shadow Road for 18 miles. This route will take you along the western border of the wilderness area.

From Highway 375, go about 3 miles north to a fork where there is a mailbox. Bear left and go past some ranch houses. Go approximately 8.7 miles further to a corral. Before the ruins of a stone house at the corral, turn right and follow the best road. From that point approximately 2 miles from the corral, bear to the left on the lesser traveled road toward the hills. Road joins a stream bed and enters a ravine. At the narrowest spot, look for the caves on the either side of the road.

The Worthington Mountain Range rises like a ship 4,000 rugged feet above dry valleys of central Nevada to almost 9,000 feet. The Worthington Mountains Wilderness Area encompasses the majority of the range. The severe limestone backbone of the mountain presents a difficult challenge to visitors with heavily dissected canyons, precipitous cliffs, knifelike limestone

surfaces, and no surface water. Those who perservere will be rewarded by endless vistas, natural arches, ancient forests, and limestone caves, **the largest being Leviathan Cave**. The Worthington Mountains feature a unique blending of flora and fauna from both the Great Basin and Mohave deserts. Wildlife species inhabiting this wilderness area include mountain lions, bobcats, mule deer, desert bighorn sheep, kit foxes, coyotes, and raptors, as well as smaller common mammal and reptile species. The vegetations includes cholla and other cactus at the lower elevations through densly forested slopes to a rocky ridgeline. Forest cover in the mountains vary juniper and pinyon pine at lower elevations while ponderosa, limber and bristlecone pines cling to the jagged peaks (the oldest tree dated at 2,100 years old). Remember that cutting or removing vegetation is not permitted. Gathering wood for campfires, when permitted, is limited to dead and down material. No other Nevada area expresses the wilderness characteristics of stark beauty, chaotic topography, and remoteness quite as well as Worthington Mountains.

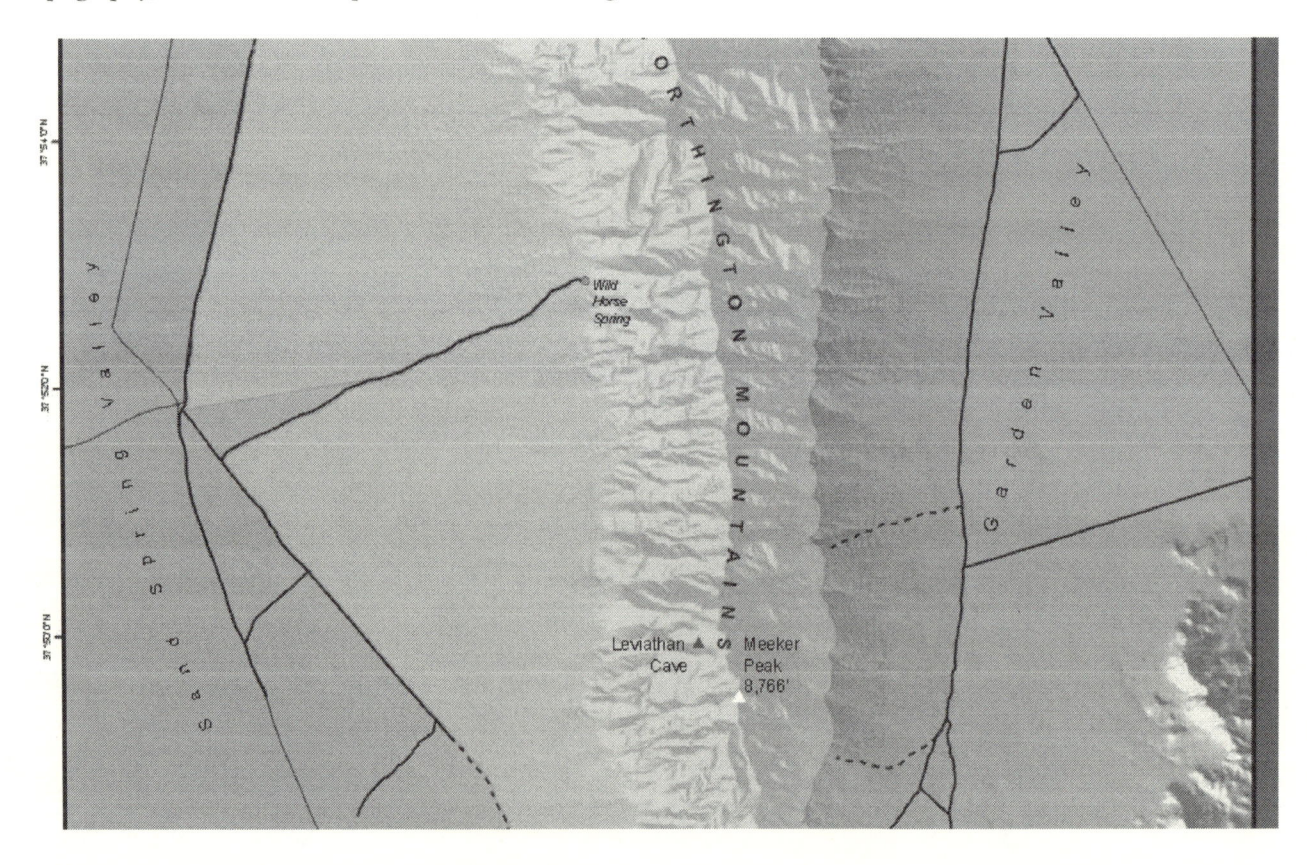

Leviathan Cave next to Meek Peak

Day Trip Exclusions leaving from *Little A'Le'Inn*

Following are some suggested day excursions leaving from the Little A'Le'Inn as your starting point. Since most of the excursions involve leaving the paved highway (375), up to date maps are very encourage. For example topographic maps, local area maps or using Google Earth (best method) if you have a data connection. Unless stated, all traveling information mentioned below are listed by direction from the Little A'Le'Inn as your point of starting reference.

Leviathan Cave in Rachel

These extensive caverns high up in the Worthington Mountains, separate from the Indian Caves. The name ought to be a very good hint here! This is said to be a world-class spelunker's cave that attracts the pros in the hiking business of recreation. It is approximately 20 miles north of Rachel (Little A'Le'Inn). There is a challenge here folks that it is supposed to be hard to get to, requiring a stiff hike up the mountain. There are several entrances. The main entrance is a sinkhole with a 20 foot drop at the entrance; unless you are very good at free-hold rock climbing, you would need ropes to get into it. Some of the folks did claim that the cave is almost endless, but a more experienced spelunker has estimated the total length at about 1500 feet. The USGS "Meeker Peak" map appears to show the main curve entrance, at an elevation of 8000' just north of Meeker Peak. Worthington Peak is a summit located in Lincoln County, NV at N37.91772° W115.61170° (NAD83) and at an elevation of 8937 ft MSL.

The closet you can get in a vehicle is probably at an elevation of about 6000 feet. You can do the entire trip in a day of course, but the long day hike each way do not leave much time to explore the cave. An overnighter would be ideal.

Leviathan Cave is located in the Worthington Range, northwest of Hiko and northeast of Rachael, about 150 miles north of Las Vegas.

From Las Vegas, drive north on Interstate-15 for 21 miles to Highway 93 (Exit 64) (Site 0674). Exit the interstate, turn left onto Highway 93, and drive north for 72 miles to Alamo (Site 0675). The Del Pueblo (Exxon Station) is the last place for food (not so good anymore), and the little motel about 1/4 mile before the Del Pueblo is acceptable if you are tired and don't want to sleep out. Continue north on Highway 93 for another 9 miles to Ash Spring. This is the last gasoline before the trailhead.

From Ash Spring, drive north on Highway 93 for 2 miles to Highway 318 (Site 0677). Turn left onto Highway 318 and drive west for about 0.7 miles to the Y-intersection with Highway 375 (Site 0676). Stay to the right on the curve and follow Highway 318 north towards Hiko. At 8.6 miles north of the 318-375 intersection, turn left onto Mail Summit Road (Site 0886), a graded dirt road. The turnoff is marked only by a stop sign. Reset your trip odometer to 0.0 here.

Drive west on Mail Summit Road. The road runs fairly straight towards the mountains. At 3.2 miles out, a road comes in from the south (left). Up to this point, the Mail Summit Road is not marked on USGS topo maps, but the road from the left is on the map.

Continue west on Mail Summit Road, trending west and north through a canyon in an old burn area. The road splits (Site 1115) where it goes up a narrow canyon. Both forks rejoin at the top of the canyon (Site 1116), and it might be wise to stay to the right both ways. At about 11.1 miles out (Site 0888), curve left (west) at an intersection of dirt roads in Coal Valley. Drive northwest over the next ridge (Murphy Gap), staying to the north (right) at a junction just over the pass (Site 0889).

This puts you in Wild Horse Valley; truly scenic high-desert country. Drive west and then north through this valley. As you pass a knob on your left, you enter Garden Valley.

When the road straightens out, you are in Garden Valley, and the trailhead is right across the valley to the west, but you need to drive north for a few miles before looping back down the other side of the valley. The mountains across the valley are the Worthington Range, and the high point on the south end of the range is Meeker Peak (8,768 ft). Leviathan Cave is on the other side of the peak, about 1,000 feet below the summit.

There are two large, limestone buttresses on the north side of the peak. One route to the cave goes up the chute between the two buttresses, over the ridge, and down the other side. The other route follows improbable ledges under the face of the western buttress and circles around to the other side.

In Garden Valley, drive north on the main road to about 29.4 miles out (Site 0890), and then turn hard to the left (southwest) on a 1-lane graded road that leads to an old water tank and a corral in the bottom of the valley, which you can see from a long way off. The corral is about 29.6 miles out (Site 1117). Continue west past the corral to the base of the mountains where a 1-lane dirt road curves left and runs south along the base of the mountains. Drive south to 33.7 miles out, where a metal T post (fence post) marks an intersection (Site 0891). Turn right and drive west up the 2-track to a large camping area at 34.3 miles out (Site 1118). A regular sedan can make it to this point. With a high-clearance vehicle, continue west for another mile to the end of the road (Site 0892; 35.2 miles out), where there is a small campsite. Park here, this is the trailhead.

There is parking for only two (maybe three) vehicles at the end of the road, so hiking groups should leave most vehicles at the big campsite and car-pool to the trailhead.

The Hike

The trailhead is located in the Pinyon-Juniper Woodland zone where fairly short trees suggest a fire long ago. Among the trees are Sagebrush, Mormon tea, grasses, and few other shrub species. From the trailhead (and from camp), you can see Meeker Peak, the two limestone buttresses that guard the north side of the peak, the chute that runs between the two crags, and the crest of the range north of the crags.

There are two ways to get to the cave: (1) straight up the chute and over the ridge, and (2) under the western buttress on improbable ledges and circling around the back. The two routes diverge about 1 hour from the trailhead.

From the trailhead (Table 2, Wpt. 01), hike southwest along the top of a low ridge towards the major canyon to the west. Ancient peoples used this area; watch the ground for obsidian flakes that they left behind. About 20 minutes out, the steep hillside forces the route off the low ridge and into the main wash (Wpt. 02). Drop into the wash and continue southwest. Parts of the wash are choked with shrubs, and it is sometimes easier to hike on the hillside above the wash. Hike up the wash for another 40 minutes to the fork in the main wash (Wpt. 03) where the gully from the chute between the buttresses meets the main wash.

At this point, decide which way you want to go... around the buttress or up the chute.

Route Around the Buttress

Continuing up the main wash, you might encounter a 500-lb bomb (Wpt. 04) lying in the bottom of the canyon and another with a tail assembly (retarding fins) a short distance farther up the canyon (Wpt. 05). This is said to be a dummy bomb, but it isn't worth investigating too closely.

In this vicinity, leave the wash, climb onto the broad ridge north of the wash, and use the ridge to gain the crest of the range (Wpt. 06). On the crest, hike south to just a couple of minutes before you would be able to touch the base of the limestone buttress (Wpt. 07). At this point, you should be able to look down the west side and see a long, steep scree chute running between the ridge and the north face of the buttress. Head down into the rocky, scree-filled chute for about 1 minute or less (more across than down), until you can start out on ledges that run horizontally across the face of the buttress. It doesn't look possible, but the airy route goes.

Head for the far side of the cliff face, aiming for a notch between the buttress and a knob on the next ridgeline (the knob and notch are visible from the crest of the ridge before you start across the ledges).

Lightly edited transcript from voice recorder: Traversed highly improbable ledge system beneath the north crag. From the ridgetop (Wpt. 07), cut down and across steep scree slope to a little ledge with an overhang, then follow ledge farther west to a larger overhang with red stains on the rocks (quite visible from a distance). Continue working across ledges and go under a big slab that broke loose and leans back against the cliff. There are ups and downs, but try to stay at the same elevation as you work across the ledges. Lots of exposure here with lots of loose rock and scree. Dangerous place. Max [one of our party] took a fall in a bad spot, and I thought he might be taking the big one.

From the notch (Wpt. 08), hike south over the next ridge and into the next canyon, staying more-or-less at the same elevation as the notch. Start by hiking southwest across the sideslope, climbing over a low ridge by passing to the west of a band of cliffs (Wpt. 09). Try not to loose more elevation than is necessary to pass the band of cliffs.

Atop the band of cliffs, continue south across the open hillside, crossing over another low ridge (Wpt. 10). From there, angle slightly to the east of south. As you approach the cave, you will either hit a drop-off or the mouth of Leviathan Cave. If you hit the cliffs, hike uphill (east) to the top of the cave opening (Wpt. 11). Arriving at the north edge of the sinkhole, traverse southeast across the top of the cave and circle around to the southwest corner (Wpt. 12). The place to get into the sinkhole is located near the bottom of the canyon on the southwest side.

Site #	Location	UTM Easting	UTM Northing	Latitude (N)	Longitude (W)	Elevation (ft)	Verified	Mileage Estimate
0674	I-15 at Hwy 93	689188	4028063	36.38091	114.89089	2,232	Yes	.
0675	Hwy 93 at Alamo	662974	4136909	37.36644	115.15960	3,452	Yes	.
0677	Hwy 93 at Hwy 318	657363	4154834	37.52891	115.21911	3,831	Yes	.
0676	Hwy 318 at Hwy 375	656355	4155179	37.53219	115.23044	3,800	Yes	.
0886	Hwy 318 at Mail Summit Rd	658154	4168556	37.65240	115.20720	4,125	Yes	0.0
1115	Mail Summit Rd Splits	650989	4172903	37.69277	115.28748	5,347	GPS	5.7
0887	Mail Summit Rd at Mail Summit	651286	4173890	37.70161	115.28391	5,686	Yes	6.4
1116	Mail Summit Rd Rejoins	651097	4173991	37.70256	115.28603	5,649	GPS	6.5
0888	Mail Summit Rd @Coal Valley Rd	648526	4180753	37.76390	115.31380	5,208	Yes	11.1
0889	Mail Summit Rd W of Murphy Gap	637066	4183185	37.78760	115.44340	5,820	Yes	18.7
0890	Mail Sum Rd @ Garden Valley Rd	628568	4195977	37.90410	115.53761	5,509	Yes	29.4
1117	Garden Valley Rd Water Tank	627753	4195183	37.89706	115.54701	5,552	GPS	30.2
0891	Garden Valley Rd@Leviathan Rd	626763	4189867	37.84930	115.55920	5,787	Yes	33.7
1118	Leviathan Rd at Camp	625840	4189618	37.84718	115.56973	5,964	GPS	34.3
0892	Leviathan Rd End	624615	4189189	37.84348	115.58373	6,349	Yes	35.2

| Wpt. | Location | UTM | UTM | Elevation | Point-to- | Cumulative | Verified |

		Easting	Northing	(ft)	Point Distance (mi)	Distance (mi)	
01	Leviathan Trailhead	624611	4189192	6,397	0.00	0.00	GPS
02	Drop into main wash	624185	4188953	6,618	0.32	0.32	GPS
03	Base of Chute	623546	4188718	6,985	0.48	0.80	GPS
04	500-pound bomb	623507	4188698	6,989	0.03	0.83	GPS
05	500-pound bomb Tail Assembly*	623406	4188704	7,075	0.10	0.93	GPS
06	Crest of the range	623078	4188775	7,603	0.34	1.27	GPS
07	Crest of the range	622979	4188469	7,825	0.23	1.50	GPS
08	Saddle on northwest ridge	622716	4188337	7,792	0.39	1.89	GPS
09	Band of Cliffs	622583	4188170	7,755	0.17	2.06	GPS
10	Low Ridge	622585	4188000	7,878	0.11	2.17	GPS
11	Top of Leviathan Cave	622649	4187852	7,717	0.13	2.30	GPS
12	Mouth of Cave	622638	4187813	7,889	0.06	2.36	GPS
13	Saddle at Top of Main Gully	622958	4188083	8,277	0.34	2.70	GPS
14	Between Buttresses	623150	4188225	7,804	0.39	3.09	GPS
03	Base of Chute	623546	4188718	6,985	0.60	3.69	GPS
02	Drop into main wash	624185	4188953	6,618	0.50	4.19	GPS
01	Leviathan Trailhead	624611	4189192	6,397	0.36	4.55	GPS

Day Trip Exclusions leaving from *Little A'Le'Inn*

Following are some suggested day excursions leaving from the Little A'Le'Inn as your starting point. Since most of the excursions involve leaving the paved highway (375), up to date maps are very encourage. For example topographic maps, local area maps or using Google Earth (best method) if you have a data connection. Unless stated, all traveling information mentioned below are listed by direction from the Little A'Le'Inn as your point of starting reference.

Ghost Towns of Keystone & Tybo

The Keystone Mine was originally discovered in the late 1860s by one of the wandering prospectors who were drawn by the Eureka boom. But there wasn't much activity until 1898 when ore was uncovered that assayed as high as 600 ounces of silver and $120 in gold per ton. The sample ore to be shipped was so carefully selected that it did not reveal the true and common value of the ore. Unfortunately, that first shipment of ore contained everything of value in the mine. Efforts to locate new deposits were fruitless and by the end of the summer most of the population had left. Only rubble marks the site today.

Take US-6 about 10 Miles N of Warm Springs.

Day Trip Exclusions leaving from *Little A'Le'Inn to Ghost Towns*

Tybo Ghost Town and Mine

The ghost town of *Tybo* is located in Tybo Canyon, on the east side of the Hot Creek Range. It is about 80 road miles or 90 minutes drive from Rachel, and well worth exploring.

After the first discoveries of ore in the Hot Creek Range in 1866 the first major discovery in Tybo was made in 1870. But it was not until 1874 that a small camp was established in Tybo Canyon. Most mines were producing lead, later also silver and zinc.

Tybo Consolidated Mining Company was founded in 1875 by several of the larger mines, and soon controlled the town. By 1876 Tybo was booming, and the population had reached 1,000. Many businesses opened, including several stores, saloons, restaurants, a hotel, a blacksmith, a school, a post office, a bank and a newspaper (the *Tybo Sun*).

In 1880 the mining company began running into problems, and by the end of 1881 the population had dwindled down to less than 100. In the following decades numerous mining companies tried to reopen and expand the old mines, but all of them failed within a few years. Since the late 1930's there has been no significant mining activity. However, even today a few people live in some of the cabins on-and-off, including a caretaker of the mine.

The remains of Tybo, including a couple of more recent mining operations, are easy accessible from the road. Some of the buildings are in fairly good condition. Especially the old general store, a wood building with a brick front, is worth exploring. Most of the mines are scattered all over the surrounding mountains and require a more or less strenuous hike. The headworks shown below are part of a more recent mine in town, and are easy to get to. There are several interesting buildings with old mining machinery in that area.

Directions

From the Little A'Le'Inn in Rachel turn left onto Hwy 375 north. Follow it for about 59 miles. At the Warm Springs junction turn right onto US-6 east. After 9.7 miles you see the Tybo historic marker on the right side of the highway. On the left side of the highway is a group of buildings and an airstrip. Follow the well-maintained dirt road past the buildings towards the mountains in the west. After 4.1 miles you come to a fork in the road. Take the left fork. After 8.6 miles you come to Tybo. Suitable for most vehicles.

Headworks of one of the more recent mines in Tybo!

The old brick school house, built in 1877 at Tybo!

GPS Coordinates

Rachel (Little A'Le'Inn)	N 37° 38.801'	W115° 44.760'
Queen City Summit	N37° 45.129'	W115° 56.733'
Warm Springs	N38° 11.447'	W116° 22.218'
Basecamp	N38° 18.705'	W116° 16.807'
Fork, keep left	N38° 21.084'	W116° 19.777'
Tybo	N38° 22.176'	W116° 24.019'

Update 2017

We have received several reports of new "No Trespassing" signs at the entrance to the Tybo Canyon. Apparently some of the roads and historic buildings have been restored, and new buildings and power lines were added.

We have no further information about the new owners or whether the signs have any legal ground, but access to Tybo may no longer be possible.

All About Nevada's Ghost Towns, A Must See Adventure!

No Adventure into Nevada can be complete without exploring Nevada's Ghost Towns and Mining Camps. Nevada's past is one of pioneers venturing west in search of a new life. Gold miners heading to Sutters Mill. Pony Express Riders battling the elements and Indians to deliver the mail. Railroaders laying track to connect our great United States. Nevada's past is a wild and glorious one.

A past of hardship, strength, perseverance, heart and soul. The California Trail, Immigrant Trail, and the Donner Trail all cross Nevada. Parts of the trails are still visible to this day. You can stand along the wagon wheel tracks and imagine yourself walking toward the mighty Sierra Nevada Mountains, uncertain what is around the next bend. Leaving possessions and loved ones along the way.

The Gold Rush to California was a trek made for promises of instant wealth that ended in tragedy for many. Few ever realized the wealth that was so talked about. With the many gold strikes discovered in Nevada, a great diversity of people came to here seeking a better, easier way of life, only to discover the harsh, brutal ways of the west.

The Chinese were among the many that were brought west to help with the railroad. There are many settlements still around Nevada that date back to the early days of the Railroad.

Nevada holds many actual mining and ghost town sites that are still visible today. Our goal here is to guide you to some sites that still have buildings, mills, and mining sites to explore. Some will not have any structures standing, but will have historical markers and history for you to visit.

*(NOTE- please check with U.S. Forest Service, & BLM on rules and regulation pertaining to removing any remains or artifacts).

Nevada is the 7th largest state in the U.S. and whenever venturing out into an area, PLEASE, be aware of where you are. Carry supplies to hold you over in case of a breakdown. Water is essential to have, dried food, nuts, a blanket, matches, and a shovel. Most important, let someone know where you are going. Even if it is the guy at the local store or gas station. You can go for hundreds of miles on Nevada's back roads without seeing a person for days. Be prepared.

Please remember to exercise caution when exploring Nevada's Ghost Towns & Mining Camps. Open shafts, drifts going into mountainsides, and old buildings, are ALL DANGEROUS.

Take a Trip to Warm Springs….Ghost Town at the End of Highway 375!

Warm Springs is located on U.S. 6, 49 miles east of Tonopah.

W116° 22.218'
N38° 11.447'

Warm Springs is an unincorporated community in the Tonopah Basin and Nye County, Nevada, near the mountain pass which divides the Kawich and Hot Creek ranges (at 38.19°N 116.37°W). It is located at the junction of U.S. Route 6 and State Route 375 (the "Extraterrestrial Highway"), around 40 miles east of Tonopah.

"Warm Springs originally was the stopping place for freighters and stages traveling to Eureka and Elko. The first settlers came to this site in 1886 and built a small stone house next to the warm soothing springs. This small settlement never really grew, but after the turn of the century a store and a logging house were built there. Warm Springs continued to serve a small number of weary desert travelers. In the 1920's the town reached its peak. On January 19, 1924, a post office, with Ethel Allred as postmaster, opened in the town. Even though it closed on June 29, 1929, there was and now still are a fairly steady number of travelers stopping at the Warm Springs.

No one lives in Warm Springs today. A small trailer park was there in the 1970's but is gone. A combined gas station and saloon have also been closed. Once the Leaching operations at Reveille and Keystone stopped, the little amount of traffic on the highways couldn't service the operations. Old buildings from Warm Springs's early days still stand. The springs are still flowing, but a small private swimming pool is off-limits to the public. But a couple of small huts are set up so that travelers can savor a warm dip in privacy."

A small stone house next to the warm, soothing springs was the first building in Warm Springs. It was built in 1866. The site originally was a stopping place for freighters and stages traveling to Eureka and Elko. It was a place where tired and weary travelers could stop and enjoy the rejuvenating waters of Warm Springs. Nobody lives at Warm Springs today. A number of old buildings from Warm Springs early days still remain. The springs still flow and there are several huts where the traveler can enjoy a warm dip in solitude.

The **Kawich Range** is a mountain range in Nye County in southern Nevada in the United States, just south of the Hot Creek Range. The southern part of the range lies on the Nellis Air Force Range. The mountains cover an area of about 250 square miles (650 km) and contain Kawich Peak, at 9,399 feet (2,865 m) above sea level. U.S. Route 6 crosses the pass between The Kawich and the Hot Creek ranges and meets State Route 375 at Warm Springs just north of the range. To the east lies the Reveille and Kawich valleys with the Reveille Range to the east of the northern portion and the Belted Range east of Quartzite Mountain at the southern end. The broad Pahute Mesa and Gold Flat lie to the south with Cactus Flat and the Cactus Range to the southwest. To the northwest across Stone Cabin Valley lies the Monitor Range. The Bureau of Land Management manages 50.3% of the mountains, and 39.7% is part of the Air Force Range. A USFWS

National Wildlife Refuge makes up 8.9% of the range.

Vegetation is primarily sagebrush scrub and piñon-juniper. The Kawich Range beardtongue (*Penstemon pudicus*) is a rare plant that is endemic to the range. The mountains are home to porcupines and several species of mice, and chipmunks, voles, squirrels, and gophers can also be found. American kestrels, MacGillivray's Warbler, Bullock's oriole, and Hairy Woodpeckers also inhabit the Kawich Range.

37°58'N 116°28'W

Kawich Range

Warm Springs, Nevada

Intersection of State Highway 375 & Route 6 at the "Infamous Ghost Town"

of "Warm Springs, Nevada!"

Buckle Up – Your Sixth Road Trip to the mysterious "Base Camp" aka Area 51 ANNEX

Base Camp and Halligan Mesa

Basecamp is located about 9.33 miles NE of Warm Springs, on the west side of Hwy 6. It includes a housing complex, a large service area for vehicles and equipment, a fire station and some radar equipment. And of course a runway, which runs parallel to the highway, in plain sight. According to the "Special Nevada Report" the "Base Camp is used as a staging and support area for field personnel and as a recreation area for military and contractor personnel." According to the same source it is usually manned by 3 to 6 people.

A (public) dirt road, leading from Hwy 6 to the abandoned mining town Tybo in the mountains, goes right through Basecamp. It divides it into the southern maintenance area and the living quarters in the north. You can drive through and take a look around, but better stay on the road. On the other side is the end of the airstrip, which leads NE from here. There are no hangars or other buildings near the ramp, and usually no planes either. Only on one occasion we have seen one of the small Beechcraft 1900 "Janets" (N20RA) sitting parked on the ramp.

Basecamp was first built as a staging area by the Atomic Energy Commission (AEC), a predecessor of the DOE, during the underground nuclear tests in the area in the late 1960s. In particular for "Project Faultless", an underground thermonuclear detonation with 67 times the energy of the bomb dropped on Hiroshima, Japan.

When the test was set off on January 19, 1968 its catastrophic results for the environment led to the immediate cancellation of any further tests.

After being abandoned by the DOE, Basecamp was taken over by the Air Force, which built a modern 7300-foot runway. In fact there is evidence that Basecamp is now owned by the Air Force Flight Test Center (AFFTC) at Edwards Air Force Base. The same department that owns the Groom Lake facility. In fact there seem to be very close relations between Basecamp and Area 51.

The runway was recently extended and improved, and it was used as test airfield for touch-and-go practice during the development of the F-117 Stealth Fighter at Area 51 and later at TTR. Also, Basecamp is almost in line with the north end of the runways at Groom, which makes it an ideal emergency airfield in case of problems during takeoff of a test flight.

A secret facility so close to the highway, and in plain sight? It makes sense when you consider that Hwy 6 only has very light traffic, especially at night. Also, everything is very casual and low-key, and to a passing traveler the whole place looks pretty deserted. Until you turn onto the dirt road, and pull your vehicle off the road near the airstrip. Within a couple of minutes a security guard in an older model pickup truck will approach you. Unlike the Groom Lake Cammos he will actually talk to you, but of course since you are on public land he has not much legal authority at that point.

Here is a typical conversation, which took place last year when I was sitting in my vehicle, on the side of the road at the end of the runway, quite visibly operating several scanners and frequency counters. Guard, pulls up next to my truck: "Sir, do you need any help?" - "No thanks, I am fine." - "What are you doing here?" - "Just sitting here." –

"No really, WHAT ARE YOU DOING HERE?" - "Just sitting here." That second confirmation must have satisfied him. After a last doubtful look at my equipment he turned his truck around and drove off, back to the camp.

About halfway down the runway you can see the Basecamp VOR transmitter. The VOR frequency is 113.900 MHz, and the Morse code ID is "AEC". Probably a reminder of the original use of the camp. One interesting thing is that the VOR is not always on.

We stop by there regularly, and on about 50% of our visits the VOR was not active. If it is, you can clearly pick it up on your scanner while driving by on the highway.

Roughly in line with the runway, a few miles away on either end are two unmanned radio facilities: A large radar dome on Halligan Mesa about 15 miles NNE and on a mountain top near Warm Springs about 11 miles SW lots of radar gear, microwave towers, satellite dishes and other antennas

Base Camp and Halligan Mesa are withdrawn by the Air Force and occupy approximately 600 acres in Hot Creek Valley in north central Nye County. Base Camp is located 60 miles east of Tonopah on U.S. 6. A county road passes through Base Camp land. Halligan Mesa is located approximately 15 miles northeast of Base Camp along U.S. Highway 6 and then 3 rniles northwest along a dirt road. There are no proposed changes in ownership, mission, boundaries, or use of Base Camp and Halligan Mesa through the year 2000.

An electronics and communications facility on Halligan Mesa, and an associated support area at Base Camp, are used for collecting data for Air Force testing programs conducted in the vicinity of the Tonopah Test Range (TTR) and the Nellis North Range. Base Camp is used as a staging and support area for field personnel and as a recreation area for military and contractor personnel. Base Camp has a recently extended and improved airstrip, several buildings for sleeping quarters, shop and maintenance buildings, and a recreation building. Base Camp is manned by three to six people. Halligan Mesa is unmanned and a helicopter pad is located near the facility.

Basecamp, seen from Hwy 6. The gray buildings on the left is the maintenance area, the tan buildings on the right the living quarters. The airstrip goes out of frame to the right of the living quarters.

US GOVERNMENT CONTRACTORS

Check for the Signs!

Aerial View of Base Camp at Highway 6 & Tybo Road.

Here are a few panoramic photos of the area. The site is so close to the highway that they really can't put anything secret there or WHY NOT!

View 2 of the Base Camp

View 3 of the Base Camp

HF Antenna System at the "Base Camp"

Now for the mysterious security cameras. Why as they mysterious? Well, the showed up for a while, then went away. The cameras were set up to monitor vehicles on the main road, the runways, and vehicles approaching from Tybo.

The cameras do not move!

I've always thought these dishes are just for satellite TV, but when you have 3 different dishes, well maybe they are used for something else...

- **GPS Coordinates**.

Obtained in the field. Error +/-100 feet.

- Basecamp main gate on Tybo Road: 38°18.700'N, 116°16.734'W
- Paved runway, south end: 38°18.937'N, 116°16.930'W
- Paved runway, north end: 38°19.989'N, 116°16.197'W
- Basecamp VOR-TAC: 38°19.382'N, 116°16.792'W
- Turnoff for Basecamp on US-6:   38°18.600'N, 116°16.519'W
- (Milepoint Nye 59.9)
- Turnoff for Radar Site on US-6: Milepoint Nye 73.7 (near Sandy Summit)
- Location of two misplaced "No Trespassing Signs" on road to Radar Site: 38°28.562'N, 116°08.983'W / 38°27.843'N, 116°08.690'W
- Radar site on Halligan Mesa (approx.):   38°30.6'N, 116°08.7'W
- Bluejay state highway maintanance station: 38°22.384'N, 116°13.511'W
- Warm Springs (junction US-6 & NV-375):   38°11.442'N, 116°22.138'W
- Air distance to Tonopah (town): 54.4 miles, bearing 252° WSW
- Air distance to Rachel: 54.7 miles, bearing 147° SE
- Air distance to Area 51 (Building 170): 78.6 miles, bearing 161° SSE (341° NNW from Area 51). *Might be different from Area 51 runway.*
- Air distance to Las Vegas: 160 miles, bearing 157° SSE

Buckle Up – You're Seventh Road Trip to the mysterious "Nuclear Test Site at Morey Flats." Called "Project Faultless" in NYE County.

Introduction...

The **Nevada National Security Site (N2S2)**, previously the **Nevada Test Site** (NTS), is a United States Department of Energy reservation located in southeastern Nye County, Nevada, about 65 miles (105 km) northwest of the city of Las Vegas. Formerly known as the **Nevada Proving Grounds**, the site was established on 11 January 1951 for the testing of nuclear devices, covering approximately 1,360 square miles (3,500 km^2) of desert and mountainous terrain. Nuclear testing at the Nevada Test Site began with a 1-kilotonne-of-TNT (4.2 TJ) bomb dropped on Frenchman Flat on 27 January 1951. Many of the iconic images of the nuclear era come from the NTS.

The Nevada Test Site contains 28 areas, 1,100 buildings, 400 miles (640 km) of paved roads, 300 miles of unpaved roads, ten heliports and two airstrips. The most-recent test was a sub-critical test of the properties of plutonium, conducted underground on December 7, 2012.

PROJECT FAULTLESS – Let's Take A Drive ….. Let's Go!

One of the history's largest underground nuclear tests, "Project Faultless," was conducted on Jan 19, 1968, not on the Nevada Test Site but on public land north of Warm Springs. (about 90 miles from Rachel.) You can actually visit **GROUND ZERO** where there is a plaque on a big concrete plug and extensive evidence of ground collapse. (Since the explosion was very deep underground, there is a very little chance of radiation). The site is accessible by roads from US-6. From Warm Springs, go north on US-6 about 25 miles to milepost 76.5, where there is a road on your left and a sign pointing to "Moore's Station." This is a well maintained road suitable for any vehicle. Follow it 12.5 miles until you reach a stop sign. Keep going straight ahead about 1.4 miles until the road ends at perpendicular road. You are very close to the site. Look for a concrete cylinder sticking out of the ground, looking like a water tank! Go right a few hundred yards and then left at the first opportunity to drive right up to the plug.

In the 1950's, when not much was known about the effects of nuclear explosions, many nuclear tests were conducted at the Nevada Test Site north of Las Vegas. The tests were conducted both above and below ground, in the beginning with little or no safety precautions. When it became obvious that the underground nuclear tests in the Nevada Test Site were a serious safety risk for nearby Las Vegas, the Atomic Energy Commission ("AEC", today known as Department of Energy "DOE") decided to conduct the most powerful tests in even more remote areas.

One of a total of 10 such locations was the "Central Nevada Test Area", in Hot Creek Valley. It is located on public land, about 70 miles northwest of Rachel.

A series of underground thermonuclear tests was planned, more powerful than any of the tests before. *Project Faultless* was the first calibration test, intended to determine the geological impact. It had a yield of approximately 1.0 megatons, about 67 times the energy of the bomb that was dropped on Hiroshima, Japan! Other, even more powerful tests were to follow later.

Project Faultless was detonated 3,200 feet underground on January 19, 1968 at 10:15am.

The results were devastating! The force of the explosion caused the ground in a radius of several miles to collapse, and created several deep fault lines that despite some "restoration" efforts by the AEC are still visible today. A steel pipe with a diameter of 7.4 feet had been drilled into the ground to place the bomb. Its top end was level with the surface before the test. After the explosion the top 9 feet of the pipe were exposed, due to the ground collapsing.

The blast also created a huge cylindrical underground cavity, a so-called nuclear rubble chimney. It is approximately 820 feet in diameter, and 2,460 feet in height. At its bottom lies over 500,000 metric tons of highly radioactive rubble, with radiation levels similar to the core of a nuclear reactor.

The completely unpredicted disastrous geological damage led to the cancellation of the entire project. The steel pipe was sealed with concrete, and all other sites that were being prepared for more, even more powerful tests were abandoned. The excavations can still be seen nearby. A bronze plaque reminding of the test was affixed to the top of the steel pipe, which now serves as a memorial, marking *Ground Zero* of the Project Faultless test.

The center of the blast, deep inside the ground, is contaminated with radiation for thousands of years. But it appears that the surface is relatively "clean", and it is safe to visit the site. However, the plaque prohibits digging in the area, or even picking up material from the ground.

On the way, about 9.7 miles past the Warm Springs junction, you see a group of buildings and an airfield on the left side of US-6. This is Basecamp, built by the Atomic Energy Commission as base camp for the Central Nevada Test Area. After the project was cancelled the USAF took over Basecamp and extended the runway to its current size. Today it is used as an auxiliary airfield for the Air Force, including secret test flights out of TTR and Area 51.

Directions

From the Little A'Le'Inn in Rachel turn left onto Hwy 375 north. Follow it for about 59 miles. At the Warm Springs junction turn right onto US-6 east. After 25.4 miles you see a small sign to "Moores Station" on the left. Turn left onto the well-maintained dirt road. After 12.2 miles you get to a 4-way intersection. Continue straight on the less developed dirt road, heading roughly west, for another 1.4 miles. Then you will see a mound of dirt directly ahead. The road splits here. Turn right, heading north. Then veer left, circling the north side of the mound. Another left turn onto a dirt track leading south brings you right to the monument shown below.

GPS Coordinates

Rachel (Little A'Le'Inn)	N 37° 38.801'	W115° 44.760'
Queen City Summit	N37° 45.129'	W115° 56.733'
Warm Springs	N38° 11.447'	W116° 22.218'
Basecamp	N38° 18.705'	W116° 16.807'
Moores Station Turnoff	N38° 28.792'	W116° 05.882'
4-way intersection	N38° 37.593'	W116° 11.402'
Project Faultless	N38° 38.058'	W116° 12.920'

Project Faultless with the Concrete Cylinder

A Must See!

Project Faultless – "The Project Faultless *PLAQUE*!"

Front View at Project Faultless at GROUND ZERO!

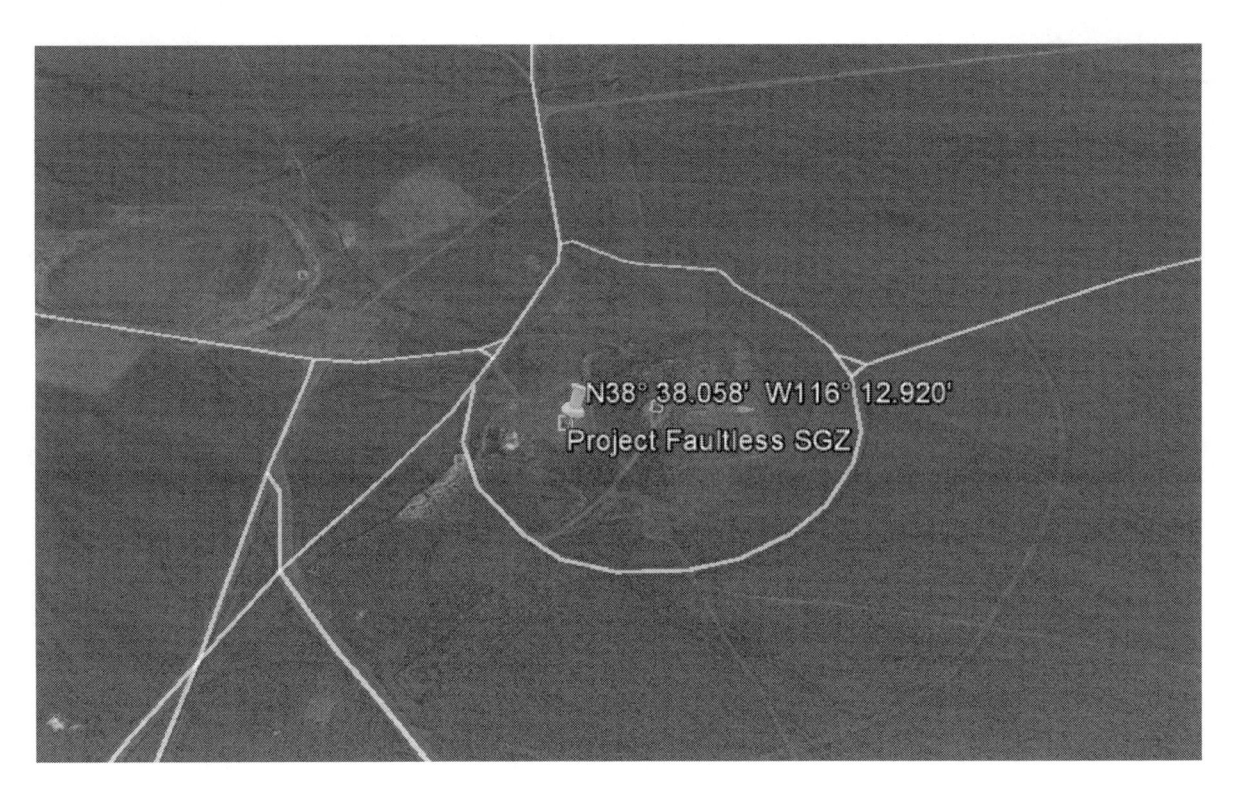

Google Earth Close Up of Project Faultless at N38° 38.058' W116° 12.920'

A Blast from the Past! Ground-Zero

Buckle Up – You're Eight Road Trip to the mysterious "Lunar Crater"

Lunar Crater National Natural Landmark is volcanic field landmark located 70 miles (110 km) east-northeast of Tonopah in Nye County, in central Nevada. It was designated a National Natural Landmark in 1973.

Location

75 miles east of Tonopah, Nevada.

38° 23' 2.29" N, 116° 4' 9" W

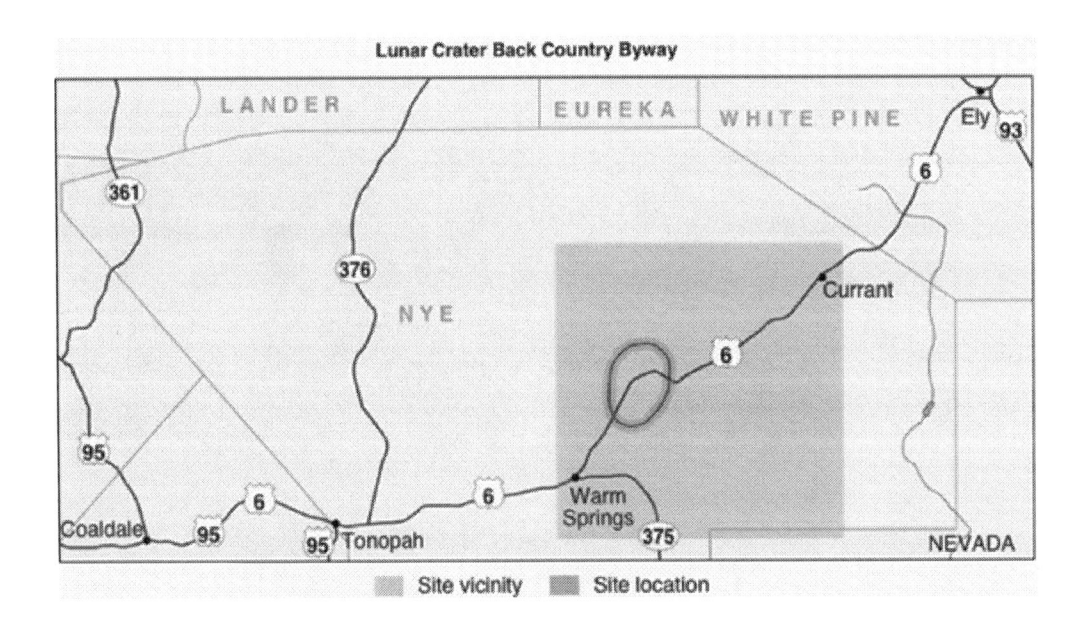

Description

Meandering among the bold volcanic features of the Lunar Crater Volcanic Field, the 24-mile byway follows an unpaved road through terrain characteristic of the Great Basin desert. Maars, cinder cones, mesas, cuestas, ash flows, lava flows, fault ridges, and alkali playas can be viewed along the route.

Directions

From Tonopah, travel 75 miles east along U.S. Highway 6. The byway forms a loop bisected by U.S. Highway 6, and is marked by signs at its eastern and western entrances along the highway.

Visitor Activities

Geologic sightseeing, hiking, picnicking, scenic drives, and off-highway driving. Although there is no wild horse and burro population within the Lunar Crater Volcanic Field, one might glimpse these animals along the way, as the Sand Springs West Herd Management Area is located on the north side of U.S. Highway 6.

Special Features

Lunar Crater, Easy Chair Crater, The Wall, Black Rock Lava Flow, Lunar Lake, and Palisade Mesa are some of the dominant landscape features that are visible from the byway. Lunar Crater, a bowl-shaped depression almost devoid of vegetation, looks more like a meteor-impact crater than what it is: a volcanic cinder cone that has collapsed in upon itself. In 1973, Lunar Crater was recognized as an outstanding example of the nation's natural heritage and designated as a National Natural Landmark.

The "Lunar Crater"

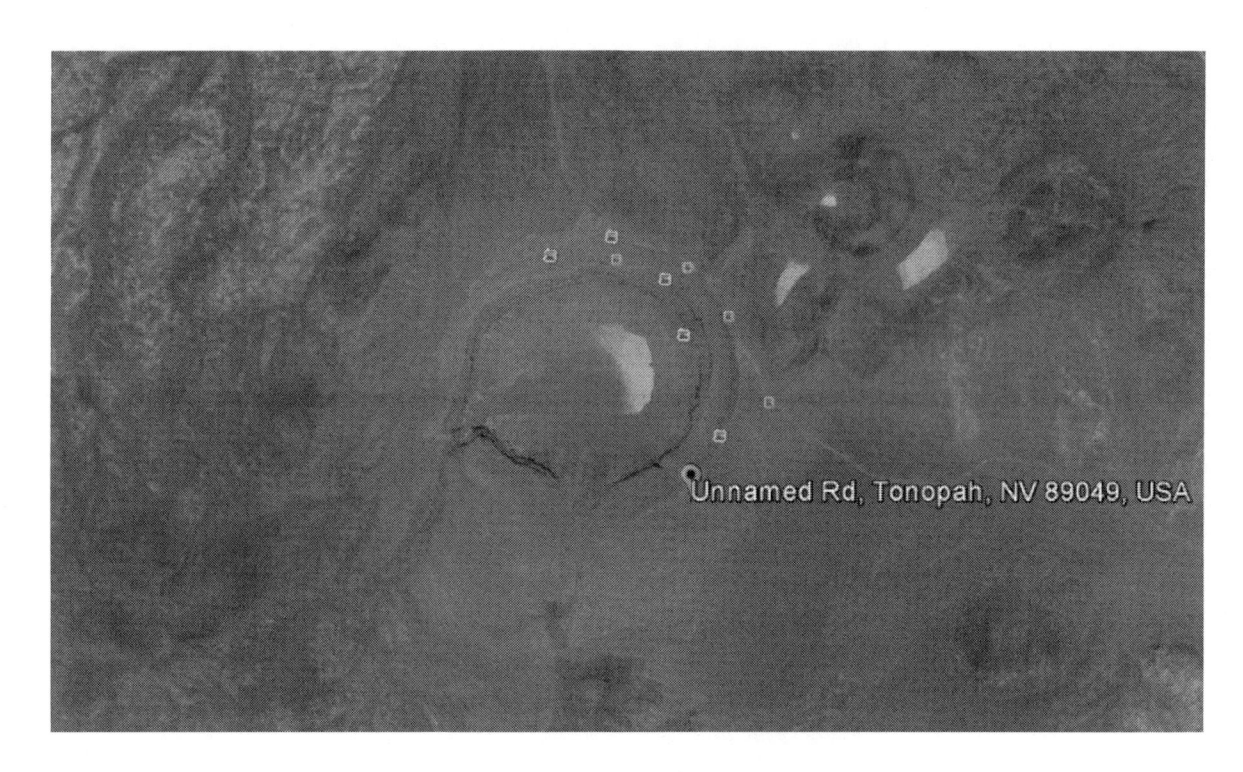

Lunar Crater View 1

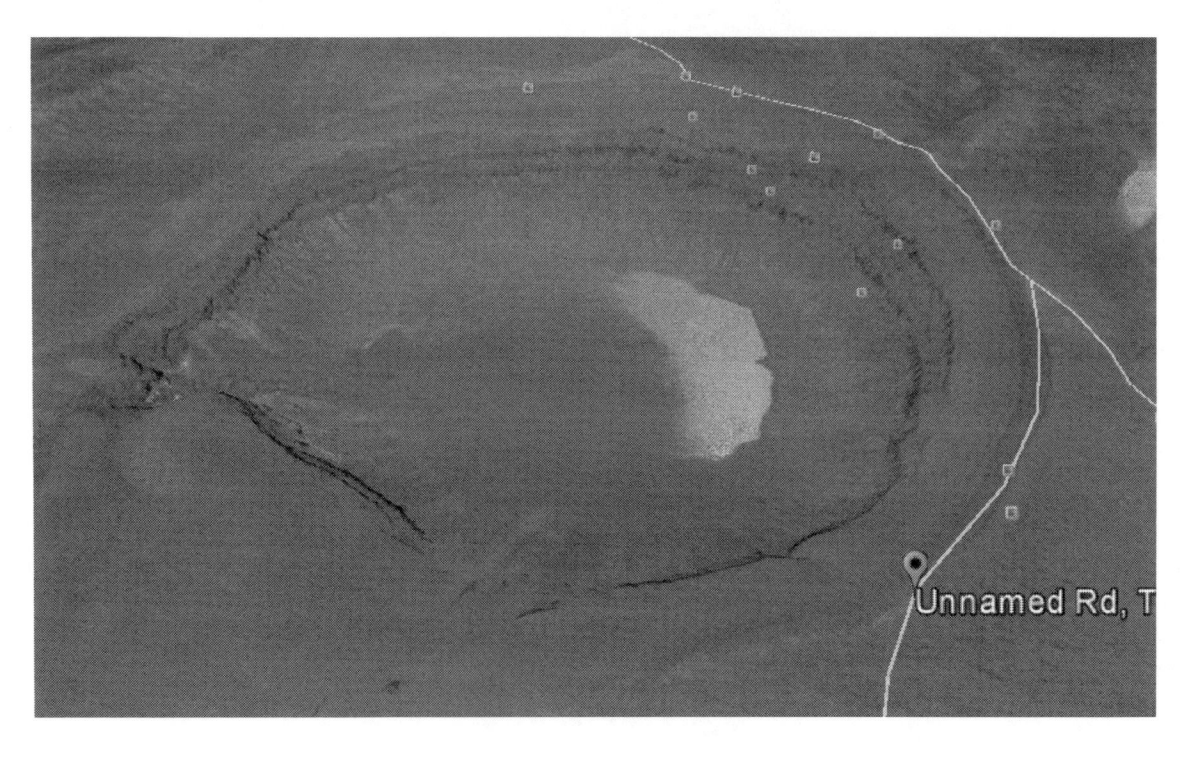

Lunar Crater View 2

Overview: Take a trip back in time! Use the AEC road, used to access the Project Faultless drill site, to visit one of Nevada's oldest orchards at a stage stop on the Belmont-Tybo-Eureda stage route.

Warning: This area is very remote and takes more self-reliance than other similar length drives/bike trips. There is no gas for 100 miles. At Moore's Station you are 17 miles from the highway. Use appropriate caution and common sense.

History: Moore's Station was established as a stage stop along the Belmont-Tybo-Eureda stage route in the early part of the 1870s at a natural spring. The spring, the creek it feeds, and the stage stop all get their name from the Moore brothers who established the ranch that would later host the stage. They knew water was scarce in central Nevada so they built a reservoir to capture the flow from the spring. They also imported fruit trees, making Moore's Station one of the earliest known orchards in the state of Nevada. Supposedly these trees still exist and producing fruit, much like the fruit trees of Lonely Dell Ranch at Lee's Ferry in Arizona. Sadly for the Moores the good times lasted for only about a decade. In the 1880s the stage route was abandoned. Owing to the perpetual water source and good shade trees, however, the ranch prospered. Today all the old buildings are fenced off and lay on private property. The ranch is still a going concern. From the road you can't see the old reservoir but it is still there according to maps and aerial photographs. The current route in abandoned the old Austin stage route down Moore's Creek for the Atomic Energy Commission's flat, graded road. This whole area was set to be turned into a nuclear test site, but the failure of the one bomb that was detonated, Project Faultless, scuttled the whole thing.

Drive/Ride: Start out on US-6. Turn north onto the signed Moore's Station road. This is a very good road - probably one of the best dirt roads in the West. Is it because it gets graded more often than it gets driven? Who can say. All I know is that 50mph is safe on this route in a truck (if you are biking your speed may be lower).

The route heads north, basically paralleling the butte to the west (take note of all that fancy electronic equipment on the top. What are they watching?). The road curves to the west and then drops down into Moore's Wash on a well-constructed incline. At the base of the incline, turn right. The road curves back across the wash bottom and parallels the eastern canyon wall. There is an opportunity to cross the wash soon after, but watch the signs. The left fork is washed out. Stick right. This same advice holds as you get to the "narrows" of Moore's Creek. Unless taking a side trip to Petroglyph Butte, stick to the right and head towards the Cottonwoods. You will see the stage house and ranch buildings on the right, tucked under all the shade trees. Once you have reached the station, you can either continue on up the road or turn around. There are some hiking opportunities in the area - make this part of a trip including Project Faultless and Petroglyph Butte for a fun afternoon in the backcountry of central Nevada!

Water Sources: Moore's Creek is flowing year-round near the station. Cows know this - if you use this water, treat it!

Camping: Camping is allowed on the surrounding BLM land. Make sure you are not camping on private property near the station.

A Road Trip inside Area 51 by the Fly Around Method

The Main Security Building inside Area 51. This building is for all check-ins before proceeding to any facility. The location of this Security Building A51 is located at 37°14'28"N 115°49'26"W.

In the figure below the Main Security Building inside Area 51 large area view. This building is for all check-ins before proceeding to any facility. The location of this Security Building A51 is located at 37°14'28"N 115°49'26"W in which you can see the route from the Back Gate to Security Building A51 which is 25.25 miles route.

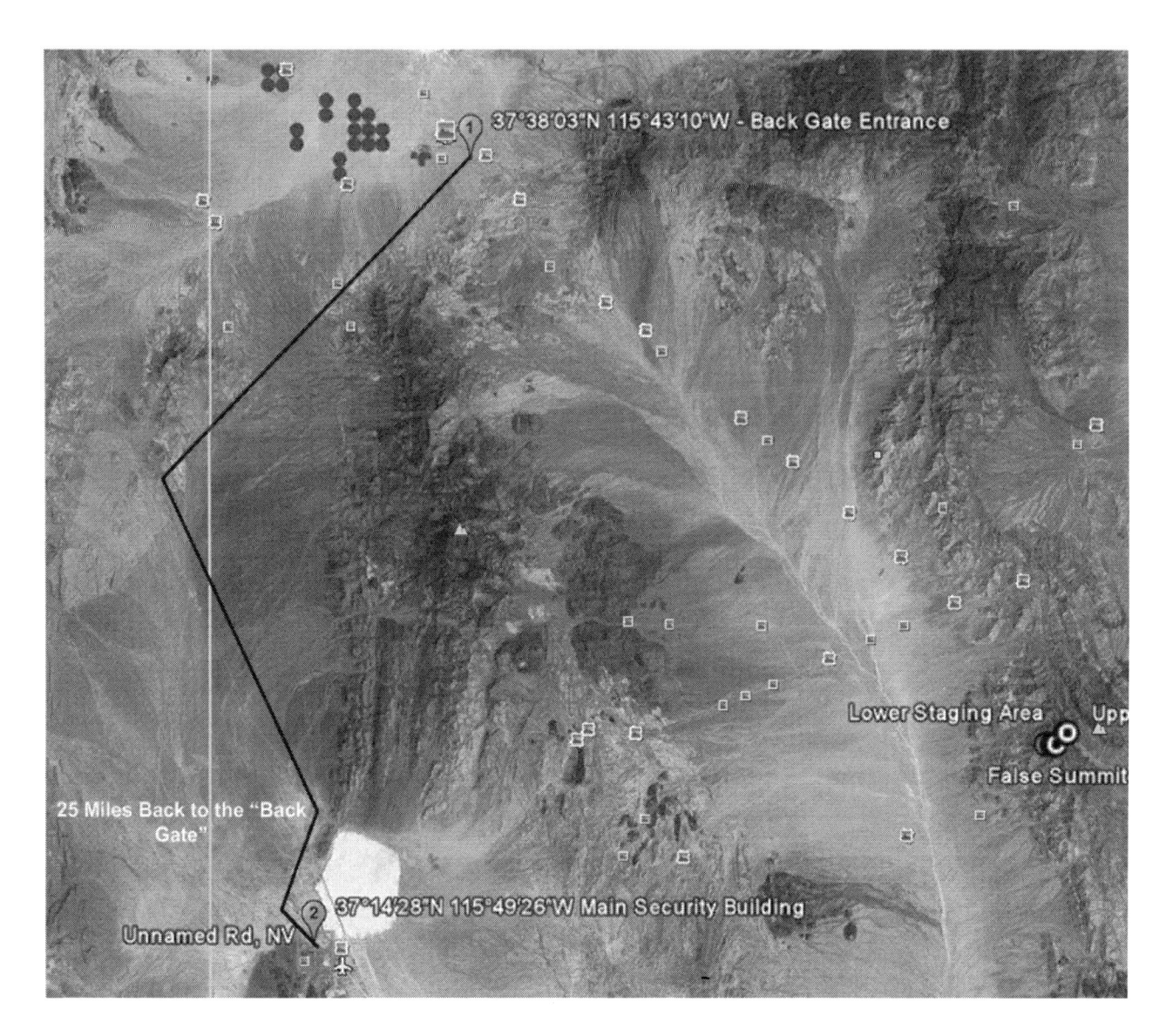

Figure 6

The Main Security Building inside Area 51 large area view. This building is for all check-ins before proceeding to any facility. The location of this Security Building A51 is located at 37°14'28"N 115°49'26"W in which you can see the route from the Back gate to Security Building A51.

What is a large Civil Engineering area, along with various equipment storage areas and workshops 37°14'25"N 115°49'10"W are visible to the southeast of that same area. A large number of white-painted, government vehicles are visible in numerous parking lots in the station area, mostly being pickup trucks, SUVs and vans.

Figure 7

The Main Civil Engineering Building inside Area 51 large area view. This building is for all structural engineering adds, moves or changes on the base.

The location of this Civil Engineering Building A51 is located at 37°14'25"N 115°49'10"W in which you can see the surrounding equipment storage buildings nearby.

The support area of the station has what appear to be several 1960s-era personnel barracks 37°14'30"N 115°49'02"W of the type formerly found on Naval shore facilities are visible. It is known internally that at least 600 hundred personnel may be stationed at Groom Lake or the length of their tour of duty. Wanted also to mention that no military family housing units are located on the base. Visible recreational facilities include a baseball diamond, tennis courts, and an indoor open mess, a type of Base Exchange, dining facility and a medical clinic. The base electrical power substation is located just to the northwest of the tennis court.

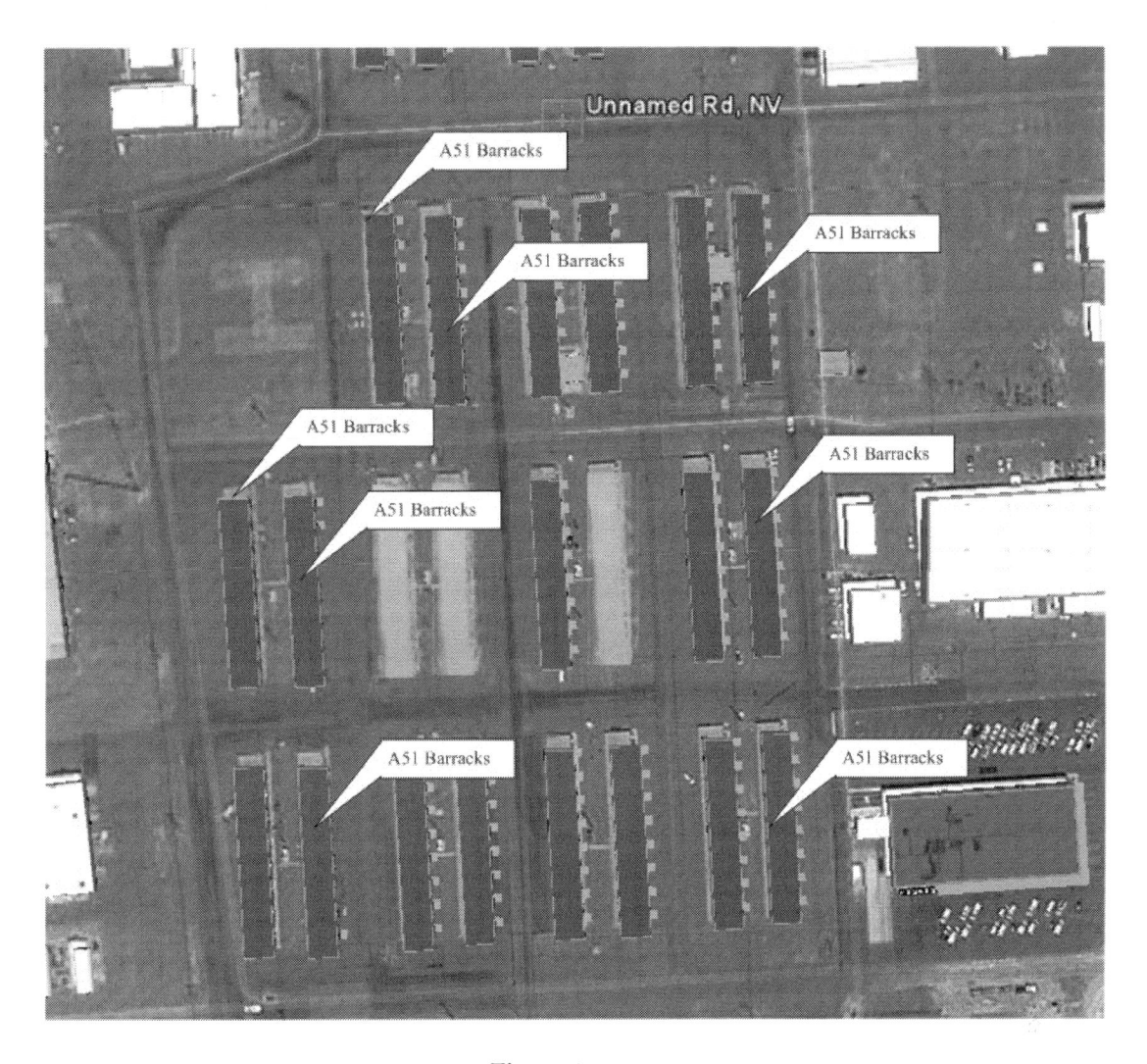

Figure 8

The Main Barrack Buildings inside Area 51 large area view. This building is for all personnel that have been assigned extended stay both military active and DoD contractor personnel. The location of Main Barrack Buildings A51 is located at 37°14'30"N 115°49'02"W in which you can see the surrounding 33 barrack buildings nearby.

What is a headquarters building appears to be located about a block to the north and west of the airfield terminal building at 37°14'27"N 115°48'50"W. It is a large, modern, multi-story office building with extensive landscaping and a parking area, which differentiates it from the other more bland, military-style buildings on the station. It is known what, if any, military designated unit is assigned to the Groom Lake facility. A large multi-storied building located just to the south of the presumed headquarters building is for auxiliary support building containing engineering labs or other facilities.

There appears to be two separate aircraft maintenance areas; one on the north side of the station, the other on the south. Numerous hangars and maintenance support buildings are located in them. Both facilities contain a very large number of hangars (four in the north area, eight in the south), far more than a normal Air Force Base or Naval Air Station would have. The large number of hangars on the station is presumably to ensure operational aircraft are kept out of view of orbiting reconnaissance satellites as well as out of the intense desert heat.

The north side maintenance area 37°14'38"N 115°48'54"W appears to be the original CIA facility, with what appear to be 1950s and 1960s era hangars and buildings, having been expanded over the years with additional buildings and four new large hangars. Several open aircraft parking ramps are visible, one having several black-painted F-16s. A helicopter parking ramp is located just to the north, with several black painted helicopters. Generally black-painted military aircraft are flown at night.

A very large tower, possibly an old airfield control tower is visible in the area.

To the north of the aircraft maintenance area appears several buildings 37°14'51"N 115°49'03"W, and two large satellite dishes, probably being the base communications facility. Several radars are visible at 37°14'52"N 115°48'50"W linked to what is likely an air defense monitoring facility. A large, triangle shaped tower 37°14'46"N 115°49'24"W is located to the west. Its unusual appearance, painted black and also unusual external features on two sides are noted, its use is undetermined.

To the south of the aircraft maintenance hangars appears to be numerous shops and support buildings 37°14'34"N 115°48'53"W, one appearing to be an administrative office complex, and a 1960s era hangar on the flightline, which has been expanded into possibly a logistics support facility and warehouse.

The south side maintenance area 37°14'03"N 115°48'47"W appears to be of relatively new construction, with modern buildings and recently-constructed aircraft taxiways and hangars of the current area. It consists of several double aircraft hangars and what are likely maintenance support buildings. A very large quad-size hangar, 37°13'53"N 115°48'54"W which appears to have four separate sets of doors, along with two other hangars are visible. One hangar just to the east of the quad-sized hangar appears to have a very high roof, twice the height of the other hangars in the area. Another large hangar, possibly several stories tall 37°13'44"N 115°48'40"W is located separately from the other facilities, it having quite wide doors, possibly capable of accommodating very large, wide winged aircraft.

What appears to be the POL (from British: "petrol, oil and lubricant" i.e. gasoline, oil, and grease) area with large above-ground fuel tanks and several aircraft fueling trucks is located on the south side of the station 37°13'24"N 115°48'54"W, along with several areas of disturbed land, possibly indicating new construction. Nearby are what appearing to be several storage tanks 37°13'44"N 115°49'24"W, along with what may be the base security police building and an outdoor rifle range.

On the extreme south end of the station appear to be several high security areas, enclosed by fences and monitored by video cameras on poles. One appears to be a munitions storage area 37°12'48"N 115°48'40"W, given what appear to be munitions storage bunkers similar to ones found on normal Air Force Bases. Two other high security areas are of undetermined use 37°12'28"N 115°48'56"W. A third fenced area, consisting of large dirt mounds are visible; the area having some natural vegetation growing on the mounds. As it is alleged that no material is allowed to leave the base, it may be a burial and disposal site.

In a sense, the government's security problem is self-inflicted. Excessive government secrecy during the Cold War, domestic spying and other scandals by the CIA, the belated declassification of the explanation of UFO sightings later explained in the Roswell report, secret radiation experiments on unwitting citizens by the Department of Energy (then Atomic Energy Commission) have contributed to an intense suspicion among some that the government is "hiding something." This perception is not unjustified given the extensive secrecy surrounding the facility. Of course the government is hiding something -- a secret flight test facility for advanced technology aircraft.

Groom Lake started out as an Army Air Corps Gunnery Range during World War II. In the mid-1950's Lockheed was searching for a remote base to test its new U-2 spy plane. Although the runway on the remote dry lake bed was unusable, the location was deemed to be ideal due to its remoteness and by the summer of 1955 construction of a 5,000 foot runway began, with two hangars and some temporary living quarters. Later surplus Navy military quarters were dismantled, shipped to Groom, and reassembled.

The first U-2 arrived on a C-124 later in 1955. The U-2 was reassembled, checked out, and on August 4, 1955 Tony Levier made the first flight test.

With the arrival of the A-12 program the runway was lengthened to 8,500 feet, fuel storage tanks capable of holding up to 1,320,000 gallon of JP-7 were added, as well as three surplus navy hangars and 100 surplus Navy housing buildings. Eight hangars at the south end of the base were built to house the A-12 spy planes.

By the 1980's a weapons storage area south of the main base was added, with five earth-covered igloos, presumably to support weapons testing for the F-117 program, and possibly the advanced cruise missile program.

Until recently, the facility was supported by one 12,400-long, 100-foot-wide hard surface runway, which extends onto the dry lake bed North, giving it a total length of 25,300 feet or 4.8 miles. Sometime in the early 1990's this runway was deactivated, and replaced by a new 11,960-foot-long, 140-foot-wide runway.

Several indicators suggest that Groom Lake's flight test activity did not end with the F-117 Stealth Fighter. First, construction of a new runway, which must have started sometime after the F-117 program had been made public. Second, the numerous reports by aviation enthusiasts and others of unusual aircraft noise and lights at night in the years since the F-117 became public. Third, the 1995 action by the Department of Interior to withdraw 3,972 acres of Bureau of Land Management land, from public access, creating a security buffer zone to prevent public viewing of military activities at Groom Lake.

Aerial View from a rented private plane showing far view of AREA 51

History of Groom Lake ….. In the Beginning….. 1950's

The Central Intelligence Agency (CIA) established the Groom Lake test facility during Project AQUATONE, through which the Lockheed U-2 spy plane was developed. Capable of flying at high altitude while carrying sophisticated cameras and sensors, the U-2 was equipped with a single jet engine and long, tapered straight wings. For security reasons, CIA officials did not believe that the new airplane should be flown at Edwards Air Force Base, California. At the request of U-2 designer *Clarence L. "Kelly" Johnson* of the Lockheed Advanced Development Projects division (better known as the Skunk Works), project pilot Tony LeVier was dispatched to scout locations around the southwestern United States for a more remote test site.

Early U2 Test Plane at Groom Lake, Nevada.

Richard M. Bissell Jr., director of the AQUATONE program, reviewed dozens of potential test sites with his Air Force liaison, *Col. Osmond J. "Ozzie" Ritland*. None seemed to meet the program's stringent security requirements. Ritland, however, recalled "a little X-shaped field" in southern Nevada that he had flown over many times during his involvement with the nuclear weapons test program.

The airstrip, called Nellis Auxiliary Field No.1, was located just off the eastern side of Groom Dry Lake, about 100 miles north of Las Vegas. It was also just outside the Atomic Energy Commission's (AEC) nuclear proving ground at Yucca Flat.

In April 1955, LeVier, Johnson, Bissell, and Ritland flew to Nevada on a two-day survey of the most promising lakebeds. After examining Groom Lake, it was obvious that this would be an ideal location for the test site, with its excellent flying weather and unparalleled remoteness. The abandoned airfield that Ritland remembered was overgrown and unusable, but the lakebed was excellent. Bissell later described the playa as "a perfect natural landing field...as smooth as a billiard table without anything being done to it."

Groom Lake aka "The Ranch" taken from Aerial Fly Over back in 1960's

Kelly Johnson originally opposed the choice of Groom Lake because it was farther from Burbank than he would have liked, and because of its proximity to the Nevada Proving Ground (later renamed Nevada Test Site). Johnson was understandably concerned about conducting a flight test program adjacent to an active nuclear test site. In fact, Groom Lake lay directly in the primary downwind path of radioactive fallout from atomic blasts.

Kelly Johnson originally opposed the choice of Groom Lake because it was farther from Burbank than he would have liked, and because of its proximity to the Nevada Proving Ground (later renamed Nevada Test Site). Johnson was understandably concerned about conducting a flight test program adjacent to an active nuclear test site. In fact, Groom Lake lay directly in the primary downwind path of radioactive fallout from atomic blasts.

Groom Lake was actually Johnson's second choice for the test location. He had already designed a base around his primary lakebed, dubbed Site I, which would have been a small, temporary camp with only the most rudimentary accommodations. Johnson estimated construction costs for such a facility at $200,000 to $225,000. Base requirements soon changed, however, calling for a permanent facility nearly 300% larger than Johnson's original design. Johnson estimated construction of a larger facility at Site I would cost $450,000. His estimate for building the same facility at Site II (Groom Lake) was $832,000. Johnson ultimately accepted Ritland's recommendation, largely because AEC restrictions would help shield the operation from public view. Bissell secured a presidential action adding the Groom Lake area to the AEC proving ground. Ritland wrote three memos to Air Force Headquarters, the AEC, and the Air Force Training Command that administered the gunnery range. Assistant Air Force Secretary for Research and Development Trevor Gardner signed the memos, this ensuring that range activities would not impinge on the new test site. Security for project AQUATONE was now assured.

During the last week of April 1955, Johnson met with CIA officials in Washington, D.C. and discussed progress on the base and the AQUATONE program. His proposal to name the base **"Paradise Ranch"** was accepted. It was an ironic choice that, he later admitted was "a dirty trick to lure workers to the program." The AQUATONE, officially designated U-2 became known as "The Angel from Paradise Ranch." The base itself was usually just called "The Ranch" by those who worked there.

On 4 May 1955, LeVier, Kammerer, and Johnson returned to Groom Lake in Lockheed's *Bonanza*. Using a compass and surveying equipment, they defined a 5,000-foot, north-south runway on the southwest corner of the lakebed and designated a site for the camp.

On 18 May 1955, Seth R. Woodruff Jr., manager of the AEC Las Vegas Field Office, announced that he had "instructed the Reynolds Electrical and Engineering Co., Inc. [REECo] to begin preliminary work on a small, satellite Nevada Test Site installation." He noted that work was already underway at the location "a few miles northeast of Yucca Flat and within the Las Vegas Bombing and Gunnery Range." Woodruff said that the installation would include "a runway, dormitories, and a few other buildings for housing equipment." The facility was described as "essentially temporary." The press release was distributed to 18 media outlets in Nevada and Utah including a dozen newspapers, four radio stations, and two television stations. This, in effect, constituted Area 51's birth announcement.

Watertown Operations

LeVier and fellow Lockheed test pilot Bob Matye spent nearly a month removing surface debris from the playa. Levier also drew up a proposal to mark four three-mile-long runways on the lakebed at a cost of $450.00. Johnson, however, refused to approve the expense, citing a lack of funds. Drilling resulted in discovery of a limited water supply, but trouble with the well soon developed. Top priorities for the test site included hangars, a road, offices, living accommodations, and various support facilities. Since Lockheed did not have a license to build on the nuclear proving ground, they gave their drawings to a contractor who did: Silas Mason Construction Company.

The Lockheed group hid their identity behind the fictional company name "CLJ", using Johnson's initials.

The fledgling base consisted of a single, paved 5,000-foot runway, three hangars, a control tower, and rudimentary accommodations for test personnel. The base's few amenities included a movie theatre and volleyball court. Additionally, there was a mess hall, several water wells, and fuel storage tanks. CIA, Air Force, and Lockheed personnel began arriving in July 1955 and Richard Newton of the CIA was assigned as base commander. The test site soon acquired a new name: Watertown. According to some accounts, the site was named after CIA director Allen Dulles' birthplace in Watertown, New York. It is still listed as a member of Alamo Township in Lincoln County.

The "Chill Area Lounge" of Groom Lake facility where the boys would relax after a hard day of flight testing.

The first U-2 was transported, disassembled, to Watertown in an Air Force C-124 cargo plane. It had no serial number and was designated Article 341. Tony LeVier made the unofficial first flight in the U-2 during a taxi test on 29 July. He piloted the first planned test flight on 4 August.

After completing Phase I (contractor) testing LeVier was replaced by Lockheed test pilots Bob Matye and Ray Goudey who expanded the airplane's altitude envelope to its operational limits. By November 1955, the test group also included Robert Sieker and Robert Schumacher.

On 17 November 1955, tragedy struck the AQUATONE project. An Air Force C-54M (44-9068) transporting personnel to the secret base crashed near the top of Mt. Charleston, about 20 miles west of Las Vegas. Nine civilians and five military personnel were killed. There were no survivors. After the accident, Lockheed assumed responsibility for transporting personnel to Watertown. A company-owned C-47 was used to ferry pilots, technicians, and special visitors to the test site.

By the beginning of 1956, four U-2 aircraft had been delivered to the Groom Lake test site. By the end of March the fleet consisted of nine aircraft, and six CIA pilots were undergoing flight training at the site. Four experienced instructor pilots trained three classes in ground school, followed by landing practice in a T-33 and, eventually, solo flights in the U-2. The second class underwent training at Groom between May and August 1956. It included Francis Gary Powers, who would later win dubious fame after being shot down and captured while flying a U-2 over the Soviet Union. The third training class was conducted in late 1956.

Several U-2 airplanes were lost in accidents including the prototype. Two CIA pilots were killed and one escaped without injury. Lockheed test pilot Robert Sieker perished in Article 341.

Atomic Blasts

Nuclear weapons testing at nearby Yucca Flat affected test and training activities at Watertown. During the first two years of the Watertown operation, the atomic proving ground had been quiet as all full-scale testing was taking place at Bikini and Eniwetok atolls in the Pacific Ocean. That changed in the summer of 1957 with Operation Plumbbob.

Because Groom Lake was downwind of the proving ground, Watertown personnel were required to evacuate the base prior to each detonation. The AEC, in turn, tried to ensure that expected fallout from any given shot would be limited so as to permit re-entry of personnel within three to four weeks. Evacuation plans included notification procedures, adequate security for classified areas, means to inform evacuees when they might return, and radiation monitoring. If a nuclear test was postponed, which occurred frequently, Watertown personnel were required to evacuate prior to each new shot date.

All personnel at the base were required to wear radiation badges to measure their exposure to fallout. AEC Radiological Safety (Rad-Safe) officers briefed Watertown personnel on nuclear testing activities and radiation safety, and presented a film called *Atomic Tests In Nevada*. They also made arrangements for radiation monitors to visit the airbase whenever fallout was anticipated in the Watertown area.

Project 57, the first shot of the new series, took place on Watertown's doorstep. On 24 April 1957, the AEC conducted a safety experiment with an XW-25 warhead just five miles northwest of Groom Lake in Area 13. Only the bottom detonator of the device was fired, simulating an accident not involving a nuclear detonation. The test was designed to disperse a known quantity of plutonium over a defined area to develop effective monitoring and decontamination procedures.

Following several delays, full-scale nuclear detonations began on 28 May. Shot BOLTZMANN, a 12-kiloton blast, was fired from a 500-foot tower on northern Yucca Flat. After more delays, two minor blasts, FRANKLIN and LASSEN, were fired during the first week of June. These tests came near the intended end of Watertown's existence as an active installation.

The base had always been considered a temporary facility. As U-2 testing began to wind down and CIA pilot classes finished their training, Watertown became a virtual ghost town.

By mid-June 1957, the U-2 test operation had moved to Edwards and operational U-2 aircraft were assigned to the 4028th Strategic Reconnaissance Squadron at Laughlin, Texas.

On 18 June 1957, a test code-named WILSON deposited fallout on Watertown. The AEC measured radiation exposure inside the evacuated buildings and vehicles at the base to study the effectiveness of various materials in shielding against fallout. In effect, Watertown served as a laboratory to determine the shielding qualities of typical building materials that might be found in any American town. WILSON was followed by the 37-kiloton PRISCILLA shot at Frenchman Flat on 24 June.

HOOD, the sixth nuclear shot of Plumbbob, was truly spectacular. It also caused substantial damage to the Groom Lake airbase. The device was lifted by balloon to a height of 1,500 feet over Yucca Flat, about 14 miles southwest of Watertown. On 5 July 1957, HOOD exploded with a yield of 74 kilotons. It was the most powerful airburst ever detonated within the continental United States. HOOD's shockwave shattered windows on two buildings at Watertown, and broke a ventilator panel on one of the dormitories.

A maintenance building on the west side of the base and the supply warehouse west of the hangars suffered serious damage as their metal roll-up doors buckled.

Despite the end of U-2 operations and the near constant rain of fallout, security at the Watertown facility remained tight. On 28 July 1957, a civilian pilot was detained after making an emergency landing at Watertown airstrip. Edward K. Current Jr., an employee of Douglas Aircraft Company, had been on a cross-country training flight when he became lost, ran low on fuel, and decided to land at Groom Lake. He was held overnight and questioned before being released.

On 20 June 1958, 38,400 acres of land encompassing the Watertown base was officially withdrawn from public access under Public Land Order 1662. This rectangular addition to the Nevada Test Site was designated Area 51. Shortly after this, the National Aeronautics and Space Administration (NASA) secured permission to designate Groom Lake as a contingency landing site for the X-15 rocket plane. It was, however, never needed for this purpose. For two years following the departure of the U-2 fleet from Watertown, the base was fairly quiet.

New Lease on Life

Dramatic changes came to Area 51 with the advent of Project OXCART, through which Lockheed's proposed successor to the U-2 was developed. The OXCART aircraft was a sleek, powerful looking aircraft with a long tapered forward fuselage with blended chines. A rounded delta wing supported two turbo-ramjet engines capable of boosting the aircraft to Mach 3.2 at altitudes in excess of 90,000 feet. Twin, inwardly canted tails and a sawtooth internal structure in the wing edges contributed to a low overall RCS. The airframe was constructed mostly of titanium, with asbestos-fiberglass and phenyl silane composites in the leading and trailing edges, chines, and tails for RCS reduction. The final designation for the OXCART aircraft was A-12, with the "A" standing for "Archangel."

The Skunk Works team in Burbank built a full-scale mock-up of the A-12 during the spring of 1959 for RCS tests to be performed by Edgerton, Germeshausen & Grier (EG&G) of Las Vegas. On 10 September, EG&G agreed to move its radar test facility from Indian Springs, Nevada, to Groom Lake for security reasons. A special pylon was constructed on a paved loop road on the west side of the lakebed. The A-12 mock-up was moved from Burbank to the test site on a specially designed trailer truck. By 18 November, the model was in place. It took 18 months of testing and adjustment before the A-12 achieved a satisfactory RCS.

Naturally, a secret location was needed for testing the triple-sonic A-12. Ten U.S. Air Force bases programmed for closure were considered, but none provided adequate security, and annual operating costs were prohibitive for most. Groom Lake was selected although it lacked personnel accommodations, fuel storage, and an adequate runway. Lockheed planners estimated cost requirements for monthly fuel consumption, hangars, maintenance facilities, housing, and runway specifications. The CIA then produced a plan for construction and engineering. A CIA cover story stated that the facilities were being prepared for radar studies to be conducted by an engineering firm with USAF support. Construction at the site, referred to as Project 51, was performed by Reynolds Electrical and Engineering Company (REECo).

Base construction began on 1 September 1960 and continued on a double-shift schedule until 1 June 1964. Workers were ferried in from Burbank and Las Vegas on C-54 aircraft. Since the existing 5,000-foot runway was incapable of supporting the weight of the A-12, a new airstrip (runway 14/32) was constructed between 7 September and 15 November 1960. The A-12 required a runway at least 8,500 feet long. About 25,000 cubic yards of concrete were poured to make the airstrip. A 10,000-foot asphalt extension, for emergency use, cut diagonally across the southwest corner of the lakebed. An Archimedes curve approximately two miles across was marked on the dry lake so that an A-12 pilot approaching the end of the overrun could abort to the playa instead of plunging the aircraft into the sagebrush. Area 51 pilots called it "The Hook." For crosswind landings two unpaved airstrips (runways 9/27 and 03/21) were marked on the dry lakebed.

Kelly Johnson had been reluctant to construct a standard Air Force runway, with expansion joints every 25-feet, because he feared the joints would set up undesirable vibrations in the OXCART aircraft. At his suggestion, the 150-foot-wide runway was constructed in segments, each made up of six 25-foot-wide longitudinal sections. The sections were 150 feet long and staggered. This layout put most of the expansion joints parallel to the direction of aircraft roll, and reduced the frequency of the joints.

Essential facilities were completed by August 1961. Three surplus U.S. Navy hangars were obtained, dismantled, and erected on the base's north side. They were designated as Hangar 4, 5, and 6. A fourth, Hangar 7, was built new. More than 130 U.S. Navy surplus Babbitt duplex housing units were transported to the base and made ready for occupancy. The original U-2 hangars were converted to maintenance and machine shops. Facilities in the main cantonment area included workshops and buildings for storage and administration, a commissary, control tower, fire station, and housing.

It was determined that 500,000 gallons of JP-7 fuel would be needed monthly to support the OXCART program. By early 1962 a fuel farm, including seven tanks 1,320,000-gallon capacity was complete. Older buildings were repaired, and additional facilities were constructed as necessary.

A reservoir pond, surrounded by trees, served as a recreational area one mile north of the base. Other recreational facilities included a gymnasium, movie theatre, and a baseball diamond. On 15 November 1961, USAF Col. Robert J. Holbury was named commander of the secret base, with the CIA's Werner Weiss as his deputy. The base was still a CIA facility, and would remain so for another 18 years.

OXCART and the *Roadrunners*

Support aircraft began arriving in the spring of 1962. These included eight McDonnell F-101B/F *Voodoos* for training and chase, a Lockheed C-130 *Hercules* for cargo transport, U-8A for administrative use, Cessna 180 for liaison use, and Kaman HH-43 helicopter for search and rescue. A Lockheed F-104A/G (56-0801) was supplied as a chase plane during the OXCART flight test period.

In January 1962, the Federal Aviation Administration (FAA) expanded the restricted airspace in the vicinity of Groom Lake. The lakebed became the center of a 600-square-mile addition to restricted area R-4808N. Restricted continuously at all altitudes, the airspace occupies the center of the Nellis Air Force Range.

The prototype A-12 (60-6924) made its unofficial first flight on 25 April 1962 with Louis W. Schalk at the controls. He flew the aircraft less than two miles at an altitude of about 20 feet. The following day, Schalk made a 40-minute flight. An official "first flight" on 30 April was witnessed by a number of dignitaries including Richard Bissell (even though he had resigned from the CIA in February) and FAA chief Najeeb Halaby.

OXCART pilot Jack Weeks nicknamed the A-12 *Cygnus* after the constellation of the swan. Initially, all 15 A-12 aircraft were based at Groom Lake and operated by the 1129th Special Activities Squadron *Roadrunners*, commanded by Col. Hugh "Slip" Slater. A-12 test aircraft (60-6924, 60-6925, 60-6928), and the TA-12 trainer (60-6927) were housed in hangars at the north end of the flightline. Operational aircraft were kept in Hangars 9 through 16 at the southern end of the base. Security was paramount. Even the existence of the A-12 was a closely guarded secret.

With the assistance of the CIA, the U.S. Air Force entered into an agreement with Lockheed to build three prototypes of an interceptor version of the A-12 under project KEDLOCK. Known as the AF-12 (later changed to YF-12A), the design included a second crew position, air-to-air missiles, and fire-control radar in the nose. The first YF-12A (60-6934) made its maiden flight on 7 August 1963 with James Eastham at the controls. After President Lyndon B. Johnson announced the existence of the aircraft in March 1964, the YF-12A test was program moved to Edwards.

Dreamland

Construction of the Area 51 facility was completed in 1965. The site population had grown to 1,835, and contractors were working three shifts a day. Lockheed-owned *Constellation* and C-47 aircraft made several flights a day ferrying personnel from Burbank and Las Vegas to Groom Lake. Hughes and Honeywell had facilities on site, and Pratt & Whitney operated an engine test stand. Perkin-Elmer set up a special building in which to work on the equipment bays in the nose of the A-12.

During the course of the OXCART program, Kelly Johnson developed an unmanned reconnaissance drone that could be launched from a modified version of the A-12. Codenamed TAGBOARD, the drone was a ramjet-powered vehicle capable of reaching 90,000 feet at Mach 3.3. Two OXCART-type aircraft (60-6940 and 60-6941) were purpose-built to launch TAGBOARD. Each was equipped with a rear seat for a Launch Systems Operator (LSO), and a dorsal launch pylon. The TAGBOARD was designated D-21 and the launch aircraft were given the unusual designation M-21. The first D-21 was launched 5 March 1966.

Unfortunately, the second M-21 was lost during the fourth TAGBOARD launch, when the drone collided with the launch aircraft. Pilot Bill Park ejected safely and was rescued 150 miles off Point Mugu, California. His LSO Ray Torick ejected but drowned before he could be rescued. The tragic loss of an aircraft and crewmember ended the use of OXCART as a launch aircraft, but it did not spell the end of TAGBOARD.

In 1967, the D-21 received a new lease on life. Under the SENIOR BOWL program, the drone was reconfigured for launch from a B-52 and redesignated D-21B. It was reconfigured for launch from inboard wing pylons and propelled to ramjet-ignition speed by a rocket booster. Two B-52H aircraft (60-0036 and 61-0021) from the 4200th Support Squadron at Beale Air Force Base, California, were sent to Groom Lake for the test program. The unofficial first flight occurred on 28 September 1967, when a D-21B was accidentally dropped due to a mechanical failure. The first actual launch attempt took place 6 November. Flight-testing continued through July 1969. The program was terminated in 1971 after only four operational flights.

At some point during the late 1960s, Area 51 gained a new nickname: DREAMLAND. This purportedly was derived from *DREAM-LAND*, a poem by Edgar Allan Poe. It describes lakes that "endlessly outspread" with waters "lone and dead." More to the point, Poe admonishes that "the traveler, traveling through it, may not-dare not openly view it; Never its mysteries are exposed, to the weak human eye unclosed." Coincidence or not, it is certainly an apt description of Area 51.

Several A-12 airplanes were deployed from Area 51 to Kadena, Japan, for Operation Black Shield reconnaissance flights over Southeast Asia in 1967. One of the airplanes was lost during a training mission and the pilot presumed killed. Four A-12s had been lost in accidents at or near Area 51, but only one of these was fatal. The surviving airframes were retired in June 1968 and placed in storage at a Lockheed facility in Palmdale. The A-12 remained unknown to the public for 12 more years while the YF-12A and later SR-71 became some of the most famous airplanes in the world.

Red Hats

Beginning in the late 1960s, and for several decades, DREAMLAND played host to a motley assortment of Soviet-built aircraft. The first such program, in 1968, involved technical and tactical evaluations of a MiG-21F-13 that the Israeli Defense Forces had acquired from an Iraqi defector. Called HAVE DOUGHNUT, the project was a joint effort of the U.S. Air Force Systems Command, Tactical Air Command, and the U.S. Navy's Air Test and Evaluation Squadron Four (VX-4). The MiG-21 was flown against nearly all U.S. combat aircraft types, allowing Air Force and Navy pilots to develop improved tactics for combating Eastern bloc aircraft.

A similar evaluation program in 1969, called HAVE DRILL/HAVE FERRY, involved two Syrian MiG-17F fighters. As in the earlier program, a small group of Air Force and Navy pilots conducted mock dogfights with the MiG-17. Selected instructors from the Navy's Top Gun school at NAS Miramar, California, were chosen to fly against the MiGs for familiarization purposes.

Testing of foreign technology aircraft continued and expanded throughout the 1970s and 1980s. Additional MiG-17, MiG-21, MiG-23, Su-7B, Su-22 and other aircraft underwent intensive evaluations. The 6513th Test Squadron *Red Hats* from the Air Force Flight Test Center (AFFTC) at Edwards conducted technical evaluation sorties. The 4477th Test and Evaluation Squadron *Red Eagles*, headquartered at Nellis Air Force Base, Nevada, performed tactical evaluations. In April 1984 Lt. Gen. Robert M. Bond, Vice Commander of Air Force Systems Command, lost his life in the crash of a MiG-23 during an orientation flight.

Area 51 also hosted another foreign materiel evaluation program called HAVE GLIB. This involved testing Soviet tracking and missile control radar systems. A complex of actual and replica Soviet-type threat systems began to grow around "Slater Lake" (the pond, which had been named after the former *Roadrunners* commander), a mile northwest of the main base. They were arranged to simulate a Soviet-style air defense complex.

The Air Force began funding improvements to Area 51 in 1977 under project SCORE EVENT. In 1979, the CIA transferred control of the test site to the AFFTC at Edwards. It was now a remote operating location of the Center, and was designated Detachment 3, AFFTC. Sam Mitchell, the last CIA commander of Area 51, relinquished command to Lt. Col. Larry D. McClain.

Pioneers of Stealth

In November 1977, a C-5 arrived at Groom Lake carrying the Lockheed HAVE BLUE prototype. HAVE BLUE was the first airplane designed to be virtually invisible to radar. The single-seat jet looked like a faceted arrowhead with two inwardly canted tail fins. Its boxy, angular fuselage and wings contributed to its low RCS. It was eventually covered with radar absorbent material (RAM). Such shaping and material treatments rendered the airplane "low observable" or "stealthy."

The first HAVE BLUE vehicle, Article 1001, was flown to demonstrate handling characteristics. The second was scheduled to carry out tests of the low observable (L.O.) characteristics. After arriving at the test site, Article 1001 underwent a few weeks of flight control, engine, and taxi tests. Every time HAVE BLUE was rolled out of its hangar, uncleared personnel at the base were sequestered to prevent them from seeing the aircraft.

HAVE BLUE first flew on 1 December 1977 with Lockheed test pilot Bill Park at the controls. Skunkworks chief Ben Rich, his predecessor "Kelly" Johnson, and Ken Perko of the Advanced Research Projects Agency were on hand to witness the event. The flight was also monitored by the White House Situation Room and Tactical Air Command Headquarters at Langley Air Force Base, Virginia. Article 1001 completed 36 flights before being lost in a non-fatal accident.

Article 1002, the low observables technology demonstrator, made its first flight on 20 July 1978 piloted by Lt. Col. Norman "Ken" Dyson. It made 52 flights against sophisticated U.S. and Soviet ground-based radars, and the E-3 Airborne Warning And Control System (AWACS). Article 1002 was lost on 11 July 1979 due to an engine fire. At the time of the accident only one final test flight had been scheduled for the HAVE BLUE program.

In October 1978, Lockheed conducted the first test of its stealth cruise missile, code named SENIOR PROM. Six prototypes were built. They somewhat resembled a subscale, unmanned version of the HAVE BLUE, but with outwardly-canted tails, narrow wings, and a single jet intake located where the cockpit would have been. The demonstrator models were launched from a DC-130. Thirteen test flights were made, and all six vehicles recovered. The recovery method involved deploying a ballistic parachute and inflating a ventral landing bag. Although the SENIOR PROM tests were successful, the contract for production of a stealthy Advanced Cruise Missile (ACM) went to the less expensive General Dynamics AGM-129A. SENIOR PROM was cancelled in 1981.

On 17 January 1981 the Lockheed test team at Groom Lake accepted delivery of the first SENIOR TREND Full Scale Development (FSD) prototype, Ship 780, designated YF-117A. Like the HAVE BLUE, it too resembled a faceted arrowhead, except that the tails were canted outward in a "V" shape. Ship 780 first flew on 18 June 1981 with Lockheed test pilot Hal Farley at the controls.

By early 1982, four more YF-117A airplanes were operating out of the southern end of the base, known as the "Southend" or "Baja Groom Lake." After finding a large scorpion in their offices, the test team adopted it as their mascot and dubbed themselves the "Baja Scorpions."

As the Baja Scorpions tested the FSD airframes, production F-117A aircraft were shipped to DREAMLAND for acceptance testing. Following functional check flights and L.O. verification, the operational airplanes were deployed to the 4450th Tactical Group at Tonopah Test Range, in the northwest corner of the Nellis Range.

While HAVE BLUE and SENIOR TREND were being put through their paces in Nevada, the Air Force, Defense Advanced Research Projects Agency, and Northrop Aircraft Corporation teamed up to develop a new aircraft. Code-named TACIT BLUE, it was originally designed as a technology demonstrator for a low-observable surveillance aircraft with a low-probability-of-intercept radar, and other sensors, that could operate close to the front line of battle with a high degree of survivability. Although plans for a stealthy surveillance aircraft were abandoned, TACIT BLUE provided important data that aided in the development of several other weapons systems. These included the B-2 advanced technology bomber, the AGM-137 Tri-Service Standoff Attack Missile (TSSAM), and the PAVE MOVER program (which led to the development of the E-8 Joint-STARS aircraft). TACIT BLUE was the first aircraft to demonstrate a low RCS using curved surfaces.

Only one complete TACIT BLUE prototype was constructed. A second, partially completed, shell was built as a back up. The aircraft featured a curved upper surface with a flush dorsal intake. Twin turbofan engines gave it a cruising speed of about 260 miles per hour. TACIT BLUE sported tapered straight wings and two square fins in a widely spaced V-tail configuration. Flat, squared "platypus bills" on the nose and tail gave it a nearly rectangular planform. From the side, TACIT BLUE resembled a whale, complete with a blowhole. In fact, the TACIT BLUE team members nicknamed it "*The Whale*," and referred to themselves as "Whalers."

The nearly complete TACIT BLUE aircraft was trucked to the test site in several large crates for final assembly in Hangar 8. Northrop test pilot Richard G. Thomas, made the first flight of TACIT BLUE on 5 February 1982. TACIT BLUE made a total of 135 sorties, flown by a team of one contractor and four Air Force pilots. Thomas made 70 of the flights, including the 100th sortie on 27 April 1984. The final flight took place on 14 February 1985. Following a highly successful test program, the one-of-a-kind aircraft was stored in the Area 51 "boneyard." In April 1996, it was declassified and delivered to the U.S. Air Force Museum in Dayton, Ohio for permanent display.

Expansion and Acquisition

Because Groom Lake's site population had grown substantially, the C-54 aircraft had become inadequate to transport all the personnel. The Air Force contracted EG&G Special Projects, McCarran Operations, in Las Vegas to transport commuters to DREAMLAND in a fleet of six Boeing 737-200s. These flights, using the call sign JANET, carried personnel and freight daily from Las Vegas, Palmdale, and Burbank to Groom Lake, and later Tonopah Test Range.

Beginning in 1979, the Air Force began actively discouraging, and at times preventing, any public or private entry to the Groom Mountains, north of Groom Lake. Air Force personnel claimed it was "in the interest of public safety and national defense." This was about the time the Air Force took control of the Groom Lake facility from the CIA. Not only were hunters and hikers excluded from the mountains north of Groom Lake, but also citizens with mining claims in the area. In 1981, the Air Force discreetly requested that 89,600 acres of land encompassing the range be legally withdrawn from public use. The process of approving this request took several years. It also resulted in a battle between the government, citizens, and various special interest groups (such as the Sierra Club). In the end, the government won.

By March 1984, government security personnel prohibited travel and controlled access along the Groom Lake road northeast of the lakebed. In August, the Groom Mountains withdrawal was approved subject to an environmental impact statement (EIS) and public hearings. Congress officially authorized the withdrawal in 1987, and the following year President Ronald Reagan signed legislation making the Groom Mountains part of the Nellis Air Force Range until 2003. None of the documentation (EIS, archeological surveys, etc.) mentioned Area 51 or the Groom Lake test facility.

As public access became increasingly restricted, facilities in the DREAMLAND complex increased dramatically in number and size. During the mid-1980s new dormitories were constructed to replace the Babbitt housing. Several large water tanks were added to supply the base. Hangar 18 was built near the south ramp. Four "Rubber Duck" temporary aircraft shelters were erected near the Southend for use by TAC personnel during F-117A acceptance tests. Many new facilities were built and, by the end of the decade the "Rubber Duck" shelters were replaced with metal hangars (Hangars 20 through 23). Recreational facilities expanded to include the softball diamond and movie theatre, as well as a swimming pool and tennis courts. The latter are located adjacent to *Sam's Place*, the local saloon and recreation center.

Runway 14/32 was extended 4,600 feet further southeast of the lakebed because the north end was subject to flooding during the rainy season. The runway now consisted of a 13,530-foot strip of concrete, 150 feet wide. The 10,000-foot hard asphalt extension and lakebed abort curve remained, but fell into disuse. The cost of maintaining the concrete runway became increasingly prohibitive. AFFTC leadership determined that the most cost effective solution would be to keep the southern half of the airstrip open until a new, parallel paved strip (runway 14L/32R) could be completed. The new concrete strip was constructed in 1991. It does not extend out onto the lakebed, but a lead-in line to the abort curve was marked on the lakebed. The northern half of the original runway (14R/32L) was closed, reducing its length to about 10,000 feet. It was finally closed along its entire length. In 2001 the South Delta Taxiway was marked as runway 12/30. It is approximately 5,420-feet-long and 150-feet-wide, with convenient access to the Southend ramp. A new central taxiway was constructed in 2003 to support runway 14L/32R.

The Groom Lake base received some unwanted publicity in 1994 when a number of former workers from the site sued the government. They claimed their health had been damaged by inhaling toxic fumes from the burning of waste materials in open trenches near the main base. For four months after the suit was filed, the government determinedly denied the existence of the base itself. Finally, however, it was forced to acknowledge that there was "an operating location at Groom Lake," but refused to provide a legal name for it citing "national security" concerns.

Air Force secretary Sheila Widnall declared that the facility "has no actual operating name per se." This was partially true. Since the Air Force had taken control of the facility in 1979 they had not used the name "Area 51," but instead simply referred to the operating location as DET 3, AFFTC,. Attorney Jonathan Turley tried on behalf of the plaintiffs to get the government to provide a legal name for the site, but was stymied at every turn.

The lawsuit forced the government to formally acknowledge the Groom Lake facility in order to keep its secrets. On 29 September 1995, President Bill Clinton signed Presidential Determination No. 95-45, which stated in part: "I find that it is in the paramount interest of the United States to exempt the United States Air Force's operating location near Groom Lake, Nevada from any applicable requirement for the disclosure to unauthorized persons of classified information concerning that operating location."

Space Invaders

Area 51's secret nature has bred rumor and speculation among fringe groups that believe the U.S. government is hiding captured extraterrestrial spacecraft, or even aliens (dead or alive) at the site. Such stories have been circulating since at least the late 1970s. Starting in 1989, groups of UFO believers began to camp out near the Nellis Range boundaries near Groom Lake to watch for "flying saucers."

As the news media caught wind of these "saucer base expeditions," print and television publicity was met with stony silence and terse denials from Air Force officials. This further fueled public speculation, spawned new rumors, and attracted still more publicity. Camera crews from around the world descended on the remote and forbidding Nevada desert. Local entrepreneurs capitalized on the situation by selling all manner of Area 51 souvenirs, videos, and visitor's guides.

The DET 3 security force, comprised of Air Force and civilian contractor personnel, worked overtime to intercept the "alien" invaders. A few civilians discovered that some nearby hilltops with a bird's-eye view of the secret base had been overlooked in the government's Groom Range land grab. Word quickly spread. Tourists sometimes camped on the hilltops 24 hours a day for days at a time. Flight test operations and even ground activities had to be postponed or cancelled. In April 1995, the Air Force seized 5,000 more acres of public land to prevent civilians from viewing the base.

Out of the Black, Into the Blue

While many current and historic programs at Dreamland remain classified, some information has been released to the public. Formal announcements, published technical papers, and official personnel biographies often reveal details of previously "black" projects. In the absence of official information, rumors abound.

The Northrop B-2 *Spirit* Advanced Technology Bomber has frequently been seen over DREAMLAND. Prototypes from the B-2 Combined Test Force at Edwards AFB and operational aircraft from a detachment of the 509th Bomb Wing at Whiteman AFB, Missouri have flown against Soviet-type radar systems and the Dynamic Coherent Measurement System (DYCOMS). Known on-site as Project 100, this airborne RCS range has been used to measure the L.O. characteristics of all U.S. stealth aircraft from the F-117A to the F/A-22A.

Project HAVE GLASS was undertaken in 1982 to significantly reduce the RCS of the General Dynamics F-16 *Fighting Falcon*. A series of modifications included RAM coatings and fillings, reflective materials, and component shape changes. The results were verified using the DYCOMS.

In 1983 AeroVironment received CIA sponsorship to build a proof-of-concept high-altitude, solar-powered, radio-controlled UAV called HALSOL. It was essentially a rectangular flying wing made from lightweight materials. Initial test flights were powered by eight electric motors using silver-zinc batteries. HALSOL made nine test flights.

Maj. Frank T. Birk piloted the first flight of a "classified technology advanced demonstration prototype" at Groom Lake in 1983. He made the first flight and two additional flights for handling qualities evaluation and performance envelope expansion testing.

On 2 October 1992, the 413th Flight Test Squadron was activated at Edwards to provide test and evaluation capability for electronic warfare (EW) systems. This change supported a consolidation of all Air Force electronic combat assets in the western United States. The mission of the 413th included planning, providing for, and organizing worldwide ground and flight tests of EW systems and equipment. A detachment of the 413th FLTS conducted EW testing at Groom Lake. In May 2004 the 413th Flight Test Squadron was inactivated as part of another consolidation and realignment of EW assets that were then absorbed by the EW Directorate at Edwards.

In the early 1990s Dennis F. "Bones" Sager was handpicked to lead a "classified prototype aircraft" called the YF-113G from design to first flight. As a fighter pilot and experimental test pilot, Sager accumulated over 2,900 flight hours in 54 aircraft types including Soviet fighters at Groom Lake. He was first Air Force pilot to fly the YF-113G.

On October 18, 2002, Boeing uncloaked its secret Bird of Prey technology demonstrator that was used to pioneer revolutionary advances in low-observables, aircraft design, and rapid prototyping. The project, initiated in 1992, remained highly classified even after its conclusion in 1999.

A Boeing spokesman announced that it had been declassified "because the technologies and capabilities developed [during the program] have become industry standards, and it is no longer necessary to conceal the aircraft's existence." Phantom Works chief test pilot Rudy Haug piloted the maiden flight of Bird of Prey in the fall of 1996. After McDonnell Douglas merged with Boeing on August 1, 1997, The Boeing Company continued to fund the project. Three pilots flew only 38 missions between 1996and 1999.

Doug Benjamin, assigned to the Special Projects Flight Test Squadron, was the only Air Force pilot to fly the Bird of Prey. He flew 21 test flights including envelope expansion, mission utility, and tactical applications sorties. Following Benjamin's retirement from the military service in 2000, it was revealed that he had flown three other classified aircraft.

Joseph A. "Broadway Joe" Lanni flew first flights of two classified prototypes during the 1990s. One of them was designated YF-24. Between 1992 and 1997 he flew hundreds of sorties in 10 different classified aircraft to evaluate performance, flying qualities, avionics, and military utility. His assignment to the "Red Hats" during this time suggests that many of these aircraft were foreign types but some may have been entirely new aircraft.

There have also been reports of Advanced Concept Technology Demonstrator (ACTD) projects undergoing flight tests at Groom Lake. Other projects at the site may include stealth helicopters, weapons development, unmanned aerial vehicles, and avionics testing.

RCS (Radar Cross Section Testing of SR71)

"LISTENING IN ON AREA 51 & BEYOND!"

WELCOME TO TECHNOLOGY SECTION OF THE BOOK.

What is a radio scanner?

The air around you is bursting with radio waves. You know that you can flip on the AM/FM radio in your car and receive dozens of stations. You can flip on a CB radio and receive 40 more. You can flip on a TV and receive numerous broadcast channels. Cell phones can send and receive hundreds of frequencies. And this is just the tip of the radio spectrum iceberg. Literally tens of thousands of other radio broadcasts and conversations are zipping past you as you read this article -- police officers, firefighters, military, ambulance drivers, paramedics, sanitation workers, space shuttle astronauts, race car drivers, and even babies with their monitors are transmitting radio waves all around you at this very moment!

To tap into this ocean of electromagnetic dialogue and hear what all of these people are talking about, all you need is a **scanner**. A scanner is basically a radio receiver capable of receiving multiple signals. Generally, scanners pick up signals in the VHF to UHF range (see How the Radio Spectrum Works for details on these frequency bands).

The 2-way radio systems heard on scanners are similar in many ways to radio signals heard on commercial FM radio and television. All radio signals are examples of electromagnetic waves, like light waves, infrared, and X-rays. The diagram below shows relationship between radio frequencies and other electromagnetic waves. The 2-way radio systems you will hear on a scanner radio are in the "VHF" and "UHF" part of the spectrum.

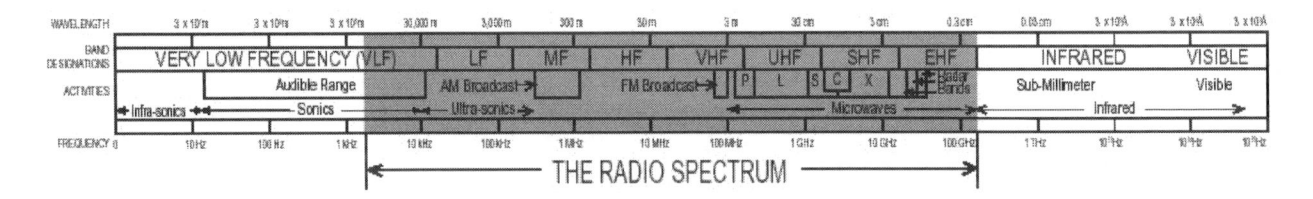

Radio scanners are very portable and affordable. In this article, we will look at the basics of scanner operation, examine radio scanning as a hobby, and show you how to get started listening to public airwaves you may not have known existed!

Scanner Basics

Scanners typically operate in three modes:

Scan

Manual scan

Search

In **scan mode**, the receiver constantly changes frequencies in a set order looking for a frequency that has someone transmitting. Lights or panel-mounted displays show what channel or frequency is in use as the scanner stops on a given frequency. The frequencies can be preprogrammed on some models or manually set on practically all models.

In **manual scan mode**, the user taps a button or turns a dial to manually step through preprogrammed frequencies one frequency at a time.

In **search mode**, the receiver is set to search between two sets of frequencies within a given band. This mode is useful when a user does not know a frequency, but wants to know what frequencies are active in a given area. If the frequency the scanner stops at during a search is interesting, the user can store that frequency in the radio scanner and use it in scan mode.

Scanner Features

Radio scanners can be either portable, with rechargeable battery packs, or desktop, like a regular radio. Scanners are gaining popularity with consumers. With the huge popularity of NASCAR racing, many people now use scanners at auto racing events to eavesdrop on the crew-driver communications at races. At a typical race, there are hundreds of frequencies in use. Each team has two or three frequencies, while race control, the sanctioning organization, the medical, fire and track crews and many others each have assigned frequencies during the race.

Some of the recently released scanners are capable of tracking municipalities and police frequencies in the 800-megahertz (MHz) range. This is known as **trunk tracking** of computer-controlled trunked radio networks.

Higher-end scanners can be controlled by the serial port [USB] of a personal computer using special software. This helps the user with the logging of stations as well as with duplicating the scanner controls within the software application.

Many models receive the NOAA weather radio broadcasts. This can be a very useful feature during pending tornadoes or hurricanes.

The **controls** on a radio scanner can vary, but practically all of them have:

Volume

Squelch - This is an adjustable control that keeps the speaker muted (quiet and free from static) when a station is not transmitting. It works whether the radio is scanning, searching or manually stepping through stored frequencies. CB radios also have this control.

WX button - This is common on some newer models. This button typically does a mini-scan of some factory-written frequencies that receive the nationwide NOAA weather broadcast reports.

Numeric keypad - This is used for entering frequencies or in combination with the "Limit" button, used for entering upper and lower ranges of a search between two frequencies. The keypad also lets you enter frequencies found during a search. More expensive models automatically store frequencies found during a search. Buy a copy of "Police Call" (you can get a used one for next to nothing at Amazon.com or download from numerous web sites) to get some frequencies for your area. **Useful Book** Scanners & Secret Frequencies by Henry L. Eisenson and Bill Cheek. Thanks to **frequency synthesizers**, most scanners can receive frequency bands in the 29-MHz to 512-MHz range. If you enter a frequency outside that range, you typically see an error indication on the display. More expensive models often have a higher range and often include military aircraft frequencies. (Earlier scanners did not have numeric keypads and required the owner to purchase individual crystals manufactured for a given frequency. Most early scanners only held six or 10 crystals. The cost of filling up a scanner with individual channel crystals often approached the cost of the scanner, much like buying ink cartridges for today's low-priced color inkjet printers.)

Search button - This starts the scanner on a continuous loop between two frequency limits, finding unknown frequencies within a given range. The searches typically are in the same automatic increments that the Federal Communications Commission (FCC) assigns for the given frequency band being searched. U.S. scanners cannot search the frequency bands assigned for analog cellular telephone calls. If you were at a car race, for example, you could do a search from 460 to 470 MHz and note when the scanner stops (or look in the race program for assigned frequencies). You could make a note of the displayed frequency or store it at that time, and then continue the search. The instruction manual that comes with a scanner typically shows what frequency bands are for government, business, aviation, and other users.

Manual button - This lets the user manually step through a range of frequencies stored in the scanner. Modern scanners have 100 to 300 channels for storing frequencies in the built-in memory. More expensive models have even more.

Scan button - This starts the scanner on a continuous loop through all of the **frequency banks** (containing stored frequencies). The scanner stops when it detects a radio signal on a stored frequency; it moves to the next stored frequency when the radio signal ends. The user can typically enable or disable certain banks of frequencies for scanning. Each bank can hold 10 to 30 frequencies, depending on the brand and model of the radio scanner. Often, banks contain frequencies according to the type of radio service. Types include emergency, police, fire, aviation, marine and business.

Delay button - This makes the scanner stall for a short duration on a frequency before moving to the next one. This delay helps the user hear the other part of the radio conversation on that frequency.

Lockout button - This temporarily disables the radio scanner from stopping on a stored frequency. For example, you might want to lockout the frequency of a busy airport tower at peak travel time during the day when you're really trying to hear the traffic helicopters in your area.

Radio scanners usually come with small whip antennas as well as an external antenna connector. An **outside antenna** or **attic antenna** enables you to hear more transmissions at a greater distance.

Scanners cannot hear everything. The typical consumer-grade scanner cannot listen in on 900-MHz cordless phones that use **digital spread spectrum** (DSS) technology. Analog cell phone frequencies are also blocked by law on all scanners.

Some law enforcement agencies also use **audio inversion** and other scrambling technologies to prevent the reception of sensitive communications. You will not be able to decipher these conversations.

Even so, there is an *unbelievable* number of radio services that use frequencies most scanners can hear.

Until you buy your own scanner, you can try out scanning frequencies on Web-controlled receivers. [http://www.qsl.net/oe3mzc/receivers.html]

Getting Started With Your Scanner

Frequency lists are easy to obtain, often via the Internet. You can find a free frequency list for your area at this Web site. [http://www.bearcat1.com/free.htm]

If you buy a portable scanner, park near an airport sometime and search the VHF AM aviation-band range, from approximately 118 MHz to 135.975 MHz, to hear all the activity that is going on. In some areas, programming 123.45 MHz into your scanner will let you hear some pilot-to-pilot communications.

In both 2-way radio systems and commercial FM radio, stations are separated by broadcasting on different frequencies. For example, a popular FM music station may be on 103.7 MHz. Another music station may be on 105.3 MHz. Your radio will tune to one station while filtering out the other station because the two stations are on different frequencies. A busy police dispatch station may be on 154.720 MHz while another may be found on 155.700 MHz. Groups of adjacent frequencies are referred to as radio bands. The FM Broadcast Radio Band is between 88 to 108 MHz while 2-way radio systems are most commonly found in the following radio bands: 30-50 MHz, 150 to 162 MHz, 450 to 470 MHz, and 851 to 869 MHz. The Radio Spectrum Diagram below shows most of the major radio bands that scanners receive. This chaptere will help you select a model that includes the radio bands and features you need.

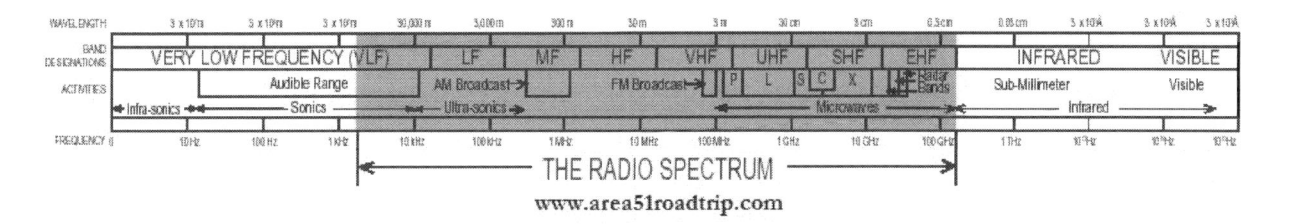

The range of 2-way radio communications depends primarily on the height of the antenna and the power used. Hand-held radios using only a few watts can only be heard by scanners from a few miles away while base stations and repeaters usually can be heard from 30-40 miles or more. Aircraft in flight can often be heard over 150 miles away, making them an easy catch for your radio scanner!

Most military aircraft communications are in the military (UHF) aircraft band, located between 225 to 400 MHz. All radio scanners in the: Continuous Coverage Scanners, can receive this band. Aircraft communications will be in AM mode while satellite communications in this band will be in NFM mode. Military aircraft sometimes also use the Civilian Aircraft Band (108 to 137 MHz), especially when flying into a civilian airport. They may also be heard in the 137 to 144 MHz and 148 to 150.8 MHz government bands. The 225-400 MHz Military Aircraft Radio Band, also known as the "UHF aero" or "UHF Air" band, is shown in purple in the radio diagram below. The 137-144 MHz and 148-150.8 MHz government bands are shown in red, while the civilian aircraft band is shown in blue.

The vast majority of local government - police, sheriffs, fire departments, and more - and business users are communicating between mobile vehicles or people. Such services are called "Land-Mobile" services. For listening to land-mobile services, what radio scanner you buy will depend on what type of system the agencies used by the agencies to which you listen - Conventional or Trunked and Analog or Digital. If you are interested in hearing any land-mobile services, follow that link below for more information.

On the other hand, if you are interested in hearing civilian aircraft, military aircraft, marine, or taking your scanner to the races, these services all use specific frequency ranges and have different scanner requirements. Follow each of the text or picture links in the table below for information specific to those topics. You may want to read all of the topics below.

Each topic will tell you which of the 6 Scanner Categories contain the radio bands and other features you need to monitor that service.

Monitoring Military Aircraft

Like commercial aircraft, military aircraft may be heard for distances of well over 100 miles, depending on the terrain and your receiving antenna. Even if you don't live near a military base you should still be able to hear some communications in this band. Unlike the civilian aircraft band (108-137 MHz), communications in the military aircraft band are far more elusive. Fewer communications will be happening at any given time, and there are far more frequencies for the communications to be spread over. As a result, it may take a significant amount of searching with your radio scanner, often for hours at a time, to hear many communications. The best way to find new frequencies is to search a small portion of the band at a time using a radio scanner with a fast search speed. You may want to leave for scanner searching while you engage in other tasks. scanner searching while you engage in other tasks.

An aerial refueling training mission involving two F-15 Eagles (twin fins), two F-16 Fighting Falcons, and a KC-135R Stratotanker: Photo by MSgt Marvin Krause, United States Air Force.

Then if you hear a conversation, you can save the frequency and continue searching.

In summary, any scanner in Continuous Coverage Scanners can monitor the 225-400 MHz Military Aircraft Radio Band. Some receivers in Categories 3, 4, and 5 can also monitor this band even though they are not Continuous Coverage receivers and therefore are not listed in Category 6; check the frequency coverage to find out. Any scanner in Categories 2, 3, 4, 5, and 6 can monitor the 108-137 MHz Civilian Aircraft Radio Band, and the 137-144 MHz and 148-150.8 MHz government radio bands and therefore may hear some military activity.

Continuous Coverage Scanners - These scanners can listen to virtually all VHF/UHF frequencies, including all major land-mobile bands. They can also tune into specialty bands not found in most scanners, like military aircraft or TV Sound. All radios in this category have continuous frequency coverage from 25-1300 MHz, except for the gap for the cellular phone band (mandated by US Federal Law) and the UHF television band (there is nothing there to hear). All have 200 to 1000 channels and allow the user to choose receive mode (NFM, WFM, AM) and search step size. Most of these radios are or were top-of-the-line scanners when produced and therefore are good-quality receivers. However, some of the older models do not have some features that are now common in high-end scanners like trunk tracking. As such, all scanners in this category have all capabilities of scanners in Categories 1, 2, and 3. Most of the newer ones also have the trunking capabilities of scanners in Categories 4, and in some cases, 5. In cases where a "Continuous Coverage" scanner also has trunking capabilities, it will be noted that the radio is also listed below.

Radio Frequency Reference Information:

RadioReference.com is the world's largest radio communications data provider, featuring a complete frequency database, trunked radio system information, and FCC license data. RadioReference is also the largest broadcaster of public safety live audio communications feeds, hosting thousands of live audio broadcasts of Police, Fire, EMS, Railroad, and aircraft communications.

With hundreds of thousands of members, RadioReference is a world leading collaboration platform for public safety communications professionals and hobbyists.

FOR COMPLETE UP-TO-DATE DETAIL ON THE LATEST FREQUENCIES PLEASE RESEARCH THE LINK BELOW:

MONITORING FREQUENCIES

https://www.radioreference.com

The Uniden BCD325P2 offers almost continuous frequency coverage of the VHF/UHF scanner bands in addition to its APCO-25 digital capability including P25 Phase 1 and Phase 2.

Frequency Coverage

- 25.0000 - 512.0000 MHz
- 758.0000 - 823.9875 MHz
- 849.0125 - 868.9875 MHz
- 894.0125 - 960.0000 MHz

Limits

All Radios in this Category feature:

- Virtually continuous frequency coverage from 25-512 and 806-1300 MHz (excluding the 824-849 and 869-894 MHz cellular phone frequencies as per US Federal Law and often the 956-1240 MHz band)
- Military Air (225-400 MHz), FM Broadcast, and VHF TV Sound (Channels 2-13);
- Selectable mode (AM, NFM, WFM) and selectable search step size
- At least 200 channels (usually 400 to 2000 channels)
- Most were Top-Of-The-Line Receivers when manufactured
- Many newer ones are also Digital or Analog Trunk-trackers and are also listed in Categories 4 or 5

The best SITE for all scanners, antennas, books and accessories is http://www.scannermaster.com/default.asp

Monitoring the Action around the Nellis U.S.A. F Ranges

During Red Flag and also other Exercises (Green Flag) that take place around the Nellis Ranges of Southern Nevada you will see and hear many fast jets and other aircraft doing air combat or just general handling and other training maneuvers.

The three trunking systems used for ground communications at Area 51, NTTR (Nevada Test and Training Range), the NNSS (Nevada National Security Site, former NTS) and Nellis/Creech AFB are **using frequencies in the UHF band, 380-400 MHz and 406-420 MHz.** The systems use two different standards: Motorola and APCO P25. They can be monitored with modern Trunking Scanners, capable of decoding APCO P25 audio. However, the Area 51 military air system uses encrypted transmissions. Each system has several repeater sites across the NTTR. All frequencies are in MHz, unless otherwise noted.

If you have a **scanner** then this opens up a completely new world of listening to the action in parallel to your visual observations including optics, spotting scopes etc.

Recommendation of required Equipment as follows:

You need two main pieces of equipment here and one cannot be used without the other because the RF signal will need to be pick up from the atmosphere.

The Scanner.

For monitoring military communications, you need a VHF and UHF scanner. Most military communications use UHF, but VHF is also used.

NOTE: VHF is used along Groom Lake Road by the local sheriff and some road sensors along Groom Lake road as well; (later we will get into the details of both)

The scanner also needs to have a fast Scan speed, preferably more that 80ch/sec and needs to be battery efficient unless you monitor from your car which can power the scanner like it would to power the lighter or your cellular phone. Most scanners take rechargeable batteries anyway plus you can also buy a spare of batteries and have them charged as a backup if you have your vehicle off, or are hiking in the area's without the vehicle. There are lots of scanners suitable for military monitoring but they vary in price range, vastly!

The Antenna Requirement

The antenna used is just as vital as the scanner. A scanner is no good unless you have a decent antenna; a decent antenna means a decent reception and a decent day of monitoring. The antenna is usually designed by the amount of gain and more specifically tuned to a certain range, for example aviation only.

Most scanners come with a decent whip/telescopic/rubber duck antenna and these are actually ideal for monitoring around the desert. They are light, small and perform well. However if you want to get brilliant performance out of your scanner, buy a small portable tri-plane discone. There are many designs on the market, small and light enough to carry round in a small bag. I do take my mobile discone everywhere I go with the mobile scanner!

Make sure the antenna is UHF capable!

Choose one which is ranged between 25 - 1300MHz which will cover everything.

My Recommended Basic Package:

Uniden BC125AT Aviation Scanner Package (W/Aviation Guide)

Like watching planes? We can help! ScannerMaster has put together the ultimate Aviation Scanner Package just for you. With the compact BC125AT handheld scanner, an antenna made specifically for the aviation band and the accessories needed to put it all together, the ScannerMaster Aviation Package is ideal for the aviation enthusiast.

Package includes:

- Uniden BC125AT Portable Scanner
- Carrying Case
- AC and DC Power Adapters
- Professional Antenna (Tuned for Aviation Band)
- FREE Aviation Frequency Guide

Link: http://www.scannermaster.com/Uniden_BC125AT_Aviation_Scanner_Package_p/01-721971.htm

A simple to use scanner for the aviation enthusiast, the BC125AT has Service Searches for both the Civil and Military Aircraft bands. Use either or both to rapidly go thru the band to find channels used in your area. You can also pre-program your airport's frequencies into memory and concentrate on known channels. You can even use Close Call RF Capture feature to find nearby transmissions that might not be listed in frequency guides.

The BC125AT may also be used for other purposes, such as railroads, the marine band (for boats and ships), weather monitoring and alerts, and even analog police, fire and EMS communications.

The BC125AT is compact enough to fit in your shirt pocket and takes up little room in your camera bag. Using the included rechargeable batteries you will have hours of use, and if they run out you can replace them with regular AA size batteries. We also provide both home and car charger adapters. The carry case protects the scanner from scratches and bumps as well as offering some drop protection.

USB AC & DC Power Pack

- Charge and power your BC125AT scanner
- Built-in standard USB port
- Input:100 to 240V AC
- Output: 5V/1A-LED power indicator

BC125 - Carrying Case
This rugged case for the Uniden Bearcat BC125AT police scanner radios provides an excellent way to protect your scanner from most scratches and falls. Includes an optional/detachable bungee cord to wrap around the scanner antenna to help secure the radio inside the case. Cutouts for speaker and access to all ports such as power and PC. Clever and handsome design.

W-901 Airband portable antenna

(Tuned Aviation Band Antenna)

- Frequency (MHz): 118-380 MHz.
- Length: 9" Material Injection Molded Antenna
- Type : Covered BNC/Helical
- Connector: Covered BNC male

Your Location is very import!

LOCATION, LOCATION, LOCATION!

Monitoring the traffic around the Ranges and Desert MOA is fairly easy; however it also depends on where you are situated especially for receiving signals that are based on mostly line-of-sight!

Military communications using the VHF (Very High Frequency) and UHF (Ultra High Frequency) spectrum are Line of Sight (LOS) only. So trying to listen to Groom Lake for example on Tikaboo Peak can only efficiently be done by actually being on the summit or the west slope side of Tikaboo Peak. Being on the eastern slope and far down the mountain won't afford you anything decent of the base communications since the RF signal which operates at line-of-sight will be reflected. See the basic diagrams below. Line-of-sight will be reflected!

See the basic diagrams below.

VHF/UHF/SHF Propogation

Frequencies above approx 50 MHz are limited to "Line of Sight" and are therefore useful for local, aviation and celestial uses.

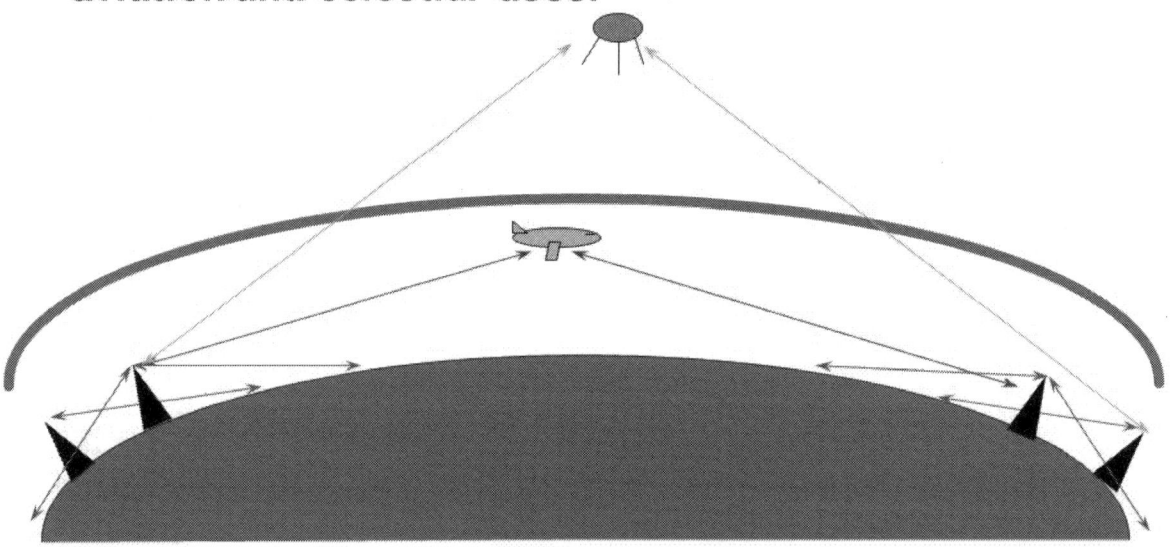

However, aircraft fly at altitude and being at ground level still affords great communication chatter and thus 'action'. Aircraft flying in between the mountains and hills will be harder to listen to, because of their flight level (FL) and terrain hugging profiles such as high elevations, for example 7,908 feet at the main summit at Tikaboo Peak.

However most of the actual 'air-war' takes place at medium to high altitudes and so monitoring this is very easy without problems. Monitoring the Strikers will be harder due to their flight level however and so sitting on a hilltop is preferred when monitoring the exercises and day to day operations from Nellis. Don't forget that sitting on the hills also affords great photos as well. But always make sure that you do not inadvertently cross the border of the restricted area!

Overall, sitting at a high elevation, and in Nevada, a mountain over 7200ft is good, offers a greatly enhanced reception and range, especially at UHF and VHF. You will hear things you never heard before at ground level and your range will increase sometimes over 100+ miles or so which means more to listen to, more to actually see and so on....that means more enjoyment.

Below are a few diagrams to explain the line of sight problems:

VHF/UHF Propagation

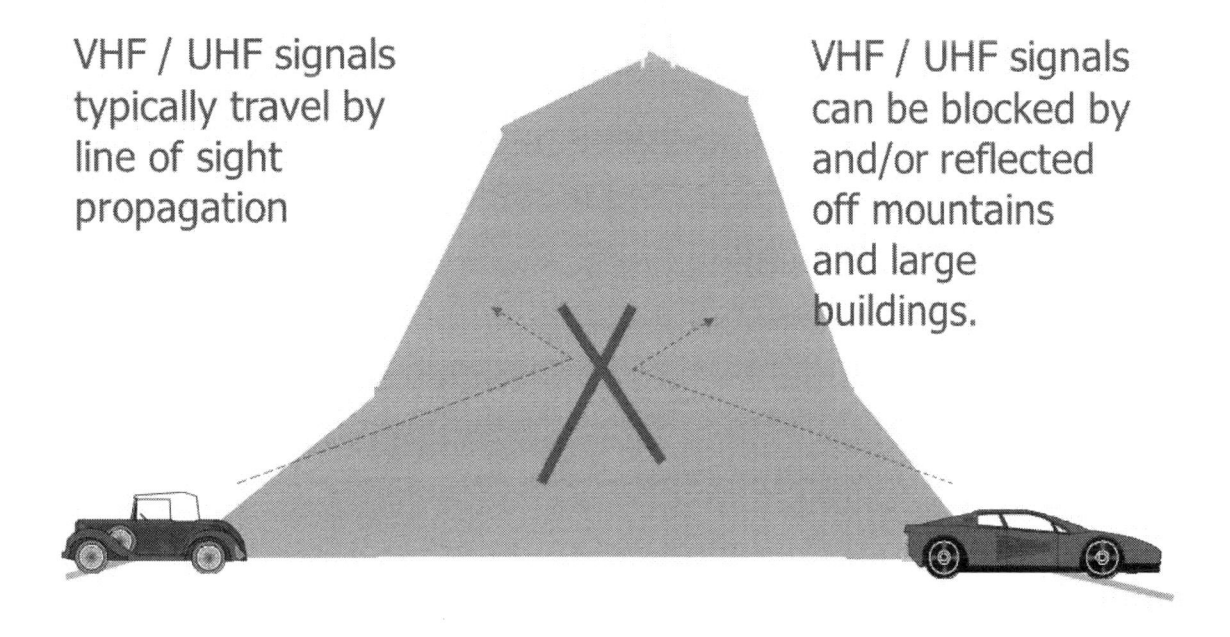

VHF / UHF signals typically travel by line of sight propagation

VHF / UHF signals can be blocked by and/or reflected off mountains and large buildings.

As mentioned **NLOS** stands for Non Line of Sight. The figure above depicts NLOS deployment scenario. As shown, wireless link is considered to be NLOS when natural and/or manmade structures block the path between aircraft and the receiving stations. In other words, NLOS communication is possible even when there is obstruction between transmitter and receiver. The signal arrives to the receiver after going through many obstructions in between. On the path, signal goes through attenuations as well as reflection, diffraction as well as penetrations. In NLOS case, wireless link can only be established if reflective path exists between base station and subscriber station as shown.

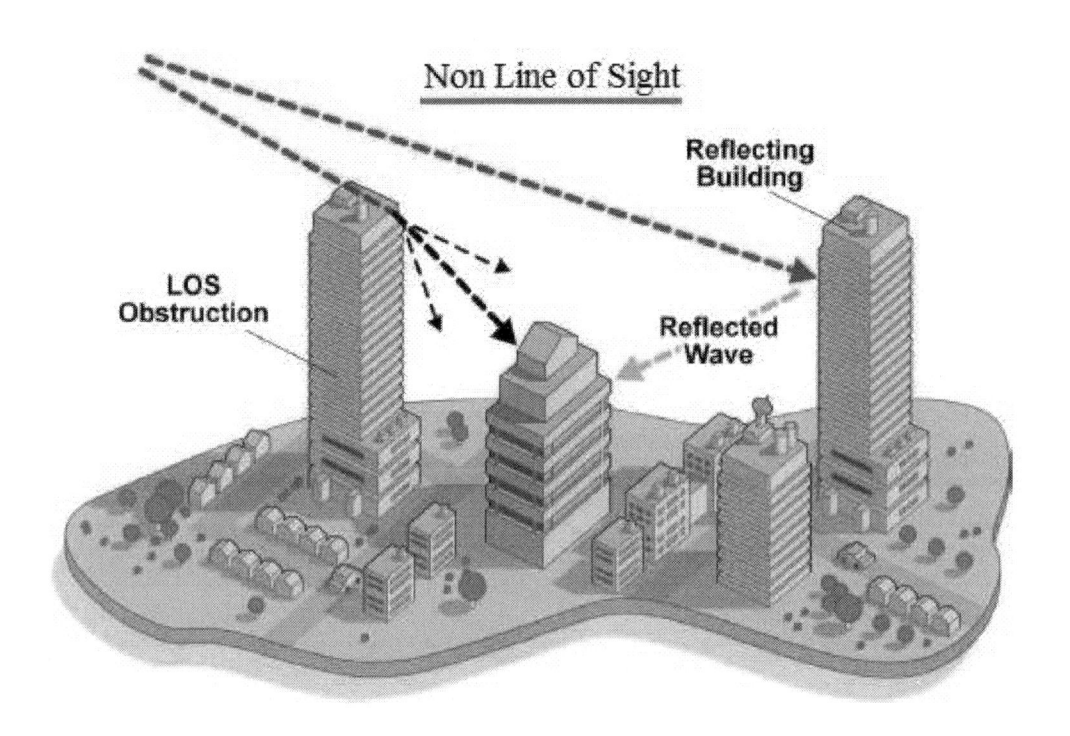

Non Line of Sight example two

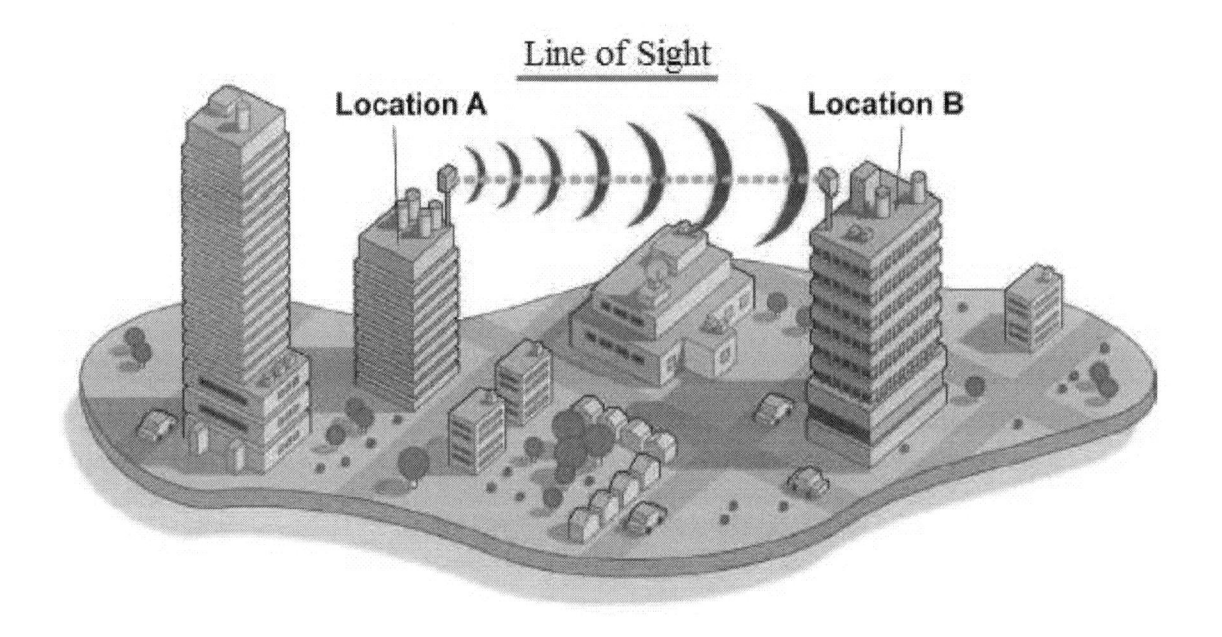

As mentioned **LOS** stands for Line of Sight. The figure above depicts line of sight communication between two transceivers. This LOS deployment is possible when there is no obstruction between base station (BS) and mobile/fixed subscriber stations (SSs). In other words, LOS communication is possible when there is no obstruction between transmitter and receiver. Due to less attenuation in the LOS communication, it offers good signal strength and higher amount of throughput compare to NLOS counterpart.

MONITORING FREQUENCIES

Also check out https://www.radioreference.com

System Name:	Nevada Test and Training Range
Location:	Groom Lake, NV
County:	2 counties
System Type:	EDACS Networked Standard
System Voice:	AEGIS Exclusive
Last Updated:	November 29, 2017, 6:00 am (Deleted news entry ID=3579)

System Frequencies

Red (c) are primary control channels | **Blue (a)** are alternate control channels | Site Map(s): FCC Callsigns RR Locations

Site	Name	County	Frequency	Frequency	Frequency	Frequency	Frequency	Frequency
001 (1)	Tonopah	Nye	01 407.500	02 407.375	03 409.975			
002 (2)	TTR	Nye	01 407.250	02 407.975	03 409.075	04 409.350	05 408.825	
003 (3)	Cedar Peak	Nye	01 407.575	02 407.1625	03 410.150	04 406.550	05 406.7625	06 410.5625
004 (4)	Basecamp	Nye	01 407.650	02 407.225	03 409.225			
005 (5)	Bald Mountain	Nye	01 409.150	02 409.650	03 407.475	04 406.9625	05 407.7625	
006 (6)	Papoose Mountain	Nye	01 407.550	02 407.225	03 409.225	04 409.425	05 410.300	
007 (7)	Angel Peak (Las Vegas)	Clark	01 408.3625	02 407.3625	03 409.3625	04 407.500	05 407.650	
008 (8)	Black Mountain or Tolicha Peak?	Nye	01 407.275	02 407.525	03 409.5625	04 406.3625	05 408.1625	
009 (9)	Stonewall Mountain?	Nye	01 407.250	02 407.975	03 409.075	04 409.350	05 408.825	

Nevada Test and Training Range – GROOM LAKE

TTR Site Details

System Name:	Nevada Test and Training Range
System Location:	Groom Lake, Nevada
Site Number:	Decimal: 002 / Hex: 2
Site Unique DB ID:	9167
Site Description:	TTR
Site County Location:	Nye
Site Neighbors:	N/A
Site Location:	N/A
Site Modulation:	N/A
Site Notes:	Confirmed LCN
Latitude	N 37.81493737606794 *(County)*
Longitude	W -116.52786254882812 *(County)*
Range	125 Miles *(County)*

Site Frequencies

407.250	407.975	408.825	409.075	409.350

Nevada Test and Training Range – BALD MOUNTAIN

Bald Mountain Site Details

System Name:	Nevada Test and Training Range
System Location:	Groom Lake, Nevada
Site Number:	Decimal: 005 / Hex: 5
Site Unique DB ID:	9039
Site Description:	Bald Mountain
Site County Location:	Nye
Site Neighbors:	N/A
Site Location:	N/A
Site Modulation:	N/A
Site Notes:	LCN Confirmed
Latitude	N 37.81493737606794 *(County)*
Longitude	W -116.52786254882812 *(County)*
Range	125 Miles *(County)*

Site Frequencies

| 406.9625 | 407.475 | 407.7625 | 409.150 | 409.650 |

Nevada Test and Training Range – PAPOOSE MOUNTAIN

Papoose Mountain Site Details

System Name:	Nevada Test and Training Range
System Location:	Groom Lake, Nevada
Site Number:	Decimal: 006 / Hex: 6
Site Unique DB ID:	9030
Site Description:	Papoose Mountain
Site County Location:	Nye
Site Neighbors:	N/A
Site Location:	N/A
Site Modulation:	N/A
Site Notes:	LCN Confirmed
Latitude	N 37.81493737606794 *(County)*
Longitude	W -116.52786254882812 *(County)*
Range	125 Miles *(County)*

Site Frequencies

| 407.225 | 407.550 | 409.225 | 409.425 | 410.300 |

Project 25 (**P25** or **APCO-25**) is a suite of standards for digital mobile radio communications designed for use by public safety organizations in North America. P25 radios are a direct replacement for analog UHF (example FM) radios but add the ability to transfer data as well as voice, allowing for a more natural implementation of encryption or messaging. P25 radios are commonly implemented by dispatch organizations, such as police, fire, Ambulance and Emergency Rescue Service, using vehicle-mounted radios combined with walkie-talkie handheld use.

Starting around 2012, products became available with the newer phase 2 modulation protocol, the older protocol known as P25 became P25 phase 1. P25 phase 2 products utilize the more advanced AMBE2+ vocoder, which allows audio to pass through a more compressed bitstream and provides two TDMA voice channels in the same RF bandwidth (12.5 kHz) that phase 1 can only provide one voice channel. The two protocols are not compatible. However, P25 Phase 2 infrastructure can provide a "dynamic transcoder" feature that translates between Phase 1 and Phase 2 as needed. In addition to this, phase 2 radios are backwards compatible with phase 1 modulation and analog FM modulation, per the standard. On the other hand, EU area created the standard for Terrestrial Trunked Radiosimilar to Project 25.

P25 systems do not have to resort to using in band signaling such as Continuous Tone-Coded Squelch System (CTCSS) tone or Digital-Coded Squelch (DCS) codes for access control. Instead they use what is called a Network Access Code (NAC) which is included outside of the digital voice frame. This is a 12 bit code that prefixes every packet of data sent, including those carrying voice transmissions.

The NAC is a feature similar to CTCSS or DCS for analog radios. That is, radios can be programmed to only pass audio when receiving the correct NAC. NACs are programmed as a three-hexadecimal-digit code that is transmitted along with the digital signal being transmitted.

Since the NAC is a three-hexadecimal-digit number (12 bits), there are 4,096 possible NACs for programming, far more than all analog methods combined.

Three of the possible NACs have special functions:

- 0x293 ($293) – the default NAC
- 0xf7e ($F7E) – a receiver set for this NAC will pass audio on any decoded signal received
- 0xf7f ($F7F) – a repeater receiver set for this NAC will allow all incoming decoded signals and the repeater transmitter will retransmit the received NAC.

The next page gives you details on one of my best recommendation on the

"RECEIVER OF RECEIVERS!"

The AOR AR-DV1 Receiver, with SDCARD slot!

AOR AR-DV1 Receiver

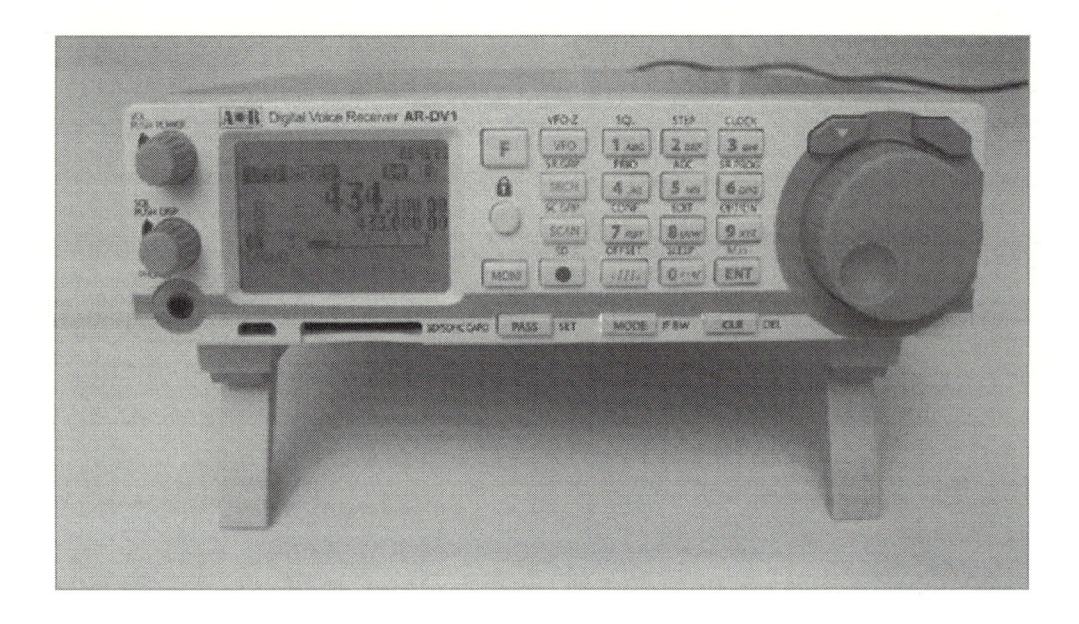

This is the best unit!

YOU CAN RECORD AND STORE ALL TRAFFIC! I HAVE THIS UNIT!

It's the FIRST multi-mode digital voice receiver to receive and decode virtually ALL popular digital modes including: MOTOTRBO(tm), DMR, dPMR(tm), APCO P25 Phase I, NXDN(tm), Icom D-Star(tm), Digital CR, Yaesu, Kenwood®, and Alinco EJ-47U as well as conventional analog signals.

With this breakthrough development, AOR offers the monitoring community a powerful new tool that receives multiple digital formats in addition to traditional analog operations in a compact receiver built for high sensitivity and selectivity.

The AOR AR-DV1B wideband communications receiver covers 100 kHz to 1300 MHz (less cellular on U.S. consumer "B" version) in traditional analog modes (SSB, CW, AM, FM, S-FM, W-FM) as well as various digital modes. In fact, we know of no other radio in this category that can decode Icom's D-Star mode, Yaesu's new C4FM mode, Alinco's digital mode, NXDN, P25 Phase1, etc.

Main Features

- 100kHz~1300MHz Wide-band reception
- Multi-mode digital demodulation
- All mode analog reception
- Memory scan
- NR, notch, digi-data display
- Built-in SD card reader (audio recording, timer recording, CSV memory data upload/download, firmware updates)
- Clock, calendar (sleep timer, alarm, timer recording, reception logging on SD)
- Compact body 7 x 2 x 8 1/2 inches
- Rear Panel: BNC antenna Jack, external speaker jack, aux jack

Receiver System

- 100kHz~18MHz : Direct conversion
- 18MHz~1300MHz: Triple superheterodyne
- Excellent image rejection and ultra-low
- internal spurii thanks to 1st I.F
- frequency set to 1.705GHz.

The NEXT couples of pages will give you P25 NTTR and the surrounding ranges the frequencies used.

NOTE: The three trunking systems used for ground communications at Area 51, NTTR (Nevada Test and Training Range), the NNSS (Nevada National Security Site, former NTS) and Nellis/Creech AFB are using frequencies in the UHF band, 380-400 MHz and 406-420 MHz. The systems use two different standards: Motorola and APCO P25. They can be monitored with modern Trunking Scanners, capable of decoding APCO P25 audio. However, the Area 51 mil. air system uses *encrypted transmissions*. Each system has several repeater sites across the NTTR. All frequencies are in MHz, unless otherwise noted.

Nevada Test and Training Range (Project 25) – PROJECT 25

System Name:	Nevada Test and Training Range (Project 25)
Location:	Rachel, NV
County:	2 counties
System Type:	Project 25 Phase I
System Voice:	APCO-25 Common Air Interface Exclusive
Last Updated:	October 2, 2014, 9:59 pm (Updated Function Tag assignments for 18 talkgroups)

System ID List

System ID	WACN
001	33744

System Frequencies

Red (c) are primary control channels | **BOLD (a)** are alternate control channels | Site Map(s): FCC Callsigns RR Locations

RFSS	Site	Name	County	Freqs	Freqs	Freqs	Freqs	Freqs	Freqs	Freqs
1 (1)	001 (1)	Tonopah	Nye	385.9125c	386.3375	386.650	387.250	387.550		
2 (2)	002 (2)	Antelope Peak	Nye	385.8125c	386.250	386.550	386.850	387.725	388.700	
4 (4)	004 (4)	Halligan Mesa	Nye	385.625	386.375c	386.700	387.2125	387.5125		
5 (5)	005 (5)	Bald Mountain	Nye	385.725c	**386.125a**	387.325a				
6 (6)	006 (6)	Papoose Mountain	Nye	**385.675a**	385.9625a	386.275a	386.575a	386.8875c		
7 (7)	007 (7)	Site 7-07	Clark	383.5625	383.850	384.250	384.5625	385.2125	385.625c	386.025
				386.175	**386.375a**	386.625	386.700a	387.2125a	387.5125a	
8 (8)	008 (8)	Site 8-08	Clark	385.8625c						
10 (A)	010 (A)	Site 10-10	Clark	386.0125c						
11 (B)	011 (B)	Site 11-11	Clark	386.8875c						

Nellis/Creech/NNSS Trunking System (P25)

System: APCO P25
WACN: 58544 / System ID: 00Fh
Band Plan: Base: 403.0000 MHz, Step: 12.5 kHz, Lo: 00-0000, Hi: 00-4095

Site#	Location	Frequencies	Peers
01	Nellis AFB	406.5000 406.7875 407.1875 407.3000 407.5000 407.8625 408.1500 408.9625 409.1125 409.5625 409.7125 410.6500	10 14
02	Creech AFB	406.3625 407.0750 407.5875 408.1750 408.7000	10
10	Angel Peak	409.3000 409.6000 409.9125 410.5500	01 02
14	Nellis AFB, Area 2	407.3500 407.7875 408.1875 409.1250 409.5500	01
21	Mercury	406.5000 406.7875 407.1875 407.5000 407.8625 408.1500 409.1125 409.5625	10
22	Checkpoint Pass	406.9875 407.3500 408.3625 409.3125 409.5250 409.7875 410.1625	-
23	Skull Mountain	406.1500 406.9750 407.5500 407.9625 408.1000 408.7625 409.1250 409.3500	-
24	Rainier Mesa	407.3000 407.4000 408.3875 410.6500	-
25	Yucca Pass, CP-1	406.7875 407.1875 407.5000 408.1500 409.1125 409.3250 409.5625	-
26	Shoshone Mtn.	406.1375 406.4000 407.1625 407.3625 408.1875 408.4250 408.9625 409.3750	-
27	LV DOE Facility	406.9875 407.3625 407.9625 408.3625 408.7625	10

Bald Mountain Site Details

37°26'59.52"N 115°44'0.87"W

Communications Coverage Area

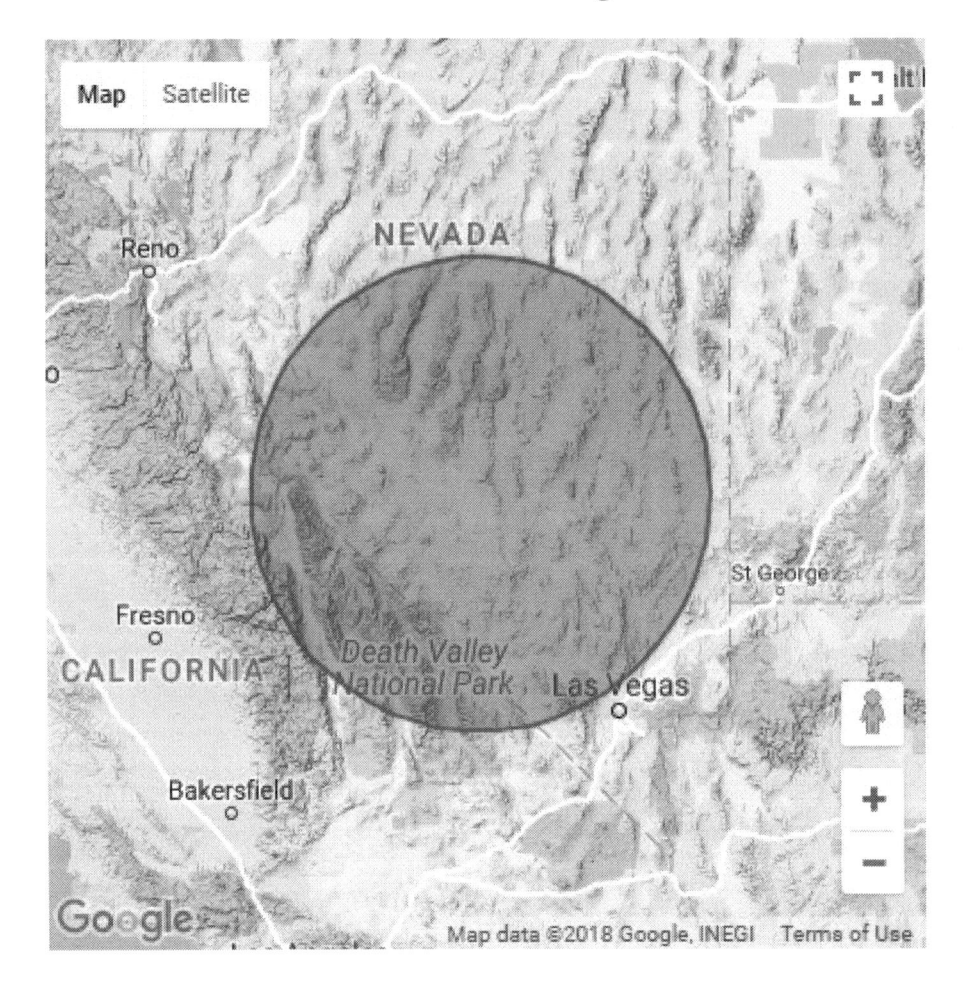

The summit is marked by a small structure and a large windbreak built from rocks and boulders. Inside the windbreak, you will find a summit register.

Roundtrip is only about 6 miles, with around 1400 ft of gain.

BALD MOUNTAIN 3D VIEW

37°26'59.52"N 115°44'0.87"W

Great Basin National Park is located approximately 50 miles east of Ely, Nevada, a few miles west of Baker, Nevada, and not far from highway 50 and the Utah border in east central Nevada.

The mountain is easily accessed just inside the park boundary via a paved road with obvious signage leading visitors to the upper campgrounds of the park. Follow the road for 12 miles or so to the parking lot just before Wheeler Peak Campground and park. Across the street from the parking lot is the trailhead for Wheeler Peak, the glacier, and a loop trail of the alpine lakes in the area.

The route is so simple that it does not even require its own route page.

Simply follow the well-signed trail from the Wheeler Peak trailhead up to the obvious saddle (approx. 11000 ft) due north of Wheeler. Once at the saddle, Bald Mountain will be the mountain to the north. While in the saddle, keep your eyes open for the bristlecone pines growing there and the huge number of deer that live in their thickets.

From the saddle, leave the trail and head north toward Bald Mountain. The grade is gentle, the terrain is never more than class 2, and it's only a mile or so to the summit.

PAPOOSE MOUNTAIN

37°10'52.94"N 115°50'34.34"W

There is a radio facility located on a peak in the Papoose Mountain Range, only a few miles southwest of Area 51, and almost certainly connected to it. Not much is known about this facility at this writing. On some maps it is marked as a microwave relay facility. Just like Area 51, it is not marked in the official Nellis Range Chart or in any of the USGS maps. One of the digitally encrypted trunking sites of the new Area 51 security radio system is located here.

The above photo is a close-up of Papoose Mountain, As you can see the entire top of the mountain has been scraped and leveled to form a plateau. Near the northern (right) edge of the plateau are several buildings and what looks like an antenna tower. On the left is a large boxy structure. It appears that the bottom is a solid building, with some sort of scaffolding towering over it. There does not seem to be much change compared to photos taken of the site in 2001.

The facility cannot be seen from Tikaboo Valley. However, it can be seen from various elevated locations, like the Powerlines Overlook, and of course from Tikaboo Peak. It is hard to spot during the day, but at night it can easily be located by the lights on the antenna tower. There is a constant white light, and a red light above it since the tower is above 200 feet and requires FAA lighting requirements.

The GPS coordinates of the tall structure on the left are: **37°12'21.95"N 115°50'23.18"W**

The GPS coordinates of the tall structure on the left are: **37°12'21.95"N 115°50'23.18"W**

This is a RESTRICTED SITE, U.S.A.F PROPERTY!

QR CODES FOR YOUR SMART PHONE:

Use the following QUICK QR Codes from your smart phone bar code scanner app to get you right into the source of information.

FLY AROUND THE GREAT TOWN OF RACHEL, NEVADA

The latest 2018 VARIOUS DRONE FOOTAGE

The *Little A'Le'Inn*

TTR Info

National Atomic Testing Museum

Travel Nevada

Nevada Energy Outreach Tours

Nevada Silver Trail

Lincoln County, Nevada

Pioche, Nevada

Extended Weather Forecast (28 mile radius of Rachel, Nevada – Extending to Tonopah, Nevada)

RadioReference

ScannerMaster

FlightRadar24

FLIGHTRADAR24

How it works – Tracking JANET Airlines

WWW827, WWW741, WWW642 and WWW715 for example

Flightradar24 is a flight tracker that shows live air traffic from around the world. Flightradar24 combines data from several data sources including ADS-B, MLAT and radar data. The ADS-B, MLAT and radar data is aggregated together with schedule and flight status data from airlines and airports to create a unique flight tracking experience on www.flightradar24.com and in Flightradar24 apps.

ADS-B

The primary technology that Flightradar24 use to receive flight information is called automatic dependent surveillance-broadcast (**ADS-B**). The ADS-B technology itself is best explained by the image to the right.
1. Aircraft gets its location from a GPS navigation source (satellite)
2. The ADS-B transponder on aircraft transmits signal containing the location (and much more)
3. ADS-B signal is picked up by a receiver connected to Flightradar24
4. Receiver feeds data to Flightradar24
5. Data is shown on www.flightradar24.com and in Flightradar24 apps

ADS-B is a relatively new technology under development, which means that today it's rarely used by Air Traffic Control (ATC). Our estimations show that roughly 70% of all commercial passenger aircraft (80% in Europe, 60% in the US) are equipped with an ADS-B transponder. For general aviation this number is probably below 20%. The percentage of aircraft equipped with ADS-B receivers is steadily increasing though, as they will become mandatory for most aircraft around the world by 2020. When mandatory, ADS-B will replace primary radar as the primary surveillance method used by ATC.

Flightradar24 has a network of more than 17,000 ADS-B receivers around the world that receive flight information from aircraft with ADS-B transponders and send this information to our servers. Due to the high frequency used (1090 MHz) the coverage from each receiver is limited to about 250-450 km (150-250 miles) in all directions depending on location. The farther away from the receiver an aircraft is flying, the higher it must fly to be covered by the receiver. The distance limit makes it very difficult to get ADS-B coverage over oceans.

On cruising altitude (above 30,000 feet) Flightradar24 covers 100% of Europe and of the USA. There is also good ADS-B coverage in Canada, Mexico, Caribbean, Venezuela, Colombia, Ecuador, Peru, Brazil, South Africa, Russia, Middle East, Pakistan, India, China, Taiwan, Japan, Thailand, Malaysia, Indonesia, Australia and New Zealand. In other parts of the world the ADS-B coverage varies. We are continually adding coverage all over the world via our FR24-receivers.

MLAT

In some regions with coverage from several **FR24-receivers** we also calculate positions of non-ADS-B equipped aircraft with the help of Multilateration **(MLAT)**, by using a method known as Time Difference of Arrival (TDOA). By measuring the the time it takes to receive the signal from aircraft with an older ModeS-transponder, it's possible to calculate the position of these aircraft. Four FR24-receivers or more, receiving signals from the same aircraft, are needed to make MLAT work. MLAT coverage can only be achieved above about 3,000-10,000 feet as the probability that four or more receivers can receive the transponder signal increases with increased altitude. Most parts of Europe and North America are today covered with MLAT above about 3,000-10,000 feet. There is also some MLAT coverage in Mexico, Brazil, South Africa, India, China, Japan, Taiwan, Thailand, Malaysia, Indonesia, Australia and New Zealand. More areas will get MLAT coverage as we continue to add new receivers to our network.

North America Radar Data

In addition to ADS-B and MLAT, we also receive additional live data for flights in the North America. This data is based on radar data (not just aircraft equipped with ADS-B transponders) and includes most scheduled and commercial air traffic in the US and Canadian airspace, as well as parts of the Atlantic and Pacific Ocean.

Flarm

Flarm is simpler version of ADS-B with a shorter range, primary used by smaller aircraft, in most cases gliders. The range of a Flarm receiver is between 20 and 100 km. Flarm receivers are often installed on small airports with a lot glider traffic to track the gliders around the airport.

Estimations

When an aircraft is flying out of coverage Flightradar24 keeps estimating the position of the aircraft for up to 2 hours if the destination of the flight is known. For aircraft without known destination, position is estimated for up to 10 minutes. The position is calculated based on many different parameters and in most cases it's quite accurate, but for long flights the position can in worst cases be up to about 100 km (55 miles) off. In settings there is an option to set for how long time you want to see estimated aircraft on map.

Aircraft visible on Flightradar24 (within ADS-B coverage)

When ADS-B was initially launched, it was primarily used in commercial passenger aircraft with 100+ passengers. An increasing number of aircraft including smaller aircraft types, are getting ADS-B transponders but, until ADS-B becomes mandatory it's up to the aircraft producer and owner to decide if an ADS-B transponder should be installed or not.

Common aircraft models that usually have an ADS-B transponder and are visible on Flightradar24 (within ADS-B coverage):

- All Airbus models (A300, A310, A318, A319, A320, A321, A330, A340, A350, A380)
- Antonov An-148 and An-158
- ATR 72-600 (most new deliveries)
- BAe ATP
- BAe Avro RJ70, RJ85, RJ100
- Boeing 737, 747, 757, 767, 777, 787
- Bombardier CRJ-900 (most new deliveries)
- Bombardier CS100 and CS300
- Embraer E190 (most new deliveries)
- Fokker 70 and 100
- McDonnell Douglas DC-10 and MD-11
- Sukhoi SuperJet 100
- Some newer Ilyushin and Tupolev (for example Il-96 and TU-204)

Common aircraft models that usually do not have an ADS-B transponder and are not visible on Flightradar24 (within ADS-B coverage):

- Antonov An-124 and An-225
- ATR 42, 72 (except most new deliveries of ATR 72-600)

- Boeing 707, 717, 727, 737-200, 747-100, 747-200, 747SP
- BAe Jetstream 31 and 32
- All Bombardier CRJ models (except most new deliveries of CRJ-900)
- All Bombardier Dash models
- All CASA models
- All Dornier models
- All Embraer models (except most new deliveries of Embraer E190)
- De Havilland Canada DHC-6 Twin Otter
- Fokker 50
- McDonnell Douglas DC-9, MD-8x, MD-90
- Saab 340 and 2000
- Most helicopters
- Most older aircraft
- Most business jets
- Most military aircraft
- Most propeller aircraft

Of course there are lots of exceptions from these rules. There are some older A300, A310, A320, B737, B747, B757, B767, MD10, MD11 aircraft flying without an ADS-B transponder, which make those aircraft invisible on Flightradar24 when in areas with ADS-B coverage only. But there are also some Twin Otters, Saab 340, Saab 2000 and MD-80 aircraft with an ADS-B transponder that are visible on Flightradar24 in areas with ADS-B coverage.

Aircraft visible on Flightradar24 (within MLAT, radar, or Flarm coverage)

In regions with MLAT, radar, or Flarm coverage most of the air traffic is tracked and visible independent of aircraft type. That includes propeller aircraft, helicopters and gliders. But as mentioned above, MLAT coverage is limited to some areas with many FR24 receivers and can normally only be achieved at altitudes above about 3,000-10,000 feet, which means that general aviation at lower altitudes may be flying below MLAT coverage. North American radar data in most cases does not include general aviation flights without a flight plan. Radar data is often missing aircraft registration information and aircraft tracked with MLAT in many cases are missing the callsign information.

Blocking

For security and privacy reasons information about some aircraft is limited or blocked. This includes most military aircraft and certain high profile aircraft, like Air Force One.

You can TRACK "JANET AIRLINES" to and from Las Vegas to Area 51, Tonopah, etc. by using the www.flightdata24.com web site! Give it a whirl!

LIVE EXAMPLE CAPTURE USING FLIGHTRADAR24 SHOWING THREE FLIGHTS TO THE RESTRICTED AREA'S [R4808N] AIRSPACE

The "LIVE CAPTURE" of three airlines circle in red above is showing flying over the RESTRICTED VARIOUS AREA'S for example, R4808N using the FLIGHTDATA24 web tool. The three airlines above are as follows:

- WWW741, WWW652 and WWW715

TYPE(B736)
Boeing 737-66N

REGISTRATION
N365SR

MODE-S CODE
A4207F

SERIAL NUMBER (MSN)
29891

AGE (JAN 2003)
15 years

N365SR Aircraft Registration

Aircraft Summary

2003 BOEING 737-66N
Fixed wing multi engine
(149 seats / 2 engines)

Owner

DEPARTMENT OF THE AIRFORCE (USAF)
HILL AFB , UT, US
(Government)

Airworthiness Class

Standard/Transport

Serial Number

29891

Engine - CFM INTL CFM56-7B22 (Turbo-fan)
Thrust: 22700lbs

Weight Over 20,000lbs

Speed Not defined

Mode S Code - 051020177 / A4207F

Certificate Issue Date - 2009-05-27

Airworthiness Date - 2009-05-19

Last Action Date

2017-05-01

Expiration

2020-09-30

Registry Source

FAA

Coverage map example showing all "live" flights at one time.

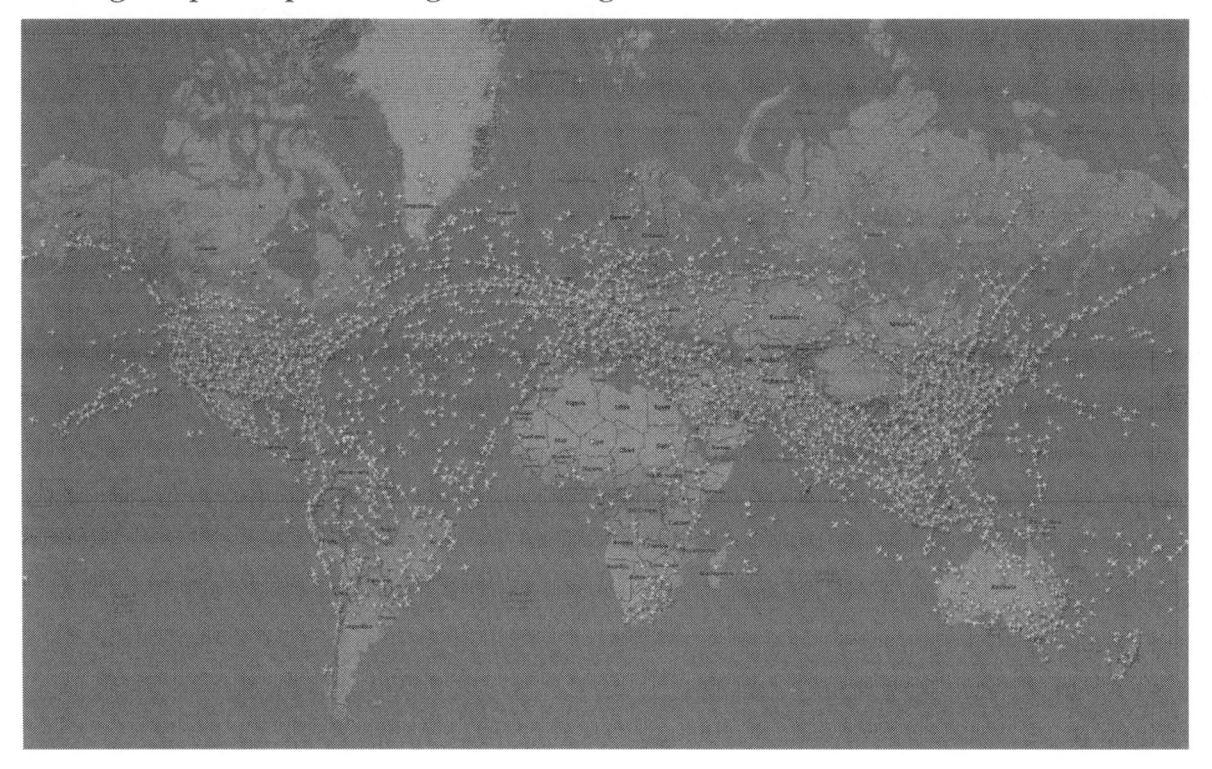

In areas where Flightradar24 normally have coverage, all major airports are marked with blue airport markers.

Flightradar24 relies on volunteers around the world for the majority of our coverage.

Find out how you can contribute and host a receiver.

Please note that coverage and aircraft visibility is dependent of many parameters including aircraft type, aircraft transponder type, aircraft altitude and terrain, so coverage can be different for different aircraft, even on the same location. If an aircraft you are looking for is not visible on Flightradar24 it either does not have a compatible transponder or it's out of Flightradar24 coverage.

INTRODUCTION TO BASIC TRANSPONDER 101

The information below assumes that your airplane isn't a balloon or glider.

Modes and Codes

Mode A. Sometimes referred to as mode 3/A. Civil Mode A is identical to military Mode 3. Mode A responds to an ATC interrogation signal with the transponder code set by the pilot.

Mode C. Refers to aircraft equipped with an altitude encoder and altimeter. With Mode C, ATC will actually see the flight level altitude on their radar screen if the transponder is operating in the Mode C or "ALT" (altitude) Mode.

Mode S. Mode S is a possible platform for a variety of other applications, such as Traffic Information Service (TIS), Graphic Weather Service, and Automatic Dependent Surveillance-Broadcast (ADS-B). Under ADS-B, each aircraft periodically broadcasts its identification, position, and altitude. Overall, Mode S provides improved surveillance quality, discrete aircraft addressing function, and digital capability. Mode S is not required for general aviation aircraft.

Squawk Codes

- **1200** Visual Flight Rules (VFR)
- **1202** Gliders
- **7500** Hijack
- **7600** Communications failure
- **7700** emergency
- **7777** military intercept code

All Controlled Airspace

According to the AIM, Section 4-1-19: In all cases, while in controlled airspace, each pilot operating an aircraft equipped with an operable ATC transponder maintained in accordance with 14 CFR section 91.413 shall operate the transponder, including Mode C if installed, on the appropriate code or as assigned by ATC.

Other Airspace Requirements

The following areas require the operation of a Mode C transponder:

- Operations within Class A, Class B, and Class C airspace.
- Operations within 30 nautical miles of the primary airport within Class B airspace from the surface to 10,000 feet msl (see airports listed below).
- Operations above the ceiling and within the lateral boundaries of Class B and C airspace.
- Operations above 10,000 feet msl in the contiguous 48 states, excluding the airspace at and below 2,500 feet agl.

- The AIM states in Section 4-1-19(a)(3) that for airborne operations in Class G airspace, the transponder should be operating unless otherwise requested by ATC.

Above 10,000 Feet

All aircraft are required to be equipped with a Mode C transponder when flying at or above 10,000 feet msl, over the 48 contiguous states or the District of Columbia, excluding that airspace below 2,500 feet agl.

Into and Out of the United States

According to 14 CFR 99.13, no person may operate an aircraft into or out of the United States, or into, within, or across an ADIZ designated in **subpart B** unless operating a transponder with Mode C. Certain exemptions might apply to aircraft that were not originally certified with an engine-driven electrical system; see 99.13(d).

Exemptions

Aircraft not originally certificated with an engine-driven electrical system or subsequently have not been certified with such a system installed, balloons, or gliders may conduct operations:

In the airspace within 30 nautical miles of the listed airports as long as operations are conducted:

- Outside of Class A, B, and C airspace.
- Below the altitude of the ceiling of a Class B or Class C airspace area designated for an airport, or 10,000 feet msl, whichever is lower.
- Above 10,000 feet msl (excluding airspace above the lateral limits of Class B and C airspace).

ATC Authorized Deviations

According to 14 CFR 91.215(d), requests for deviations must be made to the ATC facility having jurisdiction over the concerned airspace within the time periods specified as follows:

- For operation of an aircraft with an operating transponder but without operating automatic pressure altitude reporting equipment having a Mode C capability, the request may be made at any time.
- For operation of an aircraft with an inoperative transponder to the airport of ultimate destination, including any intermediate stops, or to proceed to a place where suitable repairs can be made or both, the request may be made at any time.
- For operation of an aircraft that is not equipped with a transponder, the request must be made at least one hour before the proposed operation.

SSR Mode S relies on a unique ICAO 24-bit aircraft address for selective interrogation of an individual aircraft. 16,777,214 aircraft addresses are allocated in blocks by ICAO to the state of registry, or common mark registering authority, for assignment to aircraft according to their country of registration.

Mode S transponder equipped aircraft must also incorporate an Aircraft Identification feature to permit flight crew to set the Aircraft Identification, commonly referred to as Flight ID, for transmission by the transponder. The Aircraft Identification transmission must correspond with the aircraft identification specified in item 7 of the ICAO flight plan, or, when no flight plan has been filed, the aircraft registration.

In addition to the downlinking of Aircraft Identification, which is a prerequisite for Mode S Elementary Surveillance (ELS), other specified downlink parameters (DAPs) may be acquired by the ground system to meet the requirements of Mode S Enhanced Surveillance (EHS).

The Mode S system requires each interrogator to have an Identifier Code (IC), which can be carried within the uplink and downlink transmissions (1030/1090 MHz). Responding aircraft transponder identification is achieved by acquiring the unique ICAO 24-bit aircraft address. Figure 1, below, provides an illustrative guide as to how Mode S works.

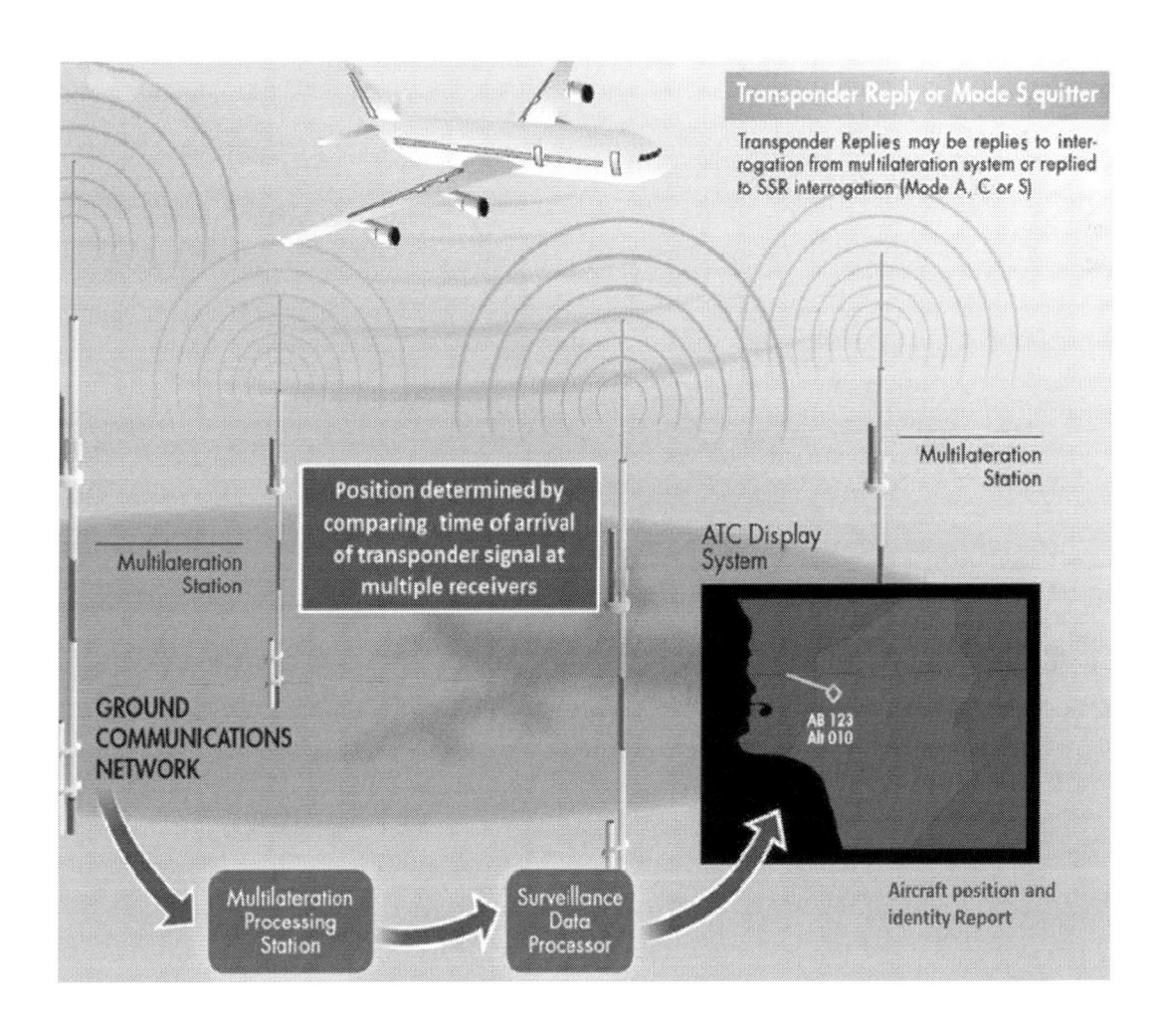

Camping Around "AREA 51"

During the early fall/spring/summer months Rachel is a popular destination for campers who come out here to explore the many old mines and ghost towns in the area, or to watch the night skies for UFOs. In fact, UFOs or not, spending a night out here in the desert, away from any light pollution, is an experience you will not forget. Many hobby astronomers come out here to take advantage of the excellent viewing conditions.

Trailer Parks at Little A'Le'Inn

The Little A'Le'Inn in Rachel has a small trailer park with full RV hookup. The rates are between $12 and $15 per day. In summer it may be a good idea to call ahead for reservations. Please use the QR CODE to get you to the Little A'Le'Inn website

Camping

Also, most of the land along the Extraterrestrial Highway is public land. There are no fences, and you can pull off the road and camp anywhere you like. If you do, please pick up all trash before you leave. There are trash barrels along the highway at Hancock Summit, Coyote Summit, Horneys Reststop and at several other locations.

Here are a few suggestions for good camp spots along the E.T. Highway (HWY 375):

- **Rachel (LN 10.0 [3])**
  Full RV hookup at the Little A'Le'Inn (see above). Also plenty of level ground near the Inn to dry-camp or to pitch your tent. Ask the friendly folks at the Inn for a good spot.

- Just before you reach Coyote Summit coming from Rachel you will see trash barrels on both sides of the highway. A dirt road intersects with the highway on the right. It leads around and to the back of a hill on the south side of the summit. There is a hidden campsite only a few hundred yards from the highway. The dirt road is suitable for most vehicles, but it dead-ends here, and turning around with a large RV may be difficult.

- **Black Mailbox (LN 29.6 [7])**
  This is a popular spot for skywatchers, and in summer there is a good chance that you will have company here. There used to be the black mailbox of a nearby ranch here, which became a traditional gathering spot for UFO watchers in the 1990's. The mailbox has since been replaced with a white box, but the location is still known as the "Black Mailbox" or simply as "The Mailbox".

- The dirt road that intersects here with the highway leads to a ranch, and also to the mysterious *Area 51*, which is just behind the hills in the southwest.

- If you camp here please do not block the intersection, or the access to the mailbox. There is a good level spot on the right, just after you turn onto the dirt road.

  For more information and some photos of the Black Mailbox see page
- **Hidden Campsite (LN 31.7)**
  This is a great hidden spot for tent or car camping. Not suitable for RV's, requires a high-clearance vehicle. Look for an unmaintained dirt road leading southwest towards a small hill. It leads around the hill to a small hidden camp area in the back. Excellent private spot for skywatching at night.
- **Gravel Area (LN 32.3 [9])**
  If you are travelling with a large RV or trailer this is an excellent campsite. Access from the highway is easy, and there is plenty of level ground for several large campers. This is an excellent place for skywatching at night, but not as private as the campsite above.
- **Campfire Hill (Groom Lake Road [near 13])**
  This campsite is located on a small hill near the perimeter of the super-secret USAF base known as *Area 51*. It is on public land, but if you camp here you can almost be certain to have perimeter security visit you at night. Take Groom Lake Road at LN 34.5. After about 12 miles you will see Campfire Hill on the right, and a road leading up to its top. Requires high-clearance 4WD.
- **Horneys Reststop (LN 38.1 [15])**
  Horneys is the only "official" reststop on the E.T. Highway. There are no facilities here, but a few trees that provide some shade. Access from the highway is possible with most trailers and RVs. This is a popular campsite in summer, and there is a good chance that you will have company here.
- **Powerlines Overlook (off hwy. [16])**
  The Powerlines Overlook is located in the mountains north of the highway. It provides an incredible view over Tikaboo Valley and the surrounding mountains. There is enough level ground for several tents. Access requires a rough 4-mile 4WD ride, and a skilled driver. Take the dirt road in the back of Horneys Reststop (see above) and keep following the main traveled road. After about 4 miles you get to the overlook, where the powerlines to Rachel cross the ridge and lead down into Tikaboo Valley.

Note: "LN..." refers to the Lincoln County mile markers along the highway. The count starts at the Nye/Lincoln county line about 10 miles north of Rachel. The numbers in refer to the location in our Tikaboo Valley Map as shown below:

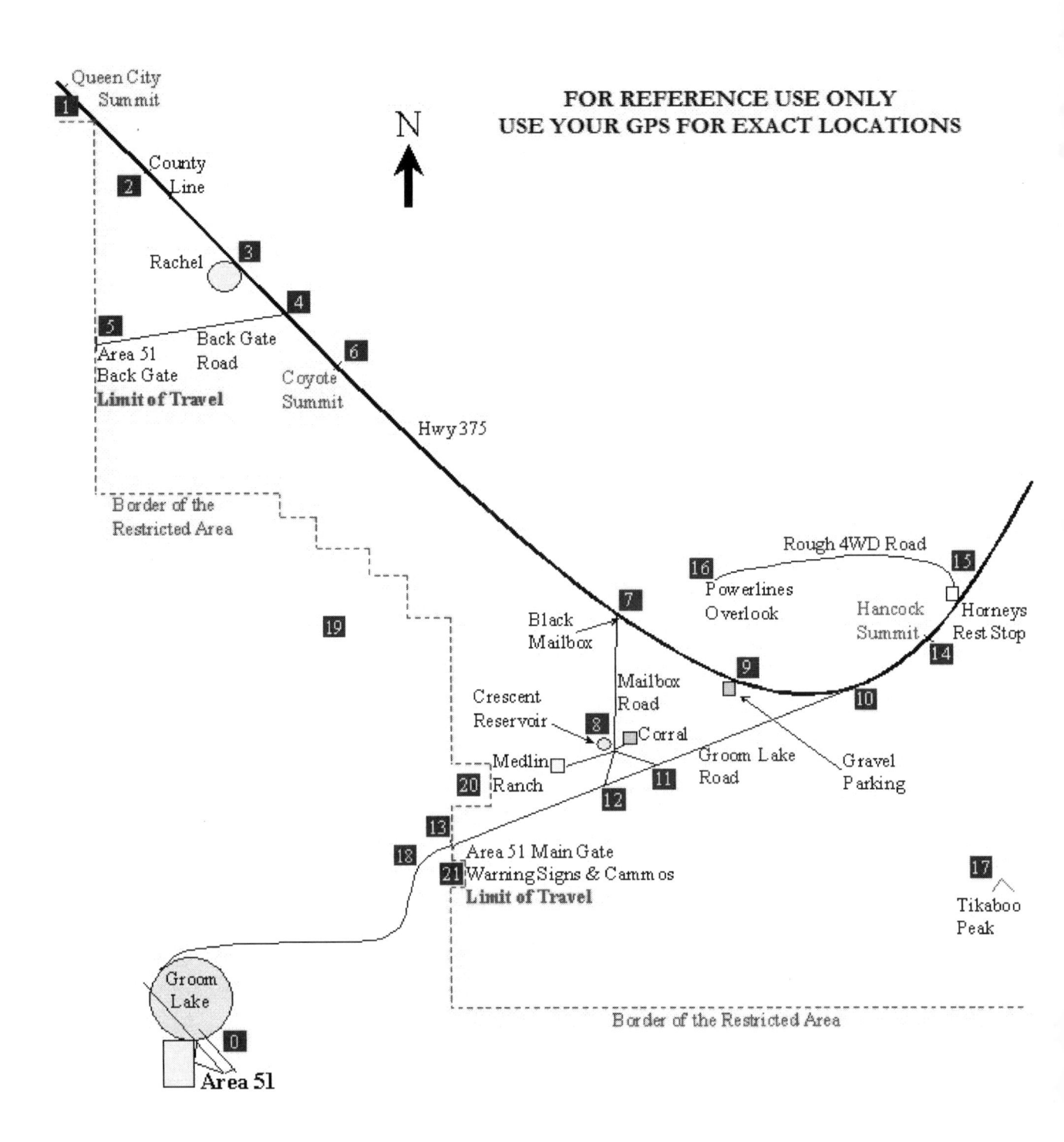

Map of Sand Spring Valley, Rachel, NV and Tikaboo Valley. It shows the location of Area 51, the Main Gate and the Back Gate, the Black Mailbox, and several other locations that may be of interest for visitors to the area. For a larger scale map and driving directions to Area 51 PLEASE USE GOOGLE EARTH for details.

In the table below NY... and LN... refers to the Nye and Lincoln County mile markers along Hwy. 375. Latitude and Longitude are the GPS coordinates of the location.

# Description	Location	Latitude north	Longitude west
0 Area 51 (Tower)		37°14.428'	115°48.528'
1 Queen City Summit (5960 ft.)	NY 45.85	37°45.129'	115°56.733'
2 Nye / Lincoln County Line	LN 0 / NY 49.36	37°43.329'	115°53.671'
3 Town of Rachel	LN 10.0	37°38.801'	115°44.760'
4 Intersection of Hwy. 375 and Back Gate Road	LN 11.4	37°38.063'	115°43.181'
5 Area 51 Back Gate (Rachel Back Gate) - Here you get to see the guard shack. It is legal to drive right up to the barrier	10.2 mi from 4	37°35.641'	115°53.924'
6 Coyote Summit (5591 ft.)	LN 16.6	37°34.331'	115°40.123'
7 Black Mailbox (now white), intersection of Hwy. 375 and Mailbox Road - Good viewing location. However, the base is right behind White Sides (the mountain with 'shoulders' on both sides) from here	LN 29.6	37°27.432'	115°28.962'
8 Crescent Reservoir - 5-way intersection. Make sure you get the right turn here. The main road leads around the reservoir and to the ranch; to get to Groom Lake Road take the second road from the right.	3.9 mi from 7	37°24.063'	115°29.573'
9 Gravel Parking Area south of Hwy. 375 - Excellent viewing location, slightly higher than the Mailbox, and better angle	LN 32.3	37°25.931'	115°26.689'
10 Intersection of Hwy. 375 and Groom Lake Road	LN 34.6	37°24.892'	115°24.586'
11 Intersection of Groom Lake Road and Ranch Road	4.2 mi from 10 1.0 mi from 8	37°23.456'	115°28.823'

#	Location	Distance	Latitude	Longitude
12	Intersection of Groom Lake Road and Mailbox Road - Coming from the Mailbox, turn right onto Groom Lake Road here	5.2 mi from 10 1.1 mi from 8	37°23.137'	115°29.826'
13	Area 51 Main Gate - Do not continue past the warning signs. Look for the cammos on nearby hills. Security cameras on the hill to your left	13.8 mi from 10	37°21.068'	115°38.813'
14	Hancock Summit (5592 ft.)	LN 37.5	37°25.832'	115°22.432'
15	Horneys Rest Stop - Roadside rest near Hancock summit, some shade, picnic tables	LN 38.1	37°26.372'	115°22.614'
16	Powerlines Overlook - Excellent high elevation view point in the mountains behind the Black Mailbox. Requires 4WD	4.3 mi from 15	37°27.541'	115°25.437'
17	Tikaboo Peak - The closest view spot for Area 51. Requires 4WD and a somewhat strenuous hike	25.8mi f.Area 51	37°20.654'	115°21.543'
18	Groom Lake Road Guard Shack - Hidden behind a curve well inside the restricted area, do not attempt to go there.	0.85 mi from 13	37°20.750'	115°39.610'
19	Bald Mountain Radio and Surveillance Facility	15.0mi f.Area 51	37°26.967'	115°44.023'
20	White Sides (Former Area 51 View Spot)	13.3mi f.Area 51	37°22.114'	115°37.681'
21	Freedom Ridge (Former Area 51 View Spot)	11.1mi f.Area 51	37°20.077'	115°38.679'

Camping Around "AREA 51"

Campfire Hill 2.26 MILES Line-of-Sight to the Groom Lake Border!

This campsite rests on top of a small hill located less than two miles from the front gates of Area 51, and because of its proximity, it exists as one of the best camping locations for your first visit to the Area.

You will have a decent view of the night sky, but you are also guaranteed to get a visit from Area 51 border security, known as the Cammo Dudes. Don't worry; you are well within public land, so their goal is likely centered on ruining your night vision with their high-powered spotlights.

Make sure you have plenty of water, food, and gas before camping at this location. Also, you might need a four-wheel-drive vehicle to make the short climb to the top of Campfire Hill; however, you can always park your car at the bottom of the hill and make the short climb to the top.

Directions: Take Hwy 375 to Lincoln County mile marker 34.6, where an unmarked-well-maintained-dirt road intersects with the Highway (37° 24.892' N, 115° 24.586' W). If you are using a GPS this road may be marked "Groom Lake Road" or simply "51 Road". In either case, follow the road about 12 miles until you see a small fork go the right. This road dead-ends shortly in a cul-du-sac, and you will see a small hill to your left. At the top is Campfire Hill.

GPS Location: 37° 21.09606869728708 N, 115° 36.383056640625 W

37°21'6.96"N 115°36'20.76"W [Area of Camping Recommendation]

Accessibility: Any two-wheel-drive vehicle in good condition should be able to make it to the base of Campfire Hill where you can easily walk to the top. You may need a four-wheel-drive vehicle if you want to drive the short road up the hill and to the actual site.

Amenities: None–it is just campsite at the top of a hill overlooking Groom Lake Road.

Distance from Area 51 Border: 2.6 Miles by Line-Of-Sight

Distance from Rachel: 33 Miles

Distance from Ash Springs: 29 Miles

Camp Fire Hill - **View from Campfire Hill towards Groom Lake Road**
37°21'6.91"N - 115°36'19.79"W

Aerial Google Earth view of Camp Hill.

The Hidden Campsite

Entrance - 37°26'16.06"N 115°27'11.21"W, this is at Highway 375!

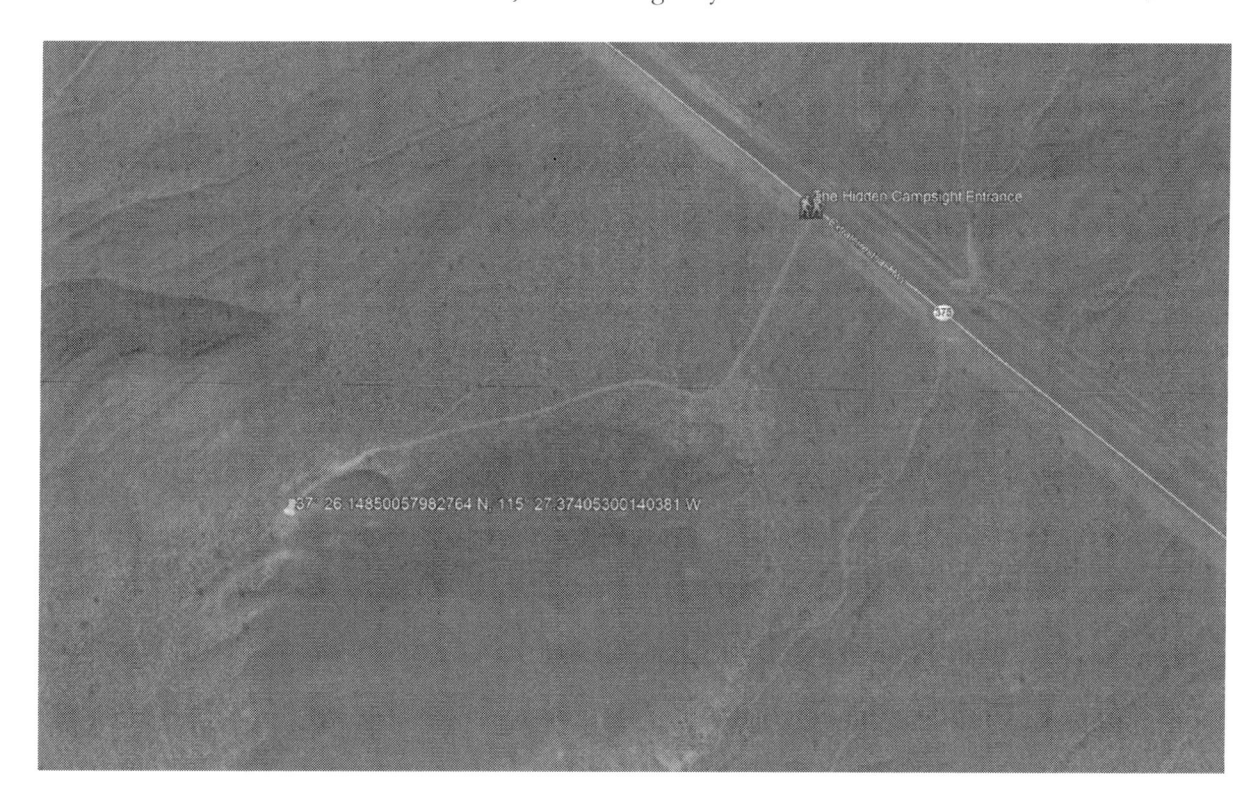

The Hidden Campsite

Entrance - 37°26'16.06"N 115°27'11.21"W at Highway 375

This campsite is located between the Black Mailbox and Gravel Parking. The advantage of this site is that it is easily accessible, yet hidden from HWY 375–so you will get an excellent view of the night skies, without anyone bothering you, and with better night vision as lights from the nearby roadway are not as bad as at the Black Mailbox.

You will still need to be prepared with water and gas as this location is at least 20 miles away from civilization. And you may need a high-clearance vehicle to follow the short dirt road to the site.

Directions: Take Hwy 375 to Lincoln County mile marker 31.3, where an unmaintained dirt road intersects with the Highway. If you are traveling North West, you should see a small hill to the right of the road. Follow the road to the back of the hill where you will find a suitable camp site.

GPS Location: 37° 26.14850057982764 N, 115° 27.37405300140381 W

Accessibility: A high-clearance vehicle is recommended, though not always necessary, to reach this site. RV access is not recommended.

Amenities: None–it is just campsite on the side of the road.

Distance from Area 51: 12 Miles

Distance from Rachel: 20 Miles

Distance from Ash Springs: 21 Miles

The Hidden Campsite

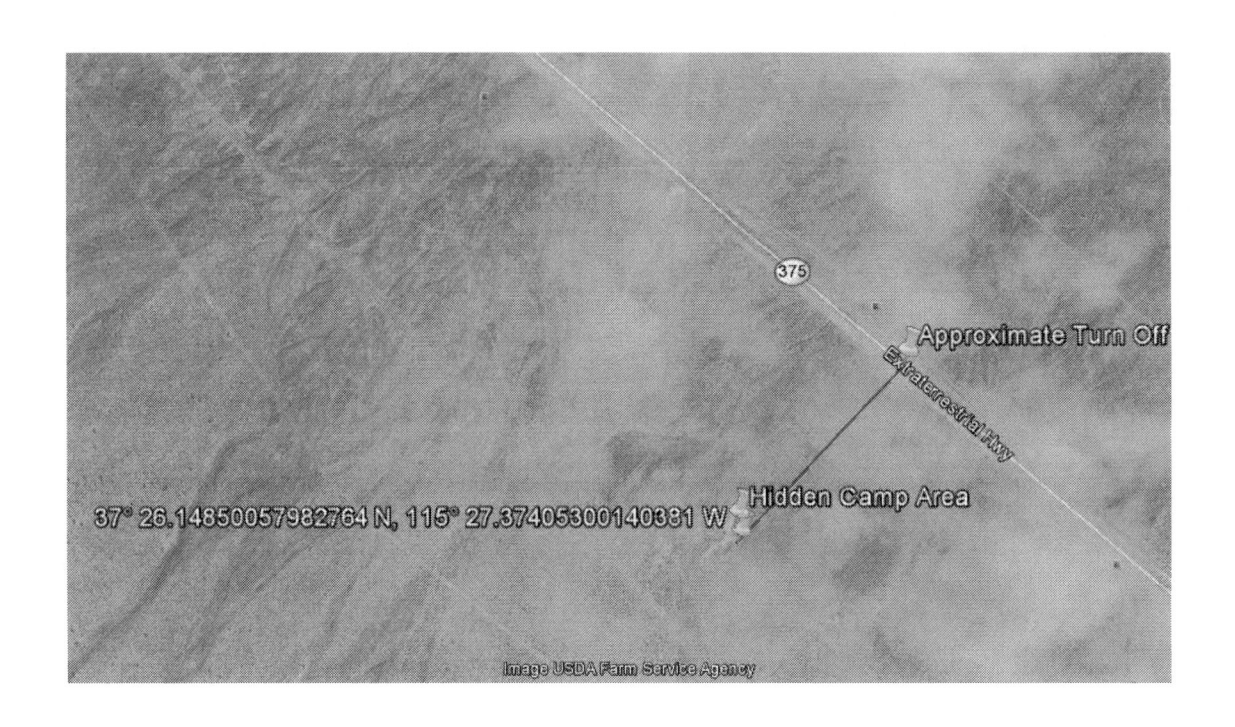

Aerial Google Earth view of the "Hidden Camp of HWY 375."

37°26'17.26"N - 115°27'12.58"W

Coyote Summit

This is a relatively easy site to get to, as it is located only miles from Rachel on Hwy 375. You'll be near civilization, and still have a somewhat private camping experience as this site is located on the south side of Coyote Summit, behind a small hill.

While you might be able to park an RV here, it may be a better idea to park at the Little A'Le'Inn, or even at the Gravel Parking area where you'll likely have a much better view of the night skies.

Directions: Take Hwy 375 to Lincoln County mile marker 16 where you'll see trash barrells on the side of the road. Take the dirt road to behind a small hill only a little ways from the highway.

GPS Location: 37° 234.331 N, 115° 40.123 W

Accessibility: Most vehicles, including RVs should be able to make it to this spot; however, turning around in an RV may be impossible, so other areas are better for RV camping.

Amenities: None–it is just campsite on the side of the road.

Distance from Area 51: 12 Miles

Distance from Rachel: 4 Miles

Distance from Ash Springs: 31 Miles

Coyote Summit

Powerlines Overlook

Powerlines Overlook, as named by the Dreamland Resort website, is one of the most spectacular campsites that you could choose for your trip to Area 51; unfortunately, it is also one of the hardest to get to.

Plan on several hours to locate and travel the trail to this site, and a reliable four-wheel-drive vehicle with an experienced driver. Do not attempt to find this site after dark, or after any substantial storm. The road is not maintained and you will be miles from civilization if you get stuck.

If you do make it to the overlook, you'll enjoy a wonderful view of the skies above Area 51, as well as a good place to pick up radio chatter from the base's tower.

Directions:

GPS Location: 37° 26.14850057982764 N, 115° 27.37405300140381 W

Accessibility: A high-clearance and four-wheel-drive vehicle is mandatory to reach this spot. If you do not have substantial experience maneuvering your vehicle in difficult terrain, then you will want to choose another camping location.

Amenities: None. This location is very remote. Make sure that you have plenty of water, food, gas, and especially a spare tire. It would also be a good idea to bring some common tools if anything goes wrong with your vehicle. Your cell phone make not work in this area and you may have to walk a substantial distance if things go wrong.

Distance from Area 51: 15 Miles

Distance from Rachel: 28 Miles

Distance from Ash Springs: 23 Miles

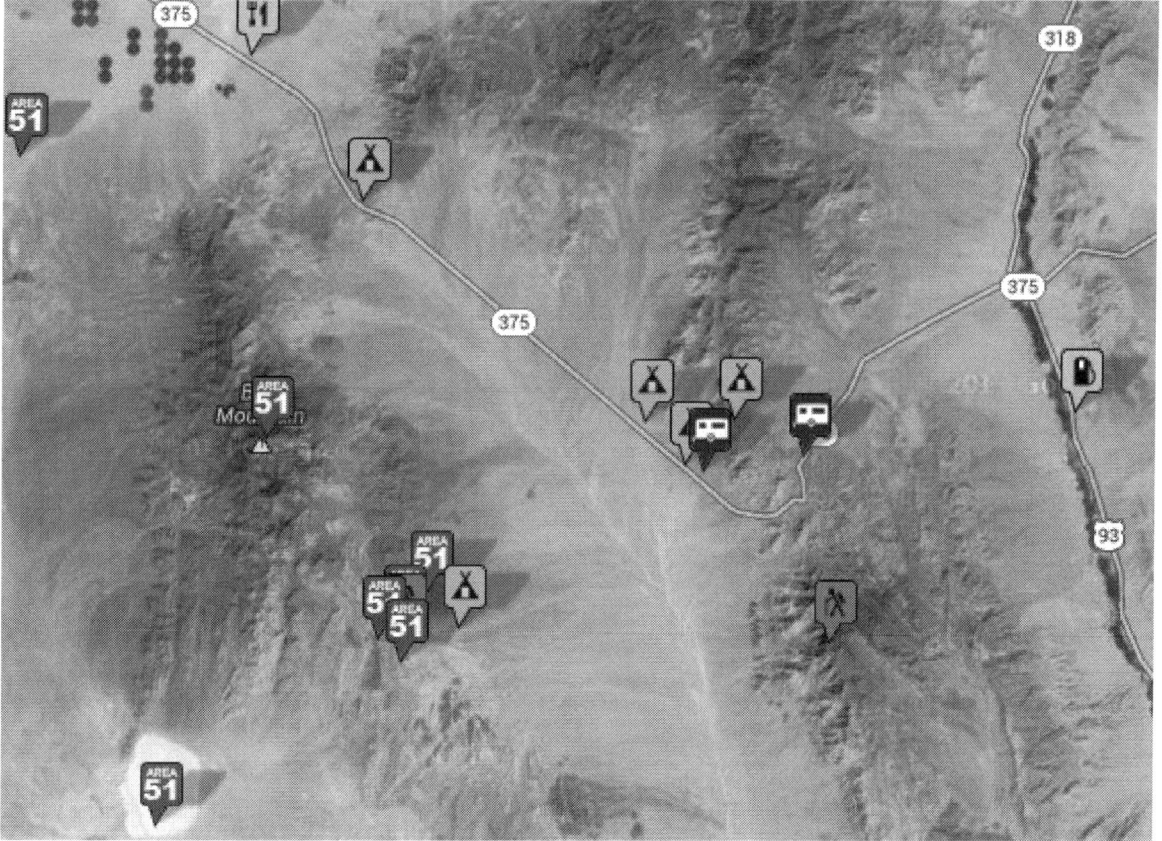

Summary of the Campsites around AREA 51 & Rachel

Camping is the best especially around AREA 51!

ENJOY!

Camping around Rachel Summary

During the summer months Rachel is a popular destination for campers who come out here to explore the many old mines and ghost towns in the area, or to watch the night skies for UFOs. In fact, UFOs or not, spending a night out here in the desert, away from any light pollution, is an experience you will not forget. Many hobby astronomers come out here to take advantage of the excellent viewing conditions.

Trailer Parks

The Little A'Le'Inn in Rachel has a small trailer park with full RV hookup. The rates are between $12 and $15 per day. In summer it may be a good idea to call ahead for reservations.

Camping

Also, most of the land along the Extraterrestrial Highway outside of Rachel is public land. There are no fences, and you can pull off the road and camp anywhere you like. If you do, please pick up all trash before you leave. There are trash barrels along the highway at Hancock Summit, Coyote Summit, Horneys Reststop and at several other locations.

Here are a few suggestions for good camp spots along the E.T. Highway:

- **Rachel (LN 10.0 [3])**:
  Full RV hookup at the Little A'Le'Inn (see above). Also plenty of level ground near the Inn to dry-camp or to pitch your tent. Ask the friendly folks at the Inn for a good spot.
  Please note: The Quik Pik trailer park was closed in late 2006.
- **Coyote Summit (LN 16.6 [6])**:
  Just before you reach Coyote Summit coming from Rachel you will see trash barrels on both sides of the highway. A dirt road intersects with the highway on the right. It leads around and to the back of a hill on the south side of the summit. There is a hidden campsite only a few hundred yards from the highway. The dirt road is suitable for most vehicles.
- **Black Mailbox (LN 29.6 [7])**:
  This is a popular spot for skywatchers, and in summer there is a good chance that you will have company here. There used to be the black mailbox of a nearby ranch here. It became part of Area 51 folklore and a traditional gathering spot for UFO watchers in the 1990's. The mailbox has since been removed but the site is still known as the "Black Mailbox" or simply as "The Mailbox". A small "shrine" has formed at the former location of the mailbox.

The dirt road that intersects here with the highway leads to a ranch, and also to the mysterious *Area 51*, which is just behind the hills in the southwest. If you camp here please do not block the intersection. There is a good level spot on the right, just after you turn onto the dirt road..

- **Hidden Campsite (LN 31.7)**:
  This is a great hidden spot for tent or car camping. Not suitable for RV's, requires a high-clearance vehicle. Look for an unmaintained dirt road leading southwest towards a small hill. It leads around the hill to a small hidden camp area in the back. Excellent private spot for skywatching at night.

- **Gravel Area (LN 32.3 [9])**:
  If you are travelling with a large RV or trailer this is an excellent campsite. Access from the highway is easy, and there is plenty of level ground for several large campers. This is an excellent place for skywatching at night, but not as private as the campsite above.

- **Campfire Hill (Groom Lake Road [near 13])**:
  This campsite is located on a small hill near the perimeter of the super-secret USAF base known as *Area 51*. It is on public land, but if you camp here you can almost be certain to have perimeter security visit you at night. Take Groom Lake Road at LN 34.5. After about 12 miles you will see Campfire Hill on the right, and a road leading up to its top. Requires high-clearance 4WD.

- **Horneys Reststop (LN 38.1 [15])**:
  Horneys is the only "official" reststop on the E.T. Highway. There are no facilities here, but a few trees that provide some shade. Access from the highway is possible with most trailers and RVs. This is a popular campsite in summer, and there is a good chance that you will have company here.

- **Powerlines Overlook (off hwy. [16])**:
  The Powerlines Overlook is located in the mountains north of the highway. It provides an incredible view over Tikaboo Valley and the surrounding mountains. There is enough level ground for several tents. Access requires a rough 4-mile 4WD ride, and a skilled driver. Take the dirt road in the back of Horneys Reststop (see above) and keep following the main traveled road. After about 4 miles you get to the overlook, where the powerlines to Rachel cross the ridge and lead down into Tikaboo Valley.
  Note: "LN..." refers to the Lincoln County mile markers along the highway. The count starts at the Nye/Lincoln county line about 10 miles north of Rachel..

Moores Station Petroglyphs

The Moores Station Petroglyph site is located in a small canyon near Moores Station, on the north side of Petroglyph Butte. Some of the petroglyphs are in excellent condition, well worth visiting. Access to the site requires a short and easy hike. The site is undeveloped, and there are no facilities.

Other petroglyph sites in the vicinity of Rachel include the Mount Irish Petroglyph Site near Hiko, accessible from Hwy. 318 and a site near Ash Springs, off US-93.

Directions

From Rachel turn left onto Hwy 375 north. Follow it for about 59 miles. At the Warm Springs junction turn right onto US-6 east. After 25.4 miles you see a small sign to "Moores Station" on the left. Turn left onto the well-maintained dirt road. After 12.2 miles you get to a 4-way intersection. Turn right here, and always follow the most traveled road when you come to a fork. After about 4 miles you will see a small canyon on the left, with Petroglyph Butte in the south. The petroglyphs are inside the canyon. Suitable for most vehicles; requires a short, easy hike.

Mount Irish Petroglyph Site

The Mount Irish Petroglyph Site is a 640-acre site in the northern Pahranagat Valley. The petroglyphs were carved into the soft reddish rock by prehistoric American Indians. The site is mostly undeveloped, and there are no facilities.

To get to the Petroglyph Site take Hwy. 318 north from the 318/375 fork. After 2.5 miles take Logan Summit Road, a dirt road leading west. The petroglyphs are spread out in an area about 8 miles from the turnoff. Look for the sign below. Access to the petroglyphs is possible with most sturdy 2WD vehicles. Many petroglyphs are within easy hiking distance from the road.

If you continue on the dirt road for another 3.5 miles you come over Logan Summit and into the northern Tikaboo Valley. On the way into the Valley you pass a beautiful wooden mining cabin that is worth a stop. The road over Logan Summit requires a 4WD high-clearance vehicle.

KXTA REFERENCE INFORMATION:

Homey Airport (KXTA)
Nevada, United States

Lat/Lng: 37° 14' 3.35" N / 115° 48' 55.56" W
37.234264 / -115.815434

Elevation: 4596'ft / 1401mMSL

ID / ICAO: KXTA

Runways: 2

Longest: 13R-31L
Concrete 8,224m / 26,981ft

Airport use: Military, Private, Permission required

Time Zone: -8UTC (-7DST)

Locl Time: 11:14 PST Tue 1-02-18

Sunrise: 06:57

Sunset: 16:37

AIRPORT DIAGRAM

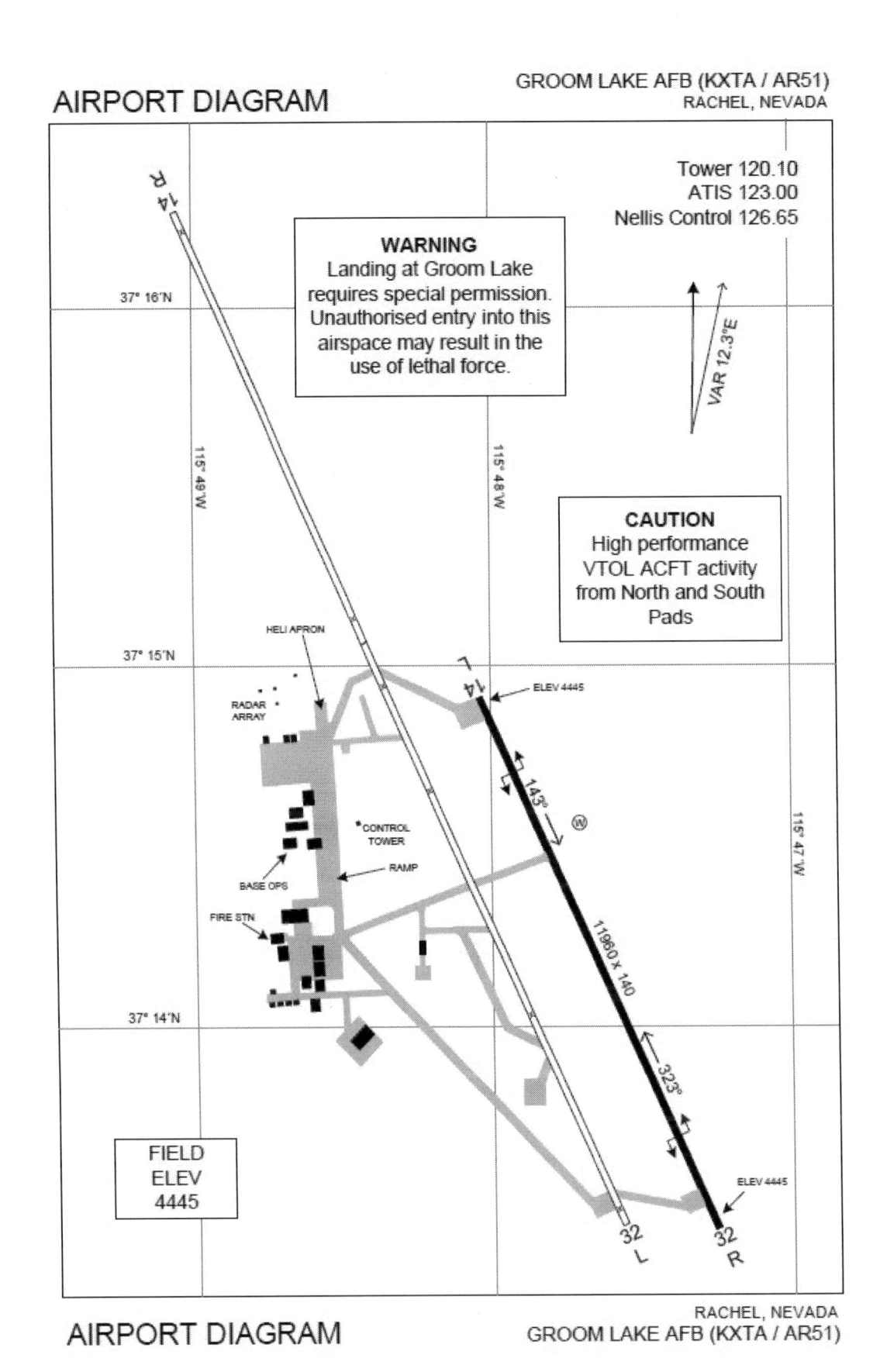

GROOM LAKE AFB (KXTA / AR51)
RACHEL, NEVADA

Tower 120.10
ATIS 123.00
Nellis Control 126.65

WARNING
Landing at Groom Lake requires special permission. Unauthorised entry into this airspace may result in the use of lethal force.

VAR 12.3°E

CAUTION
High performance VTOL ACFT activity from North and South Pads

37° 16'N
37° 15'N
37° 14'N

115° 49'W
115° 48'W
115° 47'W

14R
14L
32L
32R

ELEV 4445
143°
323°
11960 x 140
ELEV 4445

RADAR ARRAY
HELI APRON
CONTROL TOWER
BASE OPS
RAMP
FIRE STN

FIELD ELEV 4445

AIRPORT DIAGRAM

RACHEL, NEVADA
GROOM LAKE AFB (KXTA / AR51)

APPENDIX A
Area 51 Building Current Layout

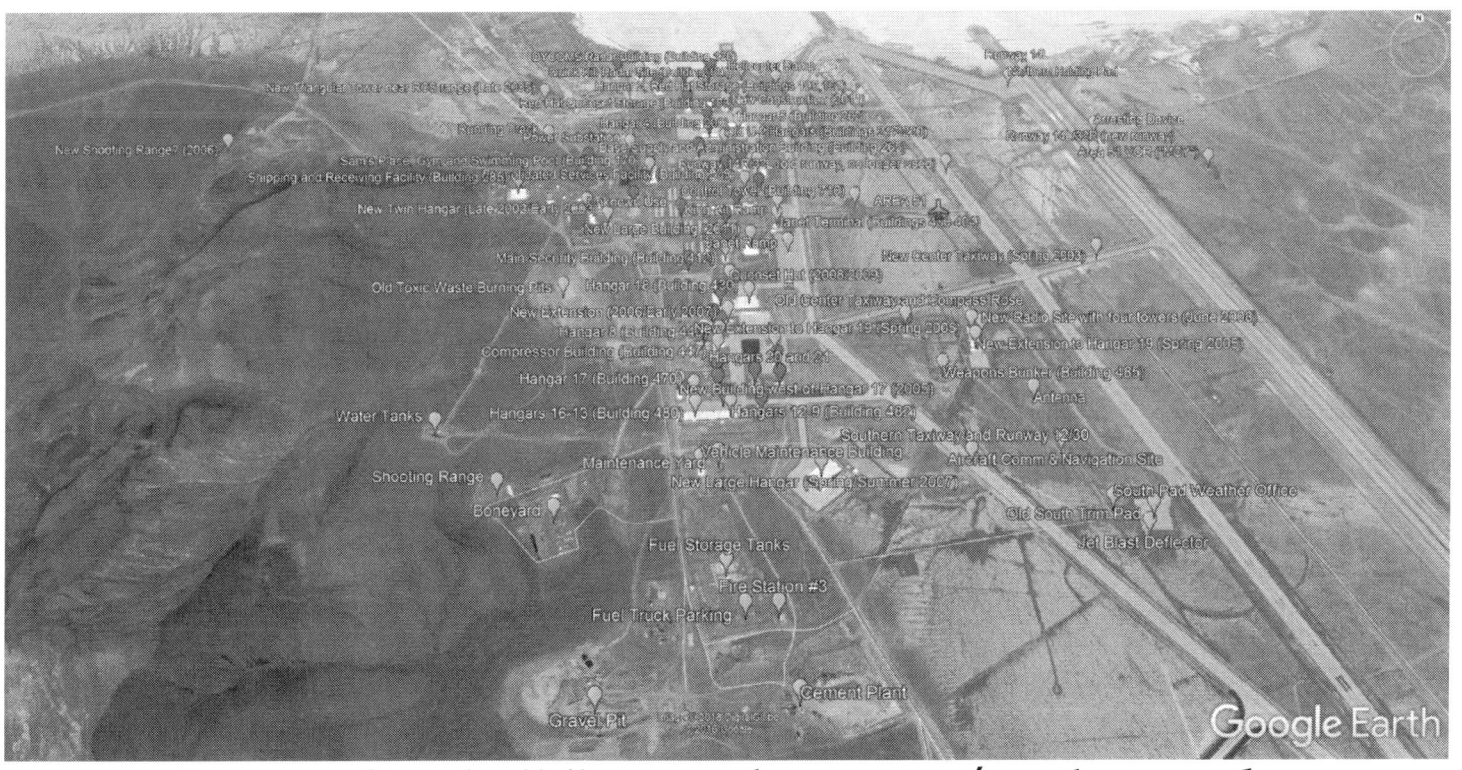

Surrounding buildings and runways/markers and other

Detailed places of Interest around Area 51

APPENDIX B

Area 51 Building Current Layout

TTR, Basecamp, some of the Gates, View Spots and other

Places of Interest around Area 51

APPENDIX C

Area 51 Back Gate

37°35'38.51"N 115°53'55.84"W

Back Gate Markers

APPENDIX D

NTTR RANGE BOUNDARY MARKERS

NTTR RANGES

The Nevada Test and Training Range land area is mostly Central Basin and Range ecoregion (cf. southernmost portion in the Mojave Desert), and smaller ecoregions (e.g., Tonopah Basin, Tonopah Playa, & Bald Mountain biomes) are within the area of numerous basin and range landforms of the NTTR.

Landforms
For the list of all NTTR landforms, see Nellis & Wildlife 5 Ranges region.

The NTTR is at the serpentine section of the Great Basin Divide in southern Nevada and uses numerous landforms for military operations, e.g., Groom Lake near the northeast NTTR border is the airstrip for Area 51, the 1955 Site II west of the lake's WWII field. Tolicha Peak and Point Bravo are the sites of for electronic combat ranges, and the Mercury Valley is the eponym for a Cold War camp that became Mercury, Nevada. The Tonopah Test Range, within the boundaries of the NTTR (e.g., "Nellis Range 75") includes Antelope Lake, Radar Hill, and the "Cactus, Antelope, and Silverbow Springs".

Northern Range

The *Northern Range* includes the Tolicha Peak Electronic Combat Range (TPECR, e.g., Range 76 targets 76-03, -05, -11, & -14) and Tonopah Electronic Combat Range (the Wildhorse Management Area encircled by the Northern Range is not part of the NTTR.)

Eastman Airfield Target

The **Eastman Airfield Target** (Target 76-14, Korean Airfield, 37°22'N 116°50'W is a Range 76 target 4.3 mi (6.9 km) northwest of the TPECR. The target has a northeastern taxiway loop, characteristic for the former Soviet Air Force base at Jüterbog Airfield in East Germany, and three ramps in front of hangars on the western side of the loop. The other taxiways have a similar layout to Jüterbog, although the runway is about 1,300 feet (400 m) shorter. There are two accompanying SAM sites, one 2.5 kilometres (1.6 mi) northwest of the airfield, and one 3.5 miles (5.6 km) northwest just like the original.

Southern Range

The **Southern Range** includes the Point Bravo Electronic Combat Range] An area of about 1,276 sq mi (3,300 km^2) of the Southern Range that was withdrawn from the Desert National Wildlife Range is co-managed by the USAF and the USFWS.

Nearby facilities

In addition to Nellis AFB, areas outside of the current NTTR land area are used for related activities, e.g., about 1,107 sq mi (2,870 km^2) of the former military range land (relinquished 1942, e.g. ranges 46-56, and c. 1953) is under the Nellis "Area A" airspace that is a Military Operations Area (MOA). The Formerly Used Defense Site north and northeast of the NTTR with "Stone Cabin, Hot Creek, Railroad, Tikaboo, and Sand Spring valleys" is a "former portion of the Tonopah Bombing Range", includes "Permit Required Confined space", and prohibits vehicles in "suspected ordnance impact area[s]" (e.g., "green markings" indicate chemical agents).

Most areas adjacent to the NTTR are managed by the Bureau of Land Management for limited non-residential use such as grazing. Temporary sites, e.g., for Patriot Communications Exercises (about "21 days per exercise"), are in the "ADA activity area" east of the NTTR with 13 empty "500 feet by 500 feet" sites for mobile electronic equipment on BLM land in the "Sand Springs Valley, Coal Valley, Delamar Valley, and Dry Lake Valley" ("general area" of the Key Pittman WMA) and "under MOA airspace".

APPENDIX E

CHEECH AIR FORCE BASE KEY MAP REFERENCES

Creech Air Force Base is a United States Air Force (USAF) command and control facility in Clark County, Nevada used "to engage in daily Overseas Contingency Operations...of remotely piloted aircraft systems which fly missions across the globe. In addition to an airport, the military installation has the Unmanned Aerial Vehicle Battlelab, associated aerial warfare ground equipment, and unmanned aerial vehicles of the type used in Afghanistan and Iraq. Creech is the aerial training site for the USAF Thunderbirds and "is one of two emergency divert airfields" for the Nevada Test and Training Range.

In addition to the airfield, the base includes the "UAV-Logistic and Training Facility", the Joint Unmanned Aerial Systems Center of Excellence, Silver Flag Alpha Regional Training Center, and other military units/facilities. The base in named in honor of retired US Air Force General Wilbur L. Creech, the former commanding officer of Tactical Air Command (TAC), the predecessor command of the current Air Combat Command (ACC).

APPENDIX F

Nellis Range Information
Link & QR CODE

Link: https://www.inplanesight.org/nellis.html

Nellis updated frequencies; GPS; Google Earth .KMZ data etc.

For example: Tikaboo Peak is one of the locations where you can view Groom Lake. These links contain two trails. One to reach the staging area. The other is the hike from the staging area to the peak. Several parking locations are indicated as waypoints. The road is dirt suitable for cars but eventually requiring SUV as you get near the end. If you have a car, your hike will be longer.

Area 51 Scanner Frequencies

NDB Band (190-535 kHz, AM)

209 kHz Basecamp NDB "AEC"
278 kHz TTR NDB "XSD" (inactive)
326 kHz Mercury NDB "MCY" (inactive)
414 kHz Groom NDB "PYD" (inactive)

HF Band (3.0 - 29.7 MHz, AM)

5.7570 >USB< Thug Common during JFEX (12/17)
18.4500 >USB< AWACS Darkstar

Low Band (29.7 - 50 MHz, NFM)

33.9000 Statewide fire / rescue
40.5000 Army Search and Rescue/FM Emergency
41.0000 Desert Radio (Bike Lake Advisory)
41.5000 Army Control Towers

TV Broadcasting Band, Channels 2 - 4 (54 - 72 Mhz, NFM)

69.4000 Mobile SAM sites in Railroad Valley during Red Flag

Aeronautical Radionavigation (108 - 118 Mhz, AM)

108.2000 North Las Vegas VOT
110.3000 McCarran Runway 25R ILS
111.7500 McCarran Runway 25L LOC/GS
113.0000 TTR VOR, ident: "TQQ" and weather info "S1"
113.9000 Basecamp VOR, ident: "AEC"
114.3000 Mormon Mesa VOR, ident: "MMM"
114.5000 Palmdale VOR, ident: "PMD"
114.7000 Beatty VOR, ident: "BTY"
116.3000 Wilson Creek VOR, ident: "ILC"
116.4000 Edwards AFB VOR, ident: "EDW"
116.7000 Boulder City VOR
116.9000 McCarran VOR
117.2000 Tonopah VOR, ident: "TPH"
117.5000 Groom Lake VOR, ident: "MCY" and weather info
117.7000 Coaldale VOR, ident: "OAL"

Civilian Aircraft Band (118 - 137 Mhz, AM)

118.0000 McCarran Clearance Delivery
118.0500 North Las Vegas ATIS
118.1250 Nellis AFB Approach/Departure (published, NW, paired with 291.7250)
118.2750 TTR Range 74 automated weather
118.3000 Creech AFB Tower and SFA (paired with 360.625)

Area 51 Scanner Frequencies

118.4000 McCarran Class B SE
118.4500 Air Exercise, targeting ops (Laser)
118.7000 Dreamland MOA Control (Janet Ops "Gold Coast")
118.7500 McCarran Control Tower (RY 01-19)
119.0000 Grand Canyon Tower
119.3500 Nellis Control West (Lee Corridor, Beatty, Goldfield, Tonopah, Warm Springs etc., paired with 254.400)
119.4000 McCarran Approach & Class B NE
119.4500 TTR Base Ops, flt. Dispatch (published, paired with 233.950)
119.9000 McCarran Control Tower (RY 08-26)
120.4500 McCarran VFR Final Approach
120.5250 NTTR Fire Fighters (air, talking to Bird Dog)
120.6500 Local Traffic (tour helicopters, main)
120.7750 Henderson Executive Airport ATIS
120.9000 Nellis AFB Clearance Delivery
121.1000 McCarran Ground Control (E OF 01R/19L)
121.1250 Creech AFB Automated Weather
121.5000 International Aircraft Emergency (International Air Distress, IAD)
121.7000 North Las Vegas Ground
121.8000 Nellis AFB Ground Control
121.9000 McCarran Ground Control (W OF 01R/19L)
121.9500 Local Traffic (tour helicopters, secondary)
122.0000 Enroute Flight Advisory Service (EFAS) ("Flightwatch"), weather advisories
122.1000 FSS (Flight Service Stations), VOR receive frequency
122.3500 Flight Service Station (FSS) in Las Vegas
122.4000 FAA Flight Service Stations
122.7000 Boulder City UNICOM
122.8000 Desert Rock (Mercury) UNICOM
122.9000 Alamo Airport CTAF, Range 63 and 64 RCO "Fatness"
122.9500 Las Vegas McCarran UNICOM
123.0000 Tonopah Airport UNICOM
123.4500 Air-to-Air
123.4750 Nellis 64 AGRS (F-16)
123.5500 Nellis Range Controller "Blackjack" VHF (paired with 377.800)
123.8250 Las Vegas McCarran Helicopter Control
124.0000 North Las Vegas Clearance Delivery
124.2000 LA Center (Cedar City, low) (NE of Vegas)
124.4000 McCarran Ramp Control (A+B+C Gates and Charter)
124.5500 Joshua Approach
124.6250 LA Center (Mount Potosi, low/high) (Vegas and NW) (Janets to TTR)
124.7500 Silverbow Tower (TTR, paired with 257.950)
124.9500 Nellis AFB Approach/Departure East and Class B
125.0250 McCarran Approach & Class B West
125.5750 Salt Lake Center (Cedar City, low + high)
125.6000 McCarran Approach & Class B East
125.7000 North Las Vegas Tower

Area 51 Scanner Frequencies

125.7500 Oakland Center (Bishop, low) (Janets to TTR)
125.9000 McCarran Departure Runways 19L/R and 26L/R
126.1500 Dreamland MOA Control/Approach (R-4808, primary, paired with UHF: 261.100)
126.2000 26 WPS (MQ-1/MQ-9) (Desert Radio, Bike Lake Advisory)
126.3000 Nevada Test Site, Mercury Approach
126.5500 Joshua Control (Edwards AFB)
126.6000 Dreamland MOA
126.6500 Nellis Control East (Sally Corridor, Wilson Creek, Las Vegas, Caliente, Mormon Mesa, paired with 317.525)
126.9500 Nellis Track (airspace controller for western 70's ranges, Hwy 95 corridor and AR-625 refueling ops during Red Flag missions, paired with 324.050)
127.1750 Oakland Center (Coaldale, low)
127.2500 TTR Ground Control
127.3500 LA Center (Cedar City, high) (NE of Vegas)
127.5000 Joshua Control (Edwards AFB)
127.9000 McCarran Ramp Control (D Gates and Cargo)
127.9250 Salt Lake Center (Wilson Creek, low)
129.0250 Private airline
129.1000 TTR Ground Control (obsolete?)
129.1750 McCarran Ramp Control (A+B+C Gates and Charter)
129.6500 Private airline
130.3500 Northwest Airlines OPS
130.5250 Red Flag: Red Team enroute
130.6500 Air Mobility Command (AMC) Primary
130.7000 Northwest Airlines, Las Vegas Ops.
131.1500 Delta Airlines, Las Vegas Ops.
131.6000 Scenic Airlines, Boulder City Ops.
131.7750 America West Airlines ("Cactus"), Las Vegas Ops.
132.0500 Oakland Center (Tonopah, high)
132.4000 McCarran ATIS Arrival/Departure
132.5500 Nellis AFB Tower
132.6250 LA Center (Mount Potosi, high) (Vegas and NW)
133.4500 Salt Lake Center (Tonopah, low/high) (Janets to TTR)
133.5500 LA Center (Barstow, high) (SW of Vegas)
133.6500 Joshua Control (Edwards AFB)
133.9500 McCarran Departure Runways 01L/R and RY 08L/R
134.1000 Creech AFB SOF
134.5250 Salt Lake Center (Wilson Creek, high)
134.6500 LA Center (Barstow, low) (SW of Vegas)
134.7000 Oakland (or Salt Lake?) Center High
135.0000 McCarran Final Approach
135.1000 Nellis AFB Approach/Departure West
135.2500 LA Center (Cedar City, high) (NE of Vegas)
135.7000 Oakland Center high altitude flight watch, above 18,000ft.
135.9000 LA Center high altitude flight watch, above 18,000ft.
136.5000 Private airline (air side)

Area 51 Scanner Frequencies

Military Land Band (138 - 144 MHz, NFM, some AM)

138.0125 >AM< 422 TES (A-10)
138.1000 >AM< Green Flag (549 CTS) Ops
138.1250 Data Carrier, Cedar Peak area
138.1500 Desert Rock Airstrip (NTS) / Range Control R-4806 / HARM Secondary
138.1750 >AM< 16 WPS (F-16)
138.2250 Federal Emergency Management Agency (FEMA), base
138.2500 >AM< 16 WPS (F-16)
138.3000 >AM< Search and Rescue, Planes
138.3750 >AM< 66 WPS (A-10)
138.5000 >AM< MAFEX Check-In, Kingfish India VHF 2
138.6000 >AM< Air Exercise, crypto check-in ("Dragnet", "Uniform")
138.7500 >AM< Red Flag Freq. "ORANGE 2"
138.7750 >AM< Red Flag Freq. "YELLOW 2" (bombing exercise)
138.8500 >AM< Red Flag AWACS
138.9500 >AM< 26 WPS (MQ-9), Red Flag Freq. "YELLOW 4"
139.1250 >AM< 16 WPS (F-16)
139.3000 >AM< Nellis AFB, Pilot to Dispatcher
139.4000 >AM< 66 WPS (A-10), 66 RQS (HH-60)
139.5500 >AM< 16 WPS (F-16)
139.5750 >AM< Green Flag (549 CTS)
139.6000 >AM< 422 TES (F-16), MAFEX Check-In, Kingfish India VHF 1
139.6250 >AM< Voice, referred someone to 377.1 MHz (LA ARTCC)
139.7500 >AM< 64 AGRS (F-16) ("Baron")
139.8000 >AM< Thunderbirds Air Show
139.8000 >AM< Red Flag Freq. "ORANGE 3"
139.8500 >AM< 64 AGRS (F-16)
139.9500 >AM< Green Flag (549 CTS)
140.1000 >AM< Green Flag (549 CTS)
140.1500 >AM< 16 WPS (F-16)
140.1750 >AM< 433 WPS (F-15C, F-22) Support
140.2250 >AM< Green Flag (549 CTS)
140.2750 >AM< 66 WPS (A-10)
140.3250 >AM< 17 WPS (F-15E) Support
140.3750 >AM< Red Flag, 66 RQS (HH-60)
140.4000 >AM< 433 WPS (F-15C, F-22) Support
140.4500 >AM< 422 TES (F-15E) Support
140.5750 >AM< Red Flag: RF 17-3: DGAR
140.7000 >AM< 433 WPS (F-15C, F-22) Support
140.8000 >AM< Red Flag: RF 17-3: DGAR
140.8250 >AM< 422 TES (F-22A)
140.9250 >AM< Red Flag: RF 17-3: DGAR
140.9500 >AM< 422 TES (F-16)
140.9750 >AM< 66 WPS (A-10) Support
141.0000 >AM< Red Flag SEAD
141.0250 >AM< 422 TES (F-22A)

Area 51 Scanner Frequencies

141.0500 >AM< Green Flag (549 CTS)
141.0750 >AM< Red Flag: RF 17-3: DGAR
141.1500 >AM< Red Flag Freq. "ORANGE 4" / CSAR Secondary
141.1750 >AM< Thunderbirds Air Show secondary (VHF Ops, take-off, landing)
141.1750 Edwards AFB, range control
141.3750 >AM< Red Flag: RF 17-3: DGAR
141.4000 >AM< Green Flag (549 CTS)
141.4750 >AM< Red Flag: RF 17-3: DGAR (White)
141.5750 >AM< Red Flag: RF 17-3: DZ/LZ 1+2
141.6000 >AM< Air exercise
141.6250 >AM< 16 WPS (F-16), 66 RQS (HH-60)
141.6500 >AM< 422 TES (F-15C) Support
141.6750 >AM< 64 AGRS (F-16)
141.7000 >AM< Restricted Area R-4806 Control
141.7750 >AM< 34 WPS (HH-60)
141.8250 >AM< Red Flag: RF 17-3: DGAR
141.9250 >AM< 422 TES (F-15E) Support
141.9500 >AM< 422 TES (F-22A)
142.1500 U.S.A.F. MARS program (Military Affiliate Radio System), Emergency/disaster preparedness, repeater input PL 100.0
142.2000 >AM< Voice, air exercise ("Fox 3")
142.2500 USAF MARS Simplex
142.2750 USAF MARS Secondary Repeater Input
142.3250 >AM< Red Flag: RF 17-3: DGAR
142.5250 >AM< Red Flag, CSAR Primary
142.5500 >AM< Red Flag, 66 RQS (HH-60)
142.7500 >AM< Supervisor of Flying (SOF) 57 FW-Bullseye Control (prim.) (UHF on 305.600 MHz)
143.3750 >AM< 66 WPS (A-10)
143.4500 U.S.A.F. MARS program (Military Affiliate Radio System), Emergency/disaster preparedness, repeater output, PL 100.0
143.6000 >AM< 422 TES (A-10)
143.7500 >AM< Red Flag, CAS ADMIN
143.7750 USAF MARS Secondary Repeater Output
143.8250 >AM< 64 AGRS (F-16)
144.4500 >AM< Red Flag Ops, launch and recovery (Handed players off to "White 8")

High Band (148 - 174 MHz, NFM, some AM)

Note: Most of the Nellis and NTS frequencies in this band are obsolete. However, they may be re-used for other purposes.

148.1000 Exercise controller "Roulette" for ground threads (SAM sites etc.)
148.1750 >AM< Creech AFB SOF
148.1750 >AM< Thunderbirds Air Show (VHF, Diamond)
148.2000 Exercise controller "Roulette" for ground threads (SAMs etc.)

Area 51 Scanner Frequencies

148.2000 >AM< Controller (AWACS?) during Air Exercise
148.2500 >AM< 66 RQS (HH-60)
148.5000 Nellis Range Controller "Blackjack" (frequency "Fox 4", repeater output), contractors etc.
148.8500 >AM< 66 WPS (A-10) Support
149.1000 >AM< Red Flag: RF 17-3: DGAR
149.1250 >AM< 422 TES (A-10)
149.3250 >AM< Dreamland MOA Ops
149.4000 >AM< Red Flag: RF 17-3: SAO/DGAR
149.5250 >AM< 64 AGRS (F-16)
149.6500 >AM< Red Flag: RF 17-3: 22 ARW, KC-135
149.8750 >AM< 26 WPS (MQ-9)
150.1750 Nellis Range Controller "Blackjack" (frequency "Fox 4", repeater input), contractors etc.
150.5000 >AM< 422 TES (F-22A)
150.6750 >AM< Red Flag, 66 RQS (HH-60)
150.9950 Lincoln County Road Department
151.0400 Cops / Highway patrol, Las Vegas area
151.0550 Nye County Sheriff (Warm Springs Repeater Output)
151.3100 NHP, Alamo repeater output
153.8450 Firefighters / paramedics (LN County 1 Repeater output, input: 154.9950)
153.9200 Alamo Fire Protection District (Repeater output, input: 155.7450)
153.9950 Clark County Animal Control
154.0100 NHP, Alamo repeater input
154.0550 NHP, Alamo repeater output
154.0700 Lincoln County Sheriff (Input, output: 155.2050)
154.6800 NHP, Alamo repeater output (same as 154.905 MHz, CTCSS 151.4 Hz)
154.7400 NHP, Alamo repeater output (CTCSS 151.4 Hz & 162.2 Hz)
154.7700 Local Law Enforcement Mutual Aid
154.7850 NHP Tonopah
154.8000 Rural Cops, Boulder City Repeater (CTCSS 173.8 Hz)
154.8300 Nye County Sheriff, Tonopah
154.8600 Lincoln County Sheriff Repeater (LN County 2, output, input: 155.5350)
154.8825 NHP, Warm Springs repeater output (CTCSS 151.4 Hz)
154.9050 NHP, Highland Peak repeater output (same as 154.680 MHz, CTCSS 151.4 Hz)
154.9875 NHP Tonopah
154.9950 Firefighters / paramedics (LN County 1 Repeater input, output: 153.8450)
155.0100 Nye County Sheriff, Tonopah (Medics tone 127.3, Cops tone 110.9)
155.0325 NHP, Warm Springs repeater output (CTCSS 151.4 Hz & 162.2 Hz)
155.1300 NHP, Highland Peak repeater output (CTCSS 151.4 Hz)
155.1450 NHP, Alamo repeater input
155.1600 Search and rescue mutual aid (LN County 3)
155.2050 Lincoln County Sheriff Repeater, APCO-25 encoded (LN County 4, output, input: 154.0700)

Area 51 Scanner Frequencies

155.3550 NHP, Alamo repeater input
155.4750 Federal Law Enforcement, mutual aid
155.5350 Lincoln County Sheriff (LN County 5, input, output: 154.8600)
155.6250 Nye County Sheriff (Warm Springs Repeater Output, CTCSS 179.9 Hz)
155.6550 Nevada Law Enforcement, statewide mutual aid
155.6850 Las Vegas Park Rangers / Parking Enforcement
155.7000 NHP, Alamo repeater output (CTCSS 151.4 Hz)
155.7450 Alamo Fire Protection District (Repeater input, output: 153.9200)
155.7900 Nye County Sheriff, Amargosa Valley Jct (CTCSS 136.5 Hz)
155.8800 Las Vegas Mc Carran airport security, morse code ID "KCE878"
158.7450 Cops, Las Vegas, northeast patrol: downtown and northeast
158.7900 Cops, Las Vegas, administration, detectives, crime scenes
158.8200 NHP, Warm Springs repeater input (DCS 115?)
158.8350 NHP, Alamo and Highland Peak repeater input (DCS 315)
158.8500 LVPD Glendale repeater (CTCSS 173.8 Hz)
158.9250 NHP, Warm Springs repeater input (DCS 115 & CTCSS 162.2 Hz)
158.9400 NHP, Highland Peak repeater input
158.9700 NHP, Alamo repeater input (DCS 315 & CTCSS 162.2 Hz)
158.9850 Lincoln County Road Department
159.0300 NHP, Alamo repeater input
159.1500 NHP, Alamo repeater output
159.4200 NHP, Alamo repeater output
162.4750 NOAA Weather info (from Utah)
162.5500 NOAA Weather info (from Las Vegas)
163.8000 USGS Seismic Sensor near Queen City Summit
168.4375 NTS Operations, repeater output
170.0250 Fire Weather (Twice daily, White Pine and Lincoln County)
170.5250 NTTR Fire Fighters, interagency, ground
171.2200 University of Nevada seismic sensor, Warm Springs Radio Site
171.7250 Tonopah Base Station, Booker Mountain (Nevada Interagency Fire Management)

Mixed Government Use Band (216 - 220 Mhz, FM)

216.7250 >FM< Nellis Air Show: Narration and Show Music
216.9750 >FM< Nellis Air Show: Cockpit voice mix

Military Aircraft Band (225 - 400 Mhz, AM)

225.3250 Red Flag AMC
225.4500 Range 65 Ops
225.5750 AWACS check-in "Mojo", (Weapons School)
225.7000 Red Flag 03/14: "Chalice on DCM, we'll act as relay for Juice"
226.1000 Creech AFB SOF
227.0500 Red Flag AWACS "Goliath" to Red Flag Ops "Galley?" (01/13)
228.0000 Range 74 Operations
228.2000 Red Flag Freq. "BEIGE 24" (Talked about drops)

Area 51 Scanner Frequencies

228.5000 Aerial refueling ? / Air Exercise
228.8000 414th Combat Training Squadron, Tactical
228.9500 Dreamland MOA AAR Mission Freq.
229.0000 Nellis 16 WPS (F-16, F-35) Ops/MX
229.2500 Red Flag FAC east, bombing ops
230.0250 26 WPS (MQ-9)
231.1000 Red Flag Joint Interface Control Officer (JICO) "Juice" (Data link and comms controller)
233.4500 Red Flag AWACS Check-In, secondary
233.6000 34 WPS (HH-60)
233.9500 TTR Base Ops, flt. Dispatch (published, paired with 119.450)
234.2500 Range 62 Operations
234.3250 Coyote MOA
234.8000 414th Combat Training Squadron, Tactical
234.9000 Red Flag Nellis Ops
235.2500 Thunderbirds Air Show (UHF, Solos, Control)
235.7500 Creech AFB SOF
236.0000 Red Flag, 66 RQS (HH-60) Ops, SAR-B (Freq. "White 2")
236.1000 Bat Ops (422nd Test and Evaluation Squadron, Nellis)
236.5000 Dreamland MOA
236.6000 Military Control Towers UHF
236.9500 Darkstar air exercise controller
238.3000 Dreamland MOA (Ops freq.) (Mission freq. on 375.8)
238.3250 Air exercise Mission (Orange 12, Paired with Ops Freq.395.150)
238.6500 Red Flag FAC east, bombing ops (Freq. "White 3")
238.7000 Nellis Range Controller
238.8000 Nellis Range Control Center "Long Shot" (R-4806E, Alamo Area)
239.4000 Red Flag Ops
239.7000 34 WPS (HH-60)
239.8000 PMSV Metro Weather
240.1000 Dreamland MOA Aerial Refueling Ops frequency (Mission: 377.250)
240.1500 voice AM, air exercise
240.3000 Aggressor secondary control
241.0000 Army National Guard
242.2000 US Air Force Air Combat Command (ACC)
243.0000 International Aircraft Emergency (Military Air Distress, MAD)
243.9000 Nellis Range Control "Baron"
245.6500 Red Flag, 66 RQS (HH-60)
251.2000 Green Flag (549 CTS) Ops
251.9000 Red Flag, 66 RQS (HH-60) Ops, SAR-A (Freq. "Red 20")
252.1000 64 AGRS (F-16) Ops (MIG Ops, "Red Team")
252.2000 voice AM, air exercise
252.5500 Red Flag: RF 17-3: VAQ-134, EA-6B
252.8000 66 RQS (HH-60)
253.4000 Tactical Control
253.7000 Red Flag Freq. "RED 3" (used fur Red Flag orientation flight)
253.7250 Red Flag: RF 17-3: SAO AirBoss

Area 51 Scanner Frequencies

254.3000 McCarran Ground Control (W OF RY 01L/19R)
254.4000 Nellis Control West (Lee Corridor, Beatty, Goldfield, Tonopah, Warm Springs etc., paired with 119.350)
254.4750 Red Flag Freq. "RED 4"
255.1250 Military aircraft enroute, Air-to-Air
255.3000 66 WPS (A-10)
255.4000 FAA Flight Service Stations / Nellis AFB UNICOM
255.5000 Dreamland MOA
255.7000 Red Flag AWACS "Darkstar"
255.7500 Aerial Refueling Operations
255.8000 Dreamland UNICOM (Base)/MOA Control (R-4808) (sec.)
255.9500 Northern Ranges MOA
256.8000 Air exercise AWACS "Tiger" to aircraft "Victory"
257.0000 Red Flag Exercise Operations
257.1000 17 WPS (F-15E) ("Orange 39")
257.3500 AMC Command post (Red Flag deployment and control)
257.8000 McCarran Control Tower
257.9500 Silverbow Tower (TTR, paired with 124.750)
258.6750 26 WPS (MQ-9)
259.0000 Red Flag, 66 RQS (HH-60) Ops
259.4000 Nellis Range Control Center "Bulls Eye"
259.8000 Red Flag: RF 17-3: VAQ-134, EA-6B
259.9500 AMC Command post (Red Flag deployment) (Freq. "RED 5")
260.1000 433 WPS (F-15C, F-22)
260.2500 Red Flag Comms.
261.1000 Dreamland MOA Control/Approach (R-4808, primary, paired with VHF: 126.150) (published)
261.3750 Red Flag: RF 17-3: VAQ-134, EA-6B
262.6500 433 WPS (F-15C, F-22A)
262.7000 Air Ex.: Mission control/ops/check-in/out for joint Nellis-Fallon ex. 10/16
262.7500 64 AGRS (F-16)
263.6000 Desert Range Control
265.5000 Red Flag Controller (giving tanker instructions for AR exercise)
265.9750 Red Flag: RF 17-3: VAQ-134, EA-6B
266.0000 Red Flag Freq. "BLUE 4" (OCA, AWACS)
266.6000 433 WPS (F-15C, F-22A)
267.1000 Red Flag: RF 17-3: VAQ-134, EA-6B, active
267.1500 Red Flag: RF 17-3: VMFA-211, F-35B
267.4750 Red Flag: RF 17-3: VMFA-211, F-35B
267.5250 Red Flag Air Drop Ops
267.6000 Red Flag AWACS "Chalice"
268.0000 Range 63 and 64 Operations (RCO "Fatness")
268.2000 Elgin MOA (Range Control Center "Barn Yard")
268.5000 Red Flag Exercise Operations
269.0000 414th Combat Training Squadron, Tactical
269.8500 Red Flag: RF 17-3: 55FS, F-16
270.0250 Red Flag MiG Ops (Red Team)

Area 51 Scanner Frequencies

270.1000 Nellis AFB ATIS ("Automatic Terminal Information Service")
270.7250 Red Flag Strike (SEAD) (Freq. "BEIGE 14")
270.8000 McCarran Ground Control (E OF RY 01R/19L)
271.6000 414th Combat Training Squadron, Tactical
272.1750 Aerial Refueling Operations (AR-641, Boom)
273.4500 Oakland Center (Tonopah, high)
273.5500 Nellis AFB Approach/Departure East and Class B
274.8750 Range 63 Operations (RCO "Fatness")
275.8000 Nellis AFB Ground Control (and Creech AFB)
275.8500 Raptor Test Flight/War Games ("Venom 1" and "Venom 2")
276.0500 Red Flag Air-Ground Strike
276.4000 Aerial Refueling Operations (AR-625h)
276.8500 Red Flag Freq. "RED 7"
277.5000 Red Flag: RF 17-3: VMFA-211, F-35B, somewhat active
277.6250 Red Flag AWACS "Darkstar", west, second. (Freq. "Magenta 12")
277.8000 414th Combat Training Squadron, Tactical, "Airboss"
278.2000 Nellis Tactical ("Barnyard" range control)
278.4000 422 TES (F-15E)
278.4250 Red Flag: RF 17-3: 393 BS, B-2
279.1500 Air Exercise Controller
279.6000 414th Combat Training Squadron, Tactical
280.0000 Range 62 Operations
280.3500 Air Exercise, air drop/strike
281.0250 Elgin MOA
282.2000 Las Vegas TRA CON (McCarran)
282.5000 US Air Force Air Combat Command (ACC)
282.8000 414th Combat Training Squadron, International Search & Rescue
283.0000 Squadron Command Post
283.7500 MAFEX Check-In, Kingfish India UHF 1
283.8000 64 AGRS (F-16) (MiG Ops)
283.9250 Red Flag: RF 17-3: VMFA-211, F-35B, active
284.0000 Air exercise (5/2010) (White 6)
284.2250 Red Flag: RF 17-3: VMFA-211, F-35B, very active
284.5500 64 AGRS (F-16)
284.6500 Joshua Control
285.3250 Red Flag: RF 17-3: 95FS, F-22, active
285.5250 Creech AFB SFA
285.6500 Air drop/air strike ops (Weapons School)
286.5000 Red Flag: RF 17-3: 95FS, F-22
287.4500 Red Flag AWACS timing signal
287.6000 414th Combat Training Squadron, Tactical
287.9000 Planes and ground controller, near Tonopah
288.2250 Range 71-76 Ops, secondary
288.6000 414th Combat Training Squadron, Tactical
288.6500 Red Flag: RF 17-3: 95FS, F-22
288.8000 Range 64 Operations (RCO "Fatness")
289.1750 MAFEX Check-In, Kingfish India UHF 2

Area 51 Scanner Frequencies

289.3000 Caliente MOA Range Control (White 12)
289.4000 Nellis AFB Clearance Delivery
289.6000 414th Combat Training Squadron, Tactical
289.7000 Aerial Refueling Operations (AR-624)
290.6000 414th Combat Training Squadron, Tactical
290.8000 414th Combat Training Squadron, Tactical (MIGs)
291.6000 Joshua Control (Edwards AFB)
291.7250 Nellis AFB Approach/Departure (published, NW, paired with 118.1250)
291.8500 Red Flag DCA
291.9000 Aerial Refueling Operations (AR-625L)
291.9750 Red Flag: RF 17-3: 95FS, F-22, somewhat active
292.0000 German Tornados during Red Flag 07-3
292.1000 17 WPS (F-15E)
292.2000 Range 61 Operations, TOSS Scoring, south
292.4500 Planes taxiing at Nellis AFB during Red Flag
293.5000 Nellis Range Control Center "Roulette", TOSS Scoring, north / HARM Primary
293.9000 Red Flag: RF 17-3: VP1, P-3C
294.7250 Red Flag: RF 17-3: 79 RQS, HC-130J
294.7750 Red Flag: RF 17-3: 95FS, F-22, very active
294.9000 Red Flag Caliente MOA ("Barnyard")
295.2000 414th Combat Training Squadron, Tactical
295.4000 Aerial Refueling Operations (AR-641, Boom)
295.6000 Red Flag AWACS, Las Vegas area, "Cylon", "Target Bullseye ..."
295.8000 Aerial Refueling Operations (AR-625h)
296.1000 414th Combat Training Squadron, Tactical
296.7000 LA Center for aircraft above 60,000 ft. (secondary)
297.0000 Air Mobility Command (AMC)
297.7000 414th Combat Training Squadron, Tactical
297.7500 Dreamland MOA Ops
300.0500 Have Quick
302.3000 Desert Radio (Bike Lake Advisory)
303.0000 Aerial Refueling Operations
303.1000 Air Exercise/Red Flag: TOT Tasking ("Disco Ops", Purple 20) (controller calls next maneuvers/positions to planes)
303.6000 Air Ex.: Primary control ("C2 common") for joint Nellis-Fallon exercise 10/16
304.6000 Range 61 Ops (Orange 18)(Blackbird, Darkstar, Raven 27)
304.8000 USAF Hurricane Hunters
304.9000 Supervisor of Flying (SOF) 57 FW-Bullseye Control (second.)
305.5000 EC East & EC West air controller (AWACS?) "Red Hook"
305.6000 Supervisor of Flying (SOF) 57 FW-Bullseye Control (prim.) (VHF on 142.750 MHz)
305.6500 422 TES (F-22A)
306.0750 Red Flag: RF 17-3: 55FS, F-16
306.2000 LA Center (AR-624)
306.5000 Red Flag: RF 17-3: 867 RS, MQ-9

Area 51 Scanner Frequencies

307.2500 McCarran Departure & Class B south-west
308.0000 Red Flag Freq. "RED 9"
308.1250 Red Flag: RF 17-3: 41 RQS, HH-60
308.5000 Red Flag: RF 17-3: LZ2
308.5500 Red Flag: RF 17-3: 55FS, F-16
308.6000 Red Flag AWACS "Chalice" ("White 8", primary check-in)
309.5000 Red Flag tactical "Blue 7"
309.7750 MiGs talking to Showtime during air exercise
310.5500 Red Flag: RF 17-3: 965 AACS, E-3
313.9000 414th Combat Training Squadron, Tactical
314.3000 voice, AM
314.3500 Red Flag: RF 17-3: 55FS, F-16
314.4000 66 RQS (HH-60)
315.2000 414th Combat Training Squadron, Tactical
315.8000 422 TES (F-15C)
316.2000 Red Flag exercise ("Chalice")
317.4500 Nellis Tac ATIS (for Red Flag and other Exercises)
317.5250 Nellis Control East (Sally Corridor, Wilson Creek, Las Vegas, Caliente, Mormon Mesa, paired with 126.650)
317.9000 Red Flag: RF 17-3: 965 AACS, E-3
318.0000 422 TES (F-15C)
318.4000 Red Flag AWACS "Bandsaw", Sally Corridor
318.5000 Air War Games AWACS
318.9000 Red Flag, 66 RQS (HH-60)
319.3000 Fighter Weapons School
319.5000 Aerial Refueling Operations (secondary all routes)
319.7000 Range 65 Operations
319.8000 Oakland Center (Bishop, low)
320.0000 Nellis AFB ACC Command Post
320.1000 Range 62 Operations
320.8000 Comms between Red Flag AWACS aircraft (Establish link in the "Red" (clear) then go "Green" (encrypted data bursts))
321.1000 Nellis SFA and in-flight emergency
321.3000 LA Center for aircraft above 60,000 ft. (secondary)
321.6000 Nellis Tactical
322.2500 433 WPS (F-15C, F-22)
322.3000 Joshua Approach (Edwards AFB)
322.3500 Air Ex.: Range Control (entry/exit) for joint Nellis-Fallon exercise 10/16
322.9500 Thunderbirds Air Show (UHF, Solo #5 and 6)
323.1750 Oakland Center (Coaldale, low)
323.2000 LA Center (AR-624)
323.3500 422 TES (F-15E)
323.8500 433 WPS (F-15C, F-22) Ops
323.9000 Nellis Metro Weather (PMSV)
324.0500 Nellis Track (airspace controller for western 70's ranges, Hwy 95 corridor and AR-625 refueling ops during Red Flag missions, paired with 126.950)
324.0500 Nellis Approach/Departure after Red Flag mission,

Area 51 Scanner Frequencies

324.4000 Weapons School exercise controller "Showtime"
324.8500 422 TES (A-10)
325.5000 USAF AWACS "Chalice", 963rd AACS
326.1250 422 TES (F-35)
326.2000 Nellis AFB Single Frequency Approach ("Charlie")
326.4000 Red Flag AWACS
326.7750 17 WPS (F-15E)
326.8000 66 WPS (A-10)
327.0000 Nellis AFB Control Tower
327.0500 Salt Lake Center (Wilson Creek)
327.1000 Oakland Center for aircraft above 60,000 ft. (primary)
327.2000 Red Flag Airborne FAC (Forward Air Controller)
327.3000 Red Flag Ops, discrete
327.6000 Red Flag: RF 17-3: High Value Airborne Asset (Primary)
327.7750 Red Flag: RF 17-3: 41/43 ECS, EC-130H
328.3000 Air Ex.: Secondary control/ops for joint Nellis-Fallon exercise 10/16
328.5000 Nellis Adversary Ops
328.5500 Red Flag: RF 17-3: 41/43 ECS, EC-130H
333.5500 Air Exercise / Orientation flight ("Bulls Eye", "Farms", "Bear Paw")
335.4500 Range 71 Operations
335.5000 TTR Ground Control
336.1000 Aerial Refueling
337.0000 Range 64 operations
337.4000 voice, AM, air exercise
337.5000 Dreamland MOA
338.4000 Red Flag AWACS "Goliath"
338.7000 Tonopah Test Range, Approach Control
340.2000 Nellis Command Post "Raymond 23"
341.2000 USSTRATCOM Air to Air
341.9250 Range 61 Operations
342.1000 414th Combat Training Squadron, Tactical
342.2000 422 TES (A-10) Support
342.5000 PMSV Metro Weather
342.6000 Air Ex.: Tactical freq. for joint Nellis-Fallon exercise 10/16
343.0000 Reveille/Desert MOA (Sally Sector) (RF 17-3: active)
343.2000 Air Exercise Operations
343.3000 Red Flag AWACS "Darkstar", Strike
343.6000 LA Center (Cedar City, low) (NE of Vegas)
343.7250 Nellis AFB Single Frequency Approach ("Alpha")
344.6000 Nellis Metro Weather (PMSV)
344.7000 Aerial Refueling Operations
344.8000 Range 71/EC West Operations (bombing exercise)
345.4000 voice, AM
347.4000 USAF AWACS "Bandsaw", 964th AACS
348.7000 Joshua Control (Edwards AFB)
349.1000 Nellis 16 WPS (F-16, F-35) Support
349.2000 Red Flag AWACS (Freq. "BLUE 11")
349.4000 US Air Force Control Towers

Area 51 Scanner Frequencies

349.5000 414th Combat Training Squadron, Tactical
349.6000 Red Flag AWACS, Strike
349.7000 Dreamland MOA Refueling Ops frequency "Bluebird"
349.9750 Red Flag: RF 17-3: High Value Airborne Asset (Secondary)
352.0500 LA Center (Mount Potosi, high) (Las Vegas area and NW)
352.6000 Aerial Refueling Operations (AR-635)
353.7000 McCarran Class B airspace south-east
354.3000 Range 76 Operations ("Ivan 2", "Ivan 4", "Jedi")
355.1000 26 WPS (MQ-9) Support
357.1000 Northern Ranges MOA
357.5000 Dreamland MOA Mission Freq. "Uniform Mission"
360.2000 USN Control Towers
360.2500 Nellis 16 WPS (F-16, F-35) Support
360.6250 Creech AFB Tower (paired with 118.300)
360.8000 Salt Lake Center (ARTCC)
361.1000 Dreamland MOA Control (R-4808)
361.5000 414th Combat Training Squadron, Tactical ("Cobra Ops")
361.6000 Range 63 Operations, air exercise ("Darkstar", RCO "Fatness")
363.9000 Range 75 Operations (bombing exercise)
364.0000 Caliente MOA
364.8000 LA Center for aircraft above 60,000 ft. (secondary)
366.1500 Green Flag (549 CTS)
369.0000 Have Quick Timing (TOD)
369.4000 422 TES (F-16)
369.9000 LA Center for aircraft above 60,000 ft. (primary)
370.8250 Red Flag Coyote MOA, AWACS "Chalice"
371.0500 422 TES (F-16)
371.6000 ECE, ECW, ECS, Tolicha Pk
372.1500 Red Flag Freq. "BEIGE 30"
372.2000 Nellis/Creech AFB Base Ops, Pilot to Dispatcher
373.5500 422 TES (F-16)
375.2000 PMSV Metro Weather
375.7000 USSTRATCOM Air Refueling Anchor
375.8000 Dreamland MOA (Mission freq.) (Ops on 238.300 or 377.850)
376.1000 Range 71-76 Ops (Air drops/strike, targeting ops)
376.1500 Nellis 16 WPS (F-16, F-35) Support
376.2000 US Air Force Air Combat Command (ACC)
376.5000 Red Flag AWACS Ops
376.9500 Red Flag, planes (British players, "Cylon")
377.1000 LA Center (Mount Potosi, low/high) (Las Vegas area and NW)
377.1750 Nellis AFB SFA
377.2500 Dreamland MOA Aerial Refueling Mission freq. (Ops: 240.100)
377.7000 414th Combat Training Squadron, Tactical
377.8000 Nellis Range Controller "Blackjack" UHF (paired with 123.550)
377.8500 Dreamland MOA (Ops. Freq.) (Mission freq. on 375.8)
378.2250 Red Flag: RF 17-3: 16 AACS, E-8C
378.3500 Red Flag: RF 17-3: DZ2

Area 51 Scanner Frequencies

378.6750 Red Flag: RF 17-3: 30 RS, RQ-170
379.0000 422 Ops Desk
379.1000 Coyote MOA, Rachel area, Air Exercise
379.1500 McCarran Approach / Class B airspace north
379.4000 Superior Valley Range (R-2509) "Baron"
379.5000 Coyote Range Control, Air Exercise
379.5500 Red Flag DCA
379.6500 Ground threat controller "Roulette", EC East, secondary
379.9250 Red Flag, foreign guest units (?)
379.9500 McCarran Clearance Delivery
381.3000 Nellis AFB Command Post (ALCP) (Raymond 22)
385.4000 Nellis AFB Approach/Departure West

Federal Government Band (406 - 420 Mhz, NFM, some AM)

406.0000 - 406.1000 New Emergency Locator Transmitters (ELTs)

UHF Band > 420 MHz (NFM)

433.9200 "Dakota Alert WMT-3000" Wireless Motion Sensor at Back Gate
451.8000 Mining operations north of Tonopah
456.8000 Mining operations north of Tonopah

Nellis AFB Aircraft Radio Preset Channels

Ch	UHF	VHF	Agency
01	A/R	A/R	Red Flag Squadron Common
02	289.400	120.900	Nellis AFB Clearance Delivery
03	275.800	121.800	Nellis AFB Ground Control
04	327.000	132.550	Nellis AFB Control Tower
05	385.400	135.100	Nellis AFB Approach/Departure West
06	273.550	124.950	Nellis AFB Approach/Departure East and Class B
07	317.525	126.650	Nellis Control East (Las Vegas Area)
08	254.400	119.350	Nellis Control West (Beatty, Restricted Areas)
09	305.600	142.750	Supervisor of Flying (SOF) 57 FW-Bullseye Control
10	321.100		Nellis Air Emergency/Single Frequency Approach
11	270.100		Nellis ATIS
12	360.625	118.300	Creech AFB Tower
13	317.450		Nellis Tac ATIS
14			Unit Option
15-19			HAVE QUICK / Unit Option
20	300.050		HAVE QUICK

Area 51 Scanner Frequencies

Red Flag

BEIGE 14: 270.725
BEIGE 24: 228.200
BEIGE 30: 372.150

BLUE 1: 233.450
BLUE 4: 266.000
BLUE 7: 309.500
BLUE 9: 327.200
BLUE 10: 343.300
BLUE 11: 349.200
BLUE 12: 349.600
BLUE 14: 379.550

INDIGO 2: 18.450

MAGENTA 2: 225.325
MAGENTA 12: 277.625

ORANGE 2: 138.750
ORANGE 3: 139.800
ORANGE 4: 141.150
ORANGE 5: 141.000
ORANGE 12: 238.325
ORANGE 18: 304.600
ORANGE 39: 257.100

RED 2: 363.900
RED 3: 253.700
RED 4: 254.475
RED 5: 259.950
RED 7: 276.850
RED 9: 308.000
RED 20: 251.900

WHITE 1: 229.250
WHITE 2: 236.000
WHITE 3: 238.650
WHITE 4: 255.700
WHITE 5: 260.250
WHITE 6: 284.000
WHITE 7: 291.850
WHITE 8: 308.600
WHITE 10: 326.400
WHITE 12: 289.300

Area 51 Scanner Frequencies

YELLOW 2: 138.775
YELLOW 4: 138.950

PURPLE 20: 303.100

VHF Air to Air (>AM<)

138.025, 138.050, 138.225, 138.275, 138.425, 138.875, 139.050, 139.100, 139.500, 139.700, 140.425, 141.900, 141.975, 142.050, 142.175, 142.225, 142.350, 142.375, 142.500, 142.850, 148.450, 149.075

Have Quick Frequencies [Channel]

225.1500 [19], 235.0500 [20], 239.9500 [17], 252.9250 [18], 257.2500 [13], 262.4500 [14], 267.8500 [15], 271.9500 [16], 279.7500 [05], 284.1500 [06], 289.0500 [07], 293.5500 [08], 298.6500 [09], 303.2750 [10], 308.7500 [11], 314.4500 [12]

Red Flag Handoff Sequence

Blue Team: 02-03-04-05/06-07-15-White 8-(Mission)-White 8-15-07-05/06-04

Red Team: 02-03-04-05/06-08-16-270.025MHz-08-05/06-04

Active mission frequencies during past Red Flag exercises

AWACS Check-In: White 8
Strike: Beige 30, Blue 9, Blue 10, Blue 12
SEAD: Orange 5
OCA: Blue 4, Blue 11
Roulette (SAM Sites): 148.1

B Security Police
163.4875 Nellis AFB Security Police (Raymond 22)
163.5125 Nellis AFB Security Police (Raymond 22)
163.5875 Nellis AFB Security Police
165.0625 Nellis AFB Security Police
165.1875 Nellis AFB Security Police (Raymond 22)
167.8250 Nellis Range/Nevada Test Site security
167.9250 NTS Fire / EMS / Radiation Safety Net
168.3500 NTS Operations
170.7500 NTS Test Operations (Frenchman Flat area)
173.5625 Nellis AFB Medical Help (Raymond 22)
173.5875 Nellis AFB Fire/Crash (Raymond 22)
173.6875 DOE/DOD Rescue/Medics (voice: "Rescue 6")
173.8375 Nellis AFB Fire/Crash

Area 51 Scanner Frequencies

225.3500 Nellis interplane communications
227.7750 Red Flag
235.2000 TTR
236.2750 Red Flag
252.4000 Skunkworks Main
260.9500 Silverbow (TTR) Approach
274.8000 Nellis AFB Emergency Air to Ground
275.2000 Skunkworks, Lockheed nationwide test frequency
283.6000 Red Flag
292.4000 Nellis Tactical Intercom
297.5000 Nellis Exercise Ops
314.6000 Skunkworks, Lockheed nationwide test frequency
316.8000 Nellis Control
338.6000 Nellis Control ("LEE", Tonopah)
349.3000 Skunkworks
361.3000 Dreamland MOA Control (R-4808)
379.9000 Skunkworks
380.3000 Nellis AFB Approach
380.3500 Salt Lake Center (Sunnyside, low/high)
381.1000 ACC Command Post Raymond 22
381.4000 USSTRATCOM Air to Air
381.4500 Salt Lake Center (Cedar City, low+high)
382.6000 Skunkworks, Lockheed nationwide test frequency
383.3000 Nellis Range Control Center "Roulette", EC West, TOSS Scoring north
384.8000 Dreamland MOA Prim. Mission / Red Flag Exercise Operations
385.5000 Nellis AFB Single Frequency Approach ("Bravo")
385.8000 Salt Lake Center (near Rachel)
387.9000 US Air Force Air Combat Command (ACC)
388.9500 Red Flag SIS/VPN
389.0000 RF 15-3 OCA Control
389.1000 Nellis Range Control Center "Jedi"
389.2000 Air exercise controller "Barnyard"
390.9000 US Air Force Air Combat Command (ACC)
391.8000 Groom Lake AWACS Aircraft "Darkstar", 965th AACS
392.1500 Nellis Control north and east ("LEE", Wilson Creek)
392.9000 Alamo Range Control Center ("Boar")
395.1500 Green Flag (549 CTS)
395.8500 Green Flag (549 CTS)
397.2000 Nellis AFB Single Frequency Approach ("Delta")
397.2500 Green Flag (549 CTS)
397.8500 Salt Lake Center (Tonopah, low/high)
398.4750 Red Flag AWACS
399.5000 Green Flag (549 CTS)
399.8500 Green Flag (549 CTS)
496.2500 Old Area 51 road sensors
497.7500 Old Area 51 road sensors

CREDITS & INFORMATION:

The following list below is given CREDIT for Information, Photo's, Insight and mostly Research Knowledge that were used in this guide book.

- UFO Seekers - https://ufoseekers.com/
- Tracey Sue - https://ufoseekers.com/
- Tim Doyle - https://ufoseekers.com/
- T.D. Barners - http://roadrunnersinternationale.com/
- Dreamland Resort www.dreamlandresort.com
- Jorge H. Arnu - Dreamland Resort Founder and Webmaster
- Chuck Clark - Dreamland Resort
- George Knapp – KLAS-TV News Reporter
- Peter Merlin - Historian and Aerospace Archeologist
- Tom Mahood - Dreamland Resort
- Norio Hayakawa - Dreamland Resort
- The LATE Art Bell (RIP) – Midnight in the Desert
- The Little A'Le'Inn – Pat, Connie and Cory & Staff!
- Wikipedia References (various references)
- National Geographic Series – Area 51 etc.
- Google Earth Tool
- USAF
- Lockheed Martin Shunk Works
- Nellis Air Force Base
- U.S. Department of Defense
- Lincoln County, Nevada
- RadioReference
- U.S.A.F.
- TTR
- NTTR Ranch
- U.S. Military
- Classified Folks - aka Colleagues that I have worked in the past

Check out more stuff at www.area51roadtrip.com

Decals, Hats, Shirts, Area 51 Passport & More!

ORDER MORE THAN ONE BOOK

AND GET A DISCOUNT!

Fourth Edition Publication: Winter, 2019

ISBN: 9781706945949

Explored, Researched & Compiled By Ron P. Milione

Formerly of UFO Hunters from the History Channel.

Do You Want to Take a Ride?

WORLDWIDE DISTRIBUTION

AMAZON / AMAZON PRIME

www.amazoon.com

Made in the USA
Las Vegas, NV
27 April 2025